Process, Sensemaking, and Organizing

CW00802161

Edited by

Tor Hernes and Sally Maitlis

OXFORD
UNIVERSITY PRESS

Great Clarendon Street, Oxford, OX2 6DP,
United Kingdom

Oxford University Press is a department of the University of Oxford.
It furthers the University's objective of excellence in research, scholarship,
and education by publishing worldwide. Oxford is a registered trade mark of
Oxford University Press in the UK and in certain other countries

First Edition published in 2010
First published in paperback 2012
Impression: 1

British Library Cataloguing in Publication Data
Data available

Library of Congress Cataloging in Publication Data
Data available

ISBN 978–0–19–959456–6 (hbk.)
ISBN 978–0–19–965556–4 (pbk.)

Printed in Great Britain
on acid-free paper by
MPG Books Group, Bodmin and King's Lynn

Contents

Contents

Acknowledgements

We would like to warmly thank the following colleagues who generously gave their time to act as reviewers for the chapters submitted for possible inclusion in this volume. Their help is greatly appreciated.

Francesca Alby, Sapienza University of Rome; Tore Bakken, Norwegian School of Management; Olga Belova, Essex Business School; Robert Chia, Strathclyde Business School; Todd Chiles, Trulaske College of Business, University of Missouri; Marlys Christianson, Rotman School of Management, University of Toronto; Roger Dunbar, Stern School of Business; Martha Feldman, University of California, Irvine; Raghu Garud, Smeal College of Business, Pennsylvania State University; Robert Gephart, University of Alberta; Hélène Giroux, HEC Montréal; Daniel Gruber, Medill at Northwestern University; Petter Holm, University of Tromsø; Alfred Kieser, Mannheim University; Ioanna Kinti, University of Oxford; Philippe Lorino, ESSEC; Steve Maguire, McGill School of Environment; Ajit Nayak, University of Bath, School of Management; Anne Nicotera, George Mason University; Brian Pentland, Michigan State University; Marshall Scott Poole, University of Illinois at Urbana-Champaign; Claus Rerup, Richard Ivey School of Business, University of Western Ontario; Linda Rouleau, HEC Montréal; Georg Schreyögg, Freie Universität Berlin; Majken Schultz, Copenhagen Business School; David Seidl, University of Zurich; John Sillince, Strathclyde Business School; Scott Sonenshein, Jesse H. Jones Graduate School of Business; Dennis Tourish, Aberdeen Business School; Harald Tuckermann, University of St. Gallen; Timothy Vogus, Owen Graduate School of Management, Vanderbilt University; Cristina Zucchermaglio, Sapienza University of Rome

List of Contributors

Irma Bogenrieder is Associate Professor of Organizational Processes at the Rotterdam School of Management, Erasmus University. Her research has appeared in leading journals, such as *Organization Studies, Business History, Research Policy, Management Learning*, and *Journal of Organizational Change Management*. Her current research addresses organizational learning, organizational routines, and endogenous change. The interrelationship between theory and practice with a focus on "How theory can help improve practice?" is a guideline in conducting her research. E-mail: ibogenrieder@rsm.nl.

Robert Chia is Professor of Management at the University of Strathclyde Business School and Emeritus Professor of Management, University of Aberdeen. He received his PhD in Organization Studies from Lancaster University and publishes regularly in the leading international journals in organization and management studies. He is the author/editor of four books and a significant number of international journal articles as well as book chapters in a variety of management sub-fields. His latest book with Robin Holt, published by Cambridge University Press in October 2009, is entitled *Strategy without Design: The Silent Efficacy of Indirect Action*. His research interests revolve around the issues of strategic leadership and foresight, complexity and creative thinking, and the impact of contrasting East–West metaphysical mindsets on executive decision-making. E-mail: robert.chia@gsb.strath.ac.uk.

Barbara Czarniawska holds a Chair in Management Studies at GRI, School of Business, Economics, and Law at University of Gothenburg, Sweden; *Doctor honoris causa* at Stockholm School of Economics, Copenhagen Business School, and Helsinki School of Economics; she is a member of the Swedish Royal Academy of Sciences, the Swedish Royal Engineering Academy, the Royal Society of Art and Sciences in Gothenburg, and Societas Scientiarum Finnica. Czarniawska takes a feminist and constructionist perspective on organizing, most recently exploring the connections between popular culture and the practice of management, and the organization of news production. She is interested in methodology, especially in fieldwork techniques and in the application of narratology to organization studies. Her recent books in English include: *A Tale of Three Cities* (2002),

Narratives in Social Science Research, (2004), *Actor-Network Theory and Organizing* (edited with Tor Hernes, 2005), *Global Ideas* (edited with Guje Sevón, 2005), *Management Education and Humanities* (edited with Pasquale Gagliardi, 2006), *Shadowing and Other Techniques of Doing Fieldwork in Modern Societies*, (2007), and *A Theory of Organizing* (2008). E-mail: Barbara.Czarniawska@gri.gu.se.

Robert P. Gephart, Jr. (PhD, University of British Columbia) is Professor of Strategic Management and Organization at the University of Alberta, School of Business. Dr Gephart is the author of *Ethnostatistics: Qualitative Foundations for Quantitative Research* and a co-editor of *Postmodern Management and Organization Theory*. He is currently Associate Editor of *Organizational Research Methods* and serves on several editorial boards including *Organization Studies* and the *Academy of Management Journal*. His research has appeared in a number of journals including the *Academy of Management Journal, Administrative Science Quarterly*, and *Organization Studies*. Gephart's current research interests include risk sensemaking, deliberative democracy, and ethnostatistics. E-mail: Robert.gephart@ualberta.ca.

Kenneth Gergen is a Senior Research Professor at Swarthmore College, USA and the President of the Taos Institute. He has published widely on such topics as social constructionist theory, the self, narrative, technology and culture, organizational process, dialogic process, and qualitative inquiry. Among his major works are *Toward Transformation in Social Knowledge, Realities and Relationships, The Saturated Self, An Invitation to Social Construction*, and most recently, *Relational Being*. Gergen's work is both controversial and widely discussed, and has merited honorary degrees in both Europe and the USA. E-mail: kgergen1@swarthmore.edu.

Tor Hernes is Professor of Organization Theory at Copenhagen Business School. Among his books is *Understanding Organization as Process: Theory for a Tangled World* (Routledge, 2007). He is currently working on a new book aiming to develop a comprehensive process theory of organization. Tor works from a combination of process philosophy, systems theory, and actor-network theory. He has previously published *The Spatial Construction of Organization: Autopoietic Organization Theory* (edited with Tore Bakken), *Actor-Network Theory and Organizing* (edited with Barbara Czarniawska) and *Managing Boundaries in Organizations* (edited with Neil Paulsen). E-mail: th.ioa@cbs.dk.

Pursey P. M. A. R. Heugens is Professor of Organization Theory at the Rotterdam School of Management, Erasmus University. He received his PhD from the same university in 2001 and has published widely in both US and European outlets, such as the *Academy of Management Review, Academy of Management Journal, Organization Studies, Journal of Management Studies*, and *Strategic Organization*. He serves on the editorial boards of *Business Ethics Quarterly, Business and Society, Corporate Reputation Review*, and other journals. His research interests include bureaucracy and institutional theories of organization, comparative corporate governance, and business ethics. E-mail: pheugens@rsm.nl.

Silvia Jordan is currently a Fellow in the Department of Accounting at London School of Economics and Political Science, UK. She received her doctorate in business studies and her diploma in psychology from the University of Innsbruck. Her research focuses on performance measurement, risk, and regulation, and organizational learning and sensemaking in the face of uncertain, complex, and ambiguous situations. She addresses these issues particularly from practice- and process-theoretical perspectives. E-mail: s.jordan@lse.ac.uk.

Ann Langley is professor of management at HEC Montréal and Canada research chair in strategic management in pluralistic settings. Her research focuses on strategic change, leadership, innovation, and the use of management tools in complex organizations with an emphasis on processual research approaches. She has published over 50 articles and two books, most recently *Strategy as Practice: Research Directions and Resources* with Gerry Johnson, Leif Melin, and Richard Whittington (Cambridge University Press, 2007). E-mail: ann.langley@hec.ca.

Sally Maitlis is an Associate Professor of Organizational Behavior in the Sauder School of Business, University of British Columbia. Her research interests include the social processes of organizational sensemaking and decision making, and narrative and discursive approaches to the study of emotion in organizations. Her work has been published in journals such as the *Academy of Management Journal, Journal of Management Studies, Journal of Organizational Behavior, MIT Sloan Management Review, Organization Science*, and *Organization Studies*. She is a member of the Editorial Boards of the *Academy of Management Journal, Academy of Management Review*, and *Organization Studies*. E-mail: maitlis@sauder.ubc.ca.

Hermann Mitterhofer is Assistant Professor at the Department of Education at the University of Innsbruck, Austria. He obtained his doctorate in Political Science from the University of Innsbruck. Hermann Mitterhofer's research interests are in the fields of empirical research methods, the philosophy of science, discourse theory, and poststructuralist subject theories and their relations to organizational processes. E-mail: hermann.mitterhofer@uibk.ac.at.

John Mullarkey was educated at University College, Dublin, University College, London, and the University of Warwick, and has taught philosophy for the last 16 years, at the University of Sunderland, England (1994–2004), and the University of Dundee, Scotland (2004 to date). He has published *Bergson and Philosophy* (1999), *Post-Continental Philosophy: An Outline* (2006), *Refractions of Reality: Philosophy and the Moving Image* (2009), and edited, with Beth Lord, *The Continuum Companion to Continental Philosophy* (2009). His work seeks new ways of engaging with "non-philosophy," believing that philosophy is a subject that gains its identity through continual challenge from outside realms, such as film, design, and animality (the three non-philosophies with which he is most acquainted). E-mail: J.Mullarkey@dundee.ac.uk.

Sergey E. Osadchiy is a PhD candidate at Rotterdam School of Management, Erasmus University, Rotterdam. He holds an MPhil degree from the same university. His research focuses on the dynamics of formal rule-based organizational structures, and on their relation to organizational memory and learning. He is also interested in the broader question of why bureaucratic structures still persist in various organizational fields. E-mail: sosadchiy@rsm.nl.

John Shotter is Emeritus Professor of Communication in the Department of Communication, University of New Hampshire, and a tutor on the Professional Doctorate in System Practice in KCCF, London. He is the author of *Social Accountability and Selfhood* (Blackwell, 1984), *Cultural Politics of Everyday Life: Social Constructionism, Rhetoric, and Knowing of the Third Kind* (Open University, 1993), *Conversational Realities: The Construction of Life through Language* (Sage, 1993), *Conversational Realities Revisisted: Life, Language, Body, and World* (Taos Publications, 2009) and *'Getting It': 'Withness'-Thinking and the Dialogical ... in Practice* (Hampton Press, 2010). E-mail: jds@hypatia.unh.edu.

Cagri Topal is a doctoral student in the School of Business at the University of Alberta, Edmonton, Canada. His major is organizational analysis. He has a BS degree in Business Administration and MS degree in Sociology from Middle East Technological University. In his dissertation, Cagri looks into the process of how business, government, and public actors construct the organizational risks caused by industrial activity. He proposes to integrate socio-cultural theories into a multi-faceted understanding of organizational risk. His other research interests include risk sensemaking, micro-processes of power within organizations, and institution-alization dynamics in nongovernmental organizations. E-mail: cagritopal@yahoo. com.

Haridimos Tsoukas is the Columbia Ship Management Professor of Strategic Management at the University of Cyprus, Cyprus and a Professor of Organization Studies at Warwick Business School, University of Warwick, UK. He has published widely in several leading academic journals and was the Editor-in-Chief of *Organization Studies* (2003–8). His research interests include: knowledge-based perspectives on organizations; the management of organizational change and social reforms; the epistemology of practice; and epistemological issues in organization theory. He is the editor (with Christian Knudsen) of *The Oxford Handbook of Organization Theory: Meta-Theoretical Perspectives* (Oxford University Press, 2003). He has also edited *Organizations as Knowledge Systems*, with N. Mylonopoulos (Palgrave Macmillan, 2004) and *Managing the Future: Foresight in the Knowledge Economy*, with J. Shepherd (Blackwell, 2004). His book *Complex Knowledge: Studies in Organizational Epistemology* was published by Oxford

University Press in 2005. He is also the author of the book *If Aristotle were a CEO* (in Greek, Kastaniotis, 2005, 2nd edn). E-mail: htsoukas@ucy.ac.cy and Hari.Tsoukas@wbs.ac.uk.

Karl E. Weick is the Rensis Likert Distinguished University Professor of Organizational Behavior and Psychology at the University of Michigan. His research interests include collective sensemaking under pressure, handoffs and transitions in dynamic events, high reliability performance, improvisation, and continuous change. E-mail: karlw@umich.edu.

Elden Wiebe (PhD, University of Alberta) is an Associate Professor of Management at The King's University College, Edmonton, Alberta, Canada. His primary research interests include time in relation to organizations, organizational change, and strategic management; and second, spirituality in the workplace. He has published in the *Journal of Management Inquiry* and *Healthcare Quarterly*. He is also the editor (with Albert J. Mills and Gabrielle Durepos) of the recently completed *Sage Encyclopedia of Case Study Research*. E-mail: elden.wiebe@kingsu.ca.

Zhen Zhang is currently a PhD student in the Department of Strategic Management and Organization in the School of Business at the University of Alberta. She obtained her bachelor's and master's degrees from the School of Business Administration, Beihang University. Her research interests are in the areas of sensemaking, identity construction and cross-cultural management. E-mail: zzhang4@ualberta.ca.

Disclaimer

While every effort was made to contact the copyright holders of material in this book, in some cases we were unable to do so. If the copyright holders contact the author or publisher, we will be pleased to rectify any omission at the earliest opportunity.

Series Editorial Structure

Series Editors

Ann Langley, HEC Montréal, Canada, ann.langley@hec.ca

Haridimos Tsoukas, University of Cyprus, Cyprus and University of Warwick, UK, process.symposium@gmail.com

Advisory Board

Editorial Officer & Process Organization Studies Symposium Administrator

Sophia Tzagaraki, process.symposium@gmail.com

Endorsements

"As we become more willing to convert reified entities into differentiated streams, the resulting images of process have become more viable and more elusive. Organization becomes organizing, being becomes becoming, construction becomes constructing. But as we see ourselves saying more words that end in 'ing,' what must we be thinking? That is not always clear. But now, under the experienced guidance of editors Langley and Tsoukas, there is an annual forum that moves us toward continuity and consolidation in process studies. This book series promises to be a vigorous, thoughtful forum dedicated to improvements in the substance and craft of process articulation."

Karl E. Weick, Rensis Likert Distinguished University Professor of Organizational Behavior and Psychology, University of Michigan, USA

"In recent years process and practice approaches to organizational topics have increased significantly. These approaches have made significant contributions to already existing fields of study, such as strategy, routines, knowledge management, and technology adoption, and these contributions have brought increasing attention to the approaches. Yet because the contributions are embedded in a variety of different fields of study, discussions about the similarities and differences in the application of the approaches, the research challenges they present, and the potential they pose for examining taken for granted ontological assumptions are limited. This series will provide an opportunity for bringing together contributions across different areas so that comparisons can be made and can also provide a space for discussions across fields. Professors Langley and Tsoukas are leaders in the development and use of process approaches. Under their editorship, the series will attract the work and attention of a wide array of distinguished organizational scholars."

Martha S. Feldman, Johnson Chair for Civic Governance and Public Management, Professor of Social Ecology, Political Science, Business and Sociology, University of California, Irvine, USA

"Perspectives on Process Organization Studies will be the definitive annual volume of theories and research that advance our understanding of process questions dealing with how things emerge, grow, develop, and terminate over time. I applaud Professors Ann Langley and Haridimos Tsoukas for launching this important book series, and encourage colleagues to submit their process research and subscribe to *PROS*."

Andrew H. Van de Ven, Vernon H. Heath Professor of Organizational Innovation and Change, University of Minnesota, USA

"The new series—*Perspectives on Process Organization Studies*—is a timely and valuable addition to the organization studies literature. The ascendancy of process perspectives in recent years has signified an important departure from traditional perspectives on organizations that have tended to privilege either self-standing events or discrete entities. In contrast, by emphasizing emergent activities and recursive relations, process perspectives take seriously the ongoing production of organizational realities. Such a performative view of organizations is particularly salient today, given the increasingly complex, dispersed, dynamic, entangled, and mobile nature of current organizational phenomena. Such phenomena are not easily accounted for in traditional approaches that are premised on stability, separation, and substances. Process perspectives on organizations thus promise to offer powerful and critical analytical insights into the unprecedented and novel experiences of contemporary organizing."

Wanda J. Orlikowski, Alfred P. Sloan Professor of Information Technologies and Organization Studies, Massachusetts Institute of Technology, USA

"The recent decades witnessed conspicuous changes in organization theory: a slow but inexorable shift from the focus on structures to the focus on processes. The whirlwinds of the global economy made it clear that everything flows, even if change itself can become stable. While the interest in processes of organizing is not new, it is now acquiring a distinct presence, as more and more voices join in. A forum is therefore needed where such voices can speak to one another, and to the interested readers. The series *Perspectives on Process Organization Studies* will provide an excellent forum of that kind, both for those for whom a processual perspective is a matter of ontology, and those who see it as an epistemological choice."

Barbara Czarniawska, Professor of Management Studies, School of Business, Economics, and Law at the University of Gothenburg, Sweden

"We are living in an era of unprecedented change; one that is character-ized by instability, volatility, and dramatic transformations. It is a world in which the seemingly improbable, the unanticipated, and the downright catastrophic appear to occur with alarming regularity. Such a world calls for a new kind of thinking: thinking that issues from the chaotic, fluxing immediacy of lived experiences; thinking that resists or overflows our familiar categories of thought; and thinking that accepts and embraces messiness, contradictions, and change as the *sine qua non* of the human condition. Thinking in these genuinely processual terms means that the starting point of our inquiry is not so much about the *being* of entities such as 'organization', but their constant and perpetual *becoming*. I very much welcome this long overdue scholarly effort at exploring and exam-ining the fundamental issue of *process* and its implications for organiza-tion studies. Hari Tsoukas and Ann Langley are to be congratulated on taking this very important initiative in bringing the process agenda into the systematic study of the phenomenon of organization. It promises to be a path-breaking contribution to our analysis of organization."

Robert Chia, Professor of Management, University of Strathclyde, UK

"This new series fits the need for a good annual text devoted to process studies. Organization theory has long required a volume specifically devoted to process research that can address process ontology, methodolo-gy, research design, and analysis. While many authors collect longitudinal data, there are still insufficient methodological tools and techniques to deal with the nature of that data. Essentially, there is still a lack of frameworks and methods to deal with good processual data or to develop process-based insights. This series will provide an important resource for all branches of organization, management, and strategy theory. The editors of the series, Professors Ann Langley and Hari Tsoukas are excellent and very credible scholars within the process field. They will attract top authors to the series and ensure that each paper presents a high quality and insightful resource for process scholars. I expect that this series will become a staple in libraries, PhD studies, and journal editors' and process scholars' bookshelves".

Paula Jarzabkowski, Professor of Strategic Management, Aston Business School, UK

1

Introducing "Perspectives on Process Organization Studies"

Ann Langley and Haridimos Tsoukas

What really exists is not things made but things in the making. Once made, they are dead, and an infinite number of alternative conceptual decompositions can be used in defining them. But put yourself *in the making* by a stroke of intuitive sympathy with the thing and, the whole range of possible decompositions coming into your possession, you are no longer troubled with the question which of them is the more absolutely true. Reality *falls* in passing into conceptual analysis; it *mounts* in living its own undivided life—it buds and burgeons, changes and creates (emphases in the original).

> William James (1909), *A Pluralistic Universe*

The classical ideal of science was to describe nature as a geometry. Now we see that nature is closer to biology and human history since there is a narrative element in nature as well—a story of paths taken or not taken. Indeed, the more we understand the structure of the universe, the more it begins to have common elements with human societies.

> Ilya Prigogine (2004), Creativity and art in nature,
> *New Perspectives Quarterly*

It is a great pleasure to present the first volume of "Perspectives on Process Organization Studies," an initiative that aims to both nurture and celebrate a more complex kind of thinking about organizations and organizing that reflects an understanding of the world as in flux, in perpetual motion, as continually in the process of becoming—where organizations are viewed not as "things made" but as processes "in the making" (Hernes, 2007).

The contributions collected in this volume emerged from the *First International Symposium on Process Organization Studies* held in Cyprus in June 2009, bringing together a diverse group of scholars energized by process ideas. Sally Maitlis and Tor Hernes co-convened the symposium and participated in the selection of papers combining more general process-based contributions with a specific track on sensemaking and organizing. In the next chapter, they present the papers specifically chosen for this volume. Here, we introduce the new series by exploring the inspiration for and origins of Process Organization Studies, specifying the rationale behind it, and identifying some of its choices and challenges and their consequences for the production of knowledge about organizations and organizing.

1.1 The Inspiration for Process Organization Studies

Simply put, Process Organization Studies addresses questions about temporally evolving phenomena. It draws inspiration from a diversity of sources—some philosophical, some humanities-driven, and some social scientific as scholars of various persuasions have in different ways confronted the need to reach beyond the dominant form of scholarship in the social sciences in which time, movement, sequence, and flux are underrepresented, and indeed in many cases, rendered invisible. Three conceptual dualities, each suggesting somewhat different modes of analysis and with different consequences for organizational scholarship, can be seen as underlying current developments in Process Organization Studies: process vs. substance metaphysics; process vs. variance theorizing; and narrative vs. logico-scientific thinking. We examine each one below.

1.1.1 Process vs. substance metaphysics

Most fundamentally, Process Organization Studies is inspired by process metaphysics—namely, the worldview that sees processes, rather than substances, as the basic forms of the universe (Whitehead, 1929; Bergson, 1946; James, 1909/1996). A process orientation prioritizes activity over product, change over persistence, novelty over continuity, and expression over determination. Becoming, change, flux as well as creativity, disruption, and indeterminism are the main themes of a process worldview.

Seeing process as fundamental, such an approach does not deny the existence of events, states, or entities, but insists on unpacking them to reveal the complex activities and transactions that take place and contribute to their constitution. As process philosopher Nicholas Rescher (1996: 29) argues, "the idea of discrete 'events' dissolves into a manifold of processes which themselves dissolve into further processes." A process point of view invites us to acknowledge, rather than reduce, the complexity of the world. It rests on a relational ontology, namely the recognition that everything that is has no existence apart from its relation to other things. Therefore, long established dualisms such as mind and body, reason and emotion, humanity and nature, individual and collective, organism and environment, agency and structure, ethics and science, need to be overcome. Focusing on *inter*-actions is preferred to analyzing self-standing actions.

Substance metaphysics recognizes the occurrence of processes but it considers them incidental and explains them in terms of substances: processes contingently *happen* to substances, but the latter are essentially unchanging in character. Consider, for example, the phrase "the student is reading" (Farmer, 1997: 64). The process of "reading" is happening to the entity "the student." The student happens to be reading but this is incidental (not essential)—it is one activity among others. The student could have been walking, listening to music, eating, etc., and would still be the same student (Farmer, 1997: 64). The process does not change the substance.

From a process metaphysical perspective, however, a different account is offered: the student is not an unchanging substance, unaffected by her experiences, but, on the contrary, is constituted by her experiences: reading is one process among others that constitutes the student. Moreover, the process of reading may be further decomposed into smaller processes such as visual perception, memory, and bodily functions. Taken to its logical limits, the student does not exist apart from her experiences—she *is* her experiences (Farmer, 1997: 65). Just as the Heraclitian individual cannot step into the same river twice, the student who was reading this morning in the library is not the self-same student who is reading in her home in the evening, since the experience of reading is different at these two points in time. As Farmer (1997: 65) observes, "the notion of the enduring substantial entity called the 'self' of the student is an abstraction to be explained in terms of the repeated patterns found in a certain series of interrelated events." Process metaphysics regards change as endemic, indeed constitutive of the world. Every event reconfigures an already established pattern, thus altering its character. Every moment is qualitatively different and should be treated as such (Pepper, 1942; Tsoukas, 1994).

3

It is not difficult to see parallels with organization studies. Mainstream accounts conceive of change as *happening to* organizations, with the latter moving along different stages in time (Tsoukas and Chia, 2002). For example, the organization is in a state X1 at point in time T1, something happens (e.g. a restructuring, or the introduction of ERP) and, as a result, the organization has moved to state X2, at point in time T2. The organization is basically the same, except for the new systems in place. The change that happened to the organization is similar to a force that may have impacted a billiard ball. The forces impacting the organization are incidental (i.e. contingent) and not essential for its constitution as a certain kind of entity.

From a process perspective, the organization is constituted by the interaction processes among its members (Cooren et al., 2006; Taylor and Van Every, 2000; Tsoukas and Chia, 2002). Weick's (1979) theory of organizing is perhaps the best known process-oriented account in the field. Shifting attention from "organization" as an already accomplished entity with certain pre-given properties to organizing, Weick underscores the process whereby ongoing, interdependent actions are assembled into sensible sequences that generate sensible outcomes (Weick, 1979: 3). Simply put, organizing is the process of reducing differences among interacting actors. Organization is an emergent outcome of the process of sensemaking through which equivocality is progressively removed. Similarly, for several communication theorists, organization as a single entity is constituted "by its emergence as an actor in the texts of the people for whom it is a present interpreted reality" (Robichaud et al., 2004: 630). From a process perspective, what we call "organization" is an abstraction which, upon closer inspection, may be explained in terms of interlocking patterns of communication. It is process all the way through.

Taking a relational ontology seriously implies that we see events and experiences grow out of other events and experiences. The past is constitutive of, or *internally related* to, the present. Whitehead (1979) used the term "prehension" to indicate the way in which one momentary experience incorporates its predecessor. Unlike substances, which do not include one another but are seen as nested, standing under one another—*sub-stantia*—experiences include other experiences and grow out of the integration of bodily and mental events into something new. Consider, for example, your experience of listening to the final chord of a musical phrase. You clearly hear that chord at a particular moment. "But," as Cobb (2007: 570) points out, "if that were all, there would be no music. You hear it as the completion of the phrase. The whole phrase resonates together. In other words, the earlier experiences of antecedent chords are also part of the present. What was there-then, is included in what is here-now. Whitehead says that, in the present moment, I prehend not only what is happening in my ears but also the earlier experiences." In other words, the way we prehend a current experience incorporates elements of past experiences.

The Whiteheadian notion of "prehension" clearly resonates with Prigogine's (2004) notion of time in complex systems and Bakhtin's (1981) notion of "dialogicality." Current experiences are partly constituted by past experiences; current conversations draw on past conversations; past "voices" are mobilized in current utterances. What was there-then is now included in what is here-now. Says Prigogine (2004): "Two people speak and then separate, but there is a remembering of the conversation. Part of the conversation is retold to others, which can be seen as an evolution of the initial conversation. This is the time of humanity, or the time of recollections, and not the time of human beings taken separately. The concept of time is dependent on a collective approach." In other words, current utterances depend essentially on past utterances.

Similarly, for Bakhtin, most of the time, language speakers use terms that are *already* defined and used by others. At the same time, speakers may renew the meaning of those terms and give them their own twist. The use of language presupposes the Other and, in that sense, it is necessarily dialogical. Thus, although utterances are the unique products of language speakers, they are not *ex nihilo* constructions, since they inescapably draw on the utterances of others (Bakhtin, 1986: 92–5). When I write or speak about a certain topic I am not the first one to do so (Bakhtin, 1986: 93). Others have expressed views about it or in relation to it and, inevitably, my topic becomes the arena in which I meet the opinions, views, and perspectives of others. Their "voices" are within mine.

A process orientation is sensitive to the constructive role of embodied-cum-embedded agency in bringing about the world we come to experience as an independent structure (Shotter, 1993, 2009). Cognition and symbolic interaction are understood to be *embedded* into forms of life and arising from *embodied* interactions with the world, mediated by artifacts. Temporality is a constitutive feature of human experience, and processes unfold in time. Human phenomena cannot be properly understood if time is abstracted away. Process thinking is intimately connected with what philosopher Stephen Toulmin (1990) calls an "ecological style" of thinking. The latter seeks to embrace complexity by reinstating the importance of the particular, the local, and the timely; it is sensitive to context, interactivity, experience, and time; and it acknowledges non-linearity, emergence, and recursivity.

1.1.2 Process vs. variance theorizing

Approaching the problem of understanding temporally ordered phenomena from the perspective of empirical science rather than constitutive ontology, it was Mohr (1982) who introduced the distinction between *"variance"* and *"process" theories*—a conception related to, but not perfectly congruent with, the distinction between substance and process metaphysics. Concretely, for Mohr, while variance theories provide explanations of phenomena in terms of relationships among dependent and independent variables, process theories provide explanations in terms of patterns in events, activities, and choices over time.

Mohr (1982) summarizes the basic features of the variance model as follows. First, a variance model deals with variables. Second, it deals with efficient causes, namely forces "conceived as *acting on* a unit of analysis (person, organization, and so on) to make it what it is in terms of the outcome variable (morale, effectiveness, and so on) or change it from what it was. It may be thought of as *push-type* causality" (Mohr, 1982: 41, italics in the original). Third, in variance models, time ordering among the antecedent independent variables is immaterial to the consequences. By contrast, a process model, according to Mohr (1982) has the following characteristics. First, a process model deals with events rather than variables. Secondly, it deals with a final cause and not efficient causes. A final cause is an end state whose existence presupposes the occurrence of a series of prior states. As Mohr (1982: 59) remarks, "a process model involves *pull-type* causality: X does not imply Y, but rather Y implies X" (italics in the original). Third, in process models, time ordering among the antecedents is crucial for the outcome.

Thus, process theories look very different from the nomothetic variable-based conceptual frameworks that still dominate most organization studies and management journals and, indeed, most of the social sciences. Unlike variance theories, process theories take sequence and ordering to be critical. An outcome is explained in terms of diachronic patterns—who does what when and what happens next—rather than in terms of the synchronic presence of higher or lower levels of specific attributes. Thus, according to Mohr (1982), process theories emphasize necessary causality rather than necessary and sufficient causality because the impact of any event will depend on what precedes it and what follows it. In practice, process theories may take the form of deterministic phase sequences, but a variety of other forms are possible including models with parallel paths, feedback loops, non-deterministic branch points, interactions and reversals. As Van de Ven (1992) notes, to warrant the label "theory" a process conceptualization also needs to be grounded in some kind of underlying logic or generative mechanism that produces the temporal patterns described.

1.1.3 Narrative vs. logico-scientific thinking

Beyond the variance-process theory distinction, the social science literature provides other conceptualizations of theoretical forms that are related to but also different from those proposed by Mohr (1982), and resonate to some extent with process metaphysics. For example, Bruner (1990, 1991) distinguishes between "logico-scientific" (or "paradigmatic") and "narrative" forms of knowing (see also Polkinghorne, 1988; Tsoukas and Hatch, 2001). Bruner (1986: 11) contrasts the two forms of knowing as follows: "the types of causality implied in the two modes are palpably different. The term then functions differently in the logical proposition 'If X, then Y' and in the narrative récit 'The king died, and then the queen died'. One leads to a search for universal truth conditions, the other for likely particular connections between two events—mortal grief, suicide, foul play."

In other words, whereas in paradigmatic knowing propositions or rules connect categories of behavior to categories of actors and situations, narrative knowing places those elements in a temporal, contextualized form with a plot, thus enlivening those characters and events, and capturing those nuances that are dropped in the abstraction process that is characteristic of paradigmatic knowing. As Tsoukas and Hatch (2001: 998) note: "In narrative we have a more concrete rendering of causality. It is historical and specific, not general and contingent. 'This happened in this way', versus 'This should happen if the following conditions hold'.... Whereas within logico-scientific thinking context becomes contingency, in narrative mode, context is situation and circumstance." Moreover, narratives preserve multiple temporalities, especially kairological (experiential, humanly relevant) time: its significance is not derived from the clock but from the meanings assigned to events by actors (Tsoukas and Hatch, 2001).

Thus, paradigmatic knowing is driven by the norms of formal scientific and logical reasoning where generalizations are made about causal influences among variables (similar to Mohr's notion of variance theory). Narrative knowing, on the other hand, incorporates temporal linkages between experienced events over time, and is a form of knowing that is used to give *meaning* to particular events drawing on culturally embedded narrative structures (e.g., the comedy, the tragedy, the fairy story, the joke, the moral fable), or any kind of recognizable story that reveals an underlying message, plot, or point. Thus, Bruner (1986, 1990, 1991) and Polkinghorne (1988) take a more subjectivist and interpretive approach to temporally arranged explanations, something absent in Mohr's (1982) notion of process theory, where a largely positivist and realist understanding of process remains dominant.

Process metaphysics, Mohr's notion of process theorizing, and the narrative forms of understanding identified by Bruner and Polkinghorne all offer handles for thinking about phenomena in ways that are sensitive to time, motion, flux, and sequence. They have all provided inspiration to organizational scholars and are contributing to the development of Process Organization Studies. And yet, as we shall see, there are clearly some distinctions in the degree to which a strong process ontology—where substances are considered to be subordinated to and constituted by processes—has been incorporated into empirical research and organizational theorizing (Chia and Langley, 2004; Van de Ven and Poole, 2005). Thus, many process scholars study phenomena such as organizational change in terms of movement from one state to another—retaining elements of the substance ontology, since change is conceptualized as happening to *things* (entities or substances) that retain their identity over time. In contrast, a deeper adherence to process metaphysics would imply viewing change in terms of the ongoing micro-processes that contribute to constituting and reproducing forms of organizing over time (Tsoukas and Chia, 2002; Hernes, 2007). We now look more closely at the origins and development of Process Organization Studies, and consider some of its variants.

1.2 Origins, Development, and Need of Process Organization Studies

Although not necessarily consolidated under a process-metaphysical label, several strands in organization studies have adopted a more or less process-oriented perspective over the years. Karl Weick's (1979, 1995) persistent emphasis on organizing and the important role of sensemaking in it is perhaps the best known process approach that has inspired several organizational researchers. Henry Mintzberg's (1978), James March's (1994), Andrew Pettigrew's (1985, 1990), Robert Burgelman's (1983, 1991) and Andrew Van de Ven's (1992; with Poole, 1990, 1995) work on the making of strategy, decision making, organizational change, venturing, and innovation respectively also shows an awareness of the importance of process-related issues and has inspired subsequent generations of organizational researchers.

Current studies that take an explicitly performative view of organizations focusing on, for example, routines (Feldman, 2000), innovation and change (Carlile, 2004), strategizing (Whittington, 2006; Jarzabkowski, 2004), naturalistic decision making (Klein, 1999), learning and knowing (Gherardi, 2006), communication (Taylor and Van Every, 2000), sensemaking (Maitlis, 2005), and the enactment of technological change in organizations (Barley, 1986; Orlikowski, 1996) have similarly adopted, to varying degrees, a process vocabulary, and have further refined a process sensibility. Indeed, the growing use of the gerund(-ing) indicates the desire to move towards dynamic ways of understanding organizational phenomena, especially in a fast-moving, inter-connected, globalized world.

Since a process worldview is not a doctrine but an orientation, it can be developed in several different directions, exploring a variety of topics in organizational research. For example, traditional topics such as organizational design, leadership, trust, coordination, change, innovation, learning and knowledge, accountability, communication, authority, technology, etc., which have often been studied as "substances," from a process perspective can be approached as situated sequences of activities and complexes of processes unfolding in time. Perspectives drawing on post-rationalist philosophies, social constructivism, discourse and narrative theory, practice theory, actor-network theory, path-dependence theory, complexity science, Austrian economics, socio-cultural, discursive, and ecological psychology, activity theory, business history, ethnomethodology, and symbolic interaction are examples of a process orientation to the study of organizational phenomena that treats them not as *faits accomplis* but as (re)created through interacting agents embedded in sociomaterial practices, whose actions are mediated by institutional, linguistic, and objectual artifacts.

The aim of this series is to stimulate the further development of these ideas. To achieve this, we bring together within each volume philosophers and social theorists who have reflected more broadly on the application of process ideas to organizations (represented by John Mullarkey, Kenneth Gergen, and John Shotter in the current volume), seminal thinkers more directly associated with process organization studies (Karl Weick, Barbara Czarniawska, and Robert Chia in the current volume), and the latest theoretical and empirical contributions from researchers in the field.

But why would one be interested adopting and promoting a process perspective? The simplest answer is that, as mentioned above, since time is an inescapable reality, process conceptualizations that take time into account offer an essential contribution to our understanding of the world that is unavailable from more traditional research-based conceptual models that tend to either ignore time completely, compress it into variables (describing decision making as fast or slow, or environments as dynamic or stable), or reduce its role to what Pettigrew et al. (2001) called "comparative statics" (re-evaluating quantitative relationships at successive times).

However, it is also important to note that process knowledge is also highly relevant to practice. Indeed, many of the management field's well-established variance theories that relate practices or organizational characteristics to performance are not as easily actionable as they appear precisely because they assume static equilibrium conditions and ignore temporal dynamics (March and Sutton, 1997; Meyer et al., 2005). For example, findings that firms with characteristic B generally perform better than those with characteristic A say nothing about how to go about moving from A to B. Moreover, substantial organizational changes aimed at moving towards B and capturing its predicted benefits generally take time and involve costs that are not and, indeed, cannot be easily included in cross-sectional conceptualizations. Finally, action under complexity interacts with its context to generate reactions, with unexpected ramifications that are absent from static models.

At a more micro level of analysis, an interesting editor's forum in the *Academy of Management Journal* discussed why established "evidence-based" human resources (HR) management knowledge is not adopted by practitioners (Rynes, 2007*a*, 2007*b*). The research findings discussed in the forum were almost all variance-based, and considerable commentary was devoted to strategies for improving their uptake. However, relatively little attention was devoted to process issues. Yet as Rynes (2007*b*: 1048) indicated in her concluding comments, "The real world of HR managers is messy, complex and filled with human drama, making it unlikely that it can be completely understood using 'hands-off' methodologies such as surveys and archival analyses." Process studies that examine how changes in practices are implemented, and how their influence spreads and interacts with existing organizational contexts offer a move closer towards a dynamic understanding of how to improve them. To achieve this, however, researchers need to get beyond a perspective that sees variance-based generalizations as the only legitimate basis for scientific advance and for practical prescription. This is not to suggest that more traditional kinds of research are not useful.

Variance-based research provides indications of what works—on average—across large samples, something that process studies are not designed to provide. And yet, without a knowledge of process, variance knowledge is very hard to use: the *how* is missing. In other words, more process organization studies are needed not simply to satisfy academic curiosity about the nature of the world, but to better understand how to act within it.

However, empirical process research and theorizing can be challenging to do well. In the next section, we explore briefly two of its choices and challenges, drawing on examples from the classic and more recent literature. These issues (*temporal orientation* and *conceptual products*) concern choices that affect the nature of the knowledge that will emerge from the research—in other words, they have important epistemological implications. The shape of Process Organization Studies as a field in the making is critically determined by the choices researchers make along these dimensions.

1.3 Conducting Process Organization Studies: Choices and Challenges

1.3.1 Temporal orientation: Past, future, or present

Time is central and ubiquitous to Process Organization Studies.[1] However, a first critical choice in conducting any study is how exactly to consider and capture time empirically. For example, process scholars may study their phenomenon by tracing it backward into the past (historical, retrospective studies), by following it forward into the future (ethnography, longitudinal case studies), by examining how it is constituted, or by doing all of these at the same time. As Leonard-Barton (1990) indicates, these options generate some important tradeoffs.

1.3.1.1 TRACING BACK

One advantage of excavating the past is that outcomes are known in advance, and the researcher has an idea about what a process study will have to explain. This focuses the data collection effort onto precisely those elements that seem directly linked to the outcome. Indeed, the outcome may well be an important motive for the research. For example, spectacular unique events such as the space shuttle catastrophes (Vaughan, 1996; Starbuck and Farjoun, 2005), or the Enron debacle (Boje and Rosile, 2003; Stein, 2007; Fleming and Zyglidopoulos, 2008) demand explanations of a process or narrative kind. Many process studies have been inspired by attempts to better understand the patterns of events leading to positive and negative outcomes (e.g., Repenning and Sterman, 2002).

Studying processes retrospectively also means economy in data collection and analysis. Real-time observation is time-consuming both in terms of person-hours spent in the field as well as in terms of elapsed time (especially when the processes spread out over many years). As long as accurate temporal chronologies can be reconstructed from archival data and extensive interviewing, retrospective studies can be an efficient and effective approach. Indeed, some interesting award-winning process analyses of change have emerged from studies that were largely retrospective. For example, Isabella's (1990) study of how managers construe critical organizational events as they evolve was based on retrospective interviews, Dutton and Dukerich's (1991) award-winning study of the interaction among image, identity, and action at the New York Port Authority was based on archival data and retrospective interviewing. More recently, another award-winning study of the emergence of an "accidental" radical change in a mission church by Plowman et al. (2007) was based on twenty-two retrospective interviews and archival data in a rare empirical application of complexity theory.

1.3.1.2 FOLLOWING FORWARD

And yet, there is nothing quite like being there in real time. Observing processes in action and wondering what will happen next is a very different experience from sifting through archival traces and second-hand narratives that have become immutable and fixed. With real-time data, there is an immeasurable gain in the richness of temporal recording, particularly so when it comes to studying interactions among people, and to recording people's perceptions and understandings at different points in time. Retrospective accounts, especially of cognitions, are subject to important limitations of memory and rationalization (making event chains seem more logical than they were at the time: Schwenk, 1985; Golden, 1992). Moreover, there are occasions when following forward in real time is a natural choice. Rather than starting with known outcomes, the researcher has access to a major change initiative that is just beginning. Here is a golden opportunity to understand how the change will interact with its context and penetrate the organization.

Yet although real-time analysis may be desirable, it can pose problems when the object of analysis is the organization as a whole, or a physically dispersed process that is hard to capture completely. The open-ended nature of longitudinal research can generate uncertainty, frustration, or a sense of there being considerable dross among the richness (see Leonard-Barton, 1990). Moreover, although the nature of real-time data may be richer and more detailed, most longitudinal process researchers have generally taken a perspective quite similar to that of retrospective researchers in analyzing their data; they have looked at it as a whole, and attempted to theorize about how the processes examined evolved up to the point where they left the field.

Yet, research in real time could also enable researchers to see events in a way that is closer to that experienced by the participants on the scene, that is sensitive to uncertainty, to activity in the present, and to the very arbitrariness of the notion of "outcome," where endings and beginnings often flow into each other (Weick, 1999). Researchers have perhaps not taken sufficient advantage of this opportunity. In doing real-time research, one might see shifts not only in the way other people construe situations, but also shifts in one's own interpretation as events unfold. Burgelman's (1991, 1994, 2002; with Grove, 2007) successive studies of Intel over a period of fifteen years are interesting in part because they show how the author himself learned and enriched his process interpretations over time as his cumulative knowledge of the firm developed. Looking at data prospectively in a systematic way would require more continuous researcher documentation, not only of site data, but also of personal theorizing (Bitektine, 2008).

1.3.1.3 RECONSTITUTING THE EVOLVING PRESENT

This brings us back to an earlier subtle ontological distinction between process studies that consider the evolution of organizations seen as entities being displaced or transformed over time, and studies that examine how organizing is dynamically and continually reconstituted by ongoing processes, that is, studies that more strongly reflect process metaphysics. Research that emphasizes the activities of people, and how these activities contribute to the creation of stable categories, comes closest to reflecting this view. Examples include Feldman's (2000, 2004) studies of the recursive yet dynamic nature of organizational routines, and Barley's (1986, 1990) classic work on how structure is regenerated through ongoing interactions surrounding technology (in this case, through the conversations between radiologists and radiation technologists in examining rooms). Such studies involve real-time ethnographic research following processes forward over a fairly long period. Yet because of the focus on reproduction and recursiveness inspired by structuration theory (Giddens, 1984), the heading "reconstituting the evolving present" better reflects their overall temporal orientation.

Indeed, some of the most intriguing ideas in Process Organization Studies are emerging from research that takes categories and concepts that are usually considered as stable, and questioning their underlying stability. For example, "identity" is one apparently stable concept that has been problematized in recent work (Gioia et al., 2000). The term "identity work" has been coined to show how individuals discursively and interactively construct their identities (Pratt et al., 2006; Maguire and Hardy, 2005). Like Weick's (1979) call for greater emphasis on verbs, adding the word "work" to any apparently static and structural concept is an interesting device for making it more dynamic, and for forcing consideration of how human agency might operate on it.

Temporal orientation is thus one critical choice with pragmatic and conceptual implications. Retrospective studies can generate sharp process conceptualizations and may be particularly useful when researchers wish to compare cases, or when the level of analysis is so broad as to render real-time analysis difficult. Real-time process research is more challenging, but likely to lead to more precise temporal data and richer understandings. Finally, work that adopts a strong process ontology concerned with understanding how the stable categories of organization such as structure, culture, and strategy are constituted through activity, offers attractive opportunities for rethinking organizational theory in more dynamic terms.

1.3.2 Conceptual products: Patterns, mechanisms, or meanings

Regardless of temporal orientation, process studies may lead to the development of some very different types of conceptual products, reflecting different notions of the nature of valuable process knowledge and some additional choices and challenges in the way process data are manipulated to produce insights. We identify three types of conceptual contributions: patterns, mechanisms, and meanings.

1.3.2.1 PATTERNS

Process analysis often seeks to identify repetitive temporal patterns among activities and events. How are events ordered? What is the typical sequence of phases? Are there different paths and cycles through the phases? What are the branch points where different paths may diverge? How are phases and activities interconnected? Examples of process research focusing on temporal patterns include the classic studies of decision-making that plot phases and subroutines (Mintzberg et al., 1976; Nutt, 1984). More recent work presenting process patterns includes James and Wooten's (2006) study of how firms handle discrimination law suits where a series of sequential paths are identified and associated with different forms of discrimination.

Gersick's (1988) in-depth study of group processes provides another classic example. She found that the task groups she studied all followed a common process pattern: at the temporal mid-point of their discussions, they all underwent a radical shift, moving from an initial stable template of behavior in their task approach to a new template that carried them through to the end. Gersick's initial study with eight naturally occurring groups was subsequently replicated on eight experimental laboratory groups generating similar findings (Gersick, 1989). Here was a robust empirical process pattern that forms the foundation for an interesting and novel contribution to knowledge about group processes.

And yet, as Gersick (1992) notes in a refreshingly reflexive piece on the initial study that formed the basis for her doctoral thesis, something is missing in this picture. Her thesis supervisor was dissatisfied when she presented her preliminary results. The first version of her award-winning paper was rejected by a major journal. The process patterns that she discovered did not have a strong theoretical grounding, a mechanism that would explain their extraordinary empirical regularity. She then found an appropriate frame in punctuated equilibrium theory, and developed an integrative theoretical paper showing how that perspective explains phenomena at a variety of different levels (Gersick, 1991).

In conducting process organization studies, detecting temporal patterns is a useful step, but it may not be enough. An empirically observed temporal pattern has a similar status to an empirically observed correlation. Without explanation, it is incomplete. The pattern needs some underlying logic that enables one to understand why progression through phases would occur in precisely this way. This is where "mechanisms" complement process patterns.

1.3.2.2 MECHANISMS

Based on an exhaustive survey of research on development and change in a variety of disciplines, Van de Ven and Poole (1995) identified four basic generative mechanisms that they suggest cover the range of theoretical motors used to explain change, either alone or in combination. These motors are labeled life cycle mechanisms (based on the idea of genetic predetermination), teleological mechanisms (based on goal-driven behaviors and learning), dialectical mechanisms (based on cycles of confrontation and resolution among opposing forces), and evolutionary mechanisms (based on the processes of variation, selection, and retention). The idea of generative motors or mechanisms derives from a realist ontology in which it is believed that underlying causal mechanisms that cannot be directly observed interact to produce empirically observed phenomena (Tsoukas, 1989; Hedström and Swedberg, 1998).

The motors identified by Van de Ven and Poole (1995) offer promising templates for generating process understandings about change. As illustrated by Gersick's (1991) review of the punctuated equilibrium model, there are often commonalities in how processes at different levels of analysis reveal the action of similar mechanisms. For example, contradiction—suggesting the action of a dialectical mechanism—has emerged as a motor for change in process studies at different levels. At the individual level, Pratt et al.'s (2006) study of identity construction among medical students found that the discrepancy between work activities and identity (work-identity integrity assessments) stimulated adaptation. At the institutional level, contradictions among institutional spheres of influence have been found to stimulate institutional entrepreneurship (Seo and Creed, 2002; Greenwood and Suddaby, 2006).

While the four mechanisms suggested by Van de Ven and Poole (1995) provide a useful starting point, it is hard to see them as exhaustive, despite the claims of the authors. Rather, they are sensitizing devices that can be tried out in attempting to understand empirical processes. Other sensitizing devices, that may or may not be reducible to the four motors, include more integrated meta-theoretical frames that are inherently processual such as structuration theory (Giddens, 1984), actor-network theory (Latour, 2005), activity theory (Engeström, 1987), sensemaking theory (Weick, 1995), and complexity theory (Stacey, 1999). Feldman (1995, 2004) describes four strategies based on ethnomethodology, semiotics, dramaturgy, and deconstruction that she uses to help see her process data in new ways. The conceptual paradigms proposed by grounded theorists (Locke, 1997) constitute yet another set of heuristic sensitizing tools. One of these paradigms is more specifically oriented towards process formulations (Strauss and Corbin, 1990).

These ideas draw attention to the nature of the conceptual work of process theorists who are not in the business of hypothesis-testing (deduction), but who aim to reach beyond the detection of common surface patterns (induction) to develop plausible explanations for temporal dynamics. This is a partly creative process (called abduction) that is hard to pin down, although it can be assisted by the sensitizing devices described in the previous paragraph, by the heuristic use of various analytical strategies (Langley, 1999), and according to Locke et al. (2008), by accepting and mobilizing doubt to allow generative thinking.

The most impressive process studies delight the reader, both by the clarity and insightfulness of their theoretical explanations and by the degree to which their empirical grounding is convincing. And yet, paradoxically, generating process theory is a creative bridging process between data and theory that is hard to program according to a set of formal procedures. The notion of "mechanism" captures the elements of explanation that process theorists mobilize, and yet the word does not necessarily reflect the interpretive and creative nature of what they are doing as they construct their accounts, however plausible. It is notable that Golden-Biddle and Locke (2006) use the term "story" to refer to the elements of qualitative research often at the centre of process studies. This brings us to another way of considering the potential conceptual contributions of process research.

1.3.2.3 MEANINGS

There are several ways in which the products of process organization studies can reflect meanings instead of, or as well as, patterns or mechanisms. At one level, many process studies take the meanings or interpretations of individuals as both their raw material and their primary object. Isabella's (1990) study of how individuals construe change events as they evolve is a typical example. The author is not interested in the objective features of these events but in what they meant to people and how this changed over time. Similarly, in their studies of identity, Dutton and Dukerich (1991), and Pratt et al. (2006), are interested in how cognitive categories such as identity evolve and how they are affected by issues and actions. Their theorizations reflect the interpretations of the people they interviewed, although the researchers' own interpretations of process patterns and mechanisms driving change are also evident.

Another way in which the products of process research can emphasize meanings is when researchers give room to multiple and competing narratives of processes. Buchanan and Dawson (2007) suggest four different ways of managing conflicting narratives in process research; normative process theory (eliminating all but a single prescriptive management story), interpretive process theory (revealing multiple stories), critical process theory (giving voice to the silenced), and dialogic process theory (emphasizing fragmentation and incoherence). Their arguments suggest a need for more intensive use of narrative methods in which individuals' or groups' stories are recognized and become the object of analysis (see also Pentland, 1999; Rhodes and Brown, 2005).

An alternative route is for process researchers to recognize explicitly the contestable nature of their interpretations, and to consider the possibility of multiple narratives or explanations—something that Langley (1999) called the "alternate templates" analytic strategy. Allison's (1971) study of the Cuban missile crisis, in which he generated three different narratives for the events based on three different theories of decision making (rational actor, organizational process, and political), is an instructive classic that has rarely been repeated so successfully. However, there are some other interesting and instructive attempts (Lapointe and Rivard, 2007; Mahring et al., 2004).

Using narrative theory directly, Boje and Rosile (2003) critically examine alternative published interpretations and explanations of the Enron meltdown. They show how the Enron story has usually been constructed as a "tragedy"—a narrative with a particular plot structure that places "key central agents and victims in situations in which their fortune is reversed and spectators get a cathartic lesson" (Boje and Rosile, 2003: 89). Based on Aristotelian definitions, the tragic narrative follows a simple storyline that is tightly coherent and ignores secondary elements to move the plot forward. The authors contrast the structure of this story with an "epic" narrative of the Enron case which has a more scattered structure involving a plurality of interacting plots and no central coherence (see Brown and Humphreys, 2003). Through this comparison, they show how the tragic narrative tends to constrain inquiry, absolving observers from blame but scapegoating the protagonists, while the epic narrative opens it up, leading in many directions and bringing in contextual elements that are connected in imprecise, chaotic, and non-convergent ways. The critical dramaturgical analysis of Boje and Rosile (2003) is a form of process theorizing that emphasizes meaning rather than patterns or mechanisms, and that draws more explicitly on the narrative vs. logico-scientific mode of reasoning described earlier.

In summary, potential empirical contributions in process organization studies take a variety of different forms. At the most basic level, process research often involves the search for empirical regularities or patterns in event sequences. However, descriptive surface patterns do not generally provide rich understanding on their own. Thus researchers will look for underlying mechanisms or combinations of mechanisms that make process sequences more understandable. Sensitizing concepts may come from a variety of sources, but the abductive process of connecting data and theory often requires creative insight. Finally the contributions of process research can also be viewed as meanings, sometimes reflecting the interpretations of respondents, or alternatively recognizing the researcher's own interpretive processes.

1.4 Conclusions

Several calls have been made in the past two decades for more dynamic approaches to the study of organizational and management phenomena. The ever intensifying forces of change in a global, inter-connected world as well as the increasing inability of traditional forms of thinking and social science that privilege stability to account for, as well as prepare us to cope with, the unfolding and often surprising processes individuals, organizations, and societies are involved in, have given impetus to the epistemological quest for dynamic understanding. Process Organization Studies, as a loosely connected network of concepts, explorations, and empirical studies that focus on the dynamic constitution of organizational and management phenomena, has always been a rich repository of ideas, whose time has come to enter the mainstream. The more we know about organizations and the way they are managed, the more we would like to know about *how* they are constituted, maintained, and change over time. Even scholars who have not adopted a particularly process-oriented approach in their work have increasingly called for more attention to be paid to processes.

For example, in strategic management, Porter (1991) argued some time ago for the need of a "dynamic theory of strategy." His four desiderata which such a theory would need to fulfill are clearly driven by process-relational concerns. A dynamic theory of strategy, he notes, should deal simultaneously with the firm and its environment; it should allow for endogenous change; it should make room for creative action; and it should acknowledge historical accident and path-dependence. In a similar vein, Greenwood and Hinings (1996: 1045) have urged researchers to study how "archetypes" (templates for organizing) are established and legitimated as well as how they change through dynamic "non-linear" processes.

Despite considerable progress made in the processual understanding of organizations and management, more imaginative, bolder, as well as more inter-disciplinary work is needed. There is a renewed appreciation of process across all social sciences, humanities, and philosophy, which potentially holds promise for our inquiries as students of organization and management. Refining an epistemology of process for organization and management studies will help boost relevant theory development, and vice versa. The more we develop process theories of organizations, the more we help refine our understanding of process at large. The aim of this series of books is to consolidate and further develop ongoing efforts to advance a sophisticated process perspective in organization and management studies. It is important for the intellectual development of the field and its relevance to the world of practice that we develop rigorous scholarship that explicitly seeks to advance how the organizational world we experience is dynamically constituted, maintained, and changed.

The series is linked to the International Symposium on Process Organization Studies, a deliberately small international conference that takes place in the Mediterranean, in the summer each year. Contributors to the Symposium may submit their work to the "Perspectives on Process Organization Studies" for double-blind reviewing. A rigorous reviewing process will ensure that a high-quality selection of papers will be published each year. Moreover, authors unconnected to the Symposium, may submit their work to the series editors (process.symposium@gmail.com) at any point in time. Reflecting the structure of the Symposium, each volume of the *Perspectives* will include both general and theme-specific process papers. The theme will vary each year.

In conclusion, "Perspectives on Process Organization Studies" aims to advance high-quality process-oriented scholarship in the field. Our collective awareness of processes is stronger than ever; the time is ripe. As Prigogine (1997: 7) notes, "We are observing the birth of a science that is no longer limited to idealized and simplified situations but reflects the complexity of the real world, a science that views us and our creativity as part of a fundamental trend present at all levels of nature". It is this kind of organization and management science we want to encourage in this series: a science that sees the social world as *chaosmos*—an ever evolving synthesis of orderly *cosmos* and recalcitrant *chaos*; an interplay between integration and multiplicity, action and structure, routine and novelty constantly renewed over time. We look forward to receiving manuscripts and working with authors on further developing their ideas. We hope the excitement that process studies create will be reflected in the submissions received, and will be further enhanced by the quality of the papers published. Join in the journey!

Note

1. This section and some of the latter parts of the previous section draw on a chapter entitled "Studying processes in and around organization" by Ann Langley, published in *The Sage Handbook of Organizational Research Methods* (eds. D. Buchanan and A. Bryman), 2009: 409–429.

References

Allison, G. E. (1971). *The Essence of Decision*, Boston: Little-Brown.

Bakhtin, M. M. (1981). *The Dialogical Imagination*, ed. M. Holquist, trans. C. Emerson and M. Holquist, Austin, TX: University of Texas Press.

Bakhtin, M. M. (1986). *Speech Genres and Other Late Essays*, eds. C. Emerson and M. Holquist, trans. V. W. McGee, Austin, TX: University of Texas Press.

Barley, S. R. (1986). Technology as an occasion for structuring: Evidence from observations of CT scanners and the social order of radiology departments, *Administrative Science Quarterly*, 31, 78–108.

Barley, S. (1990). Images of imaging: Notes on doing longitudinal fieldwork, *Organization Science*, 1(2), 220–47.

Bergson, H. (1946). *The Creative Mind*, New York: Carol Publishing Group.

Bitektine, A. (2008). Prospective case study design: Qualitative method for deductive theory testing, *Organizational Research Methods*, 11(1), 160–80.

Boje, D. & Rosile, G. A. (2003). Life imitates art: Enron's epic and tragic narration, *Management Communication Quarterly*, 17(1), 85–125.

Brown, A. D. & Humphreys, M. (2003). Epic and tragic tales: Making sense of change, *Journal of Applied Behavioral Science*, 39(2), 121–44.

Bruner, J. (1986). *Actual Minds, Possible Worlds*, Cambridge, MA: Harvard University Press.

Bruner, J. (1990). *Acts of Meaning*, Cambridge, MA: Harvard University Press.

Bruner, J. (1991). The narrative construction of reality, *Critical Thinking*, 18, 1–21.

Buchanan, D. & Dawson, P. (2007). Discourse and audience: Organizational change as a multi-story process, *Journal of Management Studies*, 44(5), 669–86.

Burgelman, R. A. (1983). A process model of internal corporate venturing in the diversified major firm, *Administrative Science Quarterly*, 28(2), 223–44.

Burgelman, R. A. (1991). Intraorganizational ecology of strategy making and organizational adaptation: Theory and field research, *Organization Science*, 2(3), 239–32.

Burgelman, R. A. (1994). Fading memories: A process theory of strategic business exit in dynamic environments, *Administrative Science Quarterly*, 39(1), 24–56.

Burgelman, R. A. (2002). Strategy as vector and the inertia of coevolutionary lock-in, *Administrative Science Quarterly*, 47(2), 325–57.

Burgelman, R. A. & Grove, A. S. (2007). Let chaos reign, then rein in chaos—repeatedly: Managing strategic dynamics for corporate longevity, *Strategic Management Journal*, 28(10), 965–80.

Carlile, P. (2004). Transferring, translating and transforming: An integrative framework for managing knowledge across boundaries, *Organization Science*, 15(5), 555–68.

Chia, R. & Langley, A. (2004). The First Organization Studies Summer Workshop: Theorizing process in organizational research (call for papers), *Organization Studies*, 25(8), 1486.

Cobb, J.B., Jr. (2007). Person-in-community: Whiteheadian insights into community and institution, *Organization Studies*, 28/4: 567–88.

Cooren, F., Taylor, J. R., and Van Every, E. J. (2006). *Communication as Organizing*, Mahwah, NJ: Lawrence Erlbaum Associates.

Dutton, J. E. & Dukerich, J. M. (1991). Keeping an eye on the mirror: Image and identity in organizational adaptation, *Academy of Management Journal*, 34(3), 517–54.

Engeström, Y. (1987). *Learning by Expanding: An Activity Theoretical Approach to Developmental Research*, Helsinki: Orienta-Konsultit.

Farmer, R. L. (1997). *Beyond the Impasse: The Promise of a Process Hermeneutic*, Macon, Georgia: Mercer University Press.

Feldman, M. S. (1995). *Strategies for Interpreting Qualitative Data*, Sage: Thousand Oaks.

Feldman, M. S. (2000). Organizational routines as a source of continuous change, *Organization Science*, 11(6), 611–29.

Feldman, M. S. (2004). Resources in emerging structures and processes of change, *Organization Science*, 15(3), 295–309.

Fleming, P. J. & Zyglidopoulos, S. C. (2008). The escalation of deception in organizations, *Journal of Business Ethics*, 81(4), 837–50.

Gersick, C. J. G. (1988). Time and transition in work teams: Toward a new model of group development, *Academy of Management Journal*, 31(1), 9–41.

Gersick, C. J. G. (1989). Marking time: Predictable transitions in work groups, *Academy of Management Journal*, 32(2), 274–309.

Gersick, C. J. G. (1991). Revolutionary change theories: A multilevel exploration of the punctuated equilibrium paradigm, *Academy of Management Review*, 16(1), 10–35.

Gersick, C. J. G. (1992). Journey 2: Time and transition in my work on teams: Looking back on a new model of group development, in P. J. Frost & R. Stablein (eds) *Doing Exemplary Research*, Newbury Park: Sage, 52–76.

Gherardi, S. (2006). *Organizational Knowledge: The Texture of Workplace Learning*, Oxford: Blackwell.

Giddens, A. (1984). *The Constitution of Society*, Berkeley, CA: University of California Press.

Gioia, D., Schultz, M., & Corley, K. G. (2000). Organizational identity, image and instability, *Academy of Management Review*, 25(1), 63–81.

Golden, B. R. (1992). The past is the past—or is it? The use of retrospective accounts as indicators of past strategy, *Academy of Management Journal*, 35(4): 848–60.

Golden-Biddle, K. & Locke, K. (2006). *Composing Qualitative Research*, Thousand Oaks: Sage.

Greenwood, R. & Hinings, C. R. (1996). Understanding radical organizational change: bringing together the old and new institutionalism, *Academy of Management Review*, 1996, 21, 1022–54.

Greenwood, R. & Suddaby, R. (2006). Institutional entrepreneurship in mature fields: The big five accounting firms, *Academy of Management Journal*, 49(1), 27–48.

Hedström, P. & Swedberg, R. (1998). *Social Mechanisms*, Cambridge, UK: Cambridge University Press.

Hernes, T. (2007). *Understanding Organization as Process*, London: Routledge.

Isabella, L. A. (1990). Evolving interpretations as change unfolds: How managers construe key organizational events, *Academy of Management Journal*, 33(1), 7–41.

James, E. H. & Wooten, L. P. (2006). Diversity crises: How firms manage discrimination lawsuits, *Academy of Management Journal*, 49(6), 1103–18.

James, W. (1909/1996). *A Pluralistic Universe*, Lincoln, NE: University of Nebraska Press.

Jarzabkowski, P. (2004). Strategy as practice: Recursiveness, adaptation, and practices-in-use, *Organization Studies*, 25(4): 529–60.

Klein, G. A. (1999). *Sources of Power: How People make Decisions*, Boston, MA: MIT Press.

Langley, A. (1999). Strategies for theorizing from process data, *Academy of Management Review*, 24(4), 691–710.

Langley, A. (2009). Studying processes in and around organizations, in D. Buchanan & A. Bryman (eds) *Sage Handbook of Organizational Research Methods*, London: Sage Publications, 409–29.

Lapointe, L. & Rivard, S. (2007). A triple take on information systems implementation, *Organization Science*, 18(1), 89–107.

Latour, B. (2005). *Reassembling the Social*, Oxford: Oxford University Press.

Leonard-Barton, D. (1990). A dual methodology for case studies: Synergistic use of a longitudinal single site with replicated multiple sites, *Organization Science*, 1(3), 248–66.

Locke, K. (1997). *Grounded Theory in Management Research*, Thousand Oaks: Sage.

Locke, K., Golden-Biddle, K., & Feldman, M. S. (2008). Making doubt generative: Rethinking the role of doubt in the research process, *Organization Science*, 19(6), 907–18.

Maguire, S. & Hardy, C. (2005). Identity and collaborative strategy in the Canadian HIV/AIDS treatment domain, *Strategic Organization*, 3(1), 11–46.

Mahring, M., Holmström, J., Keil, M., & Montealegre, R. (2004). Trojan actor-networks and swift translation: Bringing actor-network theory to IT project escalation studies, *Information Technology and People*, 17(2), 210–38.

Maitlis, S. (2005). The social processes of organizational sensemaking, *Academy of Management Journal*, 48(1), 21–49.

March, J. G. (1994). *A Primer on Decision Making*, New York: Free Press.

March, J. G. & Sutton, R. I. (1997). Organizational performance as a dependent variable, *Organization Science*, 8(6), 698–706.

Meyer, A. D., Gaba, V., & Colwell, K. (2005). Organizing far from equilibrium: Nonlinear change in organizational forms, *Organization Science*, 16(5), 456–73.

Mintzberg, H. (1978). Patterns in strategy formation, *Management Science*, 24(9), 934–48.

Mintzberg, H., Raisinghani, D., & Théorêt, A. (1976). The structure of unstructured decision processes, *Administrative Science Quarterly*, 21(2), 246–75.

Mohr, L. B. (1982). *Explaining Organizational Behavior*, San Francisco: Jossey-Bass.

Nutt, P. C. (1984). Types of organizational decision processes, *Administrative Science Quarterly*, 29(3), 414–50.

Orlikowski, W. (1996). Improvising organizational transformation over time: A situated change perspective, *Information Systems Research*, 7(1), 63–92.

Pentland, B. T. (1999). Building process theory with narrative: From description to explanation, *Academy of Management Review*, 24(4): 711–24.

Pepper, S. (1942). *World Hypotheses*, Berkeley, CA: University of California Press.

Pettigrew, A. M. (1985). *The Awakening Giant*, Oxford: Basil Blackwell.

Pettigrew, A. M. (1990). Longitudinal field research on change: Theory and practice, *Organization Science*, 1(3), 267–92.

Pettigrew, A. M., Woodman, R. W. & Cameron, K. S. (2001). Studying organizational change and development: Challenges for future research, *Academy of Management Journal*, 44(4), 697–713.

Plowman, D. A., Baker, L. T., Beck, T. E., Kulkarni, M., Solansky, S. T., & Travis, D.V. (2007). Radical change accidentally: The emergence and amplification of small change, *Academy of Management Journal*, 50(3), 515–43.

Polkinghorne, D. E. (1988). *Narrative Knowing and the Human Sciences*, Albany: State University of New York Press.

Porter, M. E. (1991). Towards a dynamic theory of strategy, *Strategic Management Journal*, 12 (special issue), 95–117.

Pratt, M. G., Rockmann, K. W., & Kaufmann, J. B. (2006). Constructing professional identity: The role of work and identity learning cycles in the customization of identity among medical residents, *Academy of Management Journal*, 49(2), 235–62.

Prigogine, I. (1997). *The End of Certainty*, New York: Free Press.

Prigogine, I. (2004). Beyond being and becoming, *New Perspectives Quarterly*, electronic access, http://www.digitalnpq.org/archive/2004_fall/01_prigogine.html, last accessed 21 April 2010.

Repenning, N. P. & Sterman, J. D. (2002). Capability traps and self-confirming attribution errors in the dynamics of process improvement, *Administrative Science Quarterly*, 47(2), 265–95.

Rescher, N. (1996). *Process Metaphysics*, New York: State University of New York Press.

Rhodes, C. & Brown, A. D. (2005). Narrative, organizations and research, *International Journal of Management Reviews*, 7(3), 167–88.

Robichaud, D., Giroux, H., & Taylor, J. (2004). The metaconversation: The recursive property of language as a key to organizing, *Academy of Management Review*, 29(4), 617–34.

Rynes, S. L. (2007*a*). Editor's foreword: Tackling the "great divide" between research production and dissemination in human resource management, *Academy of Management Journal*, 50(3), 985–6.

Rynes, S. L. (2007*b*). Editor's afterword—Let's create a tipping point: What academics and practitioners can do, alone and together, *Academy of Management Journal*, 50(3), 1046–54.

Schwenk, C. (1985). The use of participant recollection in the modeling of organizational processes, *Academy of Management Review*, 10(3), 496–503.

Seo, M.-G. & Creed, W. E. D. (2002). Institutional contradictions, praxis, and institutional change: A dialectical perspective, *Academy of Management Review*, 27(2), 222–47.

Shotter, J. (1993). *Conversational Realities*, London: Sage.

Shotter, J. (2009). Moments of common reference in dialogic communication: A basis for unconfused collaboration in unique contexts, *International Journal of Collaborative Practices*, 1, 31–9.

Stacey, R. D. (1995). The science of complexity: An alternative perspective for strategic change processes, *Strategic Management Journal*, 16(6), 477–95.

Starbuck, W. H. & Farjoun, M. (eds) (2005). *Organization at the Limit: Lessons from the Columbia Disaster*, Malden, MA: Blackwell Publishing.

Stein, M. (2007). Oedipus Rex at Enron: Leadership, oedipal struggles and organizational collapse, *Human Relations*, 60(6), 1387–410.

Strauss, A. L. & Corbin, J. (1990). *Basics of Qualitative Research*, Thousand Oaks, CA: Sage.

Taylor, J. R. and Van Every, E. J. (2000). *The Emergent Organization*, London: Lawrence Erlbaum Associates.

Toulmin, S. (1990). *Cosmopolis*, Chicago, IL: University of Chicago Press.

Tsoukas, H. (1989). The validity of idiographic research explanations, *Academy of Management Review*, 14(4), 551–61.

Tsoukas, H. (1994). Refining common sense: Types of knowledge in management studies, *Journal of Management Studies*, 31/6: 761–80.

Tsoukas, H. & Chia, R. (2002). On organizational becoming: Rethinking organizational change, *Organization Science*, 13(5), 567–82.

Tsoukas, H. & Hatch, M. J. (2001). Complex thinking, complex practice: The case for a narrative approach to organizational complexity, *Human Relations*, 54/8, 979–1013.

Van de Ven, A. H. (1992). Suggestions for studying strategy process: A research note, *Strategic Management Journal*, 13 (summer special issue), 169–88.

Van de Ven, A. H. & Poole, M. S. (1990). Methods for studying innovation development in the Minnesota Innovation Research Program, *Organization Science*, 1(3), 313–35.

Van de Ven, A. H. & Poole, M. S. (1995). Explaining development and change in organizations, *Academy of Management Review*, 20(3), 510–40.

Van de Ven, A. H. & Poole, M. S. (2005). Alternative approaches for studying organizational change, *Organization Studies*, 26(9), 1377–404.

Vaughan, D. (1996). *The Challenger Launch Decision: Risky Technology, Culture and Deviance at NASA*, Chicago: University of Chicago Press.

Weick, K. (1979). *The Social Psychology of Organizing*, Reading, MA: Addison-Wesley.

Weick, K. (1995). *Sensemaking in Organizations*, Thousand Oaks, CA: Sage.

Weick, K. E. (1999). That's moving: Theories that matter, *Journal of Management Inquiry*, 8(2), 134–42.

Whitehead, A. N. (1929/1978). *Process and Reality*, Corrected Edition. Eds. David Ray Griffin and Donald W. Sherburne, New York: Free Press.

Whittington, R. (2006). Completing the practice turn in strategy research, *Organization Studies*, 27(5), 613–34.

2

Process, Sensemaking, and Organizing: An Introduction

Tor Hernes and Sally Maitlis

2.1 Process and sensemaking

This volume is composed of chapters which all share a focus on process and organizing, some of which emphasize more particularly the notion of sensemaking. Process and sensemaking may be seen as mutually interlocking phenomena. Ever since Peirce (1878) founded what came to be known as the pragmatist tradition in philosophy, meaning and experience have been seen as cornerstones in process thinking. Importantly, meaning is located in the process itself; it is made in an ongoing present in which past experience is projected upon possible futures. Meaning is thus not received from stable concepts outside the process, such as from norms, identity, or values, but rather is made within the process itself. This is what makes sensemaking central to processes and the making of meaning an ongoing activity central to understanding organization from a process perspective:

Although process thinking in philosophy has been discussed by several writers in organization studies (e.g. Chia and King, 1998; Tsoukas and Chia, 2002; Hernes, 2007; Langley and Tsoukas, this volume), sensemaking is a relative newcomer to process thinking. It may therefore be useful to trace a brief and approximate genealogy of process thinking in order to locate the place of sensemaking as it is conceived in organization studies. We suggest four distinctions which have unfolded over the centuries and which have helped lay the groundwork for sensemaking as an integral part of understanding organization as process. These distinctions intersect with the conceptual dualities of process thinking identified by Langley and Tsoukas (this volume), while offering some additional ways helpful to understanding what process is—and is not.

An early distinction may be labeled the "change versus constancy" distinction. Heraclitus is seen as the founder of process thinking in the Western intellectual tradition, cited among other things for the statement, "All things flow", thus sensitizing us to the idea that nothing ever stays the same. Rescher (1996) contrasts Heraclitus with Parmenides, who emphasized existence as timeless, uniform, and unchanging. Instead, the world is seen as taking place in the form of a perpetual transition between fire, air, soil, and water. From this view, things elude the confines of categories because they are always on their way to becoming something else. Categories, on the other hand, are found in Aristotle's work, which laid the foundation for the classification of things, although his philosophy contains important traits of process thinking, notably through his emphasis on change (Rescher, 1996). Later writers in the process tradition have built on the early debates by privileging becoming over change and building the notions of potentiality and actuality into processes (e.g. Whitehead, 1929; Deleuze, 2004).

Sensemaking, as suggested by Weick et al. (2005), is about transience rather than constancy:

> The language of sensemaking captures the realities of agency, flow, equivocality, transience, reaccomplishment, unfolding, and emergence, realities that are often obscured by the language of variables, nouns, quantities, and structures (Weick et al., 2005: 410).

Thus, while sensemaking is about change, it is not about the step-wise type of change suggested by Lewin's (1951) model of "unfreeze—change—refreeze," which is effectively to see change as a series of immobilities (Tsoukas and Chia, 2002).

Another early and important distinction emerged between what we may label substance vs. events. Rejecting the substance view of earlier philosophers (e.g. Aristotle and Heraclitus), Lucretius (2004), subscribed to a view of the world as streams of invisible particles, called atoms, which flow but come together to form substances such as trees, water, and humans. Whereas Lucretius sided with Heraclitus on the principle of movement, he rejected a priori substances such as fire, air, soil, and water because they signified a priori defined substances, hence the contingent nature of things could not be understood. For Lucretius, movement takes place through the changing patterns of eternal particles rather than through the transformation of a priori-defined substances. Lucretius' view was based on probabilities of occurrence of events at which atoms might come together to form phenomena such as trees, water, or humans. Conceptualizing process from events as opposed to substance was later pursued by Whitehead (1929), who worked from the idea of events as occasions of experience, leading in turn to thought (Whitehead, 1929: 228). Similarly Heidegger saw being as constituted by engaging with the world. Both Whitehead and Heidegger sought to inverse the Cartesian assumption of the subject being prior to the world of experience.

The sensemaking literature typically focuses on occasions of sensemaking (Weick, 1995) rather than on the sensemakers. Sensemakers "are made" by the sense they make, not the other way round. Actors, to the extent that they are seen as entities, become "entified" through their actions, which confer identity upon them (Czarniawska, 2004).

A third distinction opposes logical empiricism (or positivism) and constructivism in relation to what provides for change and continuity in processes. Ancient philosophers discussed the metaphysics of process, exemplified by Aristotle's distinction between potentiality and actuality. In the case of building a house, for example, the ability of the builder represents potentiality whereas the process of building represents actuality. The potentiality–actuality pair of concepts helps explain continuity as well as change in processes, but from a realist standpoint, independent of how human actors experience processes. Focus on human experience became central with Bergson's (1988, 1998) conceptualization of human memory, time, and experience at the beginning of the twentieth century, which made a decisive impact upon process theorizing. Aligned with Bergson's process views are those of William James (1842–1910), who emphasized the importance of working from what he called "streams of experience" in which the world comes in "drops of experience". Similarly, in his philosophy of becoming, Whitehead (1929), while subscribing to an atomistic view analogous to that of Lucretius, replaced physical articles with "actual occasions," which were similar to William James's (1977: 104) drops of experience. Although Whitehead saw actual occasions as the "actual stuff" of processes, he argued that experience is what provides for continuity in processes, furthermore that continuity is made possible by human-made abstractions from experience, which help shape experience in turn.

In the sensemaking literature it is emphasized how sensemaking is an ongoing activity underlying the process of organizing. In his discussion of enactment Weick suggests that when *people* enact, they "undertake undefined space, time, and action, and draw lines, establish categories, and coin new labels that create new features of the environment that did not exist before" (Weick, 1995: 31). Notwithstanding the verb-like character of sensemaking which might apply to Whitehead's actual occasions and James's drops of experience, people also engage in imposing labels (Weick et al., 2005) on continuous flows of experience. In group interaction, interlocking behaviors (Weick, 1979: 4), while being intelligible to actors, help them form 'grammars' to help establish meaning.

A fourth distinction, related to, yet distinct from distinction three, concerns interpretation vs. meaning creation, or sensemaking. European continental philosophers such as Kant and Descartes located reality in the interpretive frameworks that humans apply to the world. Thus thought would serve to create a correspondence between human belief and a world "out there", forming the basis of a "representationalist epistemology" (Chia, 1999: 215). Pragmatist thinking found with Peirce (1878), Mead (1934), and Schutz (1967) opposes an interpretative view by emphasizing action as a prerequisite for meaning creation. The world cannot be known as such but is brought about by acting upon it. It does not lie there ready to be interpreted, but has to be made sense of. Thus sensemaking, argues Weick (1995, 2000), is not about interpretation, but requires action. Sense *making* is an expression that Weick uses purposely to distinguish this process from the somewhat more passive term "interpretation". Echoing views of the pragmatist philosopher William James, he argues emphatically that organizing is imposed rather than discovered, and that action *defines* cognition (Weick, 1979: 165). This key insight from pragmatist thinking has influenced other important works in organization studies, such as texts on decision making, learning, and institutions by March and colleagues (e.g. Levitt and March, 1988; Cyert and March, 1963; March and Olsen, 1989; March and Olsen, 1975).

This brief and approximate summary of the history of process thinking suggests how sensemaking is the fruit of successive streams of thought in what we might call a tradition of process thinking. But there is more to sensemaking. Weick's achievement has been to embody several of the above distinctions in his work on sensemaking. For example, the distinction between substance and events, where his work emphasizes events of making sense over sensemaking as a stable set of ideas embodied in actors. Rather than posit sense as enduring frameworks against which things are interpreted, sensemaking takes the meaning of "accepting life as ongoing events into which they are thrown ... and less ... as turf to be defended" (Weick, 1995: 188). Naturally, this does not imply that sensemaking is merely a cognitive process that accompanies the unfolding of things. On the contrary, it means confirming events as the main constituents of processes, in which forces of stabilization are played out as embodied pasts are projected upon possible futures. It means locating agency in processes, and so, locating agency in the events that make up processes.

The implications of such thinking are considerable. Perhaps the most important implication is the role played by temporality. Events of sensemaking take place in time as organizational members construct the temporality of the organization. Actors are seen as "thrown" into an existing world in which they create their own temporality as a coming together of past, present, and future (Heidegger, 1927). Temporality, in other words, does not merely mean a consideration of how things change over time. It means that actors operate "in time", and because they operate in the evanescent flow of time they are forced to establish their own temporality (Heidegger, 1927). That enables, as argued by Emirbayer and Mische (1998: 963) the agency of an embedded process of social engagement informed by the past while oriented toward the future, framed by the contingencies of the moment (see also Wiebe in this volume). Sensemaking thus becomes a process of ongoing accomplishment because the past, although necessarily formed by habit (Mead, 2002), is actually uncertain and open to choice as to what experiences to retain from the past, as well how those experiences are retained. As March (1999: 2) argues, the past is uncertain, moreover, it is experienced in ways that affect both its interpretation and the memories that are retained about it. Sensemaking, although it constitutes attempts at ordering through the evoking of causal structures, shows up the contingency of processes by providing "horizons" (Heidegger, 1927) of possibilities from which actors draw in their phantasying (Schutz, 1967) of possible future actions.

2.2 Introduction to the volume

Next, we introduce the chapters that make up the first volume of "Perspectives on Process Organization Studies". These include three pieces that explore organization process theorizing from the perspectives of philosophy, psychology, and communication, three chapters from influential organizational scholars who have long emphasized organiz*ing* over organiz*ation*, and five contributions representing new empirical or conceptual explorations of a variety of different organizational processes, including learning, change, and sensemaking. Together, the collection portrays the polyphony that characterizes Process Organization Studies, offering perspectives from different disciplines, insights from diverse theoretical traditions and contexts, and parallels made with a range of cultural forms, including art, poetry, and cookery. At the same time, we see consistency in the chapters' clear emphasis on a process ontology, process theorizing, and narrative thinking (Langley and Tsoukas, this volume). The two empirical investigations of sensemaking both reflect a strong process orientation, highlighting sensemaking as a transient and enacted process (rather than as a static outcome achieved at the end of an interpretation process), and attending to key events that provide occasions for ongoing sensemaking (rather than focusing on sense embodied in actors). Across this diverse collection, then, we see the recurrent themes that distinguish process theorizing from the more logico-scientific, variance-oriented research that dominates organization studies today.

In addition, some intriguing connections are found among the chapters. The contributions by Shotter and Weick both emphasize the poetic quality of process-sensitive practice, while Chia uses other artistic practices to illustrate how process can be beautifully captured in visual art forms that are often regarded as static entities. Gergen, Shotter, and Czarniawska beseech us to stop observing from outside and instead develop an awareness of the mutually constituting nature of our relationships with the processes we seek to understand. Mullarkey, Gephart, Topal, and Zhang, and Wiebe make temporality their central concern, while Jordan and Mitterhofer join Gephart et al. in exploring the relationship between sensemaking processes and the institutions in which they are embedded. Weick likens organizing to Shakespeare's "airy nothing," while Mullarkey notes Rorty's characterization of process thinking as "whooshing about a bit." And, of course, Heraclitus' river rises up many times.

The volume begins with contributions from scholars outside organization studies: John Mullarkey (philosophy), Kenneth Gergen (social psychology), and John Shotter (communication).

John Mullarkey's chapter, "Stop making (philosophical) sense: Notes towards a process organizational-thinking beyond 'philosophy'" considers what he calls the "inter-discipline" of process philosophy and organization studies. Preferring not to take existing philosophical models as his starting point, Mullarkey argues for Process Organization Studies as a "philosophy of the future," seeking to address the question of what philosophy will become, and comparing how recent writers in the philosophy of time have worked with the concept. He leaves us with several challenging questions that may help move us towards organizational thinking that generates its own philosophy.

In "Co-constitution, causality and confluence: Organizing in a world without entities," Kenneth Gergen argues that taking seriously a process approach to organizations requires shifts in how we study them (moving from observation to cultural participation), and in what we seek to achieve from studying them (moving from producing predictive laws to co-creating futures). Making the case that the identity of any individual or organizational "unit" is a byproduct of ongoing relational processes, he presses for a focus in organizational science not on causal explanations, but on "confluence," an array of mutually defining entities.

John Shotter builds on Gergen's ideas in his chapter, "Adopting a process orientation . . . in practice: Chiasmic relations, language, and embodiment in a living world." Here, Shotter explores practices that enable us to adopt a process orientation, and argues that this cannot be done through the intellectual, representational approaches traditionally used to understand phenomena from outside them. Rather, he speaks to the need to develop new perceptual skills, and new ways of relating—especially relating bodily— to others, and to the processes of which we must acknowledge we are a part. Looking critically at the tendency of management writers to keep us "outside" even while striving to engage us deeply in organizational processes, Shotter encourages a move from "aboutness-talk" to "withness talk," a poetic form of talk that occurs when we come into spontaneously responsive contact with another being.

Karl Weick is also drawn to poetics as a powerful way of orienting us towards process thinking and practice. His chapter, "The poetics of process: Theorizing the ineffable in organization studies," is the first of three by seminal thinkers in Process Organization Studies. In this thought-provoking chapter, Weick draws our attention to the value of "attention-drawing" in process thinking. This, he argues, allows us to appreciate the ineffable and tacit practices so important to process (but often invisible to scholars and managers) by attending to the smaller, effable episodes with which they are associated. In particular, Weick reveals what we can learn by drawing attention to images and to alternative ways of talking, and, in so doing, reveals the poetic quality of both process theorizing and of managerial work.

Robert Chia presents a different viewpoint in "Rediscovering becoming: Insights from an Oriental perspective on process organization studies," where he describes how Western ways of thinking that give primacy to permanence, stability, and being, have shaped our understandings of organizations, and the world at large. He contrasts this with the Oriental mentality of "becoming" that has at its roots change, emergence, and the continuous, natural unfolding of sequences of events—the very essence of process thinking. In an intriguing excursion into traditional Oriental artistic practices such as calligraphy and painting, Chia shows how even the "substances" produced through these art forms capture the dynamic continuity so characteristic of Oriental thinking and of a processual per-spective. Moving back to organizational life, Chia concludes by proposing that we analyze not organizations, but "organizational mentalities" which can be understood as "the reality constituting impulses underlying each socio-cultural and historical epoch."

Barbara Czarniawska, in her chapter "Going back to go forward: On studying organizing in action nets," traces process thinking in manage-ment and organization theory back in time. She relates uses of the word "process" to a variety of directions in organizational research, including systems theory, decision making, organizing, Actor-Network Theory and action-nets. Czarniawska makes a plea for a return from "theory of organi-zations" to "organization theory," making the point that organizing allows for capturing that which is not framed by formal organizations.

The final part of the volume brings chapters containing the latest theo-retical and empirical contributions from researchers in Process Organiza-tion Studies. These include two conceptual papers (Hernes; Osadchiy, Bogenrieder, and Heugens) and three empirical studies (Wiebe; Jordan and Mitterhofer; Gephart, Topal, and Zhang).

Tor Hernes' chapter "Actor-Network Theory, Callon's scallops and process-based organization studies" takes a closer look at Actor-Network Theory (ANT) and discusses its potential as a process-based theory of organization. While there is an increase in process-based work in organization studies, the field is also witnessing an increase in the application of ANT theory. ANT has intellectual roots in process thinking, while being applied to a range of organizational phenomena. Hernes works successively with three concepts: the becoming of things, heterogeneous relationality, and contin-gency and time. Michel Callon's (1986) study of the domestication of scallops in St Brieuc Bay is used as a proxy for ANT and ANT related studies. The paper concludes by suggesting that meaning structures, represented in pragmatism and phenomenology, may be used to improve its potential as a process-based theory of organization.

In "Organizational learning through problem absorption: A processual view," Sergey Osadchiy, Irma Bogenrieder, and Pursey Heugens draw on process theoretical ideas to examine how organizational rules are bent, stretched, or otherwise accommodated as new issues are confronted that demand solutions, a phenomenon called problem absorption. The authors argue that when considered processually, problem absorption does not necessarily result in rigidity as is often thought, but that it can lead instead to two different forms of organizational learning—a first form in which the meanings of distinctions and categorizations inherent in rules are recursively altered over time through the ongoing actions of adapting rules to different types of problems, and a second form that occurs as organization members reflexively make sense of their cumulative experiences of problem-fitting and rule-shifting, leading them to engage in higher-order learning and more radical forms of disruption of rule systems.

Elden Wiebe's chapter, "Temporal sensemaking: Managers' use of time to frame organizational change" responds to the importance given to temporality in process thinking. Temporality, seen as the ongoing configuration of past, present, and future, is a central theme with prominent thinkers, such as Mead, Bergson, Whitehead, and Heidegger. It locates actors *in* time rather than projecting their actions against externalized time, such as in the form of clocks or calendars. Wiebe takes this notion into the debates about organizational change. From an empirical study he constructs five distinct "worlds" of organizational change within the "same" organization. The five distinct "worlds" of change exhibit their own particular temporality, enabling a broader temporal basis than retrospection for sensemaking while contributing to our knowledge of researching and implementing organizational change.

The final two chapters are both studies of sensemaking, each exploring aspects of the relationship between sensemaking and institutions. In "Studying *metaphors-in-use* in their social and institutional context: Sensemaking and discourse theory," Silvia Jordan and Hermann Mitterhofer explore the kinds of metaphors associated with organizational members sensemaking during a strategic change initiative. To do so, they use a "contextualized metaphor" approach, which expands conceptual metaphor theory (Lakoff and Johnson, 1980) with Jürgen Link's less commonly used critical discourse analysis, to identify different understandings of the change process and to explain the differential power of certain metaphors of change. Through a careful analysis of collective symbols generated during the change process, this study provides a rare account of how organizational sensemaking is shaped by the social and institutional meanings in which it is embedded.

Robert Gephart, Cagri Topal, and Zhen Zhang's chapter, "Future-oriented sensemaking: Temporalities and institutional legitimation," takes as its focus sensemaking that works to construct intersubjective meanings that create or project images of future phenomena. This is a little studied domain in a field in which retrospection has long been the dominant temporal mode. In their chapter, Gephart and colleagues first offer a discussion of how future-oriented sensemaking is accomplished, how it relates to other temporal dimensions, and how it legitimates institutions. They then describe an ethnomethodological study of a public hearing from which several practices in future-oriented sensemaking are identified that are important in producing and sustaining institutional legitimation.

Each of the chapters in this volume both makes a unique contribution to our understanding of Process Organization Studies, and at the same time provokes many further questions. While process thinking has been around a long time, it is still relatively rare to find it at the heart of scholarly writing on organizations. Our hope for this volume is that it will energize a conversation long overdue in organization studies, and bring process thinking more fully into our writing, teaching, and practice.

References

Bergson, H. (1988). *Matter and Memory*, New York: Zone Books.

Bergson, H. (1998). The idea of duration, in D. Browning & W. T. Myers (eds) *Philosophers of Process*, New York: Fordham University Press, 137–86.

Buckley, W. (1967). *Sociology and Modern Systems Theory*, Englewood Cliffs, NJ: Prentice-Hall.

Callon, M. (1986). Some elements of a sociology of translation: Domestication of the scallops and the fishermen of St Brieuc Bay, in J. Law (ed.) *Power, Action and Belief: A New Sociology of Knowledge?* London: Routledge & Kegan Paul, 196–223.

Chia, R. (1999). A "rhizomic" model of organizational change and transformation: Perspective from a metaphysics of change, *British Journal of Management*, 10, 209–27.

Chia, R. & King, I. W. (1998). The organizational structuring of novelty, *Organization*, 5(4), 461–78.

Cyert, R. M. & March, J. G. (1963). *A Behavioural Theory of the Firm*, 2nd edn, Oxford: Blackwell.

Czarniawska, B. (2004). On time, space, and action nets, *Organization*, 11(6), 773–91.

Deleuze, G. (2004). *Difference and Repetition*, New York: Continuum Publishing Group.

Emirbayer, M. & Mische, A. (1998). What is agency? *American Journal of Sociology*, 103, 1180–98.

Ford, M. P. (1993). William James, in D. R. Griffin, J. B. Cobb, M. P. Ford, P. A. Y. Gunter, & P. Ochs (eds) *Founders of Constructive Postmodern Philosophy*, New York: State University of New York Press, 89–132.

Heidegger, M. (1927). *Being and Time*, Oxford: Blackwell.

Hernes, T. (2007). *Understanding Organization as Process: Theory for a Tangled World*, London: Routledge.

James W. (1977). *A Pluralistic Universe*, Cambridge, MA: Harvard University Press.

Lakoff, G. & Johnson, M. (1980). *Metaphors We Live By*, Chicago: University of Chicago Press.

Levitt, B. & March, J. G. (1988). Organizational learning, *Annual Review of Sociology*, 14, 319–40.

Lewin, K. (1951). *Field Theory in Social Science*, New York: Harper & Row.

Link, J. (1982). Kollektivsymbolik und Mediendiskurs. Zur aktuellen Frage, wie subjektive Aufrüstung funktioniert, *kultuRRevolution*, 1.

Link, J. (1996). *Versuch über den Normalismus. Wie Normalität produziert wird*, Göttingen: Vandenhoeck & Ruprecht.

Lucretius, T. C. (2004). *On the Nature of Things*, New York: Dover.

March, J. G. (1999). *The Pursuit of Organizational Intelligence: Decisions and Learning in Organizations*, Cambridge, MA: Blackwell.

March, J. G. & Olsen, J. P. (1975). The uncertainty of the past: Organizational learning under ambiguity, *The European Journal of Political Research*, 3, 147–71.

March, J. G. & Olsen, J. P. (1989). *Rediscovering Institutions*, New York: The Free Press.

Mead, G. H. (1934). *Mind, Self, and Society*, Chicago: University of Chicago Press.

Mead, G. H. (2002). *The Philosophy of the Present*, New York: Prometheus.

Peirce, C. S. (1878). How to make our ideas clear, *Popular Science Monthly*, 12, 286–302.

Rescher, N. (1996). *Process Metaphysics: An Introduction to Process Philosophy*, New York: State University of New York Press.

Schutz, A. (1967). *The Phenomenology of the Social World*, London: Heinemann Educational Books.

Tsoukas, H. & Chia, R. (2002). On organizational becoming: Rethinking organizational change, *Organization Science*, 13(5), 567–82.

Weick, K. E. (1979). *The Social Psychology of Organizing*, 2nd edn, New York: Random House.

Weick, K. E. (1995). *Sensemaking in Organizations*, Thousand Oaks: Sage.

Weick, K. E. (2000). *Making Sense of the Organization*, Oxford: Wiley Blackwell.

Weick, K. E., Sutcliffe, K. M. & Obstfeld, D. (2005). Organizing and the process of sensemaking, *Organization Science*, 16(4), 409–21.

Whitehead, A. N. (1929). *Process and Reality*, New York: The Free Press.

3

Stop Making (Philosophical) Sense: Notes towards a Process Organizational-Thinking beyond "Philosophy"

John Mullarkey

Abstract: What happens when a new philosophy emerges from a supposedly non-philosophical field? Must it follow the norm whereby a form of philosophy is recognized to be at work in this area (by a recognized philosopher, but one operating as an outsider), or by some kind of philosopher manqué (a native within the field) being discovered at work there (by this same outsider)? In other words, can something only be deemed "philosophical" in view of an implied subject who thinks in a particular way, discovering thoughts similar to those found in established positions of philosophy? What, alternatively, would it mean to think of a supposedly non-philosophy realm, such as process organization theory, as immanently philosophical? This chapter explores the conditions by which, far from merely illustrating or applying extant philosophy ("Theory"), Process Organization Theory might actually be seen to create its own novel philosophical thoughts, immanently. By examining the non-philosophy forwarded by François Laruelle, and the manner in which time and process resist any attempts to theorize them (to make sense out of them), we will outline a way of seeing process as a kind of resistant thinking (an idea first put forward by Henri Bergson) and, therewith, Process Organization Theory as a new form of philosophy. Interdisciplinary thought, on this view, is not about applying philosophy, but consists in philosophy renewing itself (making itself unrecognizable) by acknowledging how non-philosophical realms (art, technology, science) might be capable of creating new philosophical thoughts. With that, however, must also come a transformation of what we mean by philosophy and even thought itself.

3.1 Introduction

"Process Organization Studies." Were I to call myself a philosopher *in general* (be it in virtue of philosophizing about things in general or even about the general as such), or a process philosopher in particular (philosophizing about processes in general), the question of the nature of this inter-discipline (process philosophy and organization studies) would, typically, be the first to arise in a study such as this. Is it a meeting of "two" disciplines only (or does each harbour even more intra-disciplinarities within itself)? If so, what form of relation does this meeting constitute? To list just two options for now: is it one of *application*, where ideas from one field are used (or abused) in the field of the other; or is it one of *illustration*, where the concepts belonging to one discipline are given a more complete sense now that they find perspicuous examples in a new domain? And in which direction might such relations of application or illustration (or a merger of the two) run? Would it be *from* process philosophy *to* organization studies, or, counter-intuitively, in the opposite direction. I say "counter-intuitively," because the norm in such relations is deductive, going from the general to the particular, and so, typically, from the philosophical to the non-philosophical. But what might an *inductive* movement look like, one that generates a new philosophy specific to its own examples (in this case, organization studies)? To cut to the chase: the purpose of this chapter is to show how the normal direction from philosophy to non-philosophy can be reversed, and so, thereby, to make the case for a process organizational-thinking that does not rest on (apply or illustrate) extant models of philo-sophical thought.

How might such a reversal operate? Certainly not through arguing on the basis of a new set of *generalities* (on pain of performative contradiction). Though there are some theorists today who are interested in the non-philosophical sources of philosophy, like Alain Badiou, too often the new relation in question, whereby art, technology, or science is shown to be capable of *forcing new philosophical thoughts onto us*, is nonetheless ratified as such on account of an existing conception of what philosophical thought looks like. As such, however, nothing has really changed: only on account of an image of philosophy, *recognized by philosophers*, is the "non-philosophical" discipline allowed to create (or rather, re-create) phil-osophical concepts, categories, or methods. In this chapter, I want instead to entertain the possibility that things could be otherwise: because I *do not* already have a (process) philosophy *of* organization studies (what do I know about organization studies anyway?), nor even a fixed idea of what *any* philosophy *per se* might be (as will soon come to light), it might be possible for a genuinely *new* philosophy to be generated from process organization studies itself—to see process organization studies itself *as a philosophy of the future*.

Lest the charge of false modesty be directed towards me, let me assure the reader that I am truly convinced that I do not *know* what *is* Process Philosophy. Richard Rorty once described Henri Bergson's process thought as little more than just "whooshing about a bit" (Rorty, 1982: 182). In one respect, he might have had a point, in as much as this "whooshing" could be seen as an embodied, affective understanding of a process that does not lend itself to any static representation. Indeed, I will argue that process *makes* sense when it is enacted as an *immanent movement* rather than when it is seen as a representation of the object. This immanent movement is not an image of the object, so-called, but is a *part* of the "object"—a sensemaking that goes from the particular to the general (to reflection, to representation, and as such, to what is currently called philosophy), but only by transforming what we mean by (make sense of) philosophy itself. For, in the end, what is philosophy? As we will see, this clichéd question—the stereotypical question of the armchair philosopher—must itself also be transformed. When we reverse the direction of thought, taking (or seeing) our example, organization studies, *as* philosophical, then the question is best re-formulated as follows: *what will philosophy become*? Only by "whooshing about" in a new domain of thought may we find an answer.

At one level, then, this chapter concerns the philosophy of time, but it does so only to expose a general ignorance here—for there is no one philosophy of time, only specific, varying philosophies of something each calls "time." There are myriad different approaches to time, processual, phenomenological, and political, to name but three *very* broad categories (examples of each being treated in turn below). However, it is not my purpose to replay an old relativist tune, but rather to investigate whether these different perspectives cannot be reconciled in *another time* that does not attempt to represent them all transcendentally (as right or wrong) but that participates in each immanently. This participation might operate both in terms of how these theories resist each other (and their attempts to subsume each other) and in terms of how temporal phenomena resist such grand theories' own attempts to essentialize time. The ramifications for applying a philosophy of time (to organizations, say) would be to turn the tables on philosophy: we no longer apply a philosophy to a field, top-down, *but each field*, by resisting theory, generates a new philosophy of time through its own processes—bottom up, and immanently.

3.2 The problem of time as the need for a *theory* of time

Time has mostly been a problem for philosophers who not merely needed it to be explained, but needed it to be explained *away*. For Parmenides, only an immutable, immobile Being could explain the illusion of *all* becoming. Less radically, though still with an eye to reducing time to the atemporal, Aristotle posited the need for substance to explain movement: an unsupported movement was impossible, change is a predicate that requires a subject (movement belongs to the *thing* that moves—see Aristotle, 2004: Book Z). This need to find the condition for time, understood otherwise as unsupported change, can be seen, however, as more of a problem for philosophy than for time itself. It may be that the anathema of unconditioned becoming says more about philosophers' knowledge, about the conditions of epistemic respectability, than anything else. In Book XI of his *Confessions*, St Augustine famously wrote: 'What then is time? If no one asks me, I know, if I want to explain it to someone who asks, I do not know' (Augustine, 2008: Book XI). From this one might ask whether the *problem* of time is really only a problem of knowledge, specifically, the philosopher's model of knowledge *as a set of eternal, essential truths*? If such knowledge is timeless, then, perhaps it is the medium through which time is refracted, and thereby stripped of its inherent becoming simply in order to be understood (to stand under, in a sub-stance).

Certainly, a whole line of modern philosophers have argued that the only way to understand time is through some timeless element. In particular, there are those philosophers of time called "detensers" in virtue of the fact that they deny that the processual tenses of pastness, presentness, and futurity are real aspects of time (Smith, 1994: 1). Conversely, seeing time as a dynamic movement *makes no sense for them*, given that this process of time would itself seem to require a time *in* which to proceed, leading us on to a vicious regress. If a dimension of time like the present is itself moving, according to what measure of temporality does it move? How fast is it? Must it move in another, second-order temporality or 'super-time' (Schlesinger, 1994: 218)? Yet, even if such a second-order time existed, it too would need its own repository, another higher-level super-time, and so on *ad infinitum*. The detenser contends, therefore, that the process view of time, that it is a kind of flow from future to present to past, is an illusion of the mind. Real time belongs to a physical substratum (including the physical basis of the mind), a substratum (substance, subject) that works according to the laws of cause and effect that establish a view of time in terms of the *timeless* relations of "before," "simultaneous with," or "after," rather than the tenses of past, present, and future. There is no "flux," "dynamic," or "flow."

Despite appearances to the contrary (for many take him to be a process philosopher in the mould of Bergson), parts of Gilles Deleuze's writings reveal him to be one such detenser. In his book *Difference and Repetition*, for example, Deleuze talks of the paradox of the present as the need for a time in which to constitute or synthesize time (as the succession of past, present, and future): "*there must be another time in which the first synthesis of time can occur*" (Deleuze, 1994: 79). This time, moreover, cannot be time understood as succession, as change, or tensed, for this would just bring us back to the question of how and where such a time was constituted, how it might flow. Rather, it is empty, the time of eternity—what Deleuze calls the Virtual or *Aion*.

And here we come back to knowledge and the needs of philosophy again. For Deleuze, it is a *principle of sufficient reason* that demands that there be an "implicit" or virtual domain to make the present pass: for there to be change, there must be a *principle of* change (see Deleuze, 1993: 41–3). Process requires at least *some* kind of conceptual or logical support. This is not the same kind of support as Aristotle's substance metaphysics, of course, for at issue here is what allows us to *think* change, rather than a *thing* that is changing. But the kinship between the thing and a *logic* that supports change is noteworthy in as much as, in each case, the alternative is *unthinkable*: process without *substance or concept* is unsustainable. We need a *timeless* concept of time in order to understand time (a point that Deleuze shares, ironically, with his chief critic, Alain Badiou: to think change, one cannot begin *with* change, but outside of it; one must commence with Parmenides rather than Heraclitus—see Badiou, 2009: 542).

But what if the whole question of "support" was wrong? What if the "support" for time was always *itself*, was simply a set of indefinite *other* times nested within each other? The regress would not be a logical paradox or *aporia* whose solution requires us to stand outside of time in a virtual eternity: we could embrace the regress and naturalize it in a collection of myriad different instances of times (plural), a plethora of empirical examples, each sufficient unto itself *simply because they refuse to reduce themselves to just one, essential, eternal philosophical principle.*

Indeed, Bergson himself has a theory of the *planes* of time (or *"durée"*) that does just that: time is a stratified system of temporal rhythms running at different rates, each a condensation of other temporal rhythms (see Mullarkey, 1999: 31–61, 165–90). The pulsations of one actual time sub-sumes within itself those of other actualities in a nested *indefinite* order of ever more contractile *durées*. Time is not one unilinear succession (in need of one of other form of atemporal support), but a tiered regress of different rhythms. This regress, moreover, is not only benign: it is actually a real cosmological system of non-quantifiable scales (see Smith, 1994: 180–94). And it is on only *one* of those scales that the knowledge some call specific to philosophy itself resides.

Let me explain further. In his study of the history of process philosophy, Nicholas Rescher makes a remarkable point when describing Bergson's work: "everything in the world is caught up in a change of some sort, so that it is accurate rather than paradoxical to say that what is changing is change itself." He then adds that it would be unfaithful to the spirit of process philosophy to set *any* ontological categories that would imply concepts and positions that a process philosophy must permanently reject. However, what, we might ask, would this process philosophy be if not a changing-philosophy that must countenance the possibility of permanent transformation, even for itself? Probably to avoid such apparent *nonsense*, Rescher adds that "at the most abstract level" all true philosophical posi-tions must be the same, even for process thought (Rescher, 1996: 17, 36). For Bergson, though, this means of escape from paradox is of no help, because there is no point that can be called the highest level of abstraction: Bergson believes that abstraction is an ongoing process with no highest or lowest levels. And the so-called "examples" ("illustrations," "applications") of any one philosophy of time are themselves another level or scale of *durée*, rather than a fixed object represented by a fixed (philosophical) image. The tables have turned, and the object (art form, science, organization, . . .) generates its own temporality, and therewith a possible philosophy to accompany it.

3.3 Talking about time: sense, nonsense, and narrative

Faced by the paradox of representing time as change (which we might call "Augustine's problem"), philosophers can either posit some timeless ground that will facilitate its comprehension, its sense, or they can, as

Bergson does, embrace the paradox of multiple times as a new production of what it means to comprehend a new logic of time. And this will involve a certain revision of what we mean by philosophical knowledge. But Bergson is not alone in this endeavor. There are a number of examples we can draw upon from recent writings in the philosophy of time that make the same gesture towards a new logic of understanding, one that can even look like a logic of non-understanding, of not knowing, of not making sense of time. Nathan Widder's *Reflections on Time and Politics*, for instance, proposes a Deleuzian "ontology of sense" that involves nonsense. This idea of non-sense, he argues, should not be seen as dialectical contradiction, for that would be too abstract, and not *ontological* enough. Something beyond Hegelian contradiction is required: a "Sense" of non-sense that is under-stood through a *differential* logic (see Widder, 2008: 34, 36).[1] Such "Sense" goes beyond subject and predicate logic, being a sense that is "also non-sense," for its identity is one of self-differentiation (the becoming that comes with paradoxes of self-reference, as in Russell's famous Barber para-dox). In this respect, a paradox brings *too much sense*, being a nonsense that keeps *making sense* only by creating new types of sense (just as Russell's paradox was solved through a theory of types of meaning). As such, the Sense and nonsense of time are not opposites, but rather both "oppose the absence of sense." So far, so Bergsonian, one might say. Yet Widder's Deleuzian credentials do not allow the proliferation of such sense into typically non-Deleuzian fields such as anthropology and phenomenology: Sense is "not anthropological" because "anthropology . . . assumes, as such, the empirical discourse *of* man" (Widder, 2008: 109, 114, 36), and for Deleuzians, the discourse of man—which includes phenomenology— must be debunked.

Compare this, then, with the clearly opposed discourse of Paul Rabinow's *Marking Time: On the Anthropology of the Contemporary* (opposed, that is to say, according to Widder's ontology of what *can* make sense of the para-doxes of time). Yet on the face of things, Rabinow, like Widder, endorses the need for a certain kind of unknowing, or break with sense, that he describes in terms of an *ignorance* of time (or the "contemporary," as he puts it).[2] This comes, however, precisely through a focus on *anthropos* and *against* any *ontologizing* of time (and so contra Widder on two fronts at least). For Rabinow, anthropology is itself pluralist in essence, conveying "the dynam-ic and mutually constitutive . . . connections between figures of *anthropos* and the diverse, and at times inconsistent, branches of knowledge available during a period of time" (Rabinow, 2007: 4). He goes on (following Niklas

Luhmann), to link this pluralism with an "ecology of ignorance" and the need to acknowledge the ability to live without needing to know—"we have a responsibility to our ignorance" (Rabinow, 2007: 60–2). In his methodology, Rabinow is also attracted to John Dewey's pragmatic and nominalist approach, especially with regards to finding new modes of "thinking and writing." Yet Dewey remained too philosophical for Rabinow, being "not nominalist enough" and veering too much towards "ontologizing" (Rabinow, 2007: 6–7). Here, then, Rabinow's pluralism towards *thinking* the contemporary mode of time must stay within the anthropological and the "ontic," keeping away from fixed, ontological modes of philosophical thought.

One could regard David Wood's *Time after Time* as a "middle way" between Widder's Deleuzian ontology and Rabinow's anthropological anti-ontologism of time, given its own position within phenomenological ontology—how Being appears to us.[3] At the same time as arguing that there can no longer be any "grand narratives" concerning time, this rejection is linked to Wood's own pluralism towards time:

> I am speaking of a certain practical recognition that our theories rest on schemes and that schemes and things are not just inevitable gaps, but an abyss of difference. ... It is my bet that the "negative capability" required to function effectively in this abyss is to be found in all that work in the sciences and the humanities that can remember well enough ... to be able to welcome the event of time (Wood, 2007: 23).

Where the Christian and Enlightenment traditions tried to make sense of time, to give it a clear linearity, we now live within the "end of Time," so much so that "the breakdown of Time is one of the most thought-provoking aspects of the present age" (Wood, 2007: 12–13, 22, 20). But this allusion to Heidegger—and therewith his view that "we are still not thinking" enough about what is most important, Being—does not necessitate, according to Wood, that we "cannot tell stories" any more about time. Time can still be narrated: not in a "grand," totalizing fashion, of course, but through "open narratives": "narrativity is a democratic, elastic, sense-making activity." This renewal of time does not mean a return to linear time, but a "relaunching of time itself as intensity, possibility, as open" (Wood, 2007: 22). This open, democratic sensemaking, then, involves new models of thought and of ignorance, the reference to "negative capability" in the quotation above referring this time to John Keats's idea that "man is capable of being in uncertainties, Mysteries, doubts without any irritable reaching after fact and reason" (in Wu, 2005: 135).

3.4 Whose philosophy is it anyway?

Perhaps the question remains to be asked, however: how open can we be in this new democratic approach to time? How much of this "negative capability" can we embrace before we end up incapable of saying anything at all about time? After all, the principle of post-Heideggerian philosophy, on the contrary, has most often been to look continually for the essence of one *true* thought and *real* philosophy. This is because, as David Wood cited, for this view the most thought-provoking thing in our thought-provoking time is that "we are still not thinking." From the interdisciplinary position that I want to articulate here, however, the opposite is the case. Philosophical thinking can be found everywhere, and not merely because organization studies, say, can "ape" Plato, or reinvent Deleuze. And this for one simple reason: philosophical thought has always been a contested, multitude of examples. In other words, any one philosophy can only privilege a preferred form of thinking by *fiat*. Beyond such preferential treatment, however, there are always so many counter-examples: thinking descriptively, poetically, mathematically, affectively, embodiedly, analogically, syllogistically, fuzzily, paraconsistently; thinking through a method of questions, of problems, of dialogue, of dialectic, of genealogy, of historicism, of deconstruction … So why not a new thinking, process-organizational thinking?

We can put it this way: philosophy is that subject that has always failed to provide itself with a definition. A negative capability. Even as many practicing philosophers still endeavor to find or offer, finally, today, the one true definition of philosophical thought, so the judgment of both history and contemporary practice conspires against them: be it diachronically or synchronically, philosophy is unique amongst other disciplines in *not* possessing a definite definition, an uncontested essence. That is why, apart from its own history of agonistic examples of what it means to be a "true" or "proper" philosopher, there is no philosophy that is not at the same time a philosophy *of some other subject*, of science, of art, of history (see Mullarkey, 2006: 129–34). Philosophy is a parasite or symbiant, inherently relational. Put otherwise, however, given its own shadowy lack of content, this means that philosophy actually *belongs to other subjects* in the first instance. In that respect, the "philosophical" becomes an adjective tied to no *one* noun—it should be seen as the moment when another subject, like politics or literature, also finds itself in a state of transformation, with an identity crisis. When the subject loses its definition, then, its *own* philosophy arises, immanently (because all that philosophy itself offers as an essence is the lack of an essence, a disputed identity). But what *that* subject's philosophy looks like in detail will always be of its *own* making, a new philosophy generated through the specifics of what it calls into question, which identities it finds it must create anew. That, at least, is the optimal case whereby the philosophical status of organization studies, for instance, concerns what we mean by the practice of organization studies as much as what we mean by philosophy.

3.5 Thinking *about* time versus thinking *in* time

One retort to what I have argued thus far may take the *tu quoquoe* response, for haven't I already championed one specific philosophy in all this, namely Bergson's process philosophy. Yet my own interest in Bergson stems mainly from his metaphilosophy and its refusal to *define* (permanently) a transferable philosophical method, even for his own so-called method of intuition. At best, Bergson only gives us various quasi-definitions or pseudo-formulae, "dynamic" and "indefinite" definitions for philosophical intuition.[4] Here are a few of them: "thinking in duration" (*penser en durée*), the "inversion" of the "habitual direction of the work of thought" (*invertir la direction habituelle du travail de la pensée*), "thought and the moving" (*la pensée et le mouvant*—Bergson, 1946: 34, 190). With regard to this last formulation, if one asks after "the moving" by demanding to know "the moving *what?*", the answer that comes is that what is moving is a complexity of other movements that only appear to us as a *thing*. The appearance of substance is not denied, therefore, but what it *means* is transformed.

Bergson, consequently, does not offer us a general theory of process (indeed, for him there is no such thing as "becoming in general" but only the different processes belonging to each specific domain (Bergson, 1911: 324). The very notion of "process" itself, therefore, should be taken as only a place-holder for whatever emerges in each discipline as transformative. So calling *x* (art, history, or organizations) processual is *not* a definition. "Process" always signifies a quasi-concept at best: it marks the lack of an essence rather the positive definition of one. Indeed, it could be argued that "process philosophy should be read as a 'non-philosophy'" after the model of François Laruelle's use of the term, meaning a democratic thought (or "science"), generated from the bottom up, extensionally, within different fields. The "non-philosophy" of organization studies, consequently, is not opposed to extant "proper" philosophy, but it is what transforms it, broadens its definition. The "non-" in non-philosophy should be taken in terms similar to the meaning of the "non-" in "non-Euclidean" geometry, being part of a "mutation" that locates philosophy as only one example among a larger set of theoretical practices (Laruelle, 1989: 8, 99ff; Laruelle, 1991: 47). Nor, I should add, will what counts as "emergent" or "transformational," a "becoming" or a "process," be something for an outside, transcendent philosophy to prescribe, for these terms too are only quasi-definitions or pseudo-formulae—*they merely point to, or suggest, what cannot be defined.*

Like Bergson's process thought, Laruelle's science is completely open, or democratic, with respect to the meaning of this science or "knowing." A "non-philosophy" of organization studies would allow every theory to be partially right in as much as each is only partial, but absolutely wrong in as much as each might try to be absolute or transcendent—the very resistance of processes within organizations ensuring this irreducibility to one, transcendent account (see Mullarkey, 2006: 125–56). The theories of *x* are *a part of* the process of *x*: they relate to it mereologically rather than representationally. This is what I would call a metaphilosophical thesis, one open to the becoming-philosophical of other, *currently* non-philosophical subject-matters.

3.6 Process organizational-thinking, or, that which will become philosophy

According to Alain Badiou, there are no events in philosophy—its form is eternal, Platonic. But if one is a thoroughgoing process philosopher, there *are* such events: not only is there change everywhere, but even one's concept of process must proceed too (*pace* Rescher). Philosophy too becomes, through the forces of a (provisionally) outside "non-philosophy." Such a philosophical event will redraw the map of what counts as non-philosophy and philosophy. And its temporality is the future anterior, of that which will be or will possibly be (for such things are unforeseeable). Such Socratic unknowing—what Paul Rabinow called the responsibility to ignorance—is not about weaving mystery just for the sake of it, but is needed to facilitate the advent of something new in the name of what could become "philosophy." Hence, a process philosophy doesn't statically *reflect* the world (its history, its art, its organizations); rather, the world and its various subject-matters *refract* what philosophy is (to become) by proceeding with their *own* thinking.

For this reason, we should be open to the possibility of a "process organizational-thinking" that could constitute a philosophical event all its own through its ability to resist the ontology of any one philosophical theory (that offers us only one answer to questions such as "what is process?", "what is an organization?", and so on). "Thinking *in* organizational process" would *change* what process, organization, and even what thinking and philosophy mean, and without any need for ready-made philosophical illustration, ratification, or corroboration.[5]

So, what does (or would) process organizational thinking look like? How do (or would) we recognize it? The quick answer to that question is first this: we must stop trying to *recognize* such thinking as if we *actually knew* what thinking itself is. Practice ignorance, or unknowing. But this is not to say that one should not apply philosophy at all to organizations, or even that one should be against every illustrative use of philosophy *per se*. It is, rather, to say that one should not allow any one philosophy to essentialize what organizations are (that is, to ontologize them). We need to converge all theories and avoid the essentialism offered by any one—apply, or use, as many philosophies as possible.

The concern that some might have with such a pluralism, however, is that it would lead us down the slippery slope to relativism. But consider this description from Bergson regarding which image is best to use in order to understand process (*durée*)—the answer, again, is *all* of them:

> No image will replace the intuition of duration, but many different images, taken from quite different orders of things, will be able, through the convergence of their action, to direct the consciousness to the precise point where there is a certain intuition to seize on (Bergson, 1946: 165–6).

Or consider this quotation from Friedrich Nietzsche, the supposed godfather of contemporary relativism, on "perspective knowing":

> There is only a perspective seeing, only a perspective "knowing"; and the more affects we allow to speak about one thing, the more eyes, different eyes, we can use to observe one thing, the more complete will our "concept" of this thing, our "objectivity", be (Nietzsche, 1990: 119).

Pluralism does not have to lead us down into solipsistic silence, incommensurable frameworks, and ineffable insights. It can also be the spur to conference, to bringing together "more eyes," to multiplying the perspectives, and to taking counsel from others. The drift to a relativistic impasse is only inevitable if one takes the implied relativity to be *representational*: if, instead, one understands theories (of) organizations as immanent, processual parts of the Real (of organizations), then each theory is related to organizations mereologically rather than in epistemic terms of right (absolutism) or wrong (relativism). There is no one picture of the whole that either succeeds or fails to re-present the totality of the whole (as if there ever was a static whole standing still long enough to be pictured); rather, the part of the whole *exemplifies* or *instantiates* it through its own process (by "the convergence of their action", as Bergson put it), because the whole itself is not static either: it is a process that can be instantiated in many kinds of examples, or better, through the movement *within* and *between* many examples. (The emphasis here on including as many images or eyes as possible also precludes this pluralism from falling back into a lazy, "pick and mix" dilettantism, which would, in fact, be just as selective as any absolutist approach.)

In other words, if one materializes theory (philosophy) itself within a process ontology, then there is no need to try and find one transcendent discourse (such as Deleuzian naturalism, anthropology, phenomenology, or semiotics, cognitivism, neuroscience, . . .) that somehow has a privileged access to the Real. Materializing theory in this way shows how each philosophy is only a part, and, by that acknowledged *partiality*, opens up each part to every other part—hence, the formula: "process = pluralism."

Moreover, saying that each theory, philosophy, or sensemaking is a part of the "object" does not mean that there is *only our* construction of the object through language, our narratives (be that construction either social or individual, voluntary or involuntary). It *also* states that the object is *a part of us*, because both we and the object are processes. Participation is reciprocal. To be sure, it may well be that the effectiveness of certain popular examples within organization studies, such as the Mann Gulch episode, lies in part in how we narrate it, in how it is told as a story. But why one kind of narration works better than another, or why Mann Gulch works so well as an event for narration, must also rely on issues that are not determined by either us as representational animals, nor by any logic of narration at all. The manner of our knowing the object (or, if you prefer, "partial construction") *exemplifies* the same kind of processes as the object itself *exemplifies*—theirs is an immanent, non-representational relation.

So, with all these preliminaries and cautions in mind, what, we might now ask, would be an example of an organizational thinking that generates its own philosophy immanently, as part (theory) to whole (its "object")? To answer this we must first remember that processes are indefinite and inherently unpredictable, and as such, give us something of the essence of philosophy as an indefinite, inessential discipline. Consequently, when the essential concepts, categories, and methods of organization (studies) are in flux too, *it is precisely in virtue of this that it becomes philosophical, just as philosophy too becomes something other than "itself"—it is a reciprocal co-variation.* But, of course, this begs the question: what are the "essential concepts, categories, and methods of organization (studies)?" And to this question, no outside, supposedly transcendent respondent can answer. The response must come from *within*. Yet, admittedly, the division between inside and outside, immanence and transcendence, is not absolute but porous (it too is becoming), so perhaps some nascent intuitions can be offered through my own, limited, participation (or "whooshing about") amongst the reflections of those practicing organization studies today. Certainly, the number of images on offer of what *currently* seem (to me) like its most critical concepts, categories, and methods (if only through their sheer repeated presence *at the moment*), are multiple. A short-list of resulting questions might include the following:

1. What is an organization? A business, a public institution, a boat race team, the bodily-relation of a *Big Issue* seller to his or her customers? What other phenomena might be looked at as actual examples of organizations *(rather than as metaphors of organizations)*: slime mould; a termite hill; a performance troupe; the unemployed; protest groups; religious groups—that is, examples from the physical, plant, and animal realms; from the art world and the underworld, from politics, and from science?

2. Why is the use of dramatic examples—the fire fighters in the Mann Gulch episode, for instance—so prevalent? Are such examples tied to a competitive model of life (and death)? Must vital risk be at the heart of all examples because capitalism is both in need of risk, while also needing to tame it, being equally *excess*-risk-averse? Conversely, what is mundane sensemaking—and so what would be a supposed extra-mundane sensemaking? Is there such a thing as an "everyday" example, or is the everyday also dramatic, though at a different speed?

3. How should examples be documented? What are the losses and gains in a shift from textual documentation, to the use of diagrams, to interviews, to video, film-making, and audio-recording? Is there a working-assumption in this movement that the latter are more direct and less mediated? What use of explicitly narrational techniques can be employed? Is the use of rhetoric (or "style") always on obstacle to truth?

4. How should the investigator interact with organizations? From an objective, outside standpoint (transcendentally)? Should the investigator aim to represent events impartially, irrespective of whether that is possible or not? Or should the investigator be embedded within an organization,

relating to the object of enquiry immanently? Should research go beyond participatory observation and ethnography towards explicitly subjective modes of engagement and reporting, such as the first-person confessional, or even poetry?

5. Within the key concept of sensemaking, what is the nature of sense itself? Is it bodily, automated, and habitual? Or is it disembodied, voluntary, and reflective? Is it representational or non-representational? Informational or affective, epistemic or poetic? Is sense itself multiple, stratified along different levels?

6. And what, then, is a process anyway? How fast and how slow must a process be in order for it to be a process (or at least the *same* process)? Are processes material or immaterial, embodied or abstract, collective or individual? Or are these false dichotomies? Do we need to understand stabilities—for instance, routines, discontinuities, and interruptions of flow—as aspects of process too? Would such an incorporation entail a genuine void or irruption of non-process within process thought, or would it rather involve only a new kind, or speed, of process?

There are no conclusions to these questions, certainly none that might come from a non-practitioner like myself. But should the discipline keep on asking what currently appear (at least to me, and at least for now) to be fundamental questions, keep on both conferring, and arguing over the stakes, then, a least according to the indefinite definition of philosophy that I have outlined here, organizational-thinking will create a philosophy of its own, one with its own entirely new ideas about research, observation, documentation, sense, and even the very concept of what counts as either an organization or a process. It might even change the nature of what counts as thinking, and philosophy, itself. Nonetheless, though there may be no final resolution to any of these disputes, the lack of conclusion should not be a reason to stop enquiry. *The process is all.* The "answer" is in the multi-plication of "images" and of "eyes." As Kenneth Gergen writes, there is no last word. And nor is there a first word either—or even the guarantee that words, first or last, will possess the answers for us. And, at the risk of a performative contradiction, these words here are not final either.

Notes

1. See also Widder, 2008: 37: contra Hegel's abstractionism ("the real is the rational, and the rational the real"): "sense must present itself in the ... movement from the empirical to the conceptual and back."

2. An "anthropology of the contemporary", as Rabinow has it, intends to show both how the past continues into the present as well as how the present is a rupture with it. The contemporary is the space where old forms are given new significance in a kind of "remediation" (Rabinow, 2007: 3).
3. Wood's primary references are Heidegger and Derrida.
4. The concept indefinites or "dynamic definitions" are throughout Bergson: see Bergson, 1911: 89, 90, 111–12; Bergson, 1946: 211.
5. For a deeper exploration of another revision of thinking, this time through cinema, see Mullarkey 2009. It is worth noting that in order to write this book I had to become a fully-trained lecturer in film studies.

References

Aristotle, (2004). *The Metaphysics*, new edition, Harmondsworth: Penguin Classics.

Augustine, (2008). *The Confessions*, trans. Henry Chadwick, Oxford: Oxford Paperbacks.

Badiou, A. (2009). *Logics of Worlds*, trans. Alberto Toscano, New York: Continuum Press.

Bergson, H. (1911). *Creative Evolution*, trans. Arthur Mitchell, London: Macmillan.

Bergson, H. (1946). *The Creative Mind: An Introduction to Metaphysics*, trans. Mabelle L. Andison, New York: Philosophical Library.

Bergson, H. (1988). *Matter and Memory*, trans. Nancy Margaret Paul and W. Scott Palmer, Cambridge, MA: Zone Books.

Deleuze, G. (1993). *The Fold: Leibniz and the Baroque*, trans. Tom Conley, London: Athlone Press.

Deleuze, G. (1994). *Difference and Repetition*, trans. Paul Patton, London: Athlone Press.

Laruelle, F. (1989). *Philosophie et non-philosophie*, Liege-Bruxelles: Mardaga.

Laruelle, F. (1991). *En Tant Qu'Un: La non-philosophie éxpliquée au philosophes*, Paris: Aubier.

Mullarkey, J. (1999). *Bergson and Philosophy*, Edinburgh: Edinburgh University Press.

Mullarkey, J. (2006). *Post-Continental Philosophy: An Outline*, New York: Continuum Press.

Mullarkey, J. (2009). *Refractions of Reality: Philosophy and the Moving Image*, Basingstoke: Palgrave-Macmillan.

Nietzsche, F. (1990). *On the Genealogy of Morals and Ecce Homo*, trans. Walter Kaufmann, Reissue edn, New York: Vintage Books.

Rabinow, P. (2007). *Marking Time: On the Anthropology of the Contemporary*, Princeton, NJ: Princeton University Press.

Rescher, N. (1996). *Process Metaphysics: An Introduction to Process Philosophy*, Albany, NY: SUNY Press.

Rorty, R. (1982). Comments on Dennett, *Synthese*, LIII, 181–7.

Schlesinger, G. (1994). Temporal Becoming, in L. N. Oaklander & Q. Smith (eds) *The New Theory of Time*, New Haven, CT: Yale University Press, 214–20.

Smith, Q. (1994). The Infinite Regress of Temporal Attributions, in L. N. Oaklander & Q. Smith (eds) *The New Theory of Time*, New Haven, CT: Yale University Press, 180–94.

Widder, N. (2008). *Reflections on Time and Politics*, Philadelphia: Pennsylvania State University Press.

Wood, D. (2007). *Time after Time*, Bloomington: Indiana University Press.

Wu, D. (ed.) (2005). *Romanticism: An Anthology*, 3rd edn, Oxford: Blackwell.

4

Co-Constitution, Causality, and Confluence: Organizing in a World without Entities

Kenneth J. Gergen

Abstract: The shift in focus from entities to process in organizational theory is both theoretically challenging and rich in potential. In this chapter I first consider two major challenges to the traditional science of organizations, including a shift from research devoted to establishing empirically based covering laws to a science invested in generating futures through participatory practices. I then consider a theoretical orientation to process, one that illuminates the collaborative or co-active constitution of what we take to be entities, and the ongoing process required to sustain a world of independent events or actions. Finally, with this emphasis on co-active process in place, I take up the possibility of understanding organizational activity in terms of confluence theory. The latter emphasizes wholistic collations of co-constituting "entities" that are in motion across time. Such an orientation to understanding invites the scholar to engage in future building activities that are sensitized to the protean potentials for organizational re-constitution.

By cosmic rule, as day yields night, so winter becomes summer, war becomes peace, and plenty gives way to famine. Fire penetrates the lump of myrrh, until the fire and myrrh die away, but to rise again in the smoke called incense.

Heraclitus

It is noteworthy that we generally recognize only a handful of philosophers—Heraclitus, Bergson, and Whitehead among them—whose writings privilege ongoing process over stable substances or structure. Perhaps this should not be surprising. The major concerns of Western philosophy have long been toward establishing durable foundations—for knowledge, morality, political practices, aesthetics, and so on. In a world of process, however, there is little reason to seek enduring foundations. Indeed, it is difficult to identify the kinds of substantial entities the understanding of which would require foundations. The search for knowledge requires an object of study.

Organizational science is largely a benefactor of the tradition of substances. That is, it was born in the wake of a philosophy seeking foundations for knowledge of an enduring subject matter. In effect, one may trace the beginnings of organizational science to the twentieth-century philosophy of science, and its attempt to generate viable foundations for empirical research. The longstanding belief that sustained research will lead to increments in knowledge of the organization, and that deductions from such knowledge will favor a progressive flourishing of organizational efficacy, has been a touchstone of the discipline. Thus, in entertaining the possibility of an alternative metaphysics—one that replaces the assumption of enduring entities with a vision of continuous process—we find ourselves crossing a threshold into largely unexplored territory. If process is in the forefront, how might we envision our subject matter, the process of inquiry, and the possible implications for world practices?

These are complex issues, pregnant with possibility, and the dialogues now exploring the potentials for a process orientation to organizational study are much to be welcomed. In the present chapter, I wish to offer three inter-related entries into this dialogue. First, I will take up the more general question of what might follow if a process perspective were to be embraced by organizational science. How radical are these departures; what promise do they hold? With these preliminary remarks in hand, I will outline a process-oriented departure that has, for me, opened up a new and exciting range of inquiry. My starting point in this case will be a concern with the relational generation of meaning. Finally, I will briefly sketch an alternative to traditional causal explanation in organizational science. The focus here will be on relational confluence.

4.1 An organizational science without organizations?

The word, organization, is a noun and it is also a myth. If one looks for an organization one will not find it. What we will find is that there are events, linked together, that will transpire within concrete walls, and these sequences, their pathways, their timing, are the forms we erroneously make into substances when we talk about organizations.

Karl Weick

The presumption of enduring entities is pivotal to the traditional science of organizations. Without presuming the substantive existence of "the organization," there would be little in the way of a science. How is it possible to embrace a process orientation and sustain any form of science as we know it? In my view, a fully developed process orientation would indeed require alterations in our traditional view of behavioral science. Many of these would be radical departures. However, science is not itself a stable institution, and its beliefs and practices have not only changed over the centuries, but in markedly different directions depending on the discipline. In this sense, one might well see the shift in physics from a Newtonian to a quantum paradigm as illustrating the potentials inherent in moving from an entity to a process based cosmology. In effect, as we shift assumptions so do we stand to open up new theoretical, methodological, and practical avenues of scientific activity. At the same time, major shifts in orientation such as this are not easily achieved. What are required are the difficult tasks of self-reflexive critique, imagining alternatives, and working through the potentials and shortcomings of various practices. In what follows, I briefly center on three areas of potential transformation, and their implications:

4.2 The challenge of pure process

If we replace entities as the focus of concern with process, we are sensitized at the outset to cross-time configurations. It is not the metaphors of the organization as a pyramid or a machine that are compelling, for example, so much as metaphors of turbulent streams or conversational flows. Put in these terms, however, we can distinguish differences along a dimension varying from conservative to more radical images of process. More conservative orientations have been present since the inception of the discipline. We have long theorized, for example, that organizational functioning depends on a set of continuous bi-causal relations among various organizational entities (e.g. groups or individuals). Most systems theories embody such a view. And organizational development has long been viewed as movement from an existing (and less than optimal) condition to a more favorable one. However, such accounts are conservative in their dependence on conceptions of bounded and stable states or entities. In the case of systems formulations, for instance, one typically posits entities or states which interact, and in most organizational development sequences one moves from one bounded and identifiable state to another.

Karl Weick was perhaps among the first to propose a more radical form of process theory (Weick, 1995). His study of the Mann Gulch disaster (Weick, 1993) provides an excellent illustration of how understanding expands when we broaden our vision of process. In this study of the communication among fire-fighters under rapidly changing and life-threatening conditions, almost none of the elements remains wholly stable. The fire is in continuous motion, as well as the condition of the fire-fighters, their communication, and their equipment. Although the cross-time transformations are less rapid, much the same could be said of other, more recent process-sensitive studies. This would include inquiry into organizational discourse, conversational processes, ethnomethods, dramaturgical scenarios, rituals, and so on.

However, while extending the relational emphasis in significant ways, we also begin to approach a ceiling. At the most basic level, the units making up the sequences tend to remain inviolate. The individual actors in such accounts, for example, continue to be treated as separate or indivisible units. In this sense, whatever we view as process remains as a relationship among the independent units. In more radical form, a process orientation would challenge the very conception of boundaries. If there is continuous change, there is no indivisible "thing" to be identified. Consider, for example, in the Mann Gulch study, one might say that the fire and dry grass formed an inseparably changing agglomeration. In the process individual identities were lost. In effect, one shifts focus from things in themselves to what might be viewed as a relational forming.

At this point, however, we begin to confront the limits of scholarly expression. As scholars we rely primarily on traditions of linguistic representation. However, a language of nouns and pronouns essentially presumes a world constituted by discrete entities. To employ the language is to construct just such a world. At the same time, such a vehicle of representation cannot easily be used to describe processes in continuous motion. One may articulate particular states or stages, but not the process in motion. A space is opened now for new and innovative orientations to theoretical intelligibility. Two such possibilities will be introduced later in this chapter.

4.3 From observation to participation

In a science committed to independent entities, there is reason to maintain a clear separation between the observer and the object of observation. Objective knowledge depends on the capacity of the observer to report on the state or condition of the observed. However, as we approach the possibility of pure process, it becomes increasingly difficult to specify the boundaries separating such entities. Under these conditions the traditional view of an observational science breaks down. The border between subject and object is blurred. Preparation for such a conclusion is already extant in various corners of the social sciences. From Kuhn's (1962) classic work to contemporary inquiry in the social studies of science, it is commonly understood that the scientific observer does not function independently from the assumptions and values shared within his or her community of peers. In this sense there is no "independent" observation. Observation is always situated within a context of relationship. In effect, the independent observer melts away into communal process. At the same time, if the putative object of science is a communal construction—born of the shared paradigms or traditions of the group—then neither is there an independent object. Both subject and object become outcomes of a more basic communal process.

From a process perspective, then, we are invited to consider alternatives to the view of the scientist as an observer of an independent world. Following the above line of reasoning, at least one promising possibility is to view the organizational scientist as participating within the broader processes making up cultural life. To engage in research is a form of cultural participation. From the selection of research methods, to the concepts employed in research, and the resulting interpretations, the scientist is effectively "making culture." We swim in the river of relationship, and we cannot avoid making waves. At this point, one may appropriately inquire into the forms of cultural life that are sustained or created by various research activities. Such questions are inevitably moral and political in implication, as critical organizational scholars have properly explicated. This point is closely tied to the next.

4.4 From covering laws to co-creating futures

If one presumes a world constituted by stable entities, one can envision a science dedicated to the progressive illumination of a subject matter. In traditional terms, continuing research enables the scientist to become increasingly accurate in making predictions concerning the nature and activity of such entities. On this account, the ideal result is a set of covering laws, that is, general laws that allow precise prediction of the phenomenon under various conditions. However, in a world of inherent process, this view of a progressive science is limited. Indeed, one may view human activity as infinitely protean. And given the participation of science within the cultural flow, scientific descriptions and explanations ineluctably alter the character of social life. For example, research based on the presumption of the machine-like functioning of the organization may contribute to forms of organizational life that come to resemble a machine. In effect, social science knowledge is not cumulative in the sense of enabling the increased prediction and control of human behavior. It is essentially an agent of cultural change.

A promising alternative to the traditional aim of producing covering laws follows from the above vision of the scientist as a participant within the cultural flows. Rather than attempting to hold a "mirror up to nature" the organizational scientist is invited to engage in inquiry with the specific aim of transforming culture. At the outset this would mean inquiring into the pragmatic potential of given research projects. To what communities does the research contribute, and in what ways? No longer would it suffice to respond in terms of increments to knowledge. Rather, one may ask about the contributions to organizational functioning that might result from the research. In more radical form, the organizational scientist would turn from observational study to action research. Here the outcomes of the research are coterminous with organizational transformation. Or, as it is said, "The best way to predict the future is to invent it".

Further dialogue on these issues is surely required. Nor should discussion be limited to these. Needed, as well, are discussions of our methods of inquiry, our relationship with the worlds outside the scholarly domain, moral and political relativism, the conception of the human being, and more. Some of these concerns will indeed be reflected in the sections that follow.

4.5 The originary process of co-action

I have long been concerned with the challenge of temporal process in the social sciences.[1] The most recent adventure, however, has grown from the widely shared critique of Western individualism. Cadres of critics have deliberated on the ways in which this ideology fosters a sense of fundamental loneliness and alienation; generates a sense of pervasive doubt in oneself; invites one to think of oneself as the sole arbiter of what is good and evil; establishes a tension between self on the one hand and community on the other; defines relationships as secondary to the well-being of the self; and ultimately encourages forms of self-serving, narcissistic, and exploitative behavior. However, the major problem has been that of articulating an alternative to such a conception. Rather than pressing toward new visions of the human being, there is a tendency to revert to a pre-modern valuing of community over individuals. Yet, upon closer inspection we find that a strong communalism suffers from many of the same problems inhabiting individualism. Both propose the existence of bounded or independent units in a potential relationship of alienation. How may we conceptualize human action, then, without division as its foundation? If we can do so, we move toward the possibility of process-oriented study.

In my attempt to theorize such a world, I have found it first useful to focus on actions that are typically attributed to individual actors. We say, for example, that John is aggressive, Shirley is kind, Harold is deceitful, and so on. We have, then, what appear to be meaningful units. However, let us ask whether one's behavior is aggressive if others find it playful, or whether one is kind if others find one's action self-serving. Can the individual in himself possess attributes; can a meaningful agent exist in a social vacuum? It seems far more adequate to locate the attribute in the relationship between actor and other. And if this is so, then the identity of the unit— or the unitization—is a byproduct of an ongoing relational process. Let me expand on this possibility. I offer here a series of rudimentary propositions that place the identification of a meaningful actor, squarely within the relational matrix:

4.5.1 An individual's actions in themselves possess no meaning

We pass each other on the street. I smile and say, "Hello Anna." You walk past without hearing. Under such conditions, what am I? To be sure, I have uttered two words. However for all the difference it makes I might have stood on my head or offered a set of nonsense syllables. When you fail to acknowledge me in any way, no action has occurred. I am not an actor.

4.5.2 The potential for meaningful action is realized through the supplementary action of another

An individual's actions begin to acquire attributes when another (or others) coordinate themselves to the action, that is, when they add some form of supplementary action (whether linguistic or otherwise). Effectively, I have performed a greeting in the previous case only by virtue of Anna's response. Her utterance, "Oh, hi, good morning ... " brings me to life as one who has greeted. We thus find that becoming an identifiable actor is a privilege granted by others. If others do not treat one's utterances as meaningful, if they fail to coordinate themselves around the offering, one is reduced to a non-entity. To combine these first two proposals, we may say that one's identification as an independent actor depends on coordinated action. Indeed, our entire vocabulary of the individual—who thinks, feels, wants, hopes, and so on—is granted meaning only by virtue of coordinated activities among people. Their birth of "myself" lies within the relationship. Or more generally, individual entities acquire their existence for us (or not), depending on a process of coordination.

4.5.3 Supplementary action is itself a candidate for meaning

Any supplement functions twice, first in granting significance to what has preceded, and second as an action that also requires supplementation. In effect, the meaning it grants remains suspended until it too is supplemented. Consider an executive who advises a colleague on a decision he should take. The colleague can grant the executive existence as a meaningful agent by responding, "Yes, I can see why this might be a good idea." However, the colleague now stands idle as a meaningful agent until the executive provides a further supplement. If the executive ignored the statement, for example beginning to talk about her success as a mother, the colleague would be denied personhood. More broadly, we may say that in daily life there are no *acts in themselves*, that is, actions that are not simultaneously supplements to what has preceded. Whatever we do or say takes place within a temporal context that gives meaning to what has preceded, while simultaneously forming an invitation to further supplementation.

4.5.4 Acts and supplements are mutually constraining

If I give a lecture on organizational theory, my action is insignificant without an audience that listens, deliberates, affirms, or questions what

I have said. In this sense, every speaker owes to his or her audience a debt of gratitude; without their engagement the speaker ceases to exist. At the same time, my lecture creates the very possibility for the audience to grant me existence as a meaningful agent. In this sense, the actor's identity is not free to be itself, but is constrained by the act of supplementation. Supplementation thus operates *postfiguratively*, to create the speaker as a particular form of being. From the enormous array of possibilities, the supplement gives direction and temporarily narrows the possibilities of action. At the same time, however, I as lecturer grant to them the capacity to create me in this way. They are without existence until there is an action that invites them into being.

Yet, it is also important to realize that in practice, actions also set constraints upon the kind of supplementation that takes place. If I speak on systems theory, audience members are limited in their replies. One may ask me a question about second-order systems, but not astrophysics, the concept of repression, or my taste in mushrooms. Such constraints exist because my actions are already embedded within a *tradition of act and supplement*. I have been granted existence as a lecturer on organizational theory, by virtue of previous generations of co-actors. In this sense, actions embedded within relationships have *prefigurative* potential. The history of usage enables them to invite or suggest certain supplements as opposed to others—because only these supplements are considered intelligible within a tradition. Thus, as we speak with each other, we also begin to set limits on each other's being; to remain in the conversation is not only to respect a tradition, but to accede to being one kind of person as opposed to another. Each comment constrains the potentials of the other's being.

4.5.5 While acts/supplements are constraining, they do not determine

As proposed, our words and actions function so as to constrain the words and actions of others, and vice versa. If we are to remain intelligible within our culture, we must necessarily act within these constraints. Such constraints have their origins in a history of preceding co-actions. As people coordinate actions and supplements, and come to rely on them in everyday life, they are essentially generating a way of life. If enough people join in these coordinated activities over a long period, we may speak of a cultural tradition. Yet, it is important to underscore that our words and actions function only as *constraints*, and *not as determinants*. This is so for two important reasons: first, the conditions under which we attempt to coordinate our actions are seldom constant. We are continuously faced with the challenge of importing old words and actions into new situations. As we do so, such words and actions ever acquire new possibilities for usage. More formally, we say that all words are *polysemic*; they may be used in many different ways. And, because no two situations are identical, there is a sense in which every word is spoken for the first time. Or following Heraclitus, one cannot participate in the same sentence twice.

The preceding account briefly summarizes an orientation to organizational life in which there is no "fundamental *unit* of analysis." The defining attributes of the unit cannot be attached to any specific, spatio-temporal location. Indeed, to designate the unit is already to enter into a flow of meaning making in such a way that the unit is temporarily brought into being. It is also important here to point out the particular way in which I have made the case for a process out of which the very idea of units (persons, objects) emerge. In order to accomplish this I have had to rely on a language of nouns and pronouns to render an account of process. I have essentially described the process out of the very elements that the process denies existence. I cannot do otherwise by virtue of the fact that I rely on the English language to generate intelligibility. Thus, it is important to realize that I use the language in much the same way that Wittgenstein (1953) described the development of philosophical positions. They are ladders that enable me to bring the position into intelligibility, but which may ultimately be kicked away. In this sense, the entities employed to construct this process vision serve as temporary "place holders." They are useful in building a vision, but once in place, their participation is no longer required.

4.6 From causality to confluence

> Each thing, including each person, is first and always a nexus of relations.
>
> Brent Slife

As proposed in the initial section of this chapter, a process orientation poses a challenge to traditional explanatory practices in organizational science. In particular, reliance on causal explanation—with its presumption of independent entities lodged within a system of causal interdependency—is placed in jeopardy. This view of causal relationships—if X then Y, if not X then not Y—has ancient origins. Aristotle termed it *efficient causation*. Centuries later, under Isaac Newton's influence, one could indeed begin to conceive of the universe as "one great machine," with each of its components causally related. For every event there is a cause, and to imagine an "uncaused cause" is to step outside the realm of science. As earlier discussed, such a view laid the groundwork for a social science directed toward increasingly accurate prediction and control of human behavior.

For centuries philosophers have debated the concept of causal explanation. Remaining unsolved, however, are major questions concerning the nature of causality. Most prominent among these, how can one unit "make happen" or "produce" changes in another? We see the flame on the stove, and then we observe the boiling water. But how did the flame "make" the water boil? If you ask me to pass the salt, what if anything determines that I will pass the shaker? We are left with a mystery. As some propose, we should abandon the idea of causal force. Rather, we should simply confine ourselves to prediction. We can predict rather reliably what will happen to a pot of water placed on a flame, or a request for salt at a dinner party. The concept of causal determination is an unjustified and unnecessary addition.

There is further reason to bracket the concept of cause and effect. In significant ways the concept contributes to the presumption of enduring entities. When we search for causal explanations for a person's actions, we split the world into independent entities. There are causal units on the one hand and the units that are affected on the other. Yet, it follows from the preceding analysis that the units featured as cause and effect come into being as such through a process of co-action. What we term a "cause" is only so by virtue of our specifying an "effect." By the same token, there are no "effects" in the world unless we can point to a possible cause. If one gazes at the world about, it is impossible to separate the causes and effects. Cause and effect are co-constituting.

It is useful to expand on this point: you are walking by a park and see a man throw a ball into an open space before him. An aimless activity, you surmise, scarcely notable on a summer's day. Now, consider the same action when the ball is thrown to someone wearing a catcher's mitt. Suddenly the individual's action can be identified as "pitching." In effect, there is no pitching until there is catching, and no catching until there is pitching. We look further to find that there is a man with a bat, bags that form a diamond shape, men holding mitts in the field, and so on. At this point we might justifiably conclude that this is a "baseball game." What we traditionally view as "independent" elements—the man with the bat, the bags, the men in the field—are not meaningfully independent. They are all mutually defining. A man standing alone in the field wearing a mitt would not be playing baseball, nor would the bags constitute a game. Alone they would be virtually without meaning. It is when we bring all these elements into a mutually defining relationship that we can speak about "playing baseball." Let us then speak of the baseball game as a *confluence*, a form of life in this case that is constituted by an array of mutually defining "entities."

Let us further enrich this analytic space. In particular, it can be useful to view each of the "entities" as an arrested moment in what we may term a *vector*. The baseball player appears as a unit within the game, but he is effectively *in process*. He is not the same human who entered the playing field, nor will he be the same person who departs. His playing the game is ultimately a "moment" in the vector of what minimally can be viewed as a life cycle transformation. Similarly, the batter holds an object that was once a growing tree, then cut and trimmed, and placed into service. At some point it may be consumed by flames. It serves as a "bat" by virtue of the way it is co-constituted in the moment of the game. In this way we can view the game as a whole as a historically contingent period in which all the mutually defining "entities" are—relatively speaking—momentarily arrested.

Here we have a preliminary sketch of an approach to understanding organizational process. The identification of the independent units is always in terms of their co-constitution within a confluence. And, as all "components" of the confluence are vectoring across time, they shift their "thing-ness" along with the continuous transformation of the relational configuration. If the contours of such a formulation could be developed more fully, what would it mean for organizational understanding and practice. I briefly consider three possibilities.

4.6.1 The explanation of action

At the outset, in our attempts to understand organizational life, we may replace causal explanation with a confluence-based orientation. We may replace the metaphors of billiard balls and unmoved movers with the metaphors of baking or doing chemistry. The concern now shifts from isolated entities to the combination of ingredients. With a combination of flour, oil, eggs, milk, and a griddle, we bring about a pancake. By compounding hydrogen and oxygen atoms we have water. From this standpoint, a lighted match does not *cause* the combustion of gasoline; rather the combustion is the achievement of a particular combination of flame, gasoline vapors, and oxygen. In the same way, what scholars might define as an intellectual attack does not cause another to argue; the argument comes into being only when another responds with a defense.

In terms of organizational practice, this would mean redirecting attention from single entities to the relational confluence making up the whole. It is not the traits of the individual that count, for example, but the nature of the relational process into which the individual fits (and which might subsequently be altered by his or her presence). It is not the characteristics of a given machine technology, a benefits package, a new business opportunity, or a new office building that should rivet our attention, but the character which these "entities" acquire as they are insinuated into a particular confluence. Operationally, a sensitivity to confluence would seemingly invite more democratic workplace practices. Whether a given "entity" fits comfortably and productively within the confluence will vitally depend on the supplemental actions of the organizational participants.

4.6.2 Future building

As proposed, a confluence orientation is designed as an analytic companion to a process approach to organizations. It must first be noted, however, that there is nothing about a process orientation, or confluence theory in particular, that rules out prediction. Most commonly, the process of co-action will tend toward reliable or repeated forms of relationship. Consider the game of golf. We can predict reasonably well what club most players will select when their ball is in a sand trap, or when they find their ball is several inches from the cup. The confluence of "playing golf" is a longstanding and repetitive tradition, and its rules effectively reinforced. In this sense, the game functions as a relatively closed system. It is relatively insulated from changes in the larger culture of which it is a part. Most organizations do not enjoy such tranquility. The conditions of organizational life are in continuous motion, and with the increased speed and magnitude in the flow of information and people across the globe, the rapidity and complexity of change will only increase.

From a confluence standpoint, attention recedes from attempting to predict the future to actively creating it. Within the organization, for example, the emphasis on generating predictions of the market, and planning accordingly, would recede. Attention would be directed, instead, to asking how one might generate favorable market conditions. Organizational scientists, in this case, would be less given to assessing "the way organizations function" than to asking, for example, how they might help to create a particular kind of organization. In effect, the challenge of the organizational specialist shifts from describing and explaining what exists, to aiding in the construction of what could exist.

4.6.3 From progress to protean potentials

Related to the discussion of future building, a confluence orientation suggests a shift in approach to organizational development. In keeping with the modernist vision of infinite progress, one typically views the organization in terms of its potential for infinite strengthening and expansion. However, this view is closely linked to the traditional scientific view of prediction and control of identifiable entities. With today's increasing consciousness of the environmental threat posed by the view of infinite progress, many analysts and practitioners turn their attention to sustainability. While attractive in certain respects, the sustainability metaphor is again limited in its presumption of an identifiable entity—this time one that reaches an optimal form of stability.

From a confluence orientation, however, we may dispense both with infinite progress or stabilization of *the* organization. Rather, it is useful to view organizational processes in terms of their protean potentials. How capable is the organization in reforming itself as the conditions of confluence shift over time? Rather than emphasizing the core business that one is attempting to develop and/or sustain, for example, one may inquire into the various ways in which it may be redirected, retooled, or re-imagined, such that different opportunities may be explored. Cell phone technology provides an excellent example in this case, as an object originally designed to be a phone rapidly becomes a camera, a game board, an internet outlet, an alarm clock, a geographic position finder, and much more. In effect, the cell phone business has continued to morph over time, reforming with the changing technological and market conditions. By the same token, one may inquire into the necessity of building fixed structures, purchasing large pieces of equipment, establishing fixed operating procedures, or designating fixed job descriptions. All may represent reductions in protean potential.

4.7 Parting words

The preceding discussion has attempted to wrestle with the implications of "taking process seriously." Although world conditions today favor a shift in organizational studies toward a process orientation, there are also significant challenges to be confronted. Not only are many of the assumptions of the empiricist orientation to inquiry placed in jeopardy, but it proves difficult to conceptualize pure process in terms of the linguistic resources at our disposal. The preceding discussions represent exploratory steps in the direction of theorizing process. In the account of co-action, we began to see how relational process could bring about the conception of objects or persons as "entities." In effect, process preceded essences. In the account of confluence, the relational account was expanded. Rather than focusing on the relational dance of co-action, we began to see how an entire array of mutually defining "entities" could be formed. The emphasis on the confluence leads us into further speculations about organizational inquiry and action. It must finally be underscored, however, that these attempts are in no way thrusts toward conclusions. Rather, my greatest hope is to invite further discussion. And applying the theory of co-action, such discussion need never reach a conclusion.

Note

1. See, for example, Gergen and Gergen, 1984; Gergen, 1994.

References

Gergen, K. J. (1994). *Toward Transformation in Social Knowledge*, 2nd edn, London: Sage.

Gergen, K. J. (2009). *Relational Being: beyond Self and Community*, New York: Oxford University Press.

Gergen, K. J. and Gergen, M. (eds) (1984). *Historical Social Psychology*, Hillsdale, NJ: Erlbaum.

Kuhn, T. S. (1970). *The Structure of Scientific Revolutions*, Chicago: University of Chicago Press, 1st edn 1962.

Weick, K. E. (1993). The collapse of sensemaking in organizations: The Mann Gulch disaster, *Administrative Science Quarterly*, 38, 628–52.

Weick, K. E. (1995). *Sensemaking in Organizations*, Thousand Oaks, CA: Sage.

Wittgenstein, L. (1953). *Philosophical Investigations*, Oxford: Blackwell.

5

Adopting a Process Orientation . . . in Practice: Chiasmic Relations, Language, and Embodiment in a Living World

John Shotter

Abstract: What is involved in our adopting a process orientation, *in practice*, rather than just talking *about* it in theory? Below, I explore some of the difficulties involved in terms of Wittgenstein's (1980) distinction between difficulties of the intellect—difficulties that can be solved by rational thought—and those of the will—which require our coming to embody new ways of relating or orienting ourselves towards events happening in our surroundings. So although I begin by examining what both Whitehead (1925/1975; 1929/1978) and Bergson (1911) had to say about a process orientation, *in theory*, now, after Wittgenstein's (1953, 1969) emphasis on the fact that our utterances can only take on determinate meanings within the confines of a "language-game," I argue that our talk of various entities can only take on a determinate meaning within *a particular language-entwined practice*, and will remain indeterminate outside such practices. And straightaway, in situating us within the realm of practice and practices, this requirement re-orients us toward the importance of *poetic* forms of talk, utterances which can "touch" us and "move" us towards adopting expectations and anticipations relevant to going out to meet events happening around us with the right kind of embodied responses, at the ready, so to speak.

The elucidation of meaning involved in the phrase "all things flow," is one chief task of metaphysics.

> Whitehead (1929/1978) *Process and Reality:*
> *An Essay in Cosmology*, p. 208

Once-occurrent uniqueness or singularity cannot be thought of, it can only be participatively experienced or lived through.

Bakhtin (1993) *Toward a Philosophy of the Act*, p.13.

I'll teach you differences.
Kent's reprimand reprimand to King Lear that Wittgenstein thought of using as an epigraph for *Philosophical Investigations*.

What should we see as constituting the focal forms requiring our attention in our efforts to best understand our organizational lives? Can they be examined as self-contained entities whose properties and relations to other such entities await our investigations of them, or must we see them as already participant parts within a larger, still continuously developing whole? To adopt a process orientation is, we might say, to adopt a worldview—a way of looking out at and acting within the world around us—in which instead of substances (stuff) we see processes; instead of already existing things we see things in the making; instead of a succession of instant configurations of matter we see a unitary, holistic, continuous flow of events, we see becoming rather than merely being. But more than this, it is also to move from a dualistic view of ourselves as separate, self-contained beings living in a world conceived simply as a space full of separate objects, to a view of ourselves as inextricably entwined in with it, as being *of* the world rather than merely *in* it—this is a view of nature, in Whitehead's words (1929/1975: 92), as "a structure of evolving processes," a view that "the reality is the process." Thus central to his whole approach to our current modes of thought and inquiry is his critique of what he calls the *fallacy of misplaced concreteness*: the construction of abstractions in terms of "simply located bits of material" (1929/1975: 75). For it (mis)leads us, not only to disregard the already existing *intra*-connections[1] of things within the world around us, but also to "break up" the continuity of our experience and to conceptualize time as a sequence of self-contained "instants" like beads on a string, thus to attribute no importance to its *flow*.

This scheme of scientific ideas, as Whitehead (1975) sees it, has dominated our more intellectual and academic thought in modern times, and is still so compellingly trenchant in our more "common sense" attempts at coping with our everyday affairs that, as we shall see, it cannot easily be overcome: "It involves a fundamental duality, with material on the one hand, and on the other hand mind. In between there lie the concepts of life, organism, function, instantaneous reality, interaction, order of nature, which collectively form the Achilles heel of the whole system" (1975: 74).[2] Yet it is just these inadequately conceptualized, in-between notions that become focal in our efforts to understand our organizational lives better. Can a process orientation help us to make better sense of these somewhat vagrant terms?

Perhaps it can. But what, in actual practice,[3] is in fact involved in adopting a *process orientation*? As I see it, and as I will argue further below, to ask this question in this fashion—formulating it as having to do, not with *solving problems*, but to do with *how* we might *adopt a particular orientation* (or more likely, change an already existing one)—is already to orient (or to re-orient) ourselves in a certain fashion, to call for a very different kind of answer to the ones usually offered in answer to such a question. For clearly, to adopt a process orientation is to accept, in Niels Bohr's well-known phrase, that "we are simultaneously actors as well as spectators on the great stage of life" (Bohr, quoted in Honner, 1987: 1).

In other words, as an aspect of our adopting such an orientation we must straightaway accept that for us, there can be no "view from outside," no "external world" (Russell, 1914), no humanly independent reality as we have in fact always assumed in our more "natural scientific" moments. We are (along with every *thing* else of which we speak) ineradicably *participant parts* of and in a larger, indivisible,[4] unfolding, dynamic flow of events from which we cannot wholly separate ourselves (an ontological point of the utmost importance, as we shall see). But consequently, we can only fully benefit from our "insider's view" if we can, as Bergson (1911) puts it, fully attach ourselves to "the inner becoming of things," and stop trying to place ourselves outside them "in order to recompose their becoming artificially" (1911: 343).[5] For, as we shall see, in so *attaching* or *relating* ourselves in an *inner* fashion to the becoming of things (rather than observing them from the outside), various embodied *sensings* or *feelings* become available to us (noticeable to us) that are otherwise lost[6] or ignored if we recompose their becoming artificially—sensings or feelings which can in fact motivate, shape, and guide us as we take our next steps as we move around out in the world of our everyday practical affairs.

Whitehead and Bergson clearly set themselves the task, as individual thinkers, of *thinking* the nature of a process orientation. But another aspect of our adopting a process orientation, in practice, now, after Wittgenstein's (1953, 1969) emphasis on the fact that our utterances only take on determinate meanings within the confines of a "language-game," is our acceptance also of something very like Niels Bohr's (1958) *complementarity* principle: that our talk of various entities can only take on a determinate meaning within *a particular language-entwined practice*, and will remain indeterminate outside such practices. And straightaway, this requirement situates us within the realm of practice and practices and casts us out of the abstract, Platonic realm of thought.

5.1 Overcoming orientational difficulties: Retraining our embodied capacities

What, then, is actually involved in our adopting a process orientation? And why is it so hard for us to do? One answer is that it is hard for us because, from Descartes onwards, almost all modern thought has been in the thrall of an objectifying science. It is only by following "the secure path of a science," said Kant in his *Critique of Pure Reason* in 1787, that philosophy can become more than "a merely random groping" (1970: 17). And even now, we are still under that spell; and it leads us to believe that we already possess a suitable form or pattern of reasoning, a methodology that must be followed if we are to solve the problems, to overcome the difficulties we face in our lives. Heinrich Hertz (1894/1956) described it thus: "In endeavouring . . . to draw inferences as to the future from the past, we always adopt the following process. We form for ourselves images or symbols of external objects; and the form that we give them is such that the necessary consequents of the images in thought are always the images of the necessary consequents in nature of the things pictured" (1956: 1). In other words, we say our theories are true theories if the *predictions* we derive from them match or "picture" the *outcomes* of the "processes" we are studying. So, although we can bring off some quite spectacular results in the natural sciences by the use of this procedure, straightaway we need to note the crucial role it assigns to *symbolic representations* (theoretical structures) in our conduct of our practical affairs, and also the fact that it is solely *in terms of a theory's relation to its outcomes*, not to the whole structure of reality, that we think of a theory as being a *true* theory. Indeed, as Quine (1953) noted later, this kind of knowledge "is a man-made fabric which impinges on experience only along the edges" (1953: 42), for, as we need time and again to remind ourselves, it is a kind of knowledge fashioned in terms of idealizations—and, as we shall see, many exclusions!

Without our use of theoretical representations, then, our inquiries would seem to lack guidance, we would be fumbling around in a random fashion (or would we?—see below). But by their very nature—as idealized, already ordered schematisms—such representations offer us, not only a "thin," "frictionless" version, so to speak, of the (in fact, complex) reality in which we live, but they also, of necessity, exclude facets of it that afford very different orderings. These two difficulties, to do with the solely representational nature of much of what we try to make use of in guiding our practices of inquiry in organizational studies, will become more and more obvious as we proceed. Yet the fact is that, in many spheres of inquiry, we still labor under the spell of the assumption that there *must be* a way of setting our intellects to work, a form of symbolic reasoning that can lead to our solving the problems we face in our lives.

Wittgenstein's (1953) great achievement in his later philosophy is, I think, to have broken this spell, to have broken the hold on us of this "picture" of what we should count as *proper* knowledge. Instead, he made it very clear that many of our difficulties are *not* of the form of *problems* that can, by the application of a science-like methodology, be solved by reasoning; nor are they "empirical problems" that can be solved by discovering something currently unknown to us. They are difficulties of quite another kind, difficulties *of the will* rather than *of the intellect*, difficulties not to do with needing to be "specially trained in abstruse matters," but to do with overcoming "what most people *want* to see" (Wittgenstein, 1980: 17)—which in our case is overcoming the urge to see our world as populated solely by independently existing, countable, self-contained things. In other words, the difficulties we face are orientational or relational difficulties to do with overcoming (and changing) the embodied ways in which we spontaneously respond to features in our surroundings with appropriate expectations and anticipations as to how next to "go on" in our activities within them, thus to find our "way about"[7] without (mis)leading ourselves into taking inappropriate next steps.[8]

These difficulties, then, need to be overcome in a way quite different from those difficulties which we can formulate as *problems*, and *solve* with the aid of clever theories or appropriate frameworks of thought, by rational methods, that is difficulties of the intellect. They confront us with the task of evolving new ways of *relating* ourselves (bodily, i.e., sensitively and emotionally) to the others and othernesses around us. For how we *orient* ourselves, take up an *attitude*, or a *stance*, towards them, and adopt different *ways* of seeing, hearing, experiencing, and valuing them, influence what we perceive as the *possibilities* for action available to us within our present relations to them. Our *ways of relating* to them function in our "giving shape" to, *resolving on*, a line of action that matters to us[9] in the situation we are in.

Thus, if we now return to our original question—"What is involved, *in practice*, in adopting a process orientation?"—we find that it must involve, as Wittgenstein puts it, "a working on oneself.... On one's way of seeing things. (And what one expects of them)" (1980: 16). In other words, how can we learn to relate ourselves to our surroundings with the right kind of anticipations—process structured expectations—at the ready, so to speak, thus to "see" processes at work around us, rather than the results of actions by agents on objects? What must we do if we are to work on ourselves in this way? For as is already apparent, perhaps (or will become apparent as we explore further), it cannot be accomplished by any of the intellectual methods currently familiar to us: for all our usual representational methods—that place us over against the reality we are trying to understand—are all excluded by our primary assumption of being ourselves participant parts of a larger indivisible, unfolding, flowing unitary whole.

So how can this work on ourselves be accomplished? For, as we proceed, step-by-step, to make our way further and further into the world of process, we will find the reality we encounter there more and more difficult to understand, more and more dissimilar from what we expect or want it to be. This is because, as Wittgenstein notes: "Giving grounds, justifying the evidence, comes to an end;—but the end is not in certain propositions striking us immediately as true, i.e., it is not a kind of *seeing* on our part; it is our *acting*, which lies at the bottom of the language-game" (1969; no. 204). We find the new process orientation so difficult to adopt because our capacities to understand it are rooted and expressed in our current "forms of life" (Wittgenstein, 1953), and as we have already seen, our current forms of thought are rooted in the objectifying practices into which we have been trained in our more intellectual practices.

Overcoming our orientational difficulties, then, is not simply a matter of our having some new thoughts, some new good ideas; it is much more a matter of our training ourselves in the development of new perceptual skills, in some new practical ways of relating ourselves to our surroundings. This cannot happen in an instant. Recursively iterating a practice is involved—as, for instance, we do when we slowly "work our way into" viewing new styles of painting or listening to new forms of music, or, for instance, as many of us trained ourselves a few years ago (by converging or diverging our eyes) to "see" the 3-D visual displays made available in certain 2-D random dot stereograms. But it isn't easy. Only after an iterated series of "tryings and trying again", and returning one's achievements so far back into the original situation, does the skill finally become "second nature"[10] and available to be "applied" appropriately at will in many new situations.

5.2 The importance of ephemeral, chiasmic, relational events: Their moment-by-moment unfolding orientational function

The adoption, then, of a process orientation, in practice, has its difficulties. We cannot always adopt our well-tried methods of inquiry. So where might *we* begin? Whitehead makes two suggestions: (1) One is of the more well-known theoretical kind, in analysis: "[While] the materialistic starting-point is from independently existing substances, matter and mind. The matter suffers modifications of its external relations of locomotion, and mind suffers modifications of its contemplated objects....The organic starting-point is from the *analysis* of process as the realization of events disposed in an interlocking community.... The emergent enduring pattern is the stabilization of the emergent achievement so as to become a fact *which retains its identity throughout the process*" (Whitehead, 1925/1975: 183, my emphases). (2) Later, however, rather than with an analysis, he suggests in his description of the process of *concrescence* (that is, the process by which an actual entity comes into existence as such) a starting point of a more practical kind: as he sees it, the concrescence of a new actual entity occurs in three phases, the first of which he calls "the responsive phase" (Whitehead, 1929/1978: 245),[11] and this is where I would also like to begin—because, clearly, this takes us into the realm of practice in a way that an analysis does not.

The spontaneous responsiveness of our living responsiveness is very basic; we cannot *not be* responsive both to the others of our kind around us, as well as to all the other aspects of, or othernesses in, our surroundings. Thus, in such a spontaneously responsive sphere of activity as this, instead of one person first acting individually and independently of another, and then the second replying, by acting individually and independently of the first, we act jointly, as a *collective-we*. In so doing, we move from an *inter*-action to an *intra*-action, from an activity in which we, as separate individuals merely *coordinate* our activities, to a joint or dialogically-structured activity within which we become a *participant part* in and of a larger, unitary process.[12] And we do this bodily, in a "living" way, spontaneously, without our having first "to work out" how to respond in this manner with and to each other. This means that when someone acts, their activity cannot be accounted as wholly their own, for their acts are partly "shaped" both by the acts of the others around them, as well as by their responsiveness to other aspects of the larger situation within which they are acting (Shotter, 1980, 1984, 1993*a* and *b*). And this is what makes this kind of joint activity so special: when it occurs as an *intra-* rather than as an *inter-*action, unique, qualitatively distinct, ephemeral "somethings" emerge *within* the moment-by-moment unfolding, dynamic, *chiasmic*[13] (Merleau-Ponty, 1968) entwinings of the two or more unique "flows" of activity involved. But further, as Bakhtin (1986) notes, although what is always created "out of something given (language, an observed phenomenon of reality, an experienced feeling, the speaking subject himself, something finalized in his world view, and so forth). What is given is completely transformed in what is created" (1986: 120).

It is with the recognition of the importance of such ephemeral chiasmic events as these, along with the irreversible, transformative influences they can exert, that all the strangeness that can confront us on our adoption of a process orientation begins: for, when two or more streams of our activity, embedded within the already existing larger sphere of dynamically unfolding activity occurring out in the world between us all, begin to "run together," such comings-into-being, etc., can continually emerge amongst us, seemingly "out of the blue"—they can occur when, as Gergen (2009) puts it, we act from within a *confluence*, "an array of mutually defining relationships with each other and our surroundings" (2009: 56). In other words, what previously we took to be the rock-bottom, fixed entities in terms of which we can build up a world for ourselves, we now realize are local *achievements* (Ryle, 1949)[14]—what we now sometimes call *constructions*—arrived at by our gathering together over a period of time, from here, there, and elsewhere, fragments of experience into a unity of an, at first, non-cognitive and also of a non-observable kind, into what Whitehead (1925/1975) calls a "unity of prehension."

In gathering our fragmentary experiences into such a unity, we do not, he suggests, grasp things-in-themselves; we arrive at "*a here* and *a now*" unity of such a kind that the fragments gathered into it "have *essential reference* to other places and other times" (Whitehead, 1925/1975: 88, my emphasis). In other words, as a result of our gathering these fragmentary experiences together into an experienced unity, we arrive at a bodily sense of a "something" that supplies us with the "*presences*[15] of entities beyond itself" (1925/1975: 93, again my emphasis).

So how can we learn to "see" (or better, to sense) the influences of such vague and ephemeral chiasmic, relational events at work in our organizational activities? How can we transform these "passing singularities" into events that we can return to time and again, if we cannot "picture" them because of their incomplete, durational, or temporal nature?[16] What kind of *description* can arouse in us the kind of *orientational* understandings we require if we are to "go on" in our practical affairs with the right kind of anticipations "at the ready," so to speak?

The answer I will give to this question later, following Wittgenstein's claim that "philosophy ought really to be written only as *poetic composition*" (1980: 24), is that it needs to be of a poetic kind, a description that can "touch" or "move" us in our very being in some way. But I want to approach that question here by taking up two important ideas from Gregory Bateson: (1) One is to do with that fact that when two (or more) strands of activity intertwine, the *differences* between them can produce, as he puts it, "a difference that makes a difference" (Bateson 1973: 286)— except that I want to adapt his phrase slightly to relate it more directly to our bodily experience. For I want to focus on those events that make a difference *that matters to us*, that make a *felt* difference, a poetic difference that "touches" or "moves" us in our very way of being in the world. (2) The second idea is that in just such circumstances as these, when as Bateson (1979) notes that when the two (or more) sources of "information" (his term) become entwined in some way, they "give information of *a sort different* from what was in either source separately" (1979: 31, my emphasis)—a phenomenon of what he calls "double description" occurs, and when it does, it gives rise to "information" of a quite different "logical type"[17] from that in the two (or more) sources producing it.

This, I think, is a most important observation of Bateson's. For, just as the *intra*-play between two musical tones gives rise to "beats," or that between two similar visual arrays to moiré patterns, so also, we can expect that similar such *intra*-plays of importance will occur elsewhere in our experience. In particular, as Bateson (1979) himself notes, the chiasmic entwining of the two flows of neural activity issuing from our two eyes gives rise to binocular vision, and the slight but related *differences* between our two eyes, not only work to improve contrasts and resolution at the edges—thus to read more easily when the print is small or the illumination poor—but much more importantly, to create a sense of *depth*. Depth is itself, of course, invisible. But what we seem to see when we see "in depth," is how far or near to us things are *in relation to our bodies*, that is, what can be reached without moving, and what movements are required to reach other things. As Bateson puts it, "the *difference* between the information provided by the one retina and that provided by the other is itself information of a *different logical type*. From this new sort of information, the seer adds an extra *dimension* to seeing" (1979: 80)—a dimension that we might simply call a "relational dimension."

It is these kinds of difference which as we shall see—sequences of *differences* between what we expect and what in fact actually results—that can give us a sense, not only of an event's more *objective* aspects, but also of its more *subjective*, that is, bodily sensed or felt aspects, aspects that help to relate us or to orient us, bodily, to our surroundings.

5.3 The emergence of *prehensive unities* in the "back-and-forth" process of an *intra*-action: Differencing not causing, diffraction not reflection

Above, then, what we have been exploring is the fact that while, classically, we have studied the *finalized* 'shapes' of events occurring around us at different instants in time, at a distance, from the outside, seeking intellectually to understand the pattern of possible *past* events that might have caused them to come into existence, we are now beginning to realize that we can also enter into a continuous relationship with such events, over time—a living, bodily relationship with them of a non-intellectual kind. It is precisely this latter, more direct, bodily involvement with events in our surroundings that has been, until very recently, ignored.

Indeed, on the assumption we need to understand an *external* world full of essentially self-contained, observer-independent, *objective* things, we have taken a great deal of trouble to devise methods for actively cutting ourselves off from such engagements. But as we can see from our explorations above, not only do such methods to an extent fail (for we cannot wholly eradicate our own spontaneous responsiveness to what happens around us), when we do allow ourselves to be more fully *engaged*—that is, when we allow ourselves to have a continuous, unbroken, living contact with a state of affairs—a quite different kind of spontaneously responsive understanding becomes available to us. Indeed, in the course of such engagements, as we have seen above, as a result of the chiasmic, relational events that emerge in the *intra*-action between our outgoing actions and their incoming results, we can gain an orientational sense of how best further to act within such a situation. It is this, then—the way in which such engaged modes of *intra*-acting can orient us towards the future—that makes our engaged styles of understanding so very different from the results of our more disengaged modes.

But this leads us on into another very important distinction: what we arrive at as the result of an engagement with a situation over some period of time—think of us 'looking over' a complex panorama, or even better, feeling our way around in a darkened room—is not anything like a *reflection* of what is "out there." Another kind of process altogether, a differencing process, would seem to be involved. Indeed, as Barad makes clear: "To mirror something is to provide an accurate image or representation that faithfully copies that which is being mirrored. Hence mirrors are an often used metaphor for representationalism and related questions of reflexivity" (2007: 86)—and both these metaphors lead us back, not only into the assumption of an external world of essentially already separated things, but also back into the belief that our practices of representing have no reflexive effects on the objects represented (see Bakhtin's remark above, that the given is completely transformed in what is created). This questioning of both reflection, and especially the talk of reflexivity associated with it, is a most important and perhaps unexpected point[18]—for reflexivity still holds the world at a distance from us, whereas, we have got to re-think ourselves as in fact immersed in it. The processes involved, again as Barad (2007) notes, are much more of a *defractive* kind, to do with our picking up on differences that make a difference that matters to us within whatever situation we happen to be[19]—which involves our working on our selves—rather than merely a matter of seeking some new "good ideas."

Thus, with the importance of felt differences in mind, the beginning points for our process-oriented inquiries should, I suggest—to return to the Wittgensteinian distinction I drew earlier between difficulties of the intellect and those of the will—be in those moments situated within our practical affairs when we feel a disquiet, a confusion, bewilderment, or disorientation, when the expectations with which we go out to meet events occurring around us are not entirely fulfilled, and felt differences occur. In such moments or situations we can either (1) take flight, (2) take further thought to find an alternative framework of thought in which to try to categorize the nature of the circumstance, or (3) take the trouble to "dwell in and on" it, that is, move around in it with a set of "try out" expectations, until *its own unique nature* becomes sufficiently apparent to us.

If we take the second (classical) option, approaching our bewilderment as a problem to be solved, then we first turn to analysing it into a set of separate, identifiable elements; next we seek a pattern or order amongst them; and then we *hypothesize* a hidden agency responsible for the "discovered" order (call it the working of certain rules, principles, or laws, or the working of a story or narrative), which we then enshrine in a symbolic scheme or theory (see the reference to Hertz above) to produce an advantageous outcome which we call "the solution" to our problem.

We can then turn to "apply" the theory at will elsewhere. *As investigators we ourselves remain unchanged in this kind of process*; rather than being engaged or involved in what we are investigating, we set ourselves "over against" it.

Alternatively, if we take the third option, instead of immediately trying to analyze a bewildering circumstance into its elements, we can treat it as a felt "something" that is at first radically unknown to us, and, by "opening" ourselves to being spontaneously "moved" by it, we can "enter into" a living, dialogically-structured, back-and-forth, relationship with it—a relationship in which, if we go slowly, and allow time for the imaginative work that each response can occasion to take place, we can gain a inner sense of the "invisible landscape of possibilities" it opens up to us. Involved, as I see it, are a number of distinct phases:[20]

- we begin by being situated within a practical circumstance, and finding ourselves confused as to how to act for the best within it;
- as we "dwell in" it, as we "move around" within the confusion, a "something," an "it" begins to emerge;
- it emerges in the "time contours" or "time shapes" that become apparent to us in the dynamic relations we can sense between our outgoing activities and their incoming results;
- an image comes to us, and we find that we can express this "something," linguistically, by the use of an idiom appropriate to that image;
- but not so fast, for we can find another image, and an another, and then another—Wittgenstein uses a city, a toolbox, the controls in the driving cab of a train, and many different types of games, all as metaphors for different aspects of our experiences of the use of language.
- Having gone through a number of images, we can at last come to a sense of the landscape of possibilities giving rise to them all—indeed, we can gain such a sense of familiarity with such landscapes that ultimately, we can come to feel confident[21] of knowing our way around within them, and of being able to *resolve* on ways of *going on* within them.

As investigators, we ourselves can be radically changed in such encounters. For, in becoming involved with—that is, immersed in—the "inner life" of the others and/or othernesses around us, everything we do becomes partly shaped by being in response to what *they might do*. As a result, we (can) come to embody new "ways" of going out to meet events in our surroundings with new sets of expectations as to what we will encounter there. And in the process, the structure of our environment will gradually become incorporated into our outgoing activities in such a way that we will gradually learn how to meet our environment with the right kind of responses "at the ready." In other words, we can come to look, listen, talk, think, and act *with* the new particular prehensive unity we have arrived at in this process as a means for guiding or orienting us in our activities, as providing us with a certain *way* or *style* of looking, listening, talking, thinking, and acting.

Merleau-Ponty (1964) puts this very nicely in discussing the cave paintings of animals on the walls of Lascaux: They "are not there in the same way as the fissures and limestone formations. But they are not *elsewhere*.... I would be at great pains to say *where* is the painting I am looking at. For I do not look at it as I look at a thing; I do not fix its place. My gaze wanders in it as in the halos of Being. It is more accurate to say that I see according to it, or with it, than that I *see it*" (1964: 164). And indeed, every new circumstance that we look over can, if we dwell in it sufficiently, teach us a new way of going out to meet events in our surroundings with a readiness for them to "call out" from us new kinds of response. But to repeat, this process can only be gradual. And we will never be able to gain complete mastery over all that is around us—it will always be able to surprise us, no matter how familiar to us it has become.

It is this third option that, as we have seen, Kant (1970) wanted to avoid by adopting the secure path of science because, as he saw it, it would lead to "merely random groping." But as we have seen, in this he was wrong. It doesn't. The distinctive dynamical "somethings" that can come into existence within it can arouse in us felt sensings of a distinctive kind, what elsewhere I have called "transitional understandings" and "action guiding anticipations" of an orientational kind (Shotter, 2005). Furthermore, although they can never become finalized in clearly "pictureable" forms and thus cannot ever be represented in a theoretical symbolism of an explanatory kind, they can nonetheless result, as we have seen, in a sensed "something" of a holistic character—as Barad (2007) makes clear, they have the dynamical character of *interference* or *diffraction* effects. As such, to repeat, they have an ephemeral existence only in the bodily experience of practitioners and investigators of a practice.

What is important in this process is that every part of, and within the whole, contains within itself "essential references," as Whitehead calls them, to the other units of and within the whole. Further, to the extent that each whole has been achieved as the result of a particular *practice* or "way" of looking—where one way of language-entwined-looking (as in, say, the well-known duck–rabbit, or faces-vase ambiguous figures) *excludes* what can be seen from within another way—even though the figures themselves *are* both at once (or better, include both *possibilities* at once) we cannot ourselves in fact respond to both at once![22] We are limited, not in theory, but in practice, to responding at any one time to one or the other—only in the chiasmic unity of our dialogically-structured relations to each other, can we bring these otherwise complementary features together. Furthermore, even though the *gestalt switch* from one to another possibility in an ambiguous figure as a determinate "something" can be instantaneous once it has become "second nature," it depends upon our having first formed within ourselves appropriate unities of prehension—thus to be able to go out to meet the figures with the appropriate anticipations "at the ready."

Coming to embody such appropriate sets of anticipations, such appropriate prehensive unities, can, however, often take considerable time; not only is a great deal of imaginative work required, but often also hints from others are needed along the way, if we are to come to acquire them. It is this *embodiment work*, as we might call it, that is missed out in much organizational theorizing, and which, because of it being ignored, leads to the "up in the air," "ungrounded" character of much writing in organizational theorizing.

5.4 Rethinking organizational thought: From aboutness- to withness-thinking

"Business schools are on the wrong track," say Bennis and O'Toole (2005: 96). The trouble is that business schools have embraced "the scientific model of physicists and economists," they say, "rather then the professional model of doctors and lawyers" (2005: 98), and this leads to student managers being taught methods that "are at arm's length from actual practice, [which] often fails to reflect the way business works in real life" (2005: 99). What is needed, they suggest, is that: "The entire MBA curriculum must be infused with multidisciplinary, practical, and ethical questions and analyses reflecting the complex challenges business leaders face" (2005: 104).

While we all, I think, can agree with their account of the inappropriate nature of the MBA curriculum, will "infusing" it with "questions" and "analyses" "reflecting" the way business works in real life and the complex challenges business leaders face, change the actual *practices of management* that students come to embody in any significant way? I think not. For, if my comments above are correct, the changes we need are "deep" changes, changes not in *what* we think, but changes in "what we think with," changes in our embodied ways of being *of* the world rather than merely *in* it, changes in our language entwined practices to do with how we go out to meet our surroundings with the right kind of anticipatory responses.

Thus we need to move on from thinking that we can *start* with "analyses" (of situations into their separate parts), with the aim of arriving at "reflections" in terms of representations (static "picturings") of the complex situations from within the midst of which we must act. For both of these activities will take us back, willy-nilly, into subject–object duality and the practices of a command-and-control (cause-and-effect) form of management, and provide little guidance as to the embodied work required to orient or to relate ourselves to the unique particularities of our surroundings appropriately.

Above, I have been exploring the importance of Wittgenstein's (1953, 1969) claim that our utterances only take on determinate meanings within the confines of a "language-game," within *particular language-entwined practices*, and that they will remain indeterminate outside such practices. Or to put it another way, only within a particular practical circumstance in which there is a *clear end in view*—that is when we are operating within a *bounded* sphere of activity which we ourselves are *regulating* (and have, in effect, momentarily formed as a closed system)—can we give specific meanings to the terms we use: they are given a specific meaning against the background of the *shared* prehensive unity participants arrive at by participating within the bounded sphere of activity. Here, I want to explore the consequences of this fact (if "fact" it be) by considering a number of well-known "theoretical frameworks" or "models" thought be of central importance in our coming to an understanding of managerial activities, models which at first sight seem to be of help in our breaking free from the practices induced by more mechanistic frameworks.

5.4.1 Some examples: Still keeping us on the outside

First, let me turn to a consideration of the now famous McKinsey & Co 7-S model: Straightaway, we can note that it is presented within the idiom of a theoretical framework suitable for problem-solving: "The model is based on the theory," it is claimed, "that, for an organization to perform well, . . . seven elements need to be aligned and mutually reinforcing" (Mindtools, 2010)—the seven elements being: strategy, structure, systems, shared values, style, staff, and skills. The first three are designated as "hard" elements that, because they are easier to define or identify, can be directly influenced by management. The other four "soft" elements, however—shared values, style, staff, and skills—are more difficult to describe, and also, in being more influenced by culture are less easily influenced by management. Indeed, as Waterman, Peters, and Phillips (1980) pointed out in their first article outlining the 7-S framework, one of its values is that "it suggests the wisdom of taking seriously the variables in organizing that have been considered soft, informal, or beneath the purview of top management interest" (1980: 26). Indeed, as Taptiklis (2008) remarks in his description of Peters: "What was striking about Peters was that he demonstrated enormous curiosity about the everyday life of the organization . . . [he] wanted to get inside and even to immerse himself in organizational life. . . . Most of all, he wanted managers to notice things. Noticing things became his hallmark" (1980: 35–7).

This, of course, is all tremendously relevant and does seem to point towards what *is* needed if students are to "get into" a more "up close and personal" grasp of those details of organizational life that are usually beneath the purview of top management. However, *is* this what the framework does? What is at issue here is not, of course, whether the theory (of 7 elements) they espouse is a true theory is not. What is at issue is whether the model they derive from it is in fact a useful guide to action. Does it provide students with the orientation they need?

In assessing this we must, I think, distinguish between those moments when a model is first being presented *by an expert who already embodies the appropriate, global prehensive unity* from which the model, as an idealized expression of that unity, has been derived, and what in fact students take away with them from that presentation. Although Waterman et al. (1980) might, as they '*informally* talk the model through' (as might also other expert presenters), portray the detailed nature of managers' lives, they cannot do the whole job of provoking those in the audience into forming within themselves the relevant prehensive unity to "take away" merely through classroom talk alone. The understandings that Waterman et al. (1980) spent a considerable time in acquiring in the course of their practical investigations cannot be communicated merely as "information," as facts. So although the new forms of talk *informally* introduced by Waterman et al. (1980) might work at first in a poetic fashion, to *orient* or to *re-relate* those in their audience to notice and interconnect previously ignored features in and of their surroundings, very soon the *formal* words in the model—rather than Waterman et al.'s (1980) more spontaneously produced words in the presentation—will come to function as guides and reminders, and people then revert to their old, commonsense ways.

Indeed, let me emphasize this: As Waterman et al. (1980) say in the conclusions section of their article, they began their inquires with "the premise that...the inability of the two-variable model [working just in terms of strategy and structure] *to explain* why pathfinder organizations are so slow to adapt to change...[is because] the reasons often lie among our other *variables*: systems that embody outdated *assumptions*," (1980: 25, my emphases). In other words, formally, the model is not aimed at taking people *into* experiencing what it is like in one's managing experience to notice and to be responsive, say, to people's style—whether (at any one moment?) they are cooperative or competitive. Instead, in being aimed at defining the objective characteristics they must look for, it is precisely aimed, once again, at people standing *outside* and *separate* from those they want to understand. Indeed, it is couched in just those *process-excluding* forms of talk we use in our everyday forms of talk (see note 2) in sustaining these attitudes. No wonder that, as Taptiklis (2008) puts it in his historical review of the 7-S model: "Behind the rousing evangelical style of Peters I think that in the end, we find the same old instrumental rationality of the same old managerial elite" (2008: 41).

Here we find, then, that a workshop process explicitly aimed at changing us, not simply in the number of facts we know, but more deeply, in how we relate ourselves to our surroundings, can in the longer term easily leave us utterly unchanged. Indeed, this reversion—to "business as usual" after participation in a workshop meant to start people off on a whole new way of acting—is in fact a phenomenon quite familiar to managers attending workshops. Quite a while ago now, a participant in a workshop I was conducting, described it in terms of what he called "the good holiday phenomenon": Those in an office or business who have been on a good holiday come back full of it, and for the first few days back, they recount to everyone the special events they experienced, a few days later less so, and a week or so later no more mention of it is made; things go back to "normal." Ironically, at the very beginning of their article, Waterman et al. (1980) remark that "intellectually all managers and consultants know that much more goes on in the process of organising than the charts, boxes, dotted lines, position descriptions, and matrices can possibly depict. But all too often we behave as though we didn't know it" (1980: 14). Yet the 7-S framework is presented in two pages in a formalistic manner. Presented in this way, the great promise of the 7-S framework when it was first outlined—that it would take us into the detailed terrain of "soft" people problems—"sank like a stone" beneath the mode of expression used in "taking seriously," that is, in *formalizing* the "variables" that have been in the past considered "soft" and "informal."

I have treated the 7-S framework or model at length because the issues it raises are typical, I think, of many other frameworks or models meant to provide personnel with guidance as to what their role in the organization either requires of them, or as to how it might be developed or changed. For instance, a set of Department of Health guidelines in the UK for "the care of older people" by nurses are phrased in terms of three major headings: *People*, *Process*, and *Place*, with four "principles" under each heading. Under *Process*, for instance, we find that "process" means "delivering quality care that promotes dignity by nurturing and supporting the older person's self-respect and self worth," and that is done (among other activities) by "Communicating with the person, talking with them and listening to what they have to say." Of course, especially amongst those immersed in the communication discipline, the "point" of this principle is obvious. But is it to those of us less experienced? I think not. Acting merely by the "letter" of the principle rather than its "spirit" leaves a wide range of possibilities open in terms of which a nurse could be said to be satisfying the principle; pretty much any kind of talking and listening will do—whereas, clearly, it is the kind of *engaged*, *responsive* talking and listening we have been discussing above that is meant.

Similarly, the new Leadership Model of a major company—this time set out in terms of four overall aims with four subheadings under each—offers another set of reminders. Again we find the same "up in the air" statement of principles. To take an example, the first major principle is: *Value expertise*, which is expanded into: *Apply business rigour and judgment*; *Command respect for professional excellence*; *Generate talent for the enterprise*; and *Develop capability through continual learning*. Here the issue is not a matter of people meeting requirements by merely "paying lip service" to the principles, but of a different kind: Here the effort was to instill a new "culture" within the company. Yet rather than guidance, section managers spent considerable time being disoriented while trying to work out whether they were managing to implement the principles in their section of the company appropriately (or not), that is, in a way that *will* be rigorous, that *will* develop capability, that *will* generate talent, etc., etc. Can all these principles be grounded in activities that are, in the end, advantageous to the company? Alone, as they stand, *something more* seems to be required if they are to be of practical use—for their mode of expression seems to leave recipients unmoved. What we need are expressions that make differences within us that matter to us.

But difficulties of this kind do not just occur only in schematisms offered in companies for the instruction of their employees; we can find exactly the same difficulties emerging in the work of major organizational theorists. Let me turn now to a group of well-known theorists, Senge, Scharmer, Jaworski, and Flowers (2006), who have recently produced a popular and well-regarded book, *Presence: Exploring Profound Change in People, Organizations and Society*. For in it, it could be said, they seem to offer a neat answer to the question of what is in fact involved, in practice, in adopting a process orientation in this chapter; the answer they offer is: "We have come to believe that the core capacity needed to access the field of the future is presence" (2006: 13)—and I think, in one sense, they are exactly right. But to redirect my original question: "What, in practice, is involved in our becoming *present* within the circumstances we must deal with?"

"We first thought of presence," they say, "as being fully conscious and aware in the present moment. Then we began to appreciate presence as deep listening, of being open beyond one's preconceptions and historical ways of making sense" (2006: 13). But as they began to explore the practicalities of what was involved in the actual doing of it, they first came to discover that it involved a process of "letting go" of certain ways of acting associated with *who* they were, with their identities, with ways of acting which, as we have seen above, are oriented toward mastery and control. And this led ultimately to them seeing "all these aspects of presence as leading to a state of 'letting come', of consciously participating in a larger field for change" (2006: 13–14). And as this move, this shift, begins to occur, they say, "the subject–object duality that is basic to our habitual awareness begins to dissolve, [and] we shift from looking 'out at the world' from the viewpoint of a detached observer to looking from 'inside' what is being observed" (2006: 41)—"the key to 'seeing from the whole'," they say, "is developing the capacity not only to suspend our assumptions but to 'redirect' our awareness toward the generative process that lies behind what we see" (2006: 42).

And all of this is, of course, is precisely what we have been exploring above in trying to understand what is involved in adopting a process orientation *in practice*. What do they offer that might be a help in developing the new *capacities* we need?

Yet again, we find that it is a *theory* that is offered: the theory of the U. The deep changes we need to make in our being in and of the world can be *thought* of as moving down the left hand limb of a U in a "Sensing" phase, along the bottom of it in a "Presencing" phase, and up the right hand limb in a "Realizing" phase.[23] About the bottom phase, they say: "Standard theories of change revolve around making decisions, determining 'the vision'," whereas, they suggest, it is much more to do with, "reaching a state of clarity about and connection to what is emerging, [coming] to an 'inner knowing' where, 'in a sense, there is no decision making. What to do just becomes obvious', and what is achieved 'depends on where you're coming from and who you are as a person'" (2006: 89).

Terrific stuff! Indeed, it's just what I tried to convey as the outcome of my third "dwelling in it and on it" option when faced with a bewildering circumstance—after the phases of involvement I outline there we can come to feel confident of knowing our way around within it because we can come to be "in touch with" all the actual options it opens up to us. But what Senge et al. (2006) describe here, and in the whole of the rest of the book, are *achievements*, the final outcomes of processes. What they do not describe are the practicalities involved in carrying out the different phases in the step-by-step execution of these processes—processes which, in their execution require us to orchestrate within ourselves a complex sequence of mental activities, some to do with looking and listening, others with remembering, yet others with acting, with consulting or getting confirmation from others, and so on, and so on, each one with its own criteria of satisfaction that must be met before we can pass on to the next phase in the process. Some exemplary cases, portraying the practicalities involved in achieving *presence* in "touching" or "moving" terms, would seem to be needed. But yet again, perhaps because of the fear of only seeming to offer "anecdotal" evidence for their claims, these writers still seem to be bewitched by the embodied urge to bring their explorations to final expression (despite their conversational style) in theoretical terms. Senge et al. (2006) thus entice us with marvellous vistas of what becomes possible for us if we can learn to reorient ourselves towards our surroundings in this fashion. But how must we *work on ourselves* if we are to achieve this? They still, in my estimation, talk in a style that keeps us on the outside, "out of touch" with our own inner experiences—they are still doing what I would call *aboutness*-talk.

5.4.2 From aboutness- to withness-talk: Entering into the inner movement of things

In a now famous passage, Wittgenstein (1980) remarks: "I think I summed up my attitude to philosophy when I said: Philosophy ought really to be written only as *poetic composition*" (1980: 24), where clearly, what he meant by this was not that he wanted to argue in favor of a new set of theories, assumptions, but that he wanted—by making *remarks* that function to draw our attention to what we all too easily fail to notice and thus overlook—to "move" us to seeing ourselves and our own activities in a new light. But for this to be possible, for his remarks to be able to "move" us in this fashion, they must work on and in us, not to arouse representations within us, *but to "call out" appropriate responses from us.*

This is why he thought of his remarks as having the quality of *reminders* (Wittgenstein, 1953, no.127); for as he points out, he wants to help us overcome "the bewitchment of our intelligence by means of language" by "arranging *what we have always known*," not by trying to solve our problems "by giving new information" (no.109, rearranged, my emphasis). So although he is trying to awaken changes in us of a deep kind, he is not trying to do it by confronting us with something utterly new and utterly unfamiliar to us; instead he wants to bring to our self-awareness something that we *show* that we already know in our *use* of it, but are unaware of the fact—or to put it another way, his aim is to bring to our awareness something that we continually "*work with* it without doubting it" (Wittgenstein, 1969, no.147, my emphasis)—what in common parlance we say we "take-for-granted". This was not, however, Waterman et al.'s (1980) aim in setting up their 7-S framework. Their aim was to represent unambiguously, in general terms, just as in a scientific experiment, the *independent variables* we need to manipulate to produce desired effects in relevant *dependent variables*. Wittgenstein (1963), however, makes it very clear that he is not working in this fashion at all. He is not in his investigations proposing any theories (general or specific), offering any hypotheses, nor trying to argue for a particular new point of view. He is trying to bring to light something else altogether—our other, everyday, ways of making sense of things that are in fact obscured by our more intellectual forms of understanding.

In this light, then, what I think is inappropriate in the efforts to bring about "deep" changes in people in the cases examined above, is that the words used in these efforts are used in a *representational* fashion; speakers/writers intend readers/listeners to "get the picture," taking it that this is sufficient for the required change to happen. Consequently, their expressions do not work in a poetic fashion to remind readers/listeners of already embodied experiences relevant to the activities in question: They do not, for instance, provoke readers/listeners to explore within themselves what engaged listening actually feels like, looks like, and sounds like, and to distinguish it from merely "listening for the facts"; nor do they provoke the exploration of the kinds of human possibilities open up by engaged listening that are shut down in our more disengaged, objective versions— why the difference between them matters.

I would like to distinguish representational talking and thinking from these more poetic forms of talk and thought in terms of *aboutness*-talk and *withness*-talk. (1) *Aboutness*-talk works in terms of people "getting the picture." As Bakhtin (1984) puts it, such talk is ". . . is finalized and deaf to the other's response, does not expect it and does not acknowledge in it any *decisive* force" (1984: 293). In other words, speakers are concerned solely to express the right "picture" of a circumstance, but even if we do "get the picture" they intend, we still have to decide, intellectually, on a right course of action regarding it—the picture, in other words, still needs interpretation. (2) *Withness*-talk, on the other hand, occurs when we come into a living, spontaneously responsive contact with another's living being, with their utterances, their bodily expressions, their "works." It occurs in meetings, in the entwining of living movements in which differencing can occur. Consequently, as we have seen, it is a *diffractive* form of chiasmic *intra*-action that occurs when events occurring out in the world come to be "in touch" with each other—in which both do the touching whilst at the same time are also being touched. And it is in the relations between their outgoing touching and resultant incoming, responsive touches of the other that 'moving' differences can emerge and be sensed. Thus, it is in poetic forms of description (given in the form of reminders) that specific experiences already familiar to us can be aroused, experiences that can "orient" or "relate" us to specific new situations in such a way that we can "see" (or better, feel) the landscape of possibilities for action they open up to us. In short, withness-talk can open us up to possibilities that aboutness-talk hides from us.

5.5 Final remarks: The use of poetic forms of talk by participants living within a world of unceasing process

Right at the beginning of this chapter, I mentioned Whitehead's (1925/ 1975) *fallacy of misplaced concreteness*—which, in the light of my comments above, we can now rephrase as the misleading use of nouns (names), and noun phrases, to refer in our organizational talk (we think and hope) to self-contained, countable things existing "out there," in a world external to us. Indeed, associated with this is the phenomenon of feeling that certain words—what I will simply call "big words"—have taken up all their meaning into themselves, so that a mere mention of them will arouse in everyone the appropriate shared prehensive unity needed to make their meaning determinate. So, for example, we can hear many people at the moment saying: "If only we could get these people *into dialogue*, then they'd see how much they lose by fighting"—although, perhaps, *listening* is beginning to replace "dialogue" as the buzz-word of the moment.

However, we must now realize that we can no longer assume that the many "things" we talk *about* as being of great importance to us—such things or entities as "organizations," "leadership," "strategies," "social relations," "persons," "language," "communication," "presence," etc., etc., even "processes"—are already "out there" awaiting our description of them. Nor can we any longer assume that everyone knows perfectly well what the "it" *is* that is represented by the noun or noun phrase we happen at some moment to be using. It is not just that the concepts represented by these words are "essentially contested" concepts and involve "endless disputes about their proper use on the part of their users," as Gallie (1962: 123) claims. But that as we explore even more deeply into what is involved in our adopting a process orientation *in practice*, we begin to understand *why* such concepts *are* endlessly contested, for we now realize that the entities these words are supposed to *represent* are not, in fact, "already there" in existence in a wholly determinate form, prior to our talk "about" them. To repeat, they only come to take on determinate meanings *within a particular language-entwined material practice*—only at the moment of their use within an actual ongoing practice in which we are making something materially happen in the world.

But as Wittgenstein (1953) realized, to repeat, the "things" we suppose to be represented by many of our "big words" are not, in fact, "already in existence" in a wholly determinate form, prior to our talk "about" them. They only come to take on a determinate meaning at the moment of their use, when entwined with an actual ongoing practice in which we are making something materially happen in the world, that is within, as he termed it, a "language-game" (1953: no. 23). Indeed, he described one of the central aspects of his project thus: "When philosophers use a word—'knowledge', 'being', 'object', 'I', 'proposition', 'name'—and try to grasp the essence of the thing, one must always ask oneself: is the word ever actually used in this way in the language-game which is its original home?—What we do is to bring words back from their metaphysical [or theoretical use] to their everyday use" (1953: no. 116).

Now I have been somewhat critical of the cases I presented above, of people's efforts to effect "deep" changes in other people's ways of being in and of the world, by the use of abstract, idealized theories, models, or frameworks, for failing to take account of the importance of the embodied prehensive unities required if the terms in which they are presented are to have any determinate meanings. This could easily be extending into a critique of all such seeming talk, and mislead us into thinking that nothing of practical worth could be achieved by the use of talk alone. This would be a mistake. For as we can see, Wittgenstein (1953) himself made use of all manner of images, analogies, models, and other descriptive devices, including in particular "language-games" (Wittgenstein, 1953, no. 23)—sometimes to be used as "tools" or "instruments" in his inquiries, while at other times as "textual objects" whose properties are of descriptive importance. But the issue here hinges on *the use* he makes of his words, and, to repeat, he made a *poetic* rather than a representational use of them.

He characterized a poetic usage in this way: "A poet's words can pierce us. And that is of course *causally* connected with the use that they have in our life. And it is also connected with the way in which, conformably to this use, we let our thoughts roam up and down in the familiar surroundings of the words. . . . Do not forget that a poem, even though it is composed in the language of information, is not used in the language of giving information" (Wittgenstein, 1981, no. 155, no. 160)—the familiar surroundings being, of course, the everyday practical surroundings within which we all use these words. And he orients us in quite particular ways, towards quite particular circumstances by the use of such injunctions as "Let us imagine . . . ," or "Suppose . . . ," or "Ask yourself . . . ," or "What happens when . . . ?," and so on, where clearly these injunctions invite us to roam around within a quite precise region of our language-entwined activities. A use more oriented to triggering a shift in our noticing a previously unnoticed connection or relation than towards giving us an explanation or a new fact; more towards showing than to saying; pointing than to leading. Hence the possibility that many proposals, made and discussed in idioms appropriate to the explanatory-representational aims of the social sciences, can also work in us in a more poetic fashion and arouse, at the time of our first encounter with them, the inner roaming up and down of which Wittgenstein speaks. Tsoukas and I have discussed this issue more extensively elsewhere, along with its implications for a much more *ecological* approach to language-based change in organizations (Shotter and Tsoukas, in press).

On the use of words and word-forms as "tools" of investigation, Wittgenstein (1953) remarks: "Our clear and simple language-games are not preparatory studies for a future regularization of language—as it were first approximations ignoring friction and air-resistance. The language-games are rather set up as *objects of comparison* which are meant to throw light on the facts of our language by way not only of similarities, but also of dissimilarities. . . . For we can avoid ineptness or emptiness in our assertions only by presenting the model . . . as an object of comparison—as, so to speak, a measuring-rod; not as a preconceived idea to which reality *must* correspond. . . . [One of their uses is when] we want to establish an order in our knowledge of the use of language: an order with a particular end in view; one out of many possible orders; not *the* order. To this end we shall constantly be giving prominence to distinctions which our ordinary forms of language easily make us overlook" (nos. 130–3).

In other words (as already mentioned above), the descriptive devices he uses in his investigations are not used in a representational fashion, to help us think *about* features in the state of affairs we currently confront. They are used as orientational devices—like, say, blind persons uses a cane—as embodied prosthetic devices that we can *think with* or *act in accordance with*, thus to go out to meet events in our surroundings with a set of relevant expectations as to what we might meet there at the ready. As we see above, rather than in a static, reflective, mirroring fashion, they work to relate us to our surroundings dynamically, as we move around within them, in terms of making differences that make a difference that matters to us—a process that, as we have already seen, needs to be thought of much more either in terms of the emergence of diffraction patterns and distinction making (Barad, 2007), or in terms of the dialogically-structured (Bakhtin, 1984, 1986), back-and-forth processes at work in a practical hermeneutics (Shotter, 1984), than in terms of representing and reflecting.

This, then, is what we lose if we try (to repeat Bergson's (1911) expression) to recompose the becoming of things into sequence of "freeze-frame" snapshots within which we then try to represent, or to accurately "picture," in words. If we talk of such moments objectively, as self-contained entities, the words we use will lack any clear reference beyond themselves, *essential references* to other places and to other times will be lost. In other words, what organizational *theorists* lose if they fail to intertwine their words at the moment of their use in with any material activities, actual or imagined, is not the possible meanings of the words they use, but precisely what *they meant* in using them. As Wittgenstein (1953) remarks, with respect to our hearing a word: "In saying 'When I heard this word, it meant. to me' one refers to a *point of time* and to a *way of using the word*. (Of course, it is this combination that we fail to grasp.) . . . I speak of the essential *references* of the utterance in order to distinguish them from other peculiarities of the expression we use" (1953: 175). It is these essential references of utterances, the extra comments we make that connect what we say with *these* rather then *those* particular circumstances that allow us to make the unique meanings of our utterances clear.

The discovery of what something "is" for us, can only thus be discovered from a study—not of how we talk about it *in reflecting upon it*—but from a study of how "it" enters into and necessarily "shapes" those of our everyday communicative activities in which "it" is involved, *in practice*—an influence which, as Wittgenstein (1953) suggests, is only revealed in the "grammar" of such activities; hence the relevance of his claim that here: "Grammar tells us what kind of object anything is . . . " (no. 373). In other words, it is only *within* our actual, material practices in our daily lives that our words can have clearly determinate meanings, otherwise their meaning is left indeterminate, awaiting determination by being used within the conduct of a particular practice. Again, to repeat: "it is our *acting*, which lies at the bottom of the language-game" (Wittgenstein, 1969, no. 204). Or to put it in Bakhtin's (1993) words: "My participative and demanding consciousness can see that the world of modern philosophy, the theoretical and theoreticized world of culture, is in a certain sense actual, that it possesses validity. But what it can see also is that this world is not the once-occurrent world in which I live and in which I answerably perform my deeds" (1993: 13).

This, then, is what I think Bergson (1911) meant when he talked of our coming to possess a "second kind of knowledge" in which we followed the "flow of time . . . the very flux of the real" (1911: 343), a kind of coming to know in which we experience the very contours of those dynamic *intra-actions*, the ephemeral chiasmic relational events, within which organizing occurs. For these are the focal forms requiring our attention if we are to best understand how we manage our organizational lives. But as Bakhtin (1993) remarks, such "once-occurrent uniqueness or singularity cannot be thought of, it can only be participatively experienced or lived through" (1993: 13), thus, unless we know how to work on ourselves to rid ourselves of the charms exerted upon us by abstractions, and learn instead *what* to look for, we will fail to notice those differences, those events, that can make a difference to us that matters. But the whole point of my discussion above is that our adoption of a process orientation is not at all easy. It takes time and effort, and involves a step-by-step, iterative, recursive process in which we turn to apply our achievements so far back into the original situation of our bewilderment. As Wittgenstein (1980) put it, "the place I have to get to is the place I must already be at now. Anything that I might reach by the climbing a ladder [i.e., by being specially trained in abstruse matters] doesn't interest me" (1980: 7)—the sheer complexity of the present moment we now occupy is what we need to understand. "The disadvantage of exclusive attention to a group of abstractions, however well-founded," said Whitehead (1925/1975), "is that, by the nature of the case, you have abstracted from the remainder of things. In so far as the excluded things are important in your experience, your modes of thought are not fitted to deal with them" (1925/1975: 76).

Thus, what I have tried to capture in the discussion above, then, are some of the difficulties involved in trying to adopt a process orientation in practice, and also, the degree to which some of these difficulties can be overcome by the adoption of what I have called *withness*-talk and *withness*-thought in addition to the *aboutness*-thought and talk that is currently central to our more intellectual endeavors. Indeed, my main aim has been of a prophylactic kind in trying to pick out those forms of talk when, as Wittgenstein (1953) puts it, "language goes on holiday" (no. 38), when our words are "up in the air" without a "rooting" in a language-game shared by our listener/readers. So much of our talk- time (and printed paper) is wasted in such forms of expression. The more important exploration, to do with effective poetic forms of talk, our greater involvement in practicing practices, the exercises and other activities that might go on in classrooms that might be useful in training managers and other business people more effectively in Business Schools . . . well, that must be work for another day.

Notes

1. Why I say *intra*-connections (and later, *intra*-actions) is explained below. Also see note 10.
2. Furthermore, in our Indo-European languages, subject–object separation is reinforced in the very nature of active and passive voice verb forms, and our lack of a *middle* voice form (which existed in Homeric Greek): "In the active, the verbs denote a process that is accomplished *outside* the subject. In the middle, . . . the verb indicates a process centring in the subject, the subject being *inside* the process," notes Benveniste (1971), and he adds a few sentences later that, as a result, for us now "'to be' is a process, like 'to go' or 'to flow' in which the participation of the subject is not required" (Benveniste, 1971: 148–9). Interestingly, Wittgenstein (1980) makes a similar point, in his efforts to bring home to us the pervasive influence the use of our words can have upon us: "As long as there continues to be a verb 'to be' that looks as if it functions in the same way as 'to eat' and 'to drink', as long as we still have the adjectives 'identical', 'true', false', 'possible', as long as we continue to talk of the river of time as an expanse of space, etc. etc., people will keep

stumbling over the same puzzling difficulties and find themselves staring at something which no explanation seems capable of clearing up" (p. 15). No wonder we so easily lapse back into our *outside* accounts of processes and erase ourselves from the very activities within which we, in fact, play crucial parts.

3. I emphasize "in practice" here for two reasons: One is that, as we shall see, I want to raise *orientational* questions rather than ones to do with theories; the other is that, again as will become clear, the very nature of a process orientation, to the extent that it involves processes embedded in larger processes, ad infinitum, raises irresolvable conceptual issues to do with setting boundaries—issues that can only be resolved in practice.

4. A whole capable of being partitioned in many distinctive ways, but not already consisting of a set of countable, self-contained, basic "atomic" elements.

5. These phrases are taken from the following fuller quotation of Bergson (1911): "Instead of attaching ourselves to the inner becoming of things, we place ourselves outside them in order to recompose their becoming artificially. We take snapshots, as it were, of the passing reality, and, as these are characteristic of the reality, we have only to string them on a becoming, abstract, uniform and invisible, situated at the back of the apparatus of knowledge, in order to imitate what there is that is characteristic in this becoming itself. . . . Whether we would think becoming, or express it, or even perceive it, we hardly do anything else than set going a kind of cinematograph inside us" (p. 343).

6. See Garfinkel (2002: 265–76) for an account of "losing the phenomena" in a mode of analysis that results in a set of products (parts, units) of a different kind or character than the whole from which they have been taken as constituting.

7. "A philosophical problem has the form: 'I don't know my way about'" (Wittgenstein, 1953: no. 123).

8. Indeed, from within our involvement within an ongoing practice, I suggest that our movements can give rise to a "*shaped*" and "*vectored*" sense of our moment-by-moment changing placement in our current surroundings—engendering in us both "transitional understandings" of our current position, along with "action guiding anticipations" as to where-next we might go (Shotter, 2005).

9. My use of this phrase—of something "mattering to us"—will become clear later, in my discussion of differences that can make a difference to us *that matters*.

10. My own gradual realization of how strange dialogically structured events actually are, is a case in point. Even now, although I first began to outline the nature of "joint action" 30 years ago (Shotter, 1980), I can still be struck by a new aspect of its special nature that I had not previously realized. For instance (as I will explain more later), it was only in reading Karen Barad's (2007) book, *Meeting the Universe Halfway*, that I realized that my use of the word "*inter*-action" implied an interplay between two (or more) *already existing* individuals, and that the term "*intra*-action" was much more the term required, if we are to re-think ourselves as having to work out from within already ongoing, wholistic processes towards the constitution of distinctive (but already internally related)

individuals. I must confess that what stood in the way of me thinking this for myself was simply my lack of feeling any disquiet in my uses of the word. No matter for what strange new views of reality we might argue in our more intellectual moments, the classical Cartesian-Newtonian, mechanistic world-view is so entrenched in our everyday thought and talk that we can still lapse back into in it in our efforts to take such thought and talk out into the organizational world of everyday. Indeed, as I now see it, *arguments* for the value of a *process orientation* will fall on deaf ears in actual organizational life until the biasing effect of the classical worldview has been dealt with—for, to repeat, our incapacity to understand it is rooted and expressed in our current forms of life, hence in who and what we are to ourselves.

11. Whitehead (1929/1978) calls the other two phases the supplemental phase, and satisfaction (p. 245). The supplemental phase involves the emergence of a unity as one gathers fragments within one's movements here and there within a situation, while satisfaction is arrived at once we have a grasp of a situation in its own unique complexity. Elsewhere (Shotter, 1984), I called the back-and-forth process in which we arrive at a perceptual unity, a *practical hermeneutical process*.

12. It is our becoming a participant part within a larger whole, and as a result, our taking on a new identity as such, that makes an *intra*-action quite different from an *inter*-action in which the inter-action participants retain their original identities. I owe this point to Barad (2007).

13. In using the term *chiasmic*, I am following the lead of Merleau-Ponty (1968) who entitles chapter 4—in his book *The Visible and the Invisible*—"The Intertwining—The Chiasm." But I cannot yet pretend to say here in any comprehensive manner what "chiasmic or intertwined relations" in living processes are in fact like. But what is clear is that here is a sphere of living relations of a kind utterly different from any so far familiar to us (such as causal or logical relations) and taken by us as basic in our intellectual inquiries. All I can do here is to begin their exploration.

14. In designating our "seeings" and "hearings" as *achievements*, Ryle (1949) wanted to make a very crucial distinction, between what he called "achievement verbs" and "task verbs." For, as he remarked, "the differences, for example, between, . . . hunting and finding, . . . listening and hearing, looking and seeing, travelling and arriving, have been construed [in previous philosophies], if they have been noticed at all, as differences between coordinate species of activity or process, when in fact the differences are of quite another kind" (p. 143)—it is, as we see, the difference between unobservable, relational events and observable events.

15. See Shotter (2003).

16. Indeed, even if we could, the "over there, outside" nature of a picture would be useless to us in failing to satisfy our need for an account of their nature that would provide us, in our making use of it, with the *orientational* understandings we require.

17. Ryle (1949) gives the following example of what he calls a "category mistake" that can arise out of expecting to encounter facts as if they belonged to one logical type or category (or range of types of categories), when they actually belong to another: "A foreigner visiting Oxford or Cambridge for the first time is shown a number of colleges, libraries playing fields, museums, scientific departments and administrative offices. He then asks 'But where is the University?' . . . It has then to be explained to him that the University . . . is just the way in which all that he has already seen is organized" (pp. 17--18).

18. Although Rorty's (1979) view that "the picture which holds traditional philosophy captive is that of the mind as a great mirror, containing various representations . . ." (p. 12), and his subsequent suggestion that instead we should see "*conversation* as the ultimate context within which knowledge is to be understood" (p. 389), should, perhaps, have prepared us for it.

19. Voloshinov (1986) captures this issue very nicely in noting that "The task of understanding does not basically amount to recognizing the form used, but rather to understanding it in a particular, concrete context . . . to understanding its novelty and not to recognizing its identity. . . . Thus the constituent factor for the linguistic form, as for the sign, is not at all its self-identity as signal but its *specific variability* . . ." (pp. 68–9).

20. I see the need for more than Whitehead's (1929/1978) three phases: because of the difficulties to do with giving intelligible linguistic expression to at first only vaguely felt, distinctive "time-contours," I expand what he designates as a *supplemental* phase into a number of other distinct phases.

21. It is this kind of confidence or surety of action that Wittgenstein (1969) investigates in *On Certainty.*

22. See the mention already made above of Niels Bohr's (1958) *complementarity* principle: that *determinate* material entities only come to *be* what they *are* within the different *language entwined practices* we adopt in relating ourselves to an aspect of material reality in our attempts to render its nature visibly-rational-and-observable (to use a phrase of Garfinkel's, 1967).

23. This is a movement, of course, not too different from Whitehead's (1929/1978) original three phases of concresence, as he called it (see note 11)—the "reinvention of the wheel" (the restatement of an already well-documented process in another disciplinary idiom) is quite common, I suggest, in the realm of organization studies.

References

Bakhtin, M. M. (1984). *Problems of Dostoevsky's Poetics*, ed. and trans. Caryl Emerson. Minneapolis: University of Minnesota Press.

Bakhtin, M. M. (1986). *Speech Genres and Other Late Essays*, trans. by Vern W. McGee, Austin, TX: University of Texas Press.

Bakhtin, M. M. (1993). *Toward a Philosophy of the Act*, with translation and notes by Vadim Lianpov, ed. M. Holquist, Austin, TX: University of Texas Press.

Barad, K. (2007). *Meeting the Universe Halfway: Quantum Physics and the Entanglement of Matter and Meaning*, Durham & London: Duke University Press.

Bateson, G. (1973). *Steps to an Ecology of Mind*, London: Paladin.

Bateson, G. (1979). *Mind in Nature: A Necessary Unity*, London: Fontana/Collins.

Bennis, W. G. & O'Toole, J. (2005). How business schools lost their way, *Harvard Business Review*, May, 96–104.

Benveniste, E. (1971). *Problems on General Linguistics*, Florida: University of Miami Press.

Bergson, H. (1911). *Creative Evolution*, trans. Arthur Mitchell, New York: Henry Holt.

Bohr, N.(1958). *Atomic Physics and Human Knowledge*, New York: Wiley.

Gallie, W.B. (1962). Essentially contested concepts, in M. Black (ed.) *The Importance of Language*, Englewood Cliffs: Prentice Hall.

Garfinkel, H. (1967). *Studies in Ethnomethodology*. Englewood Cliffs: Prentice-Hall.

Garfinkel, H. (2002). *Ethnomethodology's Program: Working out Durkheim's Aphorism*, ed. and intro. Anne Warefield Rawls, New York & Oxford: Rowman & Littlefield Publishers.

Gergen, K. J. (2009). *Relational Being, beyond Self and Community*, New York: Oxford University Press.

Hertz, H. H. (1956). *The Principles of Mechanics*, New York: Dover (orig. German pub. 1894).

Honner, J. (1987). *The Description of Nature: Niels Bohr and the Philosophy of Quantum Physics*, Oxford: Clarendon Press.

Kant, I. (1970). *Critique of Pure Reason*, trans. Norman Kemp Smith, London: Macmillan's St Martin's Press.

Merleau-Ponty, M. (1964). *The Primacy of Perception and Other Essays*, ed. and intro. James M. Edie, Evanston, IL: Northwestern University Press.

Merleau-Ponty, M. (1968). *The Visible and the Invisible*, ed. Claude Lefort, trans. Alphonso Lingis, Evanston, IL: Northwestern University Press.

Mindtools (2010). *The McKinsey 7-S Framework*, downloaded from http://www.mindtools.com/pages/article/newSTR_91.htm, 5 January 2010.

Quine, W. V. (1953). Two dogmas of empiricism, in W. F. Quine, *From a Logical Point of View*, Cambridge: Cambridge University Press.

Rorty, R. (1979). *Philosophy and the Mirror of Nature*, Oxford: Blackwell.

Russell, B. (1914). *Our Knowledge of the External World*, London: Allen and Unwin.

Ryle, G. (1949). *The Concept of Mind*, London: Methuen.

Senge, P., Scharmer, O. C., Jaworski, J., & Flowers, B. S. (2006). *Presence: Exploring Profound Change in People, Organizations and Society*, London: Nicolas Brealey Publications.

Shotter, J. (1980). Action, joint action, and intentionality, in M. Brenner (ed.) *The Structure of Action*, Oxford: Blackwell, 28–65.

Shotter, J. (1984). *Social Accountability and Selfhood*, Oxford: Blackwell.

Shotter, J. (1993*a*). *Cultural Politics of Everyday Life: Social Constructionism, Rhetoric, and Knowing of the Third Kind*, Milton Keynes: Open University Press.

Shotter, J. (1993*b*). *Conversational Realities: Constructing Life through Language*, London: Sage.

Shotter, J. (2003). "Real presences": Meaning as living movement in a participatory world, *Theory & Psychology*, 13(4), 435–68.

Shotter, J. (2005). Inside processes: Transitory understandings, action guiding anticipations, and witness thinking, *International Journal of Action Research*, 1(1), 157–89.

Shotter, J. & Tsoukas, H. (in press). Complex thought, simple talk: An ecological approach to language-based change in organizations, in S. Maguire, P. Allen, & W. McKelvey (eds) *Sage Handbook of Complexity and Management*.

Taptiklis, T. (2008). *Unmanaging: Opening Up the Organization to its Own Unspoken Knowledge*, London: Palgrave Macmillan.

Voloshinov, V. N. (1986). *Marxism and the Philosophy of Language*, trans. L. Matejka & I. R. Titunik, Cambridge, MA: Harvard University Press, first pub. 1929.

Waterman, R. H., Peters, T. J., & Phillips, J. R. (1980). Structure is not organization, *Business Horizons*, 23(3), 14–26.

Whitehead, A. N. (1925/1975). *Science and the Modern World*. New York: Free Press.

Whitehead, A. N. (1929/1978). *Process and Reality: An Essay in Cosmology*, corrected edition, ed. D. R. Griffin & D. W. Sherburne, New York: Free Press.

Wittgenstein, L. (1953). *Philosophical Investigations*, trans. G. E. M. Anscombe, Oxford: Blackwell.

Wittgenstein, L. (1969). *On Certainty*, ed. G. E. M. Anscombe & G. H. von Wright, trans. D.S. Paul & G. E. M Anscombe, Oxford: Blackwell.

Wittgenstein, L. (1980). *Culture and Value*, intro. G. von Wright, trans. P. Winch, Oxford: Blackwell.

Wittgenstein, L. (1981). *Zettel*, 2nd edn, ed. G. E. M. Anscombe and G. H. von Wright, Oxford: Blackwell.

6

The Poetics of Process: Theorizing the Ineffable in Organization Studies

Karl E. Weick

Abstract: This chapter argues here for the poetics of process—the imaginative process of creating forms out of "airy nothing". Managerial work, it further notes, is akin to the work of a poet. Process thinking helps us pay attention to concrete details and the constitution of things. Through gerund forms of thinking we recover some of the process that generates nouns and gives us apparent stability. Nouns and verbs are best seen as co-evolving. Scholars who practice process theorizing accept reluctantly the ineffability underlying the stabilization of differences and reaffirm their commitment to draw attention to indications of nouns being unwound and set in motion as verbs, as well as verbs being wound into slower motion as nouns. The naming and the winding are the work of process theorizing just as they are the work of everyday life as organizing.

Try to express a feeling of "blue" or a feeling of "cold." Now, try to express a feeling of "but," a feeling of "if" or "by," a feeling of "though." You'll see what William James saw, namely, that even though conjunctions, adverbial phrases, and prepositions express shadings of relation between objects of thought, we have developed the inveterate habit of "recognizing the existence of the substantive parts alone.... Language almost refuses to lend itself to any other use" (James, 1950: 245–46). Conjunctions operate tacitly, much like the processes they shadow and enact.

Processes become the unarticulated ground while entities and states become the highlighted figure. It's tough to reverse that figure–ground relationship. Thinking processually tends to be hard to articulate, hard to disseminate, hard to apply. Hard, but not impossible. Tsoukas (2005) and D'Eredita and Barreto (2006) argue that ineffable, tacit expertise can be conveyed in fragmented form by drawing attention to salient features in episodes where the ineffable is performed. These fragments are more like a collage than a coherent depiction. They need the animation provided by conjunctions. They also need to be linked with other "similar" episodes so that observers are able to make sense of these experiences by parsing them into goals, stimuli, responses, and interpretations. Thus, an ineffable practice is conveyed piecemeal by drawing attention to smaller, effable, abridged episodes associated with a larger set of tacit, subsidiary sensitivities. This implies that a crucial stage in process thinking is attention-drawing.

Attention-drawing is exemplified by Nonaka and Takeuchi's (1995) influential case study of Matsushita's efforts to invent a bread-making machine (Tsoukas, 2005: 152–7). The crucial moves in bread making are personal knowledge that master bread makers are unable to make explicit. What they can do, and what they did for Matsushita observers, was to draw attention to specific motions made by novice bread makers that were not quite right. The master bakers were unable to put the right move into words, or to give it a context, or to make explicit what went before and after the crucial working of the dough. The best they could do was call attention to specific, observable stimuli that were felt to be part of the tacit understanding on which the baker drew.

In similar fashion, theorists who practice process are unable to make explicit how process theorizing works. For example, the author has been labeled a "process theorist" though in many ways he was among the last to discover this (e.g. the word "process" is not in the index of Weick 1995). This is true ineffability, yet that's not the whole story. I am, in Hari Tsoukas's words, a "process practitioner" (private communication, July 22, 2009). That's different from a process thinker. When I look back at what I've said, I see process thinking ("how can I know what I think until I see what I say?"). This means that the concept of process is as much an ex post articulation as it is an explicit guiding principle.

As Tsoukas put it, "the rest of us, having seen evidence of process thinking in the outcomes of your work, have labeled you a 'process theorist' and we are asking you to be true to that label (!) and tell us how you have theorized process. But the very theorizing of process is work, which is grounded on tacit understandings of process... By reflecting ex post facto on your process work, you draw our and your attention to aspects of it that constitute ways of process theorizing. What was previously ready-to-hand is now becoming present-at-hand. By seeing, ex post, patterns in your ways of theorizing (i.e. ways of doing theory work), we refine our understanding of what is involved in doing process work."

6.1 Drawing attention to images

A predictable anchor in many discussions of process is the image of a stream. When people discuss process (e.g. Hernes, 2008: 24–6) they often reach back to 500 BC and describe Heraclitus and his variously translated statement that you cannot step twice into the same river. Thus, scholars of organizational process can choose among such translations as, "The river where you set your foot just now is gone—those waters giving way to this, now this (Haxton, 2001: 27); "just as the river where I step is not the same, and is, so I am as I am not" (Haxton, 2001: 51); "new and different waters flow around those who step into the same river. It disperses and comes together . . . flows in and out . . . toward us and away" (Geldard, 2000: 158); "[Heraclitus says somewhere that] . . . all things are in process and nothing stays still, and [comparing all things to flowing waters, he says] we cannot step twice in the same river" (Geldard, 2000: 158); "according to Heraclitus one cannot step twice into the same river, nor can one grasp any mortal substance in a stable condition, but by the intensity and the rapidity of change it scatters and again gathers. Or rather, not again not later but at the same time it forms and dissolves, and approaches and departs" (Kahn, 1981: 168); and finally "Cratylus denied that you could even step in the river once, since you are changing too" (Kahn, 1981: 168). An interpretation that seems to include most translations is that "each individual's experience in the cosmos is as unique as the step into the river and yet the experience itself is universal, as the river is uniform for each individual who steps into its flow" (Geldard, 2000: 53).

A less predictable anchor, but in some ways one that is more suited for organizational studies, is found in Shakespeare's play, *A Midsummer Night's Dream*. In Act V, Scene I, Theseus says the following (Shakespeare, 1990):

> The lunatic, the lover, and the poet
> Are of imagination all compact:
> One sees more devils than vast Hell can hold,
> This is the madman; the lover, all as frantic,
> Sees Helen's beauty in the brow of Egypt.
> The poet's eye, in a fine frenzy rolling,

> Doth glance from heaven to earth, from earth to heaven;
> And as imagination bodies forth
> The forms of the things unknown, the poet's pen
> Turns them to shapes and gives to airy nothing
> A local habitation and a name.

While occasional managers may be lunatics or lovers, almost all function as poets who preside over organizing. Their work of organizing, as suggested by Theseus, consists of imagining, forming, shaping, locating, and naming. In the words of Bakken and Hernes (2006: 1601) organizing is an exercise in noun-making. The resulting noun, "organization," refers to the form, shape, location, and name of the "something" that noun-making accomplishes. What makes all of this processual is motion; both the noun and the making are impermanent. They dissolve yet can be reaccomplished (Weick, 1969: 36). Furthermore, when nouns and noun-making processes dissolve, they may do so with a reverse progression: first the name goes, then the location, the shape, the form, and finally the imagining itself. Imagination bodies forth enacted sense which eventually reverts back to airy nothing. Or, stated in more compact form, "Life is an organizing process" (Follett, 1951: 145).

The idea that imagination "bodies forth the forms of *the things* unknown," alerts us to a potential poetic error, namely, the fallacy of misplaced concreteness. Although the idea is associated with Whitehead, Jacques Barzun had coined an equivalent phrase, "misplaced abstraction," before learning of Whitehead's concept. Process theorizing can be understood from either direction. Barzun bristled at the fact that concepts "classify acts by *imposing* sameness," an act that conceals individuality. He called this "concealment by concept" and went on to say, "I used to warn my students in history against all forms of 'misplaced abstraction.' History is the realm in which the particular is the center of interest. Generalities help to organize and relate, but reification—making agents or forces out of generalities—is the unforgivable fault" (Barzun, 1984: 62). In a footnote he mentions his later discovery of Whitehead's "fallacy of misplaced concreteness" and describes Whitehead's phrase as "the more vivid and memorable phrase" while his was "more pedagogical and closer to the subject" (1984: 62). He goes on to say that "both terms, seemingly opposite, refer to the same error." You misplace concreteness when you treat an abstraction as a thing. You misplace abstraction when you treat an abstraction as a thing. The importance of avoiding the error in process theorizing is made clear by Chia (1999): "(O)rganization, therefore, is not a 'thing' or 'entity' with established patterns, *but the repetitive activity of ordering and patterning itself"* (1999: 224, italics in original). Sensemaking involves giving shape to imagined forms by locating and naming them. The temptation is often to reify the name and cling to its location, mindless that those shapes are impermanent without continuous re-accomplishment.

Theseus reminds us of additional clues that summarize and suggest tacit moments in process theorizing. Consider, for example, "airy nothing." Something like airy nothing has been discussed in the organizational literature as the root condition of organization. For example, Robert Cooper (2007) describes the social body of human organization as "the pure process of generic making and moving" that emerges from pre-sense. "Organs and senses project themselves through the body's limbs into a limbo of invisible and formless space and time out of which they make meaningful sense.... Human organs must make human sense out of the pre-human invisibility of pre-sense. This means projecting human needs, feelings and desires onto a material environment that is intrinsically insentient to human experience. Human organization begins with this originating step of human projection" (2007: 1548).

Something close to "airy nothing" also lies behind Taylor and Van Every's (2000) description of organizing as "an ongoing process of mediation in which the objective world where we live and interact both frames what we do and supplies us with the material for our own reconstruction of it. What we think of as organization is what is left over as a trace or memory of yesterday's organizing.... By the time we recognize the organization it is no longer there. What is there is our transformation of it; what makes it recognizable—re-cognizable—is precisely its no longer existing" (2000: 163). In other words, every night the organization dissolves back into airy nothing that needs to be reaccomplished the next day, through conversations that convert textual traces back into shapes and locations.

The "poet's eye" glances at airy nothing and imagines forms. So too does the eye of an entrepreneur, a forensic investigator, even a manager. The poet's eye becomes the manager's eye when we think of managing as "firstly and fundamentally the task of becoming aware, attending to, sorting out, and prioritizing an inherently messy, fluxing and chaotic world of competing demands that are placed on a manager's attention. It is creating order out of chaos. It is an art, not a science. Active perceptual organization and the astute allocation of attention is a central feature of the managerial task" (Chia, 2005: 1092).

The poet's pen creates shapes with locations and names, the manager becomes an author (e.g. Cunliffe, 2001) producing texts. This is where Whitehead's notion of noun-making draws attention to salient moments of process thinking that remind us of tacit moves of process theorizing. This, incidentally, is where my appeal to stamp out nouns (Weick, 1979: 44), suitable as it may have been in the early 1970s when reified organizations dominated the literature, was clearly only half of the story as became clearer when the interplay between organizing and sensemaking was conceptualized.

Theseus's progression from imagined forms to locations and names closely parallels a similar progression found in organizations that ranges from perception to formalization. Robert Irwin (1977) coined the phrase "compounded abstraction" to summarize the fate of initial perceptions as they are reworked in the interest of coordination and control. "As social beings, we organize and structure ourselves and our environment into an 'objective' order; we organize our perceptions of things into various pre-established abstract structures. Our minds direct our senses every bit as much as our senses inform our minds. Our reality in time is confined to our ideas about reality" (1977: 24). In Irwin's view, sensemaking moves through six stages, beginning with *perception* (synesthesia of undifferentiated sensations). The undifferentiated perceptions begin to take on meaning in the second stage, *conception*, where people isolate unnamed zones of focus. In the third stage, *form*, these zones begin to be named. And in the fourth stage, which Irwin calls *formful*, the named things are deployed relationally and are arranged in terms of dimensions like hot/cool, loud/ soft, up/down. This is basically where Theseus stops.

But Irwin adds fifth and sixth stages. These last two stages are commonplace in organizations and often signal the liminal space "betwixt and between" process and structure (Tempest et al., 2007). In the fifth stage, labeled *formal*, patterns of relations begin to be reified and treated as entities. For example, the formful relation of up/down now gets reified into the more formal relationship of superior/subordinate. And in the sixth stage, *formalize*, the reifications dictate behavior and become taken-for-granted fixtures around which people organize their activities. By the time people *formalize* their experience they are essentially estranged from direct perceptual experience. At each step in this sequence of compounded abstraction, details get lost, the concrete is replaced with the abstract, and design options get foreclosed. To practice process one dwells on the earlier stages of Irwin's formulation, which often necessitates careful attention to history (e.g. see Johnson's (2008) masterful discussion of the processes through which the Paris Opera was founded). The application of Irwin's scheme to organizational issues is illustrated in an analysis of sensemaking at NASA that resulted in the disintegration of the Columbia space shuttle over Texas in 2003 (Weick, 2005). The rapid compounding of abstraction produced formalized actions by higher level NASA personnel who concluded that the apparent foam shedding fit the general category of an "in family event that is well understood" (misplaced abstraction) while those lower in the hierarchy worried that the particulars of their perceptions, conceptions, and forms were indications of a far more serious problem that was an "out of family event not well understood" (misplaced concreteness).

6.2 Drawing attention to practice

As noted earlier, attention-drawing is one means by which aspects of tacit practice can be made explicit. It is not the practice itself that is made explicit. Instead, "what we do when we reflect on the practical activities we engage in is to re-punctuate the distinctions underlying those activities, to draw the attention of those involved to certain hitherto unnoticed aspects of those activities—to see connections among items previously thought unconnected. . . . Through instructive forms of talk (e.g. 'look at this', 'have you thought about this in that way?', 'Try this', 'Imagine this', 'Compare this to that') practitioners are moved to *re*-view the situation they are in, to relate to their circumstances in a different way. . . . [Citing from Wittgenstein Tsoukas goes on to say] Something that we know when no one asks us, but no longer know when we are supposed to give an account of it, is something that we need to *remind* ourselves of" (Tsoukas, 2005; 157).

An example of a reminder is the suggestion to "think ing" (Weick 1979: 42–7). The simple act of using more verbal nouns (e.g. "punctuating") and adding "-ing" to organizationally relevant words (e.g. "outsourcing") may seem like a frivolous tactic that does little more than feign a process mindset. At times that may be true. But if one adds "-ing" to what one is saying (e.g. organization becomes organizing), then it is also possible that when one *sees* this form of *saying*, process *thinking* gets triggered. Consider the difference between a wildland fire entrapping people and a wildland fire entrapment. An entrapment is finished. It is history, even if that history is short and recent. Entrapping is ongoing, unfolding, indeterminate, unsettled, up-for-grabs, becoming, being enacted. Entrapping has a present as well as a history. When one says "-ing," sees oneself saying "-ing," and then thinks about the associations evoked by "-ing," all of this essentially rolls a name and a location back into shapes and forms that can be imagined differently. That's true for the actors in the situation as well as the analysts who watch them. Process practitioners can't speak flux, but they can speak gerunds. A gerund is a verbal noun, a hybrid form, a clue to the movement in noun-making.

In process thinking verbs are just as important as nouns. "When some of the behaviorists tell us that 'knowledge lives in the muscles' they seem to leave out the deeper truth of the continuing activity. I am objecting here merely to the word 'knowledge.' I think it better when practicable to keep to verbs; the value of nouns is chiefly for post mortems. . . . The activity of knowing [is] a process which involves knower and known but which never looks from the windows of either. The knower knows [an active verb] the known; reality is in the knowing" (Follett, 1951: 88).

6.3 Conclusion

What would it mean for organizational studies if we took Theseus seriously?

1. It would mean that the image of manager as author would be further refined by asserting that much of managerial work is akin to the work of a poet.
2. It would reaffirm Whitehead's assertion (e.g. Hernes, 2008: 127) that nouns and verbs co-evolve, and temper those well-intentioned but misguided people who counsel scholars to stamp out nouns.
3. It would strengthen the possibility that sensemaking and process perspectives are interdependent, that each requires the other.
4. It would ground the genesis of process in the chaos of airy nothing.
5. It would assert that imagination is a necessary condition of organizing.

To draw attention to some of the tacit motions of process theorizing, one can start with images that call attention to the manager as poet, the co-evolving of nouns and verbs, actions of locating and naming, the airy nothing that founders imagine into forms, and imagining itself. Although we have listened intently to Theseus, we have not ignored Heraclitus. What we have instead is a composite that reads: "you can't step into the same process twice, nor can the stepping itself remain the same".

A hallmark of a process perspective is the basic belief that "things change." But, as Theseus suggests, that phrase can be reversed: "change things" ["thing" is a verb]. Change becomes things in the hands of poets when imagination shapes, locates, and names differences amidst the sameness. The differences that are stabilized become objects of focal awareness. The subsidiary awareness that produces stable objects remains ineffable for most people. Scholars who practice process theorizing accept ineffability with reluctance and reaffirm their commitment to draw attention to indications of nouns being unwound and set in motion as verbs as well as verbs being wound into slower motion as nouns. The naming and the winding are the work of process theorizing just as they are the work of everyday life as organizing. As my discerning co-author Kathleen Sutcliffe puts it, "Some days you see waves and some days you see particles."

References

Bakken, T. & Hernes, T. (2006). Organizing is both a verb and a noun: Weick meets Whitehead, *Organization Studies*, 27(11), 1599–616.

Barzun, J. (1984). *A Stroll with William James*, Chicago: University of Chicago.

Chia, R. (1999). A "Rhizomic" model of organizational change and transformation: Perspectives from a metaphysics of change, *British Journal of Management*, 10, 209–27.

Cooper, R. (2007). Organs of process: Rethinking human organization, *Organization Studies*, 28, 1547–73.

Cunliffe, A. L. (2001). Managers as practical authors: Reconstructing our understanding of management practice, *Journal of Management Studies*, 38(3), 351–71.

D'Eredita, M. A. & Barreto, C. (2006). How does tacit knowledge proliferate: An episode-based perspective, *Organization Studies*, 27, 1821–41.

Follett, M. P. (1951). *Creative Experience*, New York: Peter Smith.

Geldard, R. (2000). *Remembering Heraclitus*, Great Barrington, MA: Lindisfarne Books.

Haxton, B. (2001). *Heraclitus: Fragments*, New York: Penguin.

Hernes, T. (2008). *Understanding Organization as Process*, New York: Routledge.

Irwin, R. (1977). Notes Toward a Model, in *Exhibition catalog for the Robert Irwin exhibition, Whitney Museum of American Art, April 16–May 29, 1977*, New York: Whitney Museum of American Art, 23–31.

James, W. (1950). *Principles of Psychology*, New York: Dover.

Johnson, V. (2008). *Backstage at the Revolution: How the Royal Paris Opera Survived the End of the old Regime*, Chicago: University of Chicago.

Kahn, C. H. (1981). *The Art and Thought of Heraclitus*, New York: Cambridge University Press.

Nonaka, I. & Takeuchi, H. (1995). *The Knowledge-Creating Company*, New York: Oxford.

Shakespeare, W. (1990). *The Plays and Sonnets: Volume 1*, Chicago: Encyclopedia Britannica.

Taylor, J. R. & Van Every, E. J. (2000). *The Emergent Organization: Communication as its Site and Surface*, Mahwah, NJ: Erlbaum.

Tempest, S., Starkey, K., & Ennew, C. (2007). In the death zone: A study of limits in the 1996 Mount Everest disaster, *Human Relations*, 60, 1039–64.

Tsoukas, H. (2005). Do we really understand tacit knowledge? in H. Tsoukas, *Complex Knowledge*, Oxford: Oxford University Press, 141–62.

Weick, K. E. (1969). *Social Psychology of Organizing*, Reading, MA: Addison-Wesley.

Weick, K. E. (1979). *The Social Psychology of Organizing*, 2nd edn, Reading, MA: Addison-Wesley.

Weick, K. E. (1995). *Sensemaking in Organizations*, Thousand Oaks, CA: Sage.

Weick, K. E. (2005). Making sense of blurred images: Mindful organizing in Mission STS-107, in W. H. Starbuck & M. Farjoun (eds) *Organization at the Limit: Lessons from the Columbia Disaster*, Malden, MA: Blackwell, 159–78.

7

Rediscovering Becoming: Insights from an Oriental Perspective on Process Organization Studies

Robert Chia

Abstract: Process is an ambivalent term. Its use in organizational research and theorizing is widespread. Yet, there are important subtle differences in how the term is understood. Process may be construed either as an epiphenomenon of substantial organizational entities *or* as a primary condition of reality from which the phenomenon of organization spontaneously emerges. Each perspective gives rise to a different theoretical focus and agenda for the field of organization studies. In this chapter, I explore new avenues for understanding process and organization. I show that the idea of ultimate reality as formless, undifferentiated, and ceaselessly changing has been a basic intuition of the ancient Oriental world since time immemorial; one that remains widespread and influential in shaping contemporary Eastern mentalities and dispositions. I further show how this Oriental metaphysical attitude towards process, flux, and self-transformation enables us to better appreciate the phenomenon of social organization as essentially the cumulative effect of a stabilizing, simple-locating, and identity-creating human impulse. From a process organization perspective then, organization studies ought to be more concerned with analyzing the dominant organizational mentalities involved in structuring social reality than with the analysis of "organizations."

What is immediate reality before we have added the fabrication of thinking? ... At the time of pure experience. ... Reality is a succession of events that flow without stopping.

Nishida Kitaro, *An Inquiry into the Good*, 1921/1990: 47–54

7.1 Introduction

In ancient Greece the verb *eisagō* carried the meaning "to import new, strange, foreign or even heretical ideas" into a dominant orthodoxy. A book collection that explicitly encourages various *Perspectives on Process Organization Studies* offers a novel opportunity to undertake such a risky and seemingly extravagant exegesis but one perhaps timely within the context of changing global economic and political relations as we enter the second decade of the new millennium. The study of alternative *organizational mentalities*,[1] from either a different epoch or a different geographical region, and its effect on the structuring of social reality, can reflexively help us better understand contemporary Western[2] concerns with social order and organization. In this regard, the term organization is used here to denote a stabilized social form, pattern, or order of a more generic nature than a circumscribed socio-economic entity.

In this chapter, therefore, I intend to explore and examine the rich tradition of Eastern thought to show that the notion of an ever-fluxing and interminably changing reality has been deeply embedded in the unconscious collective psyche of the Oriental[3] world since time immemorial. I show that this is variously intimated and expressed through traditional Oriental cultures and practices, and in particular in the practice of the fine arts that continue to survive the onslaught of modernity. The idea of life as intrinsically chaotic, precarious, and ever-changing is a taken-for-granted, living, breathing reality in the Oriental experience. Order is regarded as a temporary respite so much so that behind all human pursuits and endeavours in the traditional Eastern world is a deeply-ingrained attitude and disposition to eschew form and organization and to pursue that Zen-like pure contact with ultimate reality. The Japanese philosopher Nishida Kitaro accurately observes that: "at the basis of Asian culture, which has fostered our ancestors for over several thousand years, lies something that can be called *seeing the form of the formless and hearing the sound of the soundless*. Our minds are compelled to seek for this" (Nishida, 1921/1990: x, my emphasis). This Oriental primordial urge to seek the form of the formless and the sound of the soundless gives rise to an ingrained and relentless self-perfecting tendency (Chia, 2003*a*) that manifests itself as a spirited restlessness and dynamism often associated with Japanese "kaizen" (continuous improvement) or as an Asian "Confucian dynamism" (Hofstede, 1991) that is used to account for the recent impressive achievements of China and the newly-developing East-Asian economies of

Singapore, Hong Kong, Taiwan, and South Korea. Yet such surface explanations do not get to the heart of the Oriental mentality, attitude, and disposition to life which derives from a fundamental metaphysics that is rooted in an alternative ontology of *becoming*. I call this process-based mentality *complex processual thinking*.

My purpose here is to show that analyzing this metaphysics of *becoming* and its associated comprehension of process, emergence, and self-transformation from *within an Oriental problematic* offers us a different way of understanding and construing organization, not as a substantial social entity but as an abstractive "world-making" bundle of micro-strategies and techniques developed by human agents to fashion out a more predictable and hence liveable world. This process of organizational world-making has been going on since the dawn of human civilization but it occurs in a variety of different ways that make for interesting comparison and a deeper appreciation of the diversity of modes of societal ordering available in practice. In this regard, an excursion that brings us into contact with a less-than-familiar Oriental mentality enables us to reflexively understand the dominant Western mentalities and preoccupations better and to appreciate how more subtle and less conspicuous self-organizing events occurring through the course of Western history have contributed immeasurably to its modern sense of order and its current ways of life. In other words, it is only by reaching out and analyzing a radically different and unfamiliar mode of social ordering, that we can come to know our own organizational tendencies afresh. Organization studies, in this regard, by taking process seriously, become more the comparative study of *organizational mentalities* than the study of "organizations" as a socio-economic entity. In this regard, it has enormous potential for illuminating the global issues and tensions currently prevalent in the world today.

7.2 The value of complex processual thinking

> Western physics not only disenchanted the universe, it devastated it.... In tearing her secrets from Nature, physics denatured the universe... hiding all that was not simplifiable, that is to say all that is disorder and organization.
>
> Morin, *Method: Towards a Study of Humankind*, 1977/1992: 373–4

We are currently experiencing an era of unprecedented global turmoil where the seemingly improbable, the unanticipated, and the downright catastrophic appear to occur with alarming regularity. What we *do not know* or *do not expect* seem intent on thwarting our best-laid plans and disrupting our everyday lives in innumerable ways. Witness the shocking events of 9/11, the Asian Tsunami disaster of December 2004, the global financial crisis of 2008–9 (and possibly beyond) precipitated by the collapse of the sub-prime mortgage sector in the United States, as well as the ever-rising tide of terrorist suicide bombers that constantly threatens to disrupt our cherished modes of existence and our ways of life by any and all means conceivable. "Black Swans" (Taleb, 2007), those outlier events that occur at the periphery of our focal attention, abound in virtually every aspect of society and in our everyday lives. Within the last decade, in particular, we have been made more painfully aware of the existence of a realm of the *unthought* and *unthinkable* that continues to confound our orthodox comprehension of events in the world. Who would have imagined a decade ago that the Chinese habit of saving excessively and the American habit of spending excessively could unexpectedly give rise to a seemingly symbiotic "chimerica" that eventually collapsed under the weight of American debts and excesses (Ferguson, 2008: 331–40)? Such an idea would have been unthinkable three decades ago. The French philosopher of complexity, Edgar Morin insists that there is an urgent need therefore to "lay siege on this unthought which commands and controls" us (Morin, 1977/1992: 16) so that we can better grasp and more adequately respond to these surprising and life-changing events occurring all around us.

A complex, perpetually changeable, and inextricably interconnected world, however, calls for complex, processual thinking: thinking that is concretely grounded in the intimacy and immediacy of pure lived experience (Morin, 1977/1992: 392–3; Ruskin, 1927, Vol. XV: 27; James, 1912/1996: 23; Nishida, 1921/1990: 3); thinking that acknowledges the reality of spontaneous, self-generated social orders, entities, and institutions (Ferguson, 1767/1966: 122; Hayek, 1948: 86: Simon, 1996: 33; Kauffman, 1993: 173); thinking that accepts and embraces the inherent messiness, contradictions, and ambiguities of reality (Morin, 2008: 6; James, 1911/1996: 50); and thinking that overflows our familiar categories of thought (Bergson, 1946/1992: 161–2; James, 1911/1996: 78–9; Whitehead, 1926/1985: 64; Morin, 1977/1992: 393). Thinking in these complex processual terms means that the starting point for organizational inquiry ought not to be the stately *being* of discrete social entities, be they "institutions," "organizations," or "individuals," but their oftentimes unexpected and precarious coming-into-presence; their *becoming* and spontaneous emergence from an undifferentiated multitude of actions, events, and interactions.

Complex processual thinking invites us to construe organization in terms of spontaneous emergence, ceaseless change, and self-transformation. It urges us to recognize that what really exists are "not things made but things in the making" (James, 1909/1996: 263). It reminds us that each instance of individuation and organization is an *exceptional* and precarious accomplishment in its own right so that social phenomena are not to be construed as naturally existing entities with state-like qualities but as relatively stabilized epiphenomena consisting of patterns of relationships and event-clusterings. Instead of thinking about organizations as "enduring totalities that resist change" (Tsoukas, 2003: 608), complex processual thinking recognizes that contingency, creativity, and complexity are fundamental to our understanding of the spontaneous emergence of organization. Organizations are "mediating networks" (Cooper and Law, 1995: 239), patterned effects of "a scattered and heterogeneous social process" (Chia, 1998: 6–7) which Karl Weick (2009) insightfully calls "organized impermanence." They are often social orders that have emerged not through any deliberate and purposeful intent on the part of wilfull agents, but as the cumulative unintended consequence of a plethora of coping actions and interactions involving a multitude of individuals none of whom have any intention to contribute to any preconceived plan. This idea of the possibility of spontaneous emergence and self-organization has been recently acknowledged by a science of complexity, but such an observation had already been made well over two hundred years ago by the Scottish Enlightenment thinkers especially in the works of Adam Smith and his lesser known contemporary Adam Ferguson. As Ferguson asserts in his study of the spontaneous emergence of societal orders:

> Mankind . . . in striving to remove inconveniences, or to gain apparent and contiguous advantages, arrive at ends which even their imagination could not anticipate . . . Every step and every movement of the multitude, even in what are termed enlightenment ages, are made with equal blindness to the future, and nations stumble upon establishments, which are *indeed the result of human action, but not the execution of any human design* (Ferguson, 1767/1966: 122, my emphasis).

This acknowledgment of the possibility of the spontaneous emergence of social, economic, and political orders was also reiterated in the observations of the French economist Claude Frédéric Bastiat (1845/2006) and more recently in the writings of the Austrian economist Friedrich Hayek (1948). Thus, in seeking to explain the emergence of organization, it is unnecessary to invoke the existence of a centralized initiating agency endowed with intention, conscious choice, and deliberate goal-oriented behavior. The accomplishment of organization need not be attributable to the pre-existence of deliberate, planned interventions. This is a central observation of complex processual thought.

Furthermore, according to complex processual thought, not only are organizations to be construed in this way as emergent, self-transforming social patterns of relations, but even individuals themselves must likewise be understood as historical effects of social relations and event-clusterings; socio-cultural practices and relationships precede identity and individuality. As Nishida Kitaro points out, the notion of an independent individual agent is an abstract concept well removed from the reality of raw experience. This is because an individual exists, not *in order to* experience but *because of* experience: "It is not that there is experience because there is an individual (agent), but that there is an individual because there is experience" (Nishida, 1921/1990: 19). Experience is *trans*-individual. The individual is not some prior-constituted entity but an emergent property of experience itself. Thus, an individual's identity and characteristics are the "condensation of histories of growth and maturation within fields of social relations" (Ingold, 2000: 3). The "coming-into-being of the person is part and parcel of the process of the coming-into-being of the world" (Ingold, 2000: 168). As social beings we are first and foremost evolving "bundles" of relationships and event-clusters not self-contained subjects. Ingold paraphrasing the Spanish philosopher Ortega y Gasset puts it especially well: "We are not things but dramas; we have no nature, only history; we *are* not, though we *live*" (Ingold, 1986: 117, emphasis original). Every individual agency emerges, lives, and dies as a locus of development within the context of a specific field of social practices. As a consequence, the human agent, like all other things, is marked by an inevitable sense of transience and perpetual striving; an immanent "pathos of things" that the Japanese call *mono no aware*.

To understand "individuals" and "organizations" in complex processual terms, therefore, is to regard them as emergent and precarious "assemblages of *organizing*" (Cooper and Law, 1995: 239), temporarily abstracted from an underlying "sea of ceaseless change" (Chia, 2003*b*: 131). Entities such as individuals and organizations are theoretical reifications that refer to slower-changing configurations of social relationships resulting from the sustained regularizing of human exchanges (Chia, 2003*b*: 123; Weick, 2009: 3). Complex processual thinking rejects what Rescher (1996: 53) calls the *process reducibility thesis* insisting that social entities and generative mechanisms are no more than "stability waves in a sea of process". Such a strong process philosophical viewpoint promotes a de-centered and dispersive view of organizational reality as a fluxing concatenation of event-clusters that resists simple location and static representation. It is a worldview that is currently experiencing a welcome revival in the West, but one that has always been deeply embedded in the traditional Oriental outlook.

7.3 Rediscovering a *becoming* worldview

Upon those who step into the same river flow other and yet other waters.

Heraclitus, *Fragments*, in Mansley Robinson, 1968: 91

there is something which exists, though it emerges from no roots.... It is real... it survives, but it has no beginning nor end.... It is born, it dies, it emerges, it returns.

Chuang Tzu, in Chan, *A Sourcebook of Chinese Philosophy*, 1963: 205

The vague intuition that "all things flow" and are in a continuous self-generating process of *becoming* and *changing* remains an abiding, albeit vague, intimation in the modern Western consciousness. Such a worldview first made its appearance as one of the key propositions of the Pre-Socratic Greek philosopher Heraclitus who insisted that the universe is in constant flux, so much so that "all things come to pass through compulsion of strife" (Heraclitus, quoted in Wheelwright, 1974: 29). For him, conflict, struggles, and temporary reconciliations are unavoidably the very stuff of life; were it not so, all of life as we understand it would cease to exist. Thus, the universe flows along of its own accord, shaping its own destiny. Human actions and interventions are therefore accorded less significance than our egos would have us believe. As Wheelwright observed: "To say that the universe flows along as it is destined . . . or that counters are moved arbitrarily and by chance, are different ways of asserting that the major occurrences in the universe lie outside the range and power of any man" (Wheelwright, 1974: 36). In this worldview there is little place for heroic acts and spectacular human achievements. Given the relative unimportance and impotence of man suggested by this worldview, it is not surprising that Heraclitus' views gave way to a Parmenidean-inspired system of thought, which elevated the importance of human agency and which emphasized the primacy of *being*, permanence, stability, and equilibrium as the stuff of reality. This privileging of *being* over *becoming* and *substance* over *process* have since provided the underlying metaphysical framework for Plato's systems of Ideals, Aristotle's system of knowledge based upon observation, and the modern, Western worldview.

Such a metaphysical attitude remains dominant notwithstanding the fact that a number of recent important thinkers, especially Henri Bergson (1911/1998, 1946/1992), and Alfred North Whitehead (1926/1985, 1929), as well as other more contemporary "process physicists" (Bohm, 1980; Prigogine, 1996) have unequivocally upheld the "flux of things" as the ultimate basis of reality. As Whitehead (1929: 295) writes: "Without doubt, if we are to go back to that ultimate integral experience, unwarped by the sophistication of theory... the flux of things is one ultimate generalization around which we must weave our philosophical system." Similarly, the physicist David Bohm insists that "Not only is everything changing, but all *is* flux. That is to say, *what is* is the process of becoming ... objects, events, entities, conditions, structures, etc., are forms that can be abstracted from this process" (Bohm, 1980: 48, emphasis original). It is this resurrecting of the primacy of movement and change (what Bohm calls the "implicate order") over that of Parmenidean substantial entities and end states that enables a radically alternative *becoming* ontology for understanding social order and organization to become more *thinkable*. This metaphysical "reversal" from *being* to *becoming* in the Western consciousness displays a surprising affinity to the rich ancient tradition of Oriental thought. As Whitehead astutely noted, it is a worldview that "seems to approximate more to some strains of Indian, or Chinese, thought than to western Asiatic, or European thought. One side makes process ultimate; the other side makes fact ultimate" (Whitehead, 1929: 9).

In the East the idea of a ceaselessly fluxing, relentlessly changing, and self-transforming reality is readily accepted as a given and finds numerous expression in the classic ancient Chinese texts including the *I Ching*, or Book of Change, and in the enigmatic writings of the Chinese philosophers Lao Tzu and Chuang Tzu, both of whom insisted on the fecundity and primacy of a pro-generative, emergent, and undifferentiated "Tao" as the ultimate basis of reality. In more recent times the Japanese philosophers Nishida Kitaro (1921/1990) and Nishitani Keiji (1982) have constructively engaged with the dominant Western philosophical thought and identified the primacy of process and "radical impermanence" as the unique founding basis for a quintessentially Oriental worldview. Similarly, Chinese philosophers such as Thomé H. Fang (1986) and He Lin (1980) a student of Alfred North Whitehead at Harvard University have both noted and explored extensively the strong affinity that exists between Whiteheadean process thought and ancient Chinese philosophy. For all of them, the world of flux and chaos that presents itself to our pristine unadulterated experience is the only reality there is. There is no presumption of some stable "Platonic" realm above or beyond it. For example, the Buddhist idea of *radical impermanence* (what the Japanese call *mujó*) is extensively expressed in the writings and sayings of the thirteenth-century Japanese Zen thinker Dôgen Kigen while for the Chinese both Chuang Tzu and Lao Tzu constantly allude to the restlessness and changefulness of nature and the heavens. For this reason, the various Oriental cultural practices and the learning of the fine arts especially the tea ceremony, flower arrangement, archery, calligraphy, and painting in both Japan and China are all aimed at self-cultivation and self-perfection to bring one into contact with this pristine, fluxing, and undifferentiated reality. As the Zen master D. T. Suzuki notes in his introduction to Eugene Herrigel's *Zen in the Art of Archery*, "One of the most significant features we notice in all the arts as they are studied in Japan and ... in other Far Eastern countries, is that they are not intended for utilitarian purposes only or for purely aesthetic enjoyment, but are meant to train the mind ... to bring it into contact with the ultimate reality" (Suzuki, in Herrigel, 1953/1985: 5).

A complex processual outlook on life remains second-nature to the Oriental mind; it is embedded in their "blood" and "veins" even as Western metaphysics, modernity, and materialism continues to make not insignificant inroads into the modern Eastern way of life. In what follows, I shall explore in greater detail how this complex processual mindset and disposition is expressed through traditional Oriental culture and artistic practices.

7.4 Oriental complex processual thinking

> For the Chinese the real world is dynamic and ultimate, an organism made up of an infinity of organisms, a rhythm harmonising an infinity of lesser rhythms.
>
> Joseph Needham, *Science and Civilisation in China*, 1962, Vol. 2: 292

In traditional Oriental culture the "three jewels," often referred to as fundamental to the Eastern emphasis on process and becoming, are calligraphy, painting, and poetry. Each of these, by their unmistakable expression of energy, vitality, and dynamism through the relentless emphasis on contrasts and renewals, exemplify a widespread attitude that embraces the inexorable necessity of change, emergence, and evolutionary self-transformation. The French sinologist Francois Jullien (1995: 131) notes that all these three

Fig. 7.1 Similarities between calligraphic strokes and Tai Chi movements
Source: Liu Xuemay, Beijing, China

cultural practices resort to the medium of the brush to "express the unfathomable vitality of the Invisible . . . through the 'actualization' of a perceptible 'configuration'." Like the art of Chinese shadow boxing (Tai Chi) or the Japanese art of archery, their aim is to convey the invisibility of breath, rhythm, and flux, through the gestures and the "uninterrupted and spiralling unfolding of contrasted movements" (Jullien, 1995: 132). This similarity of movement between calligraphy and Tai Chi is illustrated in Fig. 7.1.

In particular, calligraphy and painting, because they rely more on brush strokes than poetic words for conveying meaning, have had to develop sophisticated ways of expressing movement and life through the tip of a brush. The Chinese scholar and artist Chiang Yee, who spent considerable time painting in the English Lake district and who subsequently wrote about his aesthetic experiences, insists that the principal aim of Oriental painting and calligraphy is to capture and portray what he calls a "rhythmic vitality" whereby the superficial covering of material form is pierced to reveal the "rich inner life of the object in harmony with the artist's own soul" (Chiang Yee, 1936: 84). In the traditional Chinese worldview it is generally believed that all things in the universe are possessed of life: 'We believe that . . . a stalk of grass can feel the rhythm of life, and the artist of receptive mind can with his ready brush free the spirit imprisoned in the form' (Chiang Yee, 1936: 105–6). The skill of a painter or calligrapher is, therefore, reflected in her ability to breathe life, energy, and vitality into the piece of work by employing a variety of subtle strokes (as opposed to lines) to enable her to convey the sensuous perception within the composition of the work itself. Thus: 'Every stroke, every dot, suggest a form of Nature. If not, it would simply be a dead stroke.... All these living lines or strokes join together in harmony or in rhythm to form a scene which expresses a . . . feeling or thought' (Chiang Yee, 1936: 176). For example, in a typical Chinese painting the brush strokes are suggestively linked together through the constant emphasis on form, continuity, and outline rather than on substantial detail. Similarly, calligraphic work comprises a variety of strokes each of which in their execution is intended to convey a sense of movement, momentum, and transformation. Each type of brush stroke employed including the "dot," "dash," "hook," "iron-wire," "willow-leaf," "bamboo-leaf," "silk-threads," "bending-weeds," "earthworm," "water-wrinkles," and so on, when properly executed, has the effect of conveying this energy, rhythmic vitality, and change.

The mastery of these brush strokes and the techniques of movement associated with them, betray a deeply-cultivated sensitivity to the changefulness of reality and enables the painters and calligraphers to convey quite precisely the specific mood and feelings experienced in their aesthetic encounter with living Nature. "Chinese painting expresses the inward expression in man of that vitality, that mobility which is Nature's, and which identifies itself, for him, with his own feelings" (Chiang Yee, 1936: 186). Calligraphy and Chinese painting provide an exemplar of "dynamism *in operation*, as a coming-to-be" or *becoming*: as "registering the temporality of movement" (Jullien, 1995: 133) in all its spontaneity and fluent emergence. In particular a calligraphic brush stroke, once executed can never be subsequently touched up unlike that in a Western painting where it is not uncommon for the artist to go over several times what has already been painted. For Oriental painting and calligraphy, once that brush stroke is completed its "*dynamic continuity* remains forever active in the eyes of the beholder" (Jullien, 1995: 133) because in the execution of the stroke, there is evidently a deliberate imbalance of force applied on the brush so that the movement that ensues never becomes "stiff or frozen": "*a horizontal bar is never horizontal*, especially if it is not the final element in the character; its slight upward curve or discreet downward flick betrays the tension expressed in the continuation of the stroke" (Jullien, 1995: 134, my emphasis). The brush is impelled to move on and a continuum of strokes is created.

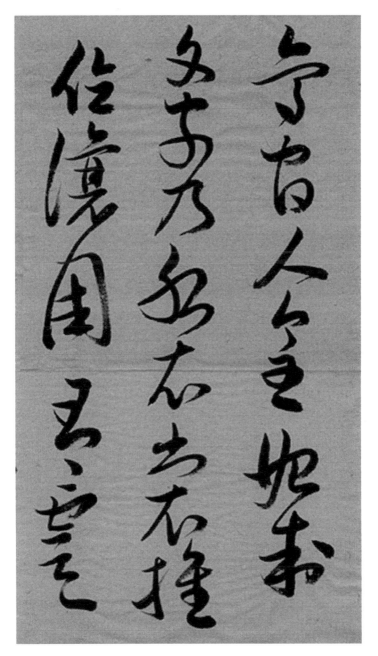

Fig. 7.2 The dynamic continuity of brush strokes
Source: Liu, Xuemay, Beijing, China

In this regard, calligraphy bears a similarity to all forms of cursive writing such as when a signature is made the impulse and momentum it initiates carries on beyond the scriptural finitude. "Even when the line is broken, the rhythmic surge is not cut off.... At one point the hand slows down, at another it speeds up, at one point the brush tip is 'incisive' at another it is 'blurred'" (Jullien, 1995: 135). This continual contrast and tension between opposing tendencies "enables each successive stroke to attract in its wake the next line" so that "the dashes, the oblique strokes, the curves and the verticals, in all their twists and arabesques, are always determined by the propensity of the impulse of energy" (Jullien, 1995: 135). Contrast and creative tension is generated so that not only does one tendency "throw the other into greater relief but also so that the former *necessarily cries out for the latter to follow it* all the more forcefully precisely because the balance needs to be restored" (Jullien, 1995: 137, my emphasis). The sublime art of calligraphy and Oriental painting consists in managing to depict the uninterrupted metamorphosis of a piece of work "*in its unceasing process*" (Jullien, 1995: 138, my emphasis). This emphasis on process is replicated in the art of Chinese poetry which places paramount importance on the vitality of the "breath" as the source of the poetic ability to make the poem unfold temporarily in the same manner as a calligraphic or painted piece of work.

In a fascinating comparative study of the methods of Western and Oriental painting, the art historian Norman Bryson (1982: 92) similarly observed that, in Oriental paintings and calligraphy "The work of production is constantly displayed in the wake of its traces" through the assiduous cultivation of what he calls "deictic markers." Calligraphy and Oriental painting do not seek to hide the "traces of the body of labour" (Bryson, 1982: 92). Mastery of the brush strokes lies in the subliminal ability to paint out the traces that have brought the piece of work into being. They "permit a maximum of integrity and visibility to the constitutive strokes of the brush" (Bryson, 1982: 89) and in so doing, as we have previously noted, allow the brush to express fully the fluidity and immediacy of living experience. For this reason, because such artistic strokes unfold in time, "calligraphic work (and Oriental painting) cannot be taken in all at once ... since it has itself unfolded within the *durée* of process" (Bryson, 1982: 94).

Western art, on the other hand, is predicated upon what Bryson calls the "*disavowal of deictic reference*" (1982: 89) whereby the individual history of the emergence and transformation of a painting into a completed piece of work is largely irretrievable because previous artistic efforts are deliberately buried in a "palimpsest of which only the final version shows through, above an interminable debris of revisions." As such, the viewer has no way of ascertaining "the degree to which other surfaces lied concealed beneath the planar display" (Bryson, 1982: 92) because the artist is solely concerned with displaying the final version. Her brush:

traces *obliteratively* . . . and whatever may have been the improvisional logic of the painting's construction, this existence of the (prior) image in its own time . . . is negated by never referring the marks on canvas to their place in the vanishing sequence of local inspiration (Bryson, 1982: 93).

The easel paintings of the West are "autochthonous, self-created, parthenogeneses, virgin-births" (Bryson, 1982: 95). In calligraphy and Oriental art, the process of *becoming* of the painting or calligraphy is incorporated into the works' display while in Western art the process is hidden or eliminated. Only its final completed state matters. The painting is placed outside duration. The entire motivation of the Western painter is to arrest and capture the flux of experience and to comprehend it "from a vantage-point outside the mobility of duration, in an eternal moment of disclosed presence" (Bryson, 1982: 94). It is this search for a Platonic atemporal *essence* which drives the Western painter.

This Western tendency to focus on and only privilege the final singular moment of revelation was also noted by the art critic John Berger. In *Ways of Seeing* (1972) he shows how, during the Renaissance period, paintings of nudes came to be increasingly objectified as a *spectacle* to an external viewer. According to him the first Renaissance nudes depicted were those of Adam and Eve which showed their evident shame at being naked in the presence of each other. This was in contrast to a prior medieval period when the story of Adam and Eve was often illustrated in a narrative sequence involving several scenes leading up to their ejection from the Garden of Eden. In these narrative sequences it was the whole story and not the singular moment of shame that was emphasized. With the advent of the Renaissance, however, "the narrative sequence disappeared, and the singular moment depicted became the moment of shame . . . now their shame is not so much in relation to one another as to the spectator . . . [they] are now naked as the spectator sees [them]" (Berger, 1972: 49). The painting no longer contains an unfolding *narrative*; it has now become a *spectacle* for an external observer. What both Berger and Bryson have usefully identified is a cultivated Western modernist penchant for the spectacular and the manifest end-state. Their analyses of Western paintings reveal an important metaphysical attitude and visual apprehension that focuses entirely on that specific moment of revelation. This is in stark contrast to an Oriental attitude that views the continuity of events as a seamless unfolding drama in time. One speaks of atemporal *essences*, the other of the finitude of *existence*. Each betrays its fundamental commitment to an underlying metaphysics; that of *being* and *becoming*. Each reflects an internalized cultural disposition that has wide-ranging implications for our understanding of the alternative *organizational mentalities* involved in dealing with human affairs.

7.5 From spectacular intervention to "allowing" silent self-transformation

[A]ncient Chinese thought is above all concerned with avoiding *confrontation* . . . it conceives of a model of efficacy based on correlation . . . detectable at the heart of the objective processes.

Francois Jullien, *The Propensity of Things*, 1995: 259

From our comparative analysis of Western and Oriental art, it is not difficult to see that the contrast between the Western emphasis on attending solely to the significant moment of consequence and the Oriental emphasis on viewing reality as a continuous unfolding flow of events brings with it different cultivated impulses and tendencies when dealing with the exigencies of life including especially issues relating to order and organization. What quintessentially characterizes the Western attitude is a cultivated penchant for the heroic, the dramatic, and the spectacular: it is the arrested moment of spectacular success or triumph that attracts most attention. The romantic appeal of an oftentimes unexpected and sensational overcoming of the odds to triumph over adversity is deeply ingrained in the Western collective psyche. This instinct is intimately allied to a cultivated preference for direct, visible engagement, and mastery in dealing with affairs of the world whether it be in warfare, politics, business, art as we have noted, or even in the seeking of personal relationships.

This penchant for the dramatic and the spectacular may be found in virtually every walk of life in the West, particularly in the United States and, increasingly, with its vast reach and global influence, in virtually every other part of the world. From the glitz and glitter of presidential campaigns to the high drama of reality television, the glamour and hero-worshipping of movie stars and sporting super-heroes, to the insatiable appetite for eye-catching and attention-grabbing marketing stunts and ultimately, in the world of business, to the irresistible tendency to lionize successful corporations and captains of industry for their impressive and often short-term achievements; all these are symptomatic of a deeply-entrenched adulation for the dramatic, the heroic, and the spectacular within the realm of human affairs. Even in the methods of art, as we have seen, it is the final spectacular and triumphant display that captures attention. The natural attitude of the democratic West, born of this ancient legacy, therefore, has been to lionize human agency and to eulogize transparency of purpose, openness of competition, and the direct and heroic mobilization of available resources and capabilities to spectacularly achieve a widely publicized end. Without doubt this overall positive attitude and disposition has provided the metaphysical outlook and ideological platform for the impressive entrepreneurial and innovative achievements of the West and in particular in the United States.

The ancient military scholar Victor Davis Hanson (1989: 224) maintains that there is much evidence to suggest that this Western penchant for the spectacular and the heroic can be traced to a decisive shift in approach to warfare initiated by the Greeks beginning from about the seventh century BC. For Hanson, it was the ancient Greeks during this period who insisted on the superiority of a face-to-face frontal clash between opposing armies as the most noble way to do battle. Henceforth, a new structure, the *phalanx*, was introduced in which two bodies of heavily armed and cuirassed hoplites were made to advance in tight formation towards the enemy with no possibility of fleeing from a direct head-on confrontation with the latter. This frontal spectacular clashing of opposing forces represented a mode of engagement that has been lionized in the conduct of warfare. It is an approach well exemplified by the "shock and awe" strategy adopted in the Allied invasion of Iraq in 2003. Heroic and spectacular actions and interventions have thus become the default *modus operandi* first in warfare and then subsequently in the conduct of human affairs especially in the world of business (Jullien, 2000). In other words, the open, direct face-to-face, and often adversarial approach employed in the battlefield has been mirrored and replicated in the dealings in human affairs so that an "*agonistic* structure of confrontation" exists "whether in the dramatic, the judicial, or the political realm" (Jullien, 2000: 44, emphasis original). Both warfare and the display of performances, whether in public debates or business competition, share the same direct confrontational *habitus* (Bourdieu, 1990) that leads to the valorizing of agency, intentionality, decisiveness, immediacy, and spectacular outcomes; it is a practice that is ennobled by the language of radical discontinuities, revelations, and revolutions. Victory is accomplished "loudly" in spectacular and triumphal terms through the visible and unequivocal overwhelming of the opposition: "it is always by *surplus*—of arguments presented, not of secret obliqueness—that a victory is won" (Jullien, 2000: 47). Thus, in virtually all aspects of Western life, it is the overt, the visible and the dramatic that captures attention and adulation and invites glorification.

This penchant for the dramatic and the spectacular contrasts with a much more subdued and inconspicuous Oriental approach which relies more on the innate *propensity of things* to realize its ambitions. Such an *obliqueness* in dealing with human affairs is what marks the difference in *organizational mentalities* between East and West. It is one which arises from a deep belief in the existence of immanent, inexorable forces driving and transforming reality and of how that can be efficaciously mobilized to one's benefit. In his study which we have previously drawn from, Bryson (1982) identified two distinct modes of visual apprehension which he called the *Gaze* and the *Glance* respectively. In the Western Gaze the preoccupation is fixing, objectifying, and representing of the object of apprehension. It is a vision primed to the dramatic and the spectacular. The Gaze intervenes and forcibly abstracts a phenomenon from its fluxing and changing context presenting it successfully as a triumphant static display. The Gaze is what creates things and entities through arresting the flux of experience and contemplating the "visual field from a vantage-point outside the mobility of duration, in an eternal moment of disclosed presence" (Bryson, 1982: 94). It relies on an "enduring, motionless and august logic of architectural form" (Bryson, 1982: 122) that speaks of mastery, control, and domination. In this cultivated disposition, therefore, Western attitudes mirror the philosophical aspirations of Western thought since the time of Plato and Aristotle; the spectacular grasping and mastery of the essences of things.

The Oriental Glance, on the other hand, is a furtive or sideways look; it seeks to *obliquely* apprehend phenomena in their necessary transience and durational temporality. It finds in itself "no counterpart to the enduring, motionless and august logic" (Bryson, 1982: 122) of Western thought. Instead, all it knows is dispersal, mobility, and fleeting configuration; the rhythmic vitality that is living Nature. What Bryson is getting at is the inevitable temporality and transience of the appearances of entities and things for the Oriental mind for whom the very concept of an entity is clearly the result of an arbitrary perceptual framing: "an optic that . . . makes a *cut* from the field and immobilizes the cut within the static framework" (Bryson, 1988: 97). In other words, the viewing of an object *qua* object requires a prior perceptual framing in order to render the object comprehensible. As soon as the frame is removed or withdrawn the object becomes inextricably entwined with its past and future as part of a mobile continuum that resists logical differentiation and isolation. A flower for instance exists only as a phase of that evolving self-transformation between seed and dust "in a continuous exfoliation or perturbation of matter" (Bryson, 1988: 97). The seed is a potential that is always already turning itself into a flower and the flower always already potentially becoming dust so that the flower "is inhabited by its past as a seed and its future as dust, in a continuous motion of postponement" (Bryson, 1988: 99). An object like a flower or an organization is never fully present to us in all its meaning and comprehension. This appreciation of the inherent and fleeting transience of things explains why in Kyoto, the ancient capital of Japan, large crowds gather each spring to wait for the blooming of the cherry blossom and to picnic under the trees. The cherry blossoms are intrinsically no more beautiful than the blossoms of, say, the pear or apple tree, but they are much more highly valued because they exemplify the inherent transience of nature and of life: they usually begin to fall within a week of their first appearing. It is precisely this evanescence that evokes the *mono no aware* in those who go there to soak up the experience.

This acute Oriental awareness of the natural *propensity of things* leads to an ingrained reluctance to overtly intervene spectacularly into human affairs and leaving them to unfold in the natural course of things. For this reason, the Oriental disposition for harmony and non-intervention is sometimes construed as a debilitating passivity which accounts for its seeming indecisiveness or lack of ambition. Francois Jullien (1995), in his extensive comparative study of the Oriental mind shows that this is far from the case. What underpins the apparent reluctance to spectacularly intervene into the course of things is a rich historical appreciation for an immanent potentiality always already at work in the configuration of reality at each particular moment in time. From the Oriental point of view, "every kind of reality . . . may be perceived as a particular deployment or arrangement of things to be relied on and worked to one's advantage" (Jullien, 1995: 15), so much so that the need for forceful spectacular intervention is readily eschewed. Timeliness of intervention, not magnitude of force, is the key to efficacious action. When, for instance, the *Tao Te Ching* alludes to "non-action", what is really meant is action that is inconspicuous and that does not create unnecessary "ripples." This preference for "silent" intervention (Jullien, 2004: 46), allowing things to take their natural course, comes from a deep appreciation of why there are significant downsides to directly intervening in a spectacular way.

For the Oriental mind, direct confrontation often result in the active *destruction* or "mutilation" of the adversary in question (Morin, 1977/ 1992: 373) because such dramatic and heroic interventions are, by definition, unavoidably *intrusive* and inevitably provoke elements of resistance or reticence that undermine its efficacy "Because it impinges from outside ... by forcing itself into the course of things, it ... tears at the tissue of things and upsets their coherence" (Jullien, 2004: 54).

Furthermore, because intervention occurs at one moment and not another, it becomes a *spectacle* that forces itself onto our attention: it becoming an "event" to be accounted for. Its *"asperity*...provides a hook on which to hang a story" (Jullien: 2004: 55) even though its overall effect may be as lasting as a momentary "shower of spray." Such spectacular actions may well satisfy our need for drama and excitement, but they are not necessarily the most efficacious or productive both in terms of deep learning and/or longer-lasting outcomes.

For these reasons, the traditional Orientals have a built-in aversion to direct engagement and confrontation. The emphasis is on achieving one's ends silently and inconspicuously by harmonizing one's actions with the internal "propensity of things" and "going with the flow" of events.

> [un]like with action, which is always "one-off" ... transformation is "without locale". Not only is it not local, as action is, but it is impossible to localize ... its effects are diffuse, all-pervading, never limited (Jullien, 2004: 57).

Because this more oblique and indirect form of engagement is less attention-grabbing, because it is more dispersed, not simply locatable, and harmonizes with the status quo and is hence non-threatening, it often surprisingly bears more productive fruit than the direct, frontal approach widely advocated. The efficacy of such an elliptical and *oblique* approach in apprehending and dealing with phenomenon is all the greater the more discreet and unnoticed it is. The notion of actively "waiting for the fruit to ripen" before intervening and grasping is widely appreciated and this again offers an implicit acknowledgment of the appropriate mode of engagement with an essentially transient and changeful reality.

What this excursion into the traditional Oriental mind reveals is an attitude towards dealing with human affairs that is wholly alien to that which characterizes the dominant Western approach; one which is inherently sensitive to the spontaneous self-transforming nature of reality and which thereby appreciates deeply the quiet efficacy of intervening *indirectly* or *obliquely* into the world of affairs, be it in politics, business, or the cultivation of human relationships. Such difference in attitude derives from a vastly different metaphysical commitment to an ontology of *becoming* and an appreciation that economy of effort and eventual success can often be realized and sustained through small, seemingly inconspicuous organizational initiatives than through large-scale organizational efforts.

Indeed, one could say that the modern organizational world is what it is today precisely because of the cumulative effect of countless and nameless events, relationships, and individuals that have wittingly or unwittingly contributed to its ultimate realization.

7.6 From analysing organizations to analysing organizational mentalities

> Fire does not burn fire. Water does not wash water. The eye does not see the eye.
>
> Nishitani Keiji, *Religion and Nothingness*, 1982: 116

The study of the phenomenon of organization is itself an organized episte-mological endeavor; one shaped by socio-cultural and historical contexts. That this is the case is not always obvious just as the eye does not normally see the eye. In inquiring into the nature of organization, therefore, we are inevitably opening ourselves up to the wider question of the organization of our forms of knowledge, our ways of understanding, and our means of intervening and engaging with the world we find ourselves in. How our worldviews, perceptions, knowledge, and modes of comprehension affect our concerns and preoccupations and shape our objects of inquiry must be correspondingly investigated if we are to begin to grasp this wider sense of organization as a generic reality-constituting activity. Organizational analysis, thus, become unavoidably meta-theoretical. In rigorosly seeking to understand the phenomenon of organization we are necessarily but almost unwittingly brought back to the question of our own philosophical roots, our habits of thought, and our organizational mentalities. And, this is perhaps as it should be, given the shifting global economic and political realities as we move into the second decade of the twenty-first century. No longer can we take for granted the theoretical agendas of the Western world in general and the United States in particular as the sole reference point for political stability, economic progress, or even as the necessary "axis for moral good." With the emergence of BRIC (Brazil, Russia, India, China) as a potential countervailing economic and political force, it is time the field of organization studies looked elsewhere for viable alternatives to our understanding of organizational processes.

What then can we say about the phenomenon of organization as a generic human impulse given our excursion into an Oriental worldview? For one thing we can begin to see that organizing as a generic process is quintessentially a social reality-constituting process involving the everyday actions and incisions of a complex multitude of individuals none of whom are deliberately intent on producing an organized or structured social order. Were they not to do so, all they would be experiencing is an "aboriginal sensible muchness" (James, 1911/1996: 50), that irreducibly dynamic, fluxing, and hence paralyzing and unliveable reality. Humans, as social beings, regardless of their culture or tradition, need a sense of collective order, stability, and predictability and it is for this purpose that organization exists as an inherently simplifying technique for arresting, fixing, and simplifying our otherwise complex and ambiguous experiences so as to make them more amenable to manipulation and control in the light of our otherwise precarious existence. Organization exists to selectively frame what would otherwise be a "blooming, buzzing confusion" (James, 1911/1996: 50), to "steer us practically in everyday life," and to make our "actions turn upon new points of emphasis" (James, 1911/1996: 73).

What this way of thinking implies is that all the social reality that we find so very familiar and necessary, and to which we often attribute an independent existence, is really only the arbitrary collective aggregation of habituated social practices, mannerisms, and behavioral codes and norms such that a regular coincidence exists between an established social representation and that which a society takes to be its reality. Thus, the slow and complex evolutionary formation of *organizational mentalities* involving modes of thought, codes of behavior, social mannerisms, dress, gestures, postures, the rules of law, ethical codes, disciplines of knowledge, and so on, serves to orient us towards ourselves, others, and to our environment in particular ways that reflect a historically-informed and culturally-situated understanding. Understood in this way, organization is not so much a social entity as it is an advantage-gaining socio-economic activity involving the "transformation, use and exchange of matter and energy" (Cooper, 1987: 406) in which the remote, the obdurate and the intractable are rendered more accessible and hence more amenable to control and manipulation. From this way of understanding organization, various historico-social analyses undertaken by writers as diverse as Max Weber (in Gerth and Mills, 1948) on rationalization, professionalization, and bureaucracy, Michel Foucault (1970) on epistemes, social epochs, and the underlying order of things, and Norbert Elias (1979–82) on the civilizing process as well as Marshal McLuhan (1967) on the effects of alphabetization and the invention of the printing press on the mentality of the Western world, all redirect our concerns with organizational analysis as the study of the reality-constituting impulses underlying each socio-cultural and historical epoch. Understood thus, it becomes the

analysis of *organizational mentalities* and not discrete socio-economic entities called "organizations" that become the primary focus of attention. We
can then revisit the concerns and preoccupations of familiar figures like
Max Weber and to appreciate that what they were preoccupied with was not
so much the study of organization or management, per se, but the study of
organizational mentalities.

Max Weber's study of the almost inexorable rationalization of modern
Western society, for instance, is one exemplary instance of this kind of
analysis. For Weber, despite the rise and fall of modern social institutions
and the changing fortunes of political and ideological affiliations, the
general drift of secular rationalization was indelibly marked by the progressive and almost inexorable *disenchantment of the world* through the method
of systematic, *instrumental rationality*. In his view, the persistence and pervasiveness of this process of disenchantment was best exemplified by the
sustained attempts to apply principles of instrumental rationality to such
an apparently subjective area of experience as music. Hence, the "fixation
of clang patterns, by a more concise notation and the establishment of the
well-tempered scale...the standardization of the quartet of woodwinds
and string instruments as the core of the symphony orchestra" (Weber,
in Gerth and Mills, 1948: 51) were all seen by Weber as telling instances of
the almost inexorable process of representational abstraction and rational
ordering taking place all around him and in every sphere of human activity.
It was this observation of the general burgeoning of an instrumental-
rationalist mindset associated with modernity that led Weber to devote
his whole life to an understanding of its wider effects on modern social life.

Likewise, Foucault's (1970) analyses of the history of ideas show that each
cultural epoch contains fundamental organizing codes that govern its
language, schemas, values, logics, and techniques of ordering as well as
hierarchies of practices which are often hidden from the view of those
immersed in their everyday activities. These *organizational mentalities* can
only be accessed through an "archaeological" exposition of the knowledge
practices of a particular cultural epoch. Foucault shows that implicit rules of
formation constitute the underlying generative code for organizing and
sensemaking for a particular epoch or episteme. These rules of formation
educate the senses, direct attention, and cause the selective focusing of
specific aspects of lived experiences to the exclusion of others since the
sensory inputs of humans are invariably abundant and overwhelming.
Each episteme therefore establishes rules that enable us to harness our
sensory perceptions in order to drive it better to fit our needs and ends. In
great part therefore, the episteme of a given epoch or culture organizes our

sensorium (McLuhan, 1967; Ong, 1967) in such a way that we are made to attend to some types of stimuli rather than others by making an issue of certain ones while relatively neglecting other ones. Each episteme allows us to think in ways foreign to the others.

Foucault shows, for example, that during the Renaissance period things were ordered and hence known through the principle of *resemblance*. The human heart for instance was often thought of as a mechanical pump because of its similarity of function. Similarly, the seeds of the aconite plant were often used as a cure for eye diseases just because their appearance was that of "tiny dark globes seated in white skinlike coverings whose appearance is much like that of eyelids covering an eye" (Foucault, 1970: 142). Likewise, walnuts were used for wounds of the pericranium because the physical appearance of the walnut resembled the human brain. We can therefore see that during the Renaissance the conception of knowledge was one involving "the essentially incomplete pursuit of an unending chain of similarities" (Gutting, 1989: 146). Science, alchemy, palmistry, and astrology all sat comfortably with one another during this period. Proximity, convenience, analogy, and emulation provided the organizing code for the creation of knowledge during the Renaissance period. What Foucault identifies are the underlying *organizational mentalities* that act as rules of formation for each epoch in the history of Western thought from the Renaissance to the present.

This same concern for an understanding of the underlying *organizational mentality* shaping societal concerns and aspirations is what defines the efforts of Marshal McLuhan. For him the invention of the printing process was a seminal moment in the shaping of the collective consciousness of the Western world for what it precipitated was a kind of "typographic thinking" that enabled the idea of mass production to become more thinkable. Thus, the invention of typography "extended the new visual stress of applied knowledge, providing the first repeatable commodity, the first assembly line and the first mass-production" (McLuhan, 1967: 124). It significantly changed the nature of the relationship between a writer and his audience. For while the previous manuscript culture was effectively conversational in that "the writer and his audience are physically related by the form of publication" (McLuhan, 1967: 84), the print culture created a clear distinction between impersonal authors and a consuming public. Conversational exchange gave way to the *commodification* of output and uniform quantification, measurability, and centralized control became important priorities in the management of economic and social life.

What these three brief examples illustrate is how a re-directing of the focus from "organizations" to *organizational mentalities* can help us open new ways by which the field of organization studies can contribute to our understanding of major complex societal issues and challenges in the modern world by showing how different epochs and different cultures wittingly or unwittingly formulate rules of engagement to deal with abiding and universal human concerns. Our excursion into the Oriental outlook and its radically different ways of dealing with human affairs should cause us to pause and ask ourselves how it is that the concerns and priorities of the Western world have come to be what they are. They sensitize us to the possibility of alternative ways of thinking and dealing with the predicaments we face in our day-to-day lives. The expanding of organization studies to include the study of the *organization of mentalities* allows us to widen the scope of our concerns beyond a narrow preoccupation with economic organizations to a concern with the wider challenges of a global and inextricably interconnected society.

7.7 Conclusion

This chapter is prompted by reflections on the fragility, vulnerability, and precariousness of human organizational accomplishments and how it is only sustained by ongoing acts of world-making. We can study organizations as a *fait accompli*, in its sanitized and easily recognizable stable state, in the luxurious settings of downtown hotels at prestigious management academy conferences, or we can alternatively examine the organization as a quintessentially human cultural achievement: a symbolic artefact precariously sustained through language, discourse, actor meanings, social interactions, and power relations. In the latter case, one acquires an intimate understanding of the ongoing practical struggles and the everyday coping strategies involved in wresting order and organization, if only temporarily, from the constant entropic tendencies of social and material reality. To recover this more intimate form of understanding, one must strive to abandon academic distance, immerse oneself in the initial flux and flow of reality and attempt to understand organizational emergence from within the phenomenon itself.

Human organized life, in all its varied forms, charts a rich and oftentimes surprising trajectory as it painstakingly and laboriously bootstraps itself into independent existence from the oftentimes debilitating and chaotic circumstance it initially finds itself in. Social organization is a human technique for appropriating nature's energy and putting it to service to enhance life chances and to expand our degrees of freedom. The taming of fire, the development of tools, oral language, and then written inscriptions, the building of homes, first in caves in mountainsides and then in tents and subsequently in more permanent, durable, and settled forms, the organization of transport mobility and communication; all these and many others constitute the gradual progression of humans' systematic overcoming of the limitations of their immediate environment and of space–time. It is a temporary triumph of order and organization over chaos and change. Whilst the history of civilizations is often presented as a tallying of the dynasties, governments, wars, and cultural transformations that have taken place over this brief period, this is not the whole picture of human progress. Instead, the attainment of modern organizational life is fundamentally a story of how humans have slowly extricated themselves from a slave-like dependence on their immediate environment by developing more and more sophisticated tools and systems in order to more efficiently exploit the latter for their own benefit. *It is this human ingenuity for devising techniques and mechanisms for trapping, conserving, retrieving, and productively utilizing energy and resources to secure and enhance our own level of existence* (Sahlins, 1960) that constitutes what we mean here by the phenomenon of ORGANIZA-TION. But, as we have been starkly reminded, yet again, by natural catastrophes such as the Asian Tsunami, the effects of Hurricane Katrina, and the tragedy of the Haitian earthquake disaster, human organizational accomplishments are never totally secure: they remain precariously balanced, perpetually in tension, and irretrievably incomplete.

Nevertheless, some modes of human organizing appear more durable in the longer-term, more sustainable, more economically justifiable, more politically acceptable, and ultimately more amenable to a richer and more fulfilling life. Why and how this is so can only be answered, if at all, by a sustained investigation of the different *organizational mentalities* which have spontaneously emerged in different socio-historical and cultural contexts. An identification of their various strengths and weaknesses can help us to forge a more realistic and comprehensive solution for dealing with the unintended consequences and challenges of globalization.

Notes

1. By *organizational mentalities* I mean the collectively cultivated ways of dealing with raw experience; the mindsets, attitudes, and dispositions that distinguish one community from another.

2. By Western I mean especially the dominant American and European ideologies and approaches especially circumscribed by the concerns with individualism, freedom, democracy, and capitalism.
3. By Oriental I mean a traditional outlook on life common to countries in the Far Eastern world including especially China, Japan, Korea, and the East Asian countries.

References

Bastiat, C. F. (1845/2006). *Fallacies of Protection*, New York: Cosimo Classic.

Berger, J. (1972). *Ways of Seeing*, London: Penguin.

Bergson, H. (1911/1998). *Creative Evolution*, Mineola, New York: Dover Publications.

Bergson, H. (1946/1992). *The Creative Mind*, New York: Citadel Press.

Bohm, D. (1980). *Wholeness and the Implicate Order*, London: Routledge.

Bourdieu, P. (1990). *The Logic of Practice*, Stanford, CA: Stanford University Press.

Bryson, N. (1982). *Vision and Painting: The Logic of the Gaze*, London: Methuen.

Bryson, N. (1988). The Gaze in the Expanded Field, in H. Foster (ed.) *Vision and Visuality*, Seattle: Bay Press.

Chan, W.-T. (1963). *A Sourcebook in Chinese Philosophy*, Princeton: Princeton University Press.

Chia, R. (1998). From complexity science to complex thinking: Organization as simple location, *Organization*, 5, 341–69.

Chia, R. (2003*a*). From knowledge-creation to perfecting action: Tao, Basho and pure experience as the ultimate ground of performance, *Human Relations*, 56(8), 953–81.

Chia, R. (2003*b*). Ontology: Organization as world-making, in R. Westwood and S. Clegg (eds) *Debating Organization: Point-counterpoint in Organization Studies*, Oxford: Blackwell, 98–113.

Chiang, Yee (1936). *The Chinese Eye*, London: Methuen & Co. Ltd.

Cooper, R. (1987). Information, communication and organization: A post-structural revision, *The Journal of Mind and Behaviour*, 8(3), 395–416.

Cooper, R. & Law, J. (1995). Organization: Distal and proximal views. *Research in the Sociology of Organization*, 13, 237–74.

Elias, N. (1979–82). *The Civilizing Process*, (2 volumes), Oxford: Blackwell.

Fang, T. (1986). *The Chinese View of Life: The Philosophy of Comprehensive Harmony*, Taipei: Linking Publishing Co.

Ferguson, A. (1767/1966). *An Essay on the History of Civil Society*, ed. Duncan Forbes, Edinburgh: Edinburgh University Press.

Ferguson, N. (2008). *The Ascent of Money*, London: Allen Lane.

Foucault, M. (1970). *The Order of Things*, London: Tavistock.

Gerth, H. H. & Mills, C. W. (1948). *From Max Weber*, London: Routledge.

Gutting, G. (1989). *Michel Foucault's Archaeology of Scientific Reason*, Cambridge: Cambridge University Press.

Hanson, V. D. (1989). *The Western Way of War*, London: Hodder and Stoughton.

Hayek, F. A. (1948). *Individualism and Economic Order*, Chicago: University of Chicago Press.

Herrigel, E. (1953/1985). *Zen in the Art of Archery*, London: Arkana.

Hofstede, G. (1991). *Culture and Organization: Software of the Mind*, New York: McGraw-Hill.

Ingold, T. (1986). *Evolution and Social Life*, Cambridge: Cambridge University Press.

Ingold, T. (2000). *The Perception of the Environment: Essays in Livelihood, Dwelling and Skill*, London, Routledge.

James, W. (1890/1983). *Principles of Psychology*, Cambridge, MA: Harvard University Press.

James, W. (1909/1996). *A Pluralistic Universe*, Lincoln and London: University of Nebraska Press.

James, W. (1911/1996). *Some Problems of Philosophy*, Lincoln: University of Nebraska Press.

James, W. (1912/1996). *Essays in Radical Empiricism*, Lincoln: University of Nebraska Press.

Jullien, F. (1995). *The Propensity of Things*, New York: Urzone, Inc.

Jullien, F. (2000). *Detour and Access: Strategies of Meaning in China and Greece*, New York: Zone Books.

Jullien, F. (2004). *A Treatise on Efficacy: Between Western and Chinese Thinking*, Honolulu: University of Hawaii Press.

Kauffman, S. (1993). *The Origins of Order: Self-Organization and Selection in Evolution*, Oxford: Oxford University Press.

Lin He (1980). Lectures on Contemporary Western Philosophy, in Wang Sijun and Li Sudong (eds) *He Lin: A Critical Biography*, Taipei: Sun Min Books.

McLuhan, M. (1967). *The Gutenberg Galaxy*, Toronto: The University of Toronto Press.

Mansley Robinson, J. (1968). *An Introduction to Early Greek Philosophy*, Boston: Houghton Mifflin Co.

Morin, E. (1977/1992). *Method: Towards a Study of Humankind*, trans. J. L. Roland Berlanger, New York: Peter Lang.

Morin, E. (2008). *On Complexity*, trans Robin Postel, New Jersey: Hampton Press.

Needham, J. (1962). *Science and Civilisation in China*, Vol. 2, Cambridge: Cambridge University Press.

Nishida, Kitaro (1921/1990). *An Inquiry into the Good*, trans. M. Abe & C. Ives, New Haven, CT: Yale University Press.

Nishitani, Keiji (1982). *Religion and Nothingness*, trans. Jan van Bragt, Berkeley: University of California Press.

Ong, W. (1967). *The Presence of the Word*, New Haven, CT: Yale University Press.

Prigogine, I. (1981). *From Being to Becoming: Time and Complexity in the Physical Sciences*, New York: W. H. Freeman & Co.

Prigogine, I. (1996). *The End of Certainty*, New York and London: The Free Press.

Rescher, N. (1996). *Process Metaphysics*, New York: State University of New York Press.

Ruskin, J. (1903–1912). *Modern Painters* Vol. XI, in E. T. Cook & Alexander Wedderburn (eds) *The Works of John Ruskin: Library Edition*. Vols VI and XI, London: Weidenfeld and Nicholson.

Ruskin, J. (1927). *The Complete Works*, Vol. XV. London: Weidenfeld and Nicholson.

Sahlins, M. D. (1960). Evolution: Specific and General, in M. D. Sahlins & E. R. Service (eds) *Evolution and Culture*, Ann Arbor: Michigan University Press, 5–21.

Simon, H. (1996). *The Sciences of the Artificial*, 3rd edn, Cambridge, MA: MIT Press.

Taleb, N. N. (2007). *The Black Swan*, London: Allen Lane.

Tsoukas, H. (2003). New times, fresh challenges: Reflections on the past and the future of organization theory, in H. Tsoukas & C. Knudsen (eds) *The Oxford Handbook of Organization Theory: Meta-theoretical Perspectives*, Oxford, Oxford University Press, 607–22.

Tsoukas, H. & Chia, R. (2002). On organizational becoming: Rethinking organizational change. *Organization Science*, 13, 567–82.

Weick, K. E. (2009). *Making Sense of Organization: The Impermanent Organization Vol 2*, New York, Wiley.

Wheelwright, P. (1974). *Heraclitus*, New York: Atheneum.

Whitehead, A. N. (1926/1985). *Science and the Modern World*, London: Free Association Books.

Whitehead, A. N. (1929). *Process and Reality*, Cambridge: Cambridge University Press.

8

Going Back to Go Forward: On Studying Organizing in Action Nets

Barbara Czarniawska

Abstract: The received view of organizations is that they are tools used to achieve collective goals. This chapter presents the possibility that, like all tools that become cumbersome, obsolete, or simply inadequate, organizations can hinder organizing. Like tools, they do have a solid existence that cannot be ignored. And just like tools, they can be put to unexpected uses: they can become an obstacle to the achievement of collective goals. A return to the generic meaning of the term "organization" as a synonym of constructed order may reveal intricacies of organizing that have been obscured by the presently ruling conceptualization.

8.1 On processes

"Process" is now *the* fashionable word in the theory and practice of management.[1] I know one university president who uses it in every sentence, tautologically if possible, as in "now we must make sure that these processes of change processes get going as soon as possible." Added to which, every gerund signifies a process (e.g. organizing), so the term is almost always used tautologically or, if one wants to be kind, in a rhetorical figure called congery—a heaping up of words.

Is "process" a new term in organization literature? Not really. Fashions tend to be cyclical, and at all times ideas are in circulation somewhere (Merton, 1965/1985). The currently fashionable Business Process Management (what else?) is a new translation of the old "workflow" that was so popular in organization theory and practice in the 1960s. Actually, one could claim that the real ancestor of the processual approach to organizing in Anglo-Saxon theory was Frederick Winston Taylor. The concept of *flow* was central to his theory, and as *workflow*, it later became a central concept in contingency theory, which built on research in industrial organizations. This research faded away when service organizations became the focus of organization studies, but returned with ICT (information and communications technology). Young researchers are now rediscovering "processual studies" (see, e.g., the special issue of *Scandinavian Journal of Management*, 2007, 23)—often seeking help from philosophers, beginning with Heraclitus and ending with Deleuze.

My plea for returning may therefore be met with suspicion—going back in time is a painful procedure. Go back far enough, and it seems that everything has already been invented. But my purpose is not to claim that organization theory should return to its roots. Rather, I would recall a certain historical turn of events that shifted the attention of organization theory from processes to structures. Such accounting for the past may make present attempts easier, perhaps even bolder.

In what follows, I first present a chain of events that in my view caused a redefinition of organization theory from a theory of organizing to a theory of organizations. I then review the negative effects of this redefinition on present organization theory. Next, I return to early processual approaches and from there to the newest of these efforts, ending with suggestions for further extensions of these approaches.

8.2 Changing definitions of "organization", with special attention to systems theory

William Starbuck (2003) has studied the etymology of the term "organization," and produced the following short history:

> The word "organization" derives from an ancient Indo-European root that also spawns the words "organ" and "work." The Roman verb "organizare" meant initially "to furnish with organs so as to create a complete human being," but later Romans gave it the broader meaning "to endow with a coordinated structure". Organizare migrated from Latin into Old French. In 1488, the French language included the word "organization," which an ancient dictionary defined self-reflectively as "the state of an organized body." ... Although dictionaries published between 1750 and 1840 do not mention this usage explicitly, around 1800 some writers began to use "organization" to describe a property of societies. (Starbuck, 2003: 56)

Also in Late Greek, the words for work (ergon) and for a tool or instrument (organon) are close (they both originated from the Proto Indo-European root -werg[2]); perhaps this proximity caused "organization" to assume various meanings from "processes" to "structures." Nevertheless, in most Indo-European languages "organization" has long meant either a state of being organized (as in "organization of the tribe") or a voluntary association (in contrast to a company, an enterprise, or an administrative unit).

And then came systems theory. With its roots in the 1920s, it came to the fore with the 1948 publication of *Cybernetics: Or the Control and Communication in the Animal and the Machine* by Norbert Wiener, a US scientist of Russian-Jewish origin. To summarize the main idea behind cybernetics, one can say that, in order to control anything—from machines to spheres of collective life—it is necessary to design a control system, imitating those plants and animals already designed by Nature.

Soon cybernetics was promoted to the status of *the* science of control, much as the creators themselves—and especially Austrian biologist Ludwig von Bertalanffy (1950)—claimed it to be. In his *General Systems Theory* from 1968, von Bertalanffy presented cybernetics as an interdisciplinary theory of the nature of all complex systems. What is more, this theory was not only universal; it was politically neutral. In 1961, Wiener's article "Science and society" was published in the most influential Soviet journal, *Voprosy Filosofii* nr 7, albeit accompanied by an appropriate Marxist commentary (Wiener, 1963). Both cybernetics and systems theory have had great success on both sides of the "iron curtain" (e.g., Rindzevičiūtė, 2008).

When systems theory arrived at the door of what was then primarily called "administration theory" (Waldo, 1961), some changes and redefinitions were required, in order to apply the new, attractive frame to the old study objects. The application of systems theory required a creation of separate units (*open systems*) divided by *boundaries* from their *environments* and related to them by *adaptation*. These units were called "organizations"—a generic term correctly derived from "formal organizations," but usefully blurring the differences among formal organizations, and suggesting their common *systemic* qualities.

Alas, as Richard Lewontin said in discussing the entry of systems theory to biology, "What is a necessary step in the construction of knowledge at one moment becomes an impediment at another" (1995: 131). From the viewpoint of the second decade of the twenty-first century, it is easy to notice that the so-called environment is not a preexisting set of problems to which an organism, or an organization, must find solutions; these organisms—or organizations—created the problems in the first place. When Weick (1988) pointed out that organizations "enact" their environment, he did not refer only to perception processes. If I may be forgiven a tautology, people *act upon their enactments*, and thus create or recreate their environments to a large extent.

What is more, the environment of organisms consists largely of other organisms, and the environment of organizations consists almost entirely of other organizations, as emphasized by Perrow (1991). Biologists such as Lewontin concluded that the notion of adaptation is misleading, for it is not the only tool for understanding the relationship between an organism and its environment. Organization theorists would do well to follow this example. Moreover, it can be claimed that biological organisms do have boundaries separating them from their environments, and that mergers, acquisitions, transnationals, and networks render tenuous the idea that organizations have preexisting borders.

"Why, then", one could ask, "would we not withdraw from a metaphor or an analogy that no longer plays its role well?" Such an operation is not as easy as it may sound. For example, James G. March and Herbert Simon introduced their classic work, *Organizations*, with such a cautionary opening in 1958:

> This book is about the theory of formal organizations. It is easier, and probably more useful, to give examples of formal organizations than to define the term. The United States Steel Corporation is a formal organization; so is the Red Cross, the corner grocery store, the New York State Highway Department. The latter organization is, of course, part of a larger one—the New York State government. But for the present purposes we need not trouble ourselves about the precise boundaries to be drawn around an organization or the exact distinction between an "organization" and "nonorganization." We are dealing with empirical phenomena, and the world has an uncomfortable way of not permitting itself to be fitted into clean classifications. (March and Simon, 1958/1993: 20)

It seems, however, that by the 1993 edition, March and Simon were worried by the commonly spread understanding of "organizations", and therefore added a definition at the very beginning of their text:

> Organizations are *systems of coordinated action* among individuals and groups whose preferences, information, interests, or knowledge differ. (March and Simon, 1993: 2)

Judging from the majority of mainstream texts up to the 1990s, this correction came too late. Organizations were seen as systems of mechanical or organic parts, in which people were either cogs or body parts (heads and hands), as Gareth Morgan pointed out in 1986, in his attempt to introduce a different set of metaphors.

By shaping "organizations" into "systems", one could argue, organization theorists did something similar to the sixteenth-century rabbi of Prague, who created a clay monster—a golem—to defend the inhabitants of the ghetto from anti-Semitic attackers. Golem fulfilled its function, and then turned around and threatened its own creators, until the rabbi disassembled it.[3]

Some readers will notice the parallel between the Golem and the Leviathan story, the latter as retold by sociologists of science and technology (Callon and Latour, 1981). Why do I need to introduce another mythical figure? There are certain similarities between the stories of Leviathan and Golem—both were created to defend against anarchy and violence. But although the Leviathan stands for the sovereign, and is created by the same people from the same people, Golem is a mindless warrior, sent to fight against the enemy.

> In order to grow, we must enrol other wills by translating what they want and by reifying this translation in such a way that none of them can desire anything else any longer. Hobbes restricted this process of translation to what we now call "political representation." The scattered wills are recapitulated in the person of the sovereign who says what we want, and whose word has force of law and cannot be contradicted. (Callon and Latour, 1981: 296)

What enemy should the organizational Golem fight? It could be that organization theorists thought that systems theory would help them to defend themselves from economists, who always claimed a monopoly on explaining economic organizations. Like sociologists and political scientists who black boxed the Leviathan, however, organization theorists have certainly helped to maintain and solidify their Golem, which has enjoyed great success among practitioners.

Now that Golem is out, is there any way to call it back? And, perhaps more importantly, is there a reason for disassembling the creature? My answer is yes, as the insistence on studying "organizations" can obscure key instances of organizing: organizing without organizations; organizing among organizations; and organizing in spite of organizations.

8.3 Studying "organizations" can obscure critical instances of organizing

8.3.1 Organizing without organizations

Clay Shirky's *Here Comes Everybody: The Power of Organizing Without Organizations* (2008) can be dismissed by many readers as Internet hype. Here is an author who believes, like many others, that the Web will revolutionize our lives—the standard prediction accompanying any new technology. Shirky, however, does not claim that everything enabled by the Internet must necessarily be good—only that certain organizing attempts, once impossible without the support of a formal organization, all of a sudden are possible. To create a historical contrast, one can recall Bengt Jacobsson's (1994: 68) reading of August Strindberg's *The Red Room*, which he saw "as a story about the origins of the modern, organised Sweden." One of its heroes tours across political organizations, bureaucracies, companies, newspapers, and workers' associations, and comes to the bitter conclusion that "greed and selfishness was always hidden behind more idealistic facades" (1994: 75). Yet whenever the Swedes wanted to do something, they formed an organization. For Strindberg, the evil behind formal organization was called collectivism; the remedy lay in extreme individualism.

One of the curses of the second part of the twentieth century was an identification made between collectivism and collective action, an identification supported and encouraged by the two main ideological powers. Either one did things alone, or one was guilty of "collectivism." Drowned now and again under the weight of old-fashioned individualism is the obvious observation that people are social animals (Aronson, 1972/2007, now in its tenth edition), and that even Robinson Crusoe's actions were collective, in the sense of being based on collective knowledge and memory. And yet it is collective action that is the main core of human life, and the Internet does permit organization without the intermediation of formal organizations.

Shirky's first example was the simple exchange of information and opinions, made possible by blogging. His next example was the collaborative creation of knowledge, of which Wikipedia is the best example. Finally, he quoted examples of organizing mass actions, such as political protests.

Megens and Martin (2003), in their review of "cybermethods," pointed out that such methods glide across diverse arenas. Their list of arenas for the application of cybermethods begins with "conventional economics, politics, war, law," in which the methods are most certainly used by formal

145

organizations; continues with the new areas of e-commerce, e-politics, information warfare, and e-law, in which both formal organizations and ad hoc organized groups may be involved; and ends with e-life, cyberreality, and Matrix-world, in which formal organizations, albeit still present, are more or less hidden under the multitude of various organizing initiatives.

Once again, there is no a priori moral valuation involved. Blogging may be contributing to a growing number of heart attacks (apparently bloggers do not get enough sleep), and it certainly contributes to information overload. Wikipedia contains a great deal of incorrect information, but so do most encyclopedias—only the latter do not admit it, but hide behind the authority of formal organizations. Last but not least, football hooligans use the Internet to organize their fights with hooligan fans from the opposing team. Even murder can be organized this way, as in Günter Grass's *Crabwalk* (2003). Thus, the point is not the moral superiority of organizing without organizations, and certainly not a point for individualism and against collectivism. As Robert Michels said and Jacobsson repeated, so often, "from a means, organization becomes an end" (Michels, 1949: 390, after Jacobsson, 1994: 83).

Sweden has undergone little change since Strindberg's times—in this aspect, at least. A recent TV series on a fashionable topic of organizing in the face of risk and threat (directed against the government and its seat in central Stockholm) showed, as a first step, the creation of a formal organization. This organization becomes immediately involved in arranging a series of meetings, the purpose of which is a division of formal responsibilities (Czarniawska, 2007). In the meantime, the terrorist plans and performs unencumbered.

8.3.2 Organizing among organizations

Much organizing happens between and among organizations, be it in form of alliances and similar cooperative efforts (see e.g., Smith Ring and Van De Ven, 1992), networks (Håkansson and Johansson, 2001), or mergers and acquisitions (DePamphilis, 2008). Perhaps the most common and least noted is the cooperation among various parts of different formal organizations, with the purpose of performing a joint action. City management can be cited as the most obvious example (Czarniawska, 2002). Although there is always a large formal organization called "city administration," it is a multi-faceted hybrid, with parts ranging from the purely political to the purely productive, and everything in between. But the city is an arena for a great many other formal organizations, from companies to citizens' voluntary associations, and in order to undertake any activity on the terrain of the city—anything from formal permission to active cooperation may be required.

Thus an urban recovery project in Rome in the rundown district of Magliana along the River Tiber required the removal of 43 companies, and included plans for 32 new interventions, 22 of public and 10 of private organizations (Czarniawska, 2010b). The problems and obstacles related to the actualization of this project had to do partly with the fact that it was almost impossible to ascertain if the number 43 was correct, and to contact all involved parties; and partly with the city's problem of maintaining the will to cooperate among the 32 parties, especially as their planned interventions had to wait until the formalities were resolved. Not all projects are necessarily this complex, but there is no doubt that organizations are constantly cooperating; that their cooperation is not always easy, precisely because of the formalities involved; and that the issue tends to be ignored in conventional organization studies, keen as its authors are on remaining "within" an organization.

8.3.3 Organizations obstruct organizing

Much as I am against reifying organizations (in the sense of seeing them as structures, units with borders, containers), I find the conceptualization of organizations as tools for collective action (Perrow, 1986) to be extremely convincing. Organizations can then be seen as virtual artifacts (actants rather than macro actors, to use the vocabulary of actor-network theory, in which an actant is anything in a narrative that acts or is acted upon). From that perspective, an organization can be seen as combining the functions of *dispatcher* (Latour, 1998) and that of *translator* in a machine that has been given a legal personality (Lamoreaux, 2004). An organized collective action means that the right things and the right humans must be in the right places at the right times, doing the right things. To be able to send objects and humans to the right places at the right time, the dispatcher must know how to contact them and know how to explain what to do. Thus the dispatcher depends on translator services. The translator is needed because there is a movement of people and objects; had they stayed at the same place, there would be no need for translation (Czarniawska and Sevón, 1996, 2005).

Humans are not "cogs" in this machine, any more than they are chips in their computers. They constructed this machine—this tool—with help of other co-constructors (thus "social construction"), but once constructed, the machine continues to construct them. In such a perspective, organizations are literally instrumental: either they work, or they do not. If they do not, they should be repaired or exchanged (and eventually dropped, as Karl Weick (1996) has suggested). What is more, they can be designed better or worse, but they cannot be designed perfectly.

Elaine Scarry's (1985) theory explains convincingly why that is so. According to her, an artifact's "reciprocation" (the ways in which it can be used) always exceeds the designer's projection (the intentions of the designer projected into the object). As much as they may wish to, the designers cannot control the use of their artifact because they design more than they know (the institutional order speaks through them), and they cannot foresee all the contexts of use (Czarniawska, 2009a). My favorite example is again taken from this not-formally organized source of knowledge called the Internet, and it concerns the known uses of computers at a workplace, collected partly through surveys, and partly through observation.[4]

- elements of decoration;
- surfaces on which to place decorative elements;
- notice boards (outside and inside);
- computation devices (including household bills);
- communication devices (including private e-mails, chatting, and looking for a partner);
- graphic art creation devices (including subversive art);
- video/audio composition devices (including subversive music and videos);
- video/audio reproducing devices (TV, DVDs);
- word processing (including private texts);
- desktop publishing;
- scheduling (calendars);
- programming devices;
- doors to virtual worlds;
- picture frames (screens);
- weapons;
- objects for unloading aggressive feelings;
- half-products for hard covers and folders;
- beds for growing grass (on other people's dirty keyboards).

The analogy is obvious: organizations, like computers and other tools, can be used for varying purposes. Refusing to account for the functionality of an organization or accounting only for its formally stated purposes can overshadow the many unexpected uses of organizations, such as the obstruction of organizing.

When the Municipality of Rome faced the challenge of hosting the influx of pilgrims arriving at the Vatican for the celebration of the Third Millennium of Christianity in 1999, they reasoned along organizational lines. A list was made of all municipal and regional organizations to be involved, and their representatives invited to a meeting. After the meeting dissolved in a quarrel over the relative importance of various units in the future actions, the organizers decided to change tack. They prepared a list of necessary actions, established how they need to be connected, and only then contacted potential executors (Pipan and Porsander, 2000).

8.4 Breaking Golem into pieces: Studying organizing

It could be said that I exaggerate the performativity of organization theory, weak as it is compared to the performativity of economics (McKenzie et al., 2007). Economists construct economies according to their prescriptions. But does it really matter for the practice of management and organizing how the theoreticians have conceptualized it? More importantly, it can be claimed that it is actually the practitioners of organizing who reified the concept in its present, common rendition, because it suited their political purposes.

It may well be so. But it does not follow that the theoreticians should take this reification for granted and follow the lead of practitioners unreflectively. I am far from the first to state the need to problematize this construct. In fact, it can be claimed that the processual view of organizing is older than the structural one, and that it continues unabashed, in spite of temporary fashions that may dictate a focus on structures. What follows is not a complete list of examples, but one that contains works that had directed my attention to processes of organizing.

8.4.1 The Theory of Work Harmonization (1898)

Karol Adamiecki was a Polish engineer, educated at the Technical Institute in Petersburg.[5] After graduation, he returned to his hometown of Dąbrowa Górnicza in Silesia, a region that hosts most of the mining and industrial towns in southern Poland. There, he accepted employment at Bank Smelting Mills, first as a draughtsman, and then as the assistant manager of the rolling mill. He became intensely interested in the possibilities of increasing production output. He maintained and developed this interest in several other jobs he held in Russian mills, not least in order to defend the honor of Polish workers, who were seen as unproductive by the mill owners. His theory of work harmonization from 1898 preceded F. W. Taylor's by a couple of months, but he wrote only in Polish and Russian. In 1903 he delivered a paper, "Principles of Collective Work," to the Society of Russian Engineers in Ekaterinoslav, which allegedly caused a sensation in Russian technical circles (Urwick, 1956; after Marsh, 1975).

Adamiecki's contribution became known as "the harmonogram," a form of graphic analysis based on his theory of work harmonization, the aim of which was to increase the visibility of the interdependence of various production processes. Apparently, the introduction of the harmonogram in various mills resulted in 100–400 per cent increases in output (Urwick, 1956). His theory became widely known after the publication of his "Harmonograf" article in 1931 (Adamiecki, 1931; Marsh, 1975). By that time, however, Henry Gantt, whose charts have become known in the Anglo-Saxon world through his 1910 and 1915 publications, had invented a similar method. Yet according to Marsh (1975), it was Adamiecki's harmonogram rather that Gantt's charts that became the basis of later methods such as PERT (Program Evaluation and Review Technique) and the Critical Path Method.

Adamiecki's theory of work harmonization postulated that good management is based on three types of harmony:

- harmony of choice (all production tools should be compatible with each other, with special regard to their output production speed);
- harmony of doing (the importance of time coordination, schedules, and timetables);
- harmony of spirit (the importance of creating a good team).[6]

In 1925, Adamiecki founded the Polish Institute of Scientific Management in Warsaw, and in 1974, the newly created University of Economics in Katowice was named after him (the college from which it was created had already been named after him in 1972).

I cannot say that Adamiecki was the hero of my youth; studying industrial psychology, I read him along with many other authors, part of the burden of obligatory assignments. All this sentimental "harmonization" talk seemed to be a thing of the past, and not for my generation. But among some of the things that struck me was his attention to processes (another was an admiration for things that function well); workflow, in the vocabulary of the time, was at the center of researchers' attention in the 1970s.

Indeed, neo-contingency theorists cherished the notion of workflow long after the theory itself went out of fashion.

> Workflow is the process whereby inputs, including raw materials, manufactured components and parts, machine capacity and human effort are organized in order to transform them into output. It presupposes differentiated arrays of machines, jobs, organizational sub-units, people with specific skills and knowledge, and it consists of the technical and social arrangements that allow human effort, machine capacity and material inputs to be brought together to achieve output goals.... "Work" may be done by machines or by humans or by a combination of the two. In the course of technical change, boundaries between human and machine work are changed, and combinations of the two also change. Variables should therefore be able to reflect such shifts rather than be biased by them. (Sorge, 1989: 27)

The variables favored by the neo-contingency theorists were so abstract ("workflow continuity," "product variability"), however, that although possibly useful as evaluation variables, they did not work as explanatory variables. This may have been unavoidable, given that they relied upon ostensive rather than performative definitions (variables were treated like physical attributes), and aimed at structural correlations, even by scholars who were focusing on processes (Joerges and Czarniawska, 1998).

8.4.2 Garbage Can Model

Michael D. Cohen, James G. March, and Johan P. Olsen suggested in their famous article from 1972, "A Garbage Can Model of Organizational Choice," that a garbage can is a good analogy for decision-making in "organized anarchies"—organizations in which preferences are problematic, technology is unclear, and participation in decision making is fluid. Up to the present day, readers have been divided into those who believe that this description fits all organizations, and those who believe that only universities and such half-professional and half-political organizations can be accommodated under that label. March and his collaborators, insisting on the earlier assumption that it is the *allocation of attention* that explains actual decision making, posited formal organizations as garbage cans, in which accessible problems, solutions, decision-making opportunities, and participants meet randomly, producing outcomes/decisions.

To my reading, the garbage can theory can indeed be a model for organization studies, serving as a protoplot—applying Kenneth Burke's dramatist pentad in order to emplot reports of research on organizing (Czarniawska, 1999). Instead of focusing on "an open system" metaphor, the garbage can suggests a focus on the chronology of events (or chronology of attention shifts), in which the garbage can, or formal organization, is only a stage on which the drama of organizing evolves—where the choice opportunities arise.[7]

Does all of this make it a processual approach? According to Bendor et al. (2001), who undertook an evaluation of the impact of the model on organizational research, absolutely so:

> As problems, solutions, and participants move independently about the organization, various combinations find themselves dumped into these cans, and the decisions coming out (if any) depend on whatever mixtures the intersecting streams happen to generate. The organization's basic structure (notably, its rules) channels and constrains this multifarious action, thereby shaping the organization's patterns of choice and problem solving. But the driving force of the garbage can explanation is process. (Bendor et al., 2001: 71)

Whereas Bendor et al. continued to suggest improvements along the lines of enriching the garbage can model with more structural elements, my suggestions would be the opposite—possibly because Bendor et al. have a very different opinion on the role of metaphors in the social sciences. To me, the next step would be to focus exactly on processes; after all, whatever is being produced in garbage cans is produced as a result of chemical processes set to work by a meeting of various elements. Their composition, though changing, is far from unpredictable; sociological and anthropological studies of garbage show clear dependence on the contents of garbage cans on class, neighborhood, and economic situation (Rathje and Murphy, 1992). Thus, whereas the contents of a particular garbage can at a particular moment may be primarily accidental, there is a pattern across time and space, and therefore some chemical-like processes must be more frequent than other. Do problems, solutions, and participants "dissolve"? Do they "consume" one another, or perhaps "corrode"?

Here, once again, I agree with Bendor et al. (2001): the garbage can model must be put to a more specific use. A protoplot is not yet a plot, and settling labels on problems, solutions, participants, and choice opportunities cannot serve as a final explanation. A given process must be emplotted in a way specific to it. The garbage can is a starting point, not an end result.

8.4.3 Organizing

Among the authors who did the most to introduce systems theory to organization theory were Charles West Churchman (e.g. Churchman

1971, 1979) and two social psychologists, Daniel Katz and Robert L. Kahn (1966).[8] I translated their book *The Social Psychology of Organizations* into Polish, and was completely convinced by it: open systems were the answer! True, there were "throughput" processes, but the important thing was to identify various parts of a system and find feedback loops and input and output ratios. Adamiecki was forgotten. Once the structure was in place and couplings were tight, the processes would follow automatically. What a surprise, then, to see a book so clearly alluding to the same group of problems but provocatively turning everything upside down: *The Social Psychology of Organizing* (Weick, 1969/1979). Still not translated into Polish, Weick's book was to many organization theorists a startling reminder of what needs to be studied. For inspiration, Weick went back to an older social psychologist, F. H. Allport (1954), who suggested studying the "structure of events" (an intriguing name for a process). Reformulating these suggestions in another vocabulary, Weick defined organizing as the process of assembling "ongoing interdependent actions into sensible sequences that generate sensible outcomes" (Weick, 1979: 3). The result of organizing is interlocked cycles, which can be represented as causal loops rather than as a linear chain of causes and effects. Speaking about "interlocked cycles" or "looped chains of events" may offer a way out of the growing emptiness of the term "process."

Weick's way of conceptualizing organizing also meant that organizing is, and must be, an ongoing encounter with ambiguity, ambivalence, and equivocality. It is part of a larger attempt to make sense of life and the world, and it should be studied as such—not merely as a move from "organizations" to "organizing," but also as a move from "decision making" to "sense making" (Weick, 1995)—another dramatic shift in attention allocation, to borrow March's words. On this point, the two theoreticians agree: they both take ambiguity as a given, and consider the idea of "uncertainty reduction" as relevant but, as are all attempts at ordering, of short duration.

8.4.4 *Actor-Network Theory*

Actor-network theory (ANT) originated in Studies of Science and Technology, and was the result of a felicitous crossing-over between narratology (in the version of Lithuanian-French semiotician Algirdas Greimas, see e.g. Greimas and Courtés, 1982) and studies of successful inventions (Latour, 1988). It has recently trickled across[9] to organization studies, although for the most part in the version of "actors and their networks." This version is not, however, what the approach proposed to accomplish.

ANT is narratology at the service of understanding how the social is assembled, based on a fruitful analogy between a fictitious narrative and a research report. In a fictitious narrative, it is not known at the outset who is a hero and who is a villain (unless it is a sequel). Initially unprepossessing figures conquer kingdoms after having successfully accomplished their narrative trajectory, whereas various signs of power and authority (formal titles, golden treasures) may change owners and remake some characters while dismembering others. Thus a lesson for studying organizing: if it is known at the outset who has power, who is a hero, and who is a villain, research is a waste of time. A study that truly purports to provide information that did not exist before begins with the identification of actants (those that act and are acted upon) in a given case (that is, an occurrence of a phenomenon), follows a narrative trajectory (a series of programs and anti-programs), and shows how actants that established associations and stabilized them became actors, or even macro actors. After all, macro actors are but large networks that are hiding their networked character by presenting themselves through one voice of a representative speaker.

Although ANT can be of great use in organization theory (see e.g. Czarniawska and Hernes, 2005; Latour, 2005), it does not cover every case of organizing, because ANT was constructed for a different purpose. It focuses on macro actors, if only to show how they were assembled. It does not focus on organizing that does not lead to the construction of actors or on the macro actors that disassemble. It could be that the latter do not provide for good stories,[10] but even such unglamorous organizing is necessary for organization theorists to learn about. What is needed is to extend the focus of research to organizing that does not lead to the construction of macro actors—sometimes because it is not meant to, and sometimes because it fails. In narratological terms, one could say that there is a need to focus on pieces of discourse that do not become stories.

8.4.5 Action Nets

For the last ten years or so, I have suggested that instead of studying "organizations", building-like units, or even "networks"—connections between well-defined points—organization scholars should be studying connections among actions (Czarniawska, 1997, 2004, 2008). My plea is to study organizing as the connection, re-connection, and disconnection of various collective actions to each other, either according to patterns dictated by a given institutional order or in an innovative way. Such collective actions need not be performed within the bounds of a formal organization;

an action net can involve actions performed by several formal organizations or by assemblies of human and non-human actants. The actions can be connected loosely or temporarily.

For a genealogy of this idea, the most obvious connection is the connection to actor-network theory, although in a variation that focuses on the evolving of the narration itself,[11] rather than on one of its effects such as the construction of characters (actors, including formal organizations). I also spiced actor-network theory with a pinch of new institutionalism: in a given institutional order, certain collective actions seem obvious or even necessary candidates for being connected to others (producing to selling, for example), whereas other connections may seem alien or innovative.

Going back in time, I need to mention Karl Weick's work (1969/1979) as being of central importance, due also to his innovative updating of some insights known to me previously from social psychology.

Finally, I need to recall my early fascination with graph theory and the Critical Path Method, which I later abandoned as too mechanistic and therefore unrealistic. I have also realized that studies of workflow were part of my education, first in industrial and later in organizational psychology. But only recently (Czarniawska, 2009b) have I discovered in the notion of action nets a trace of Adamiecki's main conviction: that connecting "doings" to one another is the main trait of organizing. "Organizations" are legal units; a "network" can exist, yet do nothing; in order to do anything, "doings" are necessary, and they have to be coordinated—not in parallel, but by connections, which need to be stabilized, etc., etc., etc.

Thus, either the tools are doing their work, and should be kept and maintained, or they should be dropped and replaced. In the meantime, the critical question is: "What is being done?" and possibly "What needs to be done?" rather than "Who is doing what?"

8.5 Some postulates

The recent fashion favoring "processes" and "practices" in organization studies makes me feel somewhat like the character from Molière's *The Bourgeois Gentleman* (1670), Monsieur Jourdain, who did not know that he had been speaking prose all of his life before being told. Well, I did know that I studied processes, and if I did not study practices it depended on the fact that in many languages other than English the word in the plural has a distinctly different meaning ("practitioners" in Swedish and "shady activities" in Polish, for instance). What I care about most is a return from the "theory of organizations" to "organization theory": an explanation of how an organized state is achieved. One version of such an explanation concentrates on human agents only. As Martin Parker described it:

> Organization here refers to the process of making more or less stable patterns—the use and continual revision of recipes, interpretive frameworks, accounts, ethno-methods and so on that enable human beings to perform and order (Parker, 1998: 506).

But as Parker pointed out, in agreement with such authors as Law (1994) and Latour (2005), this process cannot take place if no machines, objects and quasi-objects, cybermethods, and so on are added—those that enable humans and non-humans to perform and to order. Organizing, then, is a social process (beings and objects associated with one another) of accomplishing a collective action in a somewhat orderly manner.

What about "organizations," then? First of all, processes of organizing need to be separated from the sites where they take place. Organizing may occur within formal organizations, but it is rarely contained within their borders, and imposing such a frame from the outset ("organizing is a process taking place in formal organizations") possibly excludes many fascinating new phenomena related to organizing. The liberation of organizing from the artificial frame imposed by the (virtual) limits of a formal organization will help researchers to scrutinize organizing that is hidden by a focus on organizations. One obvious example is the organizing and managing of consumers, clients, and patients in "services"—whoever is at the receiving end of the products of formal organizations. The hospital where I have been a patient organized my life much more thoroughly and effectively than my boss or my employer does; yet organization theory focused on formal structures only allows for study at the macro level—"the organizing of a university" and "the organizing of a hospital." Furthermore, such non-obvious organizing techniques as accounting and marketing need to be scrutinized more closely than they have been.

As to "organizations," I would be in favor of giving them back their proper names. Even if they are tools, tools differ, not least in their purpose (e.g. company vs. city administration vs. association). So back to companies, federations, clubs, societies, utilities, states, regions... as to whether or not they perform any organizing, it is and will remain an empirical question.

Notes

1. Some of the topics discussed here have been developed in another context in "Organizations as obstacles to organizing," Czarniawska (forthcoming).
2. http://www.myetymology.com/greek/, accessed 7 January 2010.
3. For a feminist version of the story, see Marge Piercy's *He, She and It* (in Europe known as *Body of Glass*), 1991.
4. http://www.bls.gov/opub/ted/2005/aug/wk5/art05.htm, "The Many Uses of Computers." 123HelpMe.com. http://www.123HelpMe.com/view.asp?id=26706, both accessed 12 February 2008.
5. At the time, Poland was divided among three occupying forces: Russia, Germany, and the Austro-Hungarian Empire.
6. http://en.wikipedia.org/wiki/Karol-Adamiecki, accessed 27 September 2008.
7. I differ here from Bendor et al. (2001) who see choice opportunities as garbage cans, ignoring the fact that the former are transient, and the latter solid.
8. Under the influence of Talcott Parsons, Chester Barnard (1938) used systems theory much earlier, but this element of his work went mostly unnoticed.
9. More about ideas trickling down, up, and across in Czarniawska (2005).
10. Although I am of an opinion that Mark Twain's "Aurelia's unfortunate young man" (written about 1865) is an excellent story, posing as it does the poignant question: When does an actor cease to be an actor?
11. More on the analogy between organizing and narrating in Czarniawska (2008).

References

Adamiecki, K. (1931). Harmonograf, *Przegląd Organizacji* (1).

Allport, F. H. (1954). The structuring of events: Outline of a general theory with applications to psychology, *Psychological Review*, 61: 281–303.

Aronson, E. (1972/2007). *Social Animal*, New York: Worth Publishers.

Barnard, C. (1938/1968). *The Functions of the Executive*, Cambridge, MA: Harvard University Press.

Bendor, J., Moe, T. M., & Shotts, K. W. (2001). Recycling the garbage can: An assessment of the research program, *The American Political Science Review*, 95(1), 169–90.

Bertalanffy, L. von (1950). An outline of general system theory, *British Journal for the Philosophy of Science*, 1, 139–64.

——(1968). *General System Theory: Foundations, Development, Applications*, New York: George Braziller.

Callon, M. & Latour, B. (1981). Unscrewing the big Leviathan: How actors macro-structure reality and how sociologists help them to do so, in A. V. Cicourel, & K. Knorr Cetina (eds) *Advances in Social Theory and Methodology: Towards an Integration of Micro- and Macro-sociologies*, London: Routledge and Kegan, 277–303.

Churchman, C. W. (1971). *The Design of Inquiring Systems: Basic Concepts of Systems and Organizations*, New York: Basic Books.

——(1979) *The Systems Approach and its Enemies*, New York: Basic Books.

Cohen, M. D., March, J. G., & Olsen, J. P. (1972). A garbage can model of organizational choice, *Administrative Science Quarterly*, 17, 1–25.

Czarniawska, B. (1997). *Narrating the Organization: Dramas of Institutional Identity*, Chicago, IL: University of Chicago Press.

——(1999). *Writing Management: Organization Theory as a Literary Genre*, Oxford: Oxford University Press.

——(2002). *A Tale of Three Cities: Or the Glocalization of City Management*, Oxford: Oxford University Press.

——(2004). On time, space and action nets, *Organization*, 11(6), 777–95.

——(2005). Fashion in organizing, in B. Czarniawska & G. Sevón (eds) *Global Ideas: How Ideas, Objects and Practices Travel in the Global Economy*, Malmö/Copenhagen: Liber/CBS, 129–46.

——(2007). Organisering i TV-rutan, *Kommissionen*, in B. Czarniawska, A. Diedrich, T. Engberg, U. Eriksson-Zetterquist, E. Gustavsson, K. Lindberg, L. Norén, D. Renemark, L. Walter, & P. Zackariasson *Organisering kring hot och risk*, Lund: Studentlitteratur, 195–213.

——(2008). *A Theory of Organizing*, Cheltenham: Edward Elgar.

——(2009a). How institutions are inscribed in technical objects and what it may mean in the case of the Internet, in F. Contini & G. F. Lanzara (eds) *ICT and Innovation in the Public Sector: European Studies in the Making of e-government*, Basingstoke, UK: Palgrave Macmillan, 49–87.

——(2009b). My forgotten predecessors, in K. Sahlin, L. Wedlin, & M. Grafström (eds) *Exploring the Worlds of Mercury and Minerva*, Uppsala: Acta Universitatis Upsaliensis (51), 101–12.

——(2010). Translation impossible? Accounting for a city project, *Accounting, Auditing and Accountability Journal*, 23(3), 420–37.

——(forthcoming). Organizations as obstacles to organizing. Paper presented at "What is an Organization? Materiality, Agency and Discourse" Conference (2008 05 21), HEC-Montréal and Université de Montréal, Montreal, Québec, Canada.

——& Hernes, T. (eds) (2005). *Actor-Network Theory and Organizing*, Malmö: Liber.

——& Sevón, G. (eds) (1996). *Translating Organizational Change*, Malmö/Copenhagen: Liber/CBS.

——& Sevón, G. (eds) (2005). *Global Ideas: How Ideas, Practices and Artifacts Travel in the Global Economy*, Malmö/Copenhagen: Liber/CBS.

DePamphilis, D. (2008). *Mergers, Acquisitions, and Other Restructuring Activities*, New York: Elsevier

Górski, P. (2005). *Między inteligencką tradycją a menedżeryzmem*, Kraków: Wydawnictwo Uniwersytetu Jagiellońskiego.

Grass, G. (2003). *Crabwalk*, Orlando, FL: Houghton Mifflin Harcourt.

Greimas, A. J. & Courtés, J. (1982). *Semiotics and Language: An Analytical Dictionary*. Bloomington, IN: Indiana University Press.

Håkansson, H. & Johansson, J. (eds) (2001). *Business Networking Learning*, Oxford: Pergamon Press.

Jacobsson, B. (1994). On evil organizations and illusory reforms, in B. Czarniawska & P. Guillet de Monthoux (eds) *Good Novels, Better Management: Reading Organizational Realities in Fiction*, Reading, UK: Harwood Academic Publishers, 65–92.

Joerges, B. & Czarniawska, B. (1998). The question of technology, or how organizations inscribe the world, *Organization Studies*, 19(3), 363–85.

Katz, D. & Kahn, R. L. (1966). *The Social Psychology of Organizations*, New York: Wiley.

Kunda, G. (1992). *Engineering Culture*, Philadelphia, PA: Temple University Press.

Lamoreaux, N. R. (2004). Partnerships, corporations, and the limits on contractual freedom in U.S. history: An essay in economics, law and culture, in K. Lipartito & D. B. Sicilia (eds) *Constructing Corporate America: History, Politics, Culture*, New York: Oxford University Press, 29–65.

Latour, B. (1988). *The Pasteurization of France*, Cambridge, MA: Harvard University Press.

Latour, B. (1998). *Artefaktens återkomst*, Stockholm: Nerenius & Santérus.

Latour, B. (2005). *Reassembling the Social*, Oxford: Oxford University Press.

Law, J. (1994). *Organizing Modernity*, Oxford: Blackwell.

Lewontin, R. C. (1995). Genes, environments and organisms, in R. B. Silvers (ed.) *Hidden Histories of Science*, New York: New York Review of Books, 115–40.

McKenzie, D. A., Muniesa, F., & Siu, L. (eds) (2007). *Do Economists Make Markets? On the Performativity of Economics*, Princeton, NJ: Princeton University Press.

March, J. G. & Simon, H. A. (1958/1993). *Organizations*, New York: Wiley.

Marsh, E. J. (1975). The harmonogram of Karol Adamiecki, *The Academy of Management Journal*, 18(2), 358–64.

Megens, H. & Martin, B. (2003). Cybermethods: An assessment, *First Monday*, 8(2). (http://firstmonday.org/issues/issue8_2/megens/index.html, accessed 6 January 2010).

Merton, R. (1965/1985). *On the Shoulders of Giants*, Chicago, IL: Chicago University Press.

Morgan, G. (1986). *Images of Organizations*, London: Sage.

Parker, M. (1998) Judgment day: Cyborganization, humanism and postmodern ethics, *Organization*, 5(4), 503–18.

Perrow, C. (1986). *Complex Organizations: A Critical Essay*, New York: McGraw-Hill.

Perrow, C. (1991). A society of organizations, *Theory and Society*, 20, 725–62.

Piercy, M. (1991). *Body of Glass*, London: Penguin.

Pipan, T. & Porsander, L. (2000). Imitating uniqueness: How big cities organize big events, *Organization*, 21(1), 1–27.

Rathje, W. & Murphy, C. (1992). *Rubbish! The Archeology of Garbage*, New York: Harper Collins.

Rindzevičiūtė, E. (2008). *Constructing Soviet Cultural Policy: Cybernetics and Governance in Lithuania after World War II*, Linköping: Linköping University, Department for Studies of Social Change and Culture.

Scandinavian Journal of Management (2007). 23(3).

Scarry, E. (1985). *The Body in Pain: The Making and Unmaking of the World*, New York: Oxford University Press.

Shirky, C. (2008). *Here Comes Everybody: The Power of Organizing Without Organizations*, London: Allen Lane.

Smith Ring, P. & Van De Ven, A. (1992). Structuring cooperative relationships between organizations, *Strategic Management Journal*, 13(7), 483–98.

Sorge, A. (1989). An essay on technical change: Its dimensions and social and strategic context, *Organization Studies*, 10/1, 23–44.

Starbuck, W. H. (2003). The origins of organization theory, in H. Tsoukas & C. Knudsen (eds) *The Oxford Handbook of Organization Theory: Meta-theoretical Perspectives*, Oxford, UK: Oxford University Press, 143–82.

Twain, M. (Samuel Clemens) (1865). *Aurelia's Unfortunate Young Man*. http://www.readbookonline.net/readOnLine/1519/, accessed 6 January 2010.

Waldo, D. (1961). Organization theory: An elephantine problem, *Public Administration Review*, 21, 210–25.

Weick, K. E. (1969/1979). *The Social Psychology of Organizing*, 2nd edn, New York: Addison-Wesley.

Weick, K. E. (1976). Educational organizations as loosely coupled systems, *Administrative Science Quarterly*, 21, 1–19.

Weick, K. E. (1988). Enacted sensemaking in crisis situations, *Journal of Management Studies*, 25, 305–17.

Weick, K. E. (1995). *Sensemaking in Organizations*, Thousands Oaks, CA: Sage.

Weick, K. E. (1996). Drop your tools: An allegory for organization studies, *Administrative Science Quarterly*, 21, 1–19.

Wiener, N. (1948). *Cybernetics: Or the Control and Communication in the Animal and the Machine*, Cambridge, MA: MIT Press.

Wiener, N. (1963). *God and Golem, Inc.* Cambridge, MA: The MIT Press.

Wojdak, M. (1983). Sylwetki profesorów Politechniki Warszawskiej: Karol Adamiecki, Warszawa: Prac. Hist.BGPW, 233-4-83-D.

9

Actor-Network Theory, Callon's Scallops, and Process-Based Organization Studies

Tor Hernes

Abstract: This chapter presents a comparison between Actor-Network Theory (ANT) and process thinking, with the aim of understanding the potential contribution of ANT to process-based organization studies. Such a comparison is important, given the increased focus on process thinking and the growing interest in ANT in organization studies. The chapter suggests three topics of comparison between the two, all of which are central to process thinking. They are as follows: the becoming of things, heterogeneous relationality, and contingency and time. It seems clear from the comparison that ANT has much to offer process-based organization studies. Most importantly, ANT works from an ontology of becoming rather than assuming that entities can be defined in terms of pre-given competencies and capabilities. Where ANT has limitations for the study of organization is at the level of actor networks and their conceptualization of meaning making. The chapter seeks to address this by introducing the notion of meaning structures. ANT tends to take a flat view of actor networks, where cohesion depends on the strength of associations between actors and the meanings that actors make of their respective connections, rather than the wholeness of the network. The chapter suggests that meaning structures, inherent to the process thinking represented in pragmatism and phenomenology, may be used to adapt ANT, making it more appropriate for process-based organization studies. Meaning structures imply that actors sense both wholeness and parts, enabling meaning making to transcend the level of local connections. Whereas this capacity is reserved to human actors, it does not necessarily violate the ANT principle of symmetry between human and material actors.

9.1 Process thinking, organization, ANT, and Callon's study

The aim of this chapter is to assess the potential of Actor-Network Theory (ANT) as a process-based theory of organization. An increasing number of works in organization studies examine the nature of processes and discuss how to apply process thinking to organization and management. There is also a marked increase in the application of ANT theory within organization studies. Given ANT's roots in process thinking, its potential for process-based organization studies warrants closer examination. In order to explore ANT as a process-based organization theory, I work successively with three topics: the becoming of things, heterogeneous relationality, and contingency and time. I apply these three concepts in turn to process thinking and organization studies, and then to ANT and Callon's (1986) study of the domestication of scallops in St Brieuc's Bay. In his paper, Callon spelled out the processes of translation, a key term in ANT, in ways that qualify his paper as foundational for ANT. Callon's study is used in this chapter as a proxy for ANT and ANT-related studies due to the way it articulated translation processes in an empirical setting, which may legitimately be described as a process of organizing, as this chapter will illustrate.

Process thinking is a body of ideas whose history is entangled by a more than two-millennia-old lineage of various philosophical works, sometimes referred to as "process philosophy" (Whitehead, 1929/1978) or "process metaphysics" (Rescher, 1996). A range of philosophers are associated with these schools of thought, from ancient philosophers (Heraclitus, Aristotle, Lucretius) to nineteenth- and twentieth-century pragmatists (such as James, Peirce, Dewey, and Mead), process thinkers (such as Whitehead and Bergson), twentieth-century phenomenologists (such as Heidegger and Alfred Schutz) and post-modernist writers (such as Foucault and Deleuze). Drawing upon thinkers such as these, recent efforts have been made in organization studies directed at understanding organization as process (e.g. Chia and King, 1998; Chia, 1999; Carlsen, 2006; Cooper, 2005; Tsoukas and Chia, 2002; Chia and Holt, 2009; Styhre, 2004; Clegg et al., 2005; Bakken and Hernes, 2006; Hernes, 2007).

The gist of recent process thinking in organization studies is to think of organization as attempts at ordering, amid a world of flux, ambiguity, and uncertainty, but without assuming stable external referents against which organizing may be held up. Thus attempts focus on capturing the ongoing and ever-mutating character of organizational life (Weick, 1979; Tsoukas and Chia, 2002), but without assuming the existence of organizations as stable frames of human action and sensemaking (Czarniawska, 2004). In Chia's (1999: 210) words, "[a process view] pits a metaphysics of change, in which primacy is accorded to movement, change and transformation, against the still-dominant Parmenidean-inspired metaphysics of substance which elevates stability, permanence and order." In this state of flux, ambiguity, and uncertainty, organization is seen as linking and connecting that which would otherwise be separated (Cooper and Law, 1995). The work of connecting is not about connecting existing entities in a stable state, but about actualizing things in the making; bringing them from virtuality to actuality (Deleuze, 2004). Importantly, as pointed out by Tsoukas and Chia (2002), organizational phenomena are not treated as entities, but as enactments of processes involving actors making choices interactively, in inescapably local conditions, by drawing on *broader rules and resources*. The enactments mentioned by Tsoukas and Chia can be seen as taking place through the work of connecting, of activating connections (Cooper, 2005) between heterogeneous materials (Chia and King, 1998). Tsoukas and Chia's emphasis on acting locally while drawing on broader resources is important because it literally takes activities of organization out of the confines of "the organization." Instead, organization becomes a situated activity of connecting heterogeneous entities in the making, whether or not they belong structurally within the confines of the organization. Such thinking turns conventional assumptions about organizations on their head. Organization is not seen as an existing circumscribed system within which actions occur, and which has to change in order for new patterns of action to emerge. Instead organization is the work (Czarniawska, 1997) of imposing some sense of stabilization upon a world on the move.

The implications of such views are substantial and invite consideration of the merits of ANT as a way to understand organization as process. ANT is an application of a process view to areas of technology, economics, and organization, where a basic tenet is the emergent character of entities, and where ordering consists of the work of connecting entities in the making. Ever since early studies (e.g. Latour and Woolgar, 1979), passing via Callon (1986) and restated in Latour (2005) a guiding principle of ANT studies has been to follow the work of actors assembling seemingly disparate and heterogeneous entities into intelligible assemblies (Latour, 2005). ANT represents a process view by several accounts, as will be demonstrated in this chapter. It is also becoming a significant stream of thought in organization studies (Czarniawska, 2004, 2009; Law, 1994, 2004; Law and Hassard, 1999; Calas and Smircich, 1999; Czarniawska and Hernes, 2005; Hernes, 2007). For example, ANT frameworks and concepts have been applied in studies of innovation and organization (Akrich, Callon and Latour, 2002*a*, 2002*b*; Hoholm, 2009), institutional theory (Czarniawska and Sevon, 1996, 2005), accounting and strategy (Skærbæk and Tryggestad, 2009), and practice studies (Gherardi and Nicolini, 2002).

ANT's potential as a theory of organization lies primarily in its focus on how material and human actors connect into durable wholes. It shares the principle of connecting and stabilization with theories of organizing as they are found in organization studies. However, whereas theories of organizing privilege the sensemaking of human actors, ANT works from a different assumption about the human–material relationship, which is that of translation between material and human actors. Whereas theories of organizing operate mainly with a view of human actors attempting to impose order on other human actors, and technologies, ANT studies how human and material entities acquire their identities through the mutual work of connecting. Thus ANT may be applied to demonstrate how phenomena intrinsic to organizing and organizations come into existence and stabilize organizational actions, as shown by Skærbæk and Tryggestad (2009) in the case of accounting systems. Skærbæk and Tryggestad, working from a performative view of accounting devices, demonstrate how these devices play an active part in a corporate strategy formulation process.

If we accept a process-based understanding of organization as being about the ordering of heterogeneous entities, Callon's (1986) study becomes a suitable representative study of a process of organization. It recounts how researchers, scallops, and fishermen were connected into an organized system of collective aims; namely the domestication of scallops in the St Brieuc Bay in France. The main human actors in this case consisted of a small group of French marine biologists, and their project of ordering involved "domesticating" scallops, which are unable to grow and proliferate in a wild state in the St Brieuc's Bay. In order to achieve their goals, they also have to negotiate with local fishermen and enlist their cooperation. The researchers go about their jobs without devoting particular attention to scallops, fishermen in the St Brieuc's Bay dredge the ocean floor for scallops all-year-round, without allowing them time to reproduce, and marine predators feed on scallop larvae (in contrast to Japan, where scallops were cultivated from the larvae stage, protected from predators). These, and other processes, were initially unconnected to one another. For example, Callon notes that there was no direct relationship between larvae and fishermen in St Brieuc's Bay in the early 1970s. Through the efforts of the marine researchers, links were progressively established as they observed processes which they established, deflected, or imported into the context of St Brieuc's

Bay. They also assumed ownership of these processes. Callon's analysis then focuses on how the chosen processes are progressively shaped into an actor-network around the domestication of the scallops.

Callon's study is not one of "organizations," but of a process of organization in the sense of connecting actors across time and space. It responds somewhat to Weick's (1974, 1979) appeal to shun the noun "organization" and to replace it with the verb "organizing." Whereas Weick has provided studies of groups focusing on sensemaking processes, however, Callon's study does not confine the organizing processes to the group, but considers a broader network of diverse actors. Callon's study is explicitly based on a heterogeneous view whereby materials and humans shape each other in a process of mutual translation. The temporary and indeterminate outcome of these translations is the actor-network, which directs attention to how actors actually perform their work of stabilization. Unlike Weick's work, however, stabilization does not reside in sensemaking, nor does disruption of the network result from loss of sensemaking, but relates more to the interests of individual actors in being enrolled into the network.

9.2 The becoming of things

9.2.1 The becoming of things, process thinking, and process-based organization studies

Key to process thinking is the replacement of being by becoming (Whitehead, 1929/1978; Hartshorne, 1965; Rescher, 1996). Whatever "things" we talk about, they are in the making rather than given a priori qualities, and whatever states we talk about, they are temporary outcomes rather than inputs to processes. Rescher (1996) appropriately describes a common assumption of process thinking in philosophy as follows:

> For the process philosopher is, effectively, by definition, one who holds that what exists in nature is not just originated and sustained by processes but is in fact ongoingly and inexorably *characterized* by them. On such a view, process is both pervasive in nature and fundamental for its understanding. (Rescher, 1996: 8)

The pervasiveness of process suggests that nothing can be defined with a priori characteristics, because whatever "thing" we talk about is forever in the process of becoming, along with all other "things" to which it is related, regardless of whether they are human or non-human actors. Most importantly, it implies that there is no fixed point outside the process against which the process—and its outcomes—may be understood, such as culture, identity, markets, technology, institutions, or financial resources. In the absence of external fixed points that may be seen to influence the process, explanations are sought in the dynamics of the process itself.

Whitehead's (1929/1978) process thinking was embedded in what is called a "Philosophy of becoming" (Hartshorne, 1965), in an attempt to avoid what he famously referred to as "the fallacy of misplaced concreteness" (Whitehead, 1929/1978: 2). According to Whitehead, it is essential to recognize that abstractions are never present in a final state, but rather are perpetually in the process of becoming. Nothing can ever be as we perceive it, nor can it become as we want it to be. Everything is in the process of becoming, perpetually. The conceptualization of becoming was an issue among ancient philosophers, who were more concerned with nature in its brute state than with the role of human perception in the constitution of nature. In his *Metaphysics*, Aristotle alerted us to the constant interplay between actuality and potentiality; between that which is there and that which may become. From a different angle, Heraclitus pointed out how the world is in a perpetual state of becoming. "All things flow" is frequently cited from Heraclitus' work. The sentence simply tells us not to expect anything to stay in its place. Even when things may remain pretty much unchanged over a period of time, their *meaning* changes with time. His statement that "the sun is new every day" was echoed by Hume's point that repetition changes nothing in the object repeated, but does change something in the mind that contemplates it (Hume, in Deleuze, 2004: 90). For all intents and purposes, the sun is the same every day, but we may infer that having looked at it once, looking at it again is not the same experience because it has already been looked at. The changing meaning of the "same" things is a major tenet of process thinking as it relates to phenomenology.

Later, Roman poet and philosopher, Lucretius (2004) criticized Heraclitus' "naïve" ideas that nature consisted of a priori defined substances such as fire, air, soil, and water. Instead, Lucretius subscribed to an atomic view, seeing the world as streams of invisible particles, called atoms, which flow but come together to form phenomena such as trees, water, and humans. In his philosophy of becoming, Whitehead, while subscribing to an atomistic view, replaced physical articles with "actual occasions," similar to William James's (1977: 104) "drops" of experience. According to Whitehead, actual occasions are the basic units of direct, lived, experience. They are what he called "event particles" (i.e. the basic units) of processes (Whitehead, 1920: 172). Thus Whitehead's notion of becoming was not about the becoming of physical shapes, such as with Lucretius, but the becoming of experience in the form of actual occasions. In a world of atomistic events, Whitehead's project was centered on explaining continuity of experience, and continuity is provided through the capacity of humans to abstract from concrete lived experience, and thus provide a sense of stabilization over multiple actual occasions. Entities that emerge as unities out of processes are abstractions. They arise from processes, and they form in turn the basis for further processes. Abstractions are always "becoming" rather than "being"; they are always in formation, and do not exist as entities in themselves.

Putting a stronger emphasis on temporality and the human construction of past experience, Bergson, whose conception of time and consciousness influenced other process theorists, such as Whitehead and James, viewed time as a series of successions of "pure states" (Bergson, 1998: 153). Yet Bergson also made the point that the ego would not endure if it forgot its former states; it needs its former states in order to form the past and present into an organic whole (Bergson, 1998: 153). As Whitehead pointed out, progress (in terms of creating future possibilities) does not result from concrete experience alone. We need abstractions for experiences to make sense, which is only possible with the help of time. Experiences make sense by being referred to a former state, via abstractions, just as abstractions make for the emergence of a new state.

In organization studies Chia and King (1998: 472), building on Whitehead and Bergson, formulate organization as follows: "[organization as process] redirects our attention towards organization as an *ontological* activity of reality-construction: of slowing down, punctuating, arresting, and regularizing what is essentially an undifferentiated fluxing reality, indifferent to our causes, into a novel, ordered, liveable world." Weick (1995: 107) suggests, in a similar vein, that ordering attempts take place through the imperfect imposition of discrete labels on continuous subject matter. We may infer from this that because the subject matter is continuously on the move, the imposition of labels cannot but be tentative and in the making. Rather, a sense of stability is created by the ongoing association of entities that take part in the process. As actors, be they human, organizational, or institutional, strive to reproduce those features that create a sense of stability, they become part of—and change with—those processes that they try to influence. Thus actors cannot stand outside processes, but change and move with them. The sense of stability is created as actors form recognizable relational wholes in interaction with other entities, such as technologies, products, markets, and firms.

9.2.2 The becoming of things, ANT, and Callon's scallops

Chia and King (1998) see ANT as viewing actors as temporarily stabilized effects of networking processes. ANT is founded on a principle of indeterminate entities that are given their identities and roles through the work performed in relation to other entities. To underline the indeterminacy of entities, Latour (1987, 1999, 2005) draws upon Greimas's (Greimas and Courtés, 1982) semiotics in which he speaks of "grammatical subjects," which may or may not reveal themselves as persons. Accordingly, Greimas adopted the term "actant," which applies not only to human beings but also to animals, objects, or concepts. Thus, central to ANT is the idea that entities, instead of being endowed with pre-given qualities, reveal themselves through their processes of mutual translation. The term "entities" includes not just tangible entities, but also concepts. As Czarniawska (2009) notes, words are things, not the other way around; and as things they can be used to construct or destruct.

Callon's work, as reflected in actor-network theory, has a flow-like character reflected by process thinking. In his paper, Callon (1986) is explicit about the nature of things as being in a state of indeterminate, yet not accidental, flux. While suggesting that groups of actors have a real existence, he asserts, "But reality is a process. Like a chemical body it passes through successive states." The groups or categories considered in the study (scallops, fishermen, researchers) are subjected to processes of translation over time, passing through what he calls "moments." Moments represent transitions in time whereby the representations of actors in relation to the network, change. For example, as Callon writes,

> The scallops are transformed into larvae, the larvae into numbers, the numbers into tables and curves which represent easily transportable, reproducible, and diffusable sheets of paper. . . . Instead of exhibiting the larvae and the towlines to their colleagues at Brest, the three researchers show graphic representations and present mathematical analyses. The scallops have been displaced. They are transported into the conference room through a series of transformations. (Callon, 1986: 14)

In his paper, Callon follows the successive transformation of entities and their relationships, and explains a temporary state (i.e. the stabilization of researchers, scallops, and fishermen connected into an actor network) in the light of how transformations of entities takes place. The process that Callon describes is the formation of the network in which no entities are considered to have stable values, but where their respective identities are constantly subject to negotiation. Key to Callon's paper is the idea that actors (people, technologies, institutions, organizations) are continually in the process of formation, thus putting focus on the processes by which actors perform the translation of other actors, while enrolling them into networks of actors involved in the process:

> The approach proposed here differs from this in various ways: first, as will be suggested below, the list of actors is not restricted to social entities; but second, and most important, because the definition of groups, their identities and their wishes are all constantly negotiated during the process of translations. Therefore, these are not pregiven data, but take the form of an hypothesis (a problematisation) that is introduced by certain actors and is subsequently weakened, confirmed or transformed. (Callon, 1986: 227–8)

Callon thus exemplifies the becoming of things and how the becoming of entities (in this case researchers, scallops, and fishermen) is indeterminate but subjected to the work of translation performed by the actors. The scallops case exemplifies how the becoming of things takes place in processes of organizing actors around an ambition of combining research and testing with commercial exploitation. It shows how this is performed through work such as, for example, by the use of graphical means, such as numbers, curves, and table, mentioned in the above citation from Callon's paper.

9.3 Heterogeneous relationality

9.3.1 Heterogeneous relationality, process thinking, and process-based organization studies

Chia and King (1998: 467) claim that what they call the "heterogeneous becoming" of things—rather than their manifest outcomes—is descriptive of several process theories, including Whitehead, Bergson, Derrida, Deleuze, and Serres (Serres' work has had considerable influence on the sociology of translation developed by Callon and Latour (Middleton and Brown, 2005)). The idea of heterogeneity presupposes that the things of the world are seen to belong to different kinds. Although in its "pure" state the world may be seamless, in the sense that there are no real limits between the entities that make it up, socially meaningful frameworks are based on the assumption that things are perceived to exist distinctly from one another. The delineation of things from one another enables them to be connected into relational wholes in which they make sense in relation to one another, as well as to the whole. A table, for example, standing on its own in an empty room, is merely a physical structure upon which things may be placed. However, with people seated around it and with food on it, the table takes on meaning in a relational whole consisting of table, people, chairs, food, and rituals, as the individual entities connect into the ritual of a meal. The actual table may remain a simple physical structure, but during a meal it acquires meaning by being part of a composite whole in which the boundaries between elements become blurred as they interact with each other. The whole thus created is heterogeneous, consisting of technical artifacts (chairs, table), natural artifacts (food), individual persons, and social relationships. This heterogeneous whole is not the same if one element is taken away and another is added. Nor is it the same if relationships are changed. For example, it may matter whether the eldest person is served first. In order to understand "what is going on," the table and the meal is viewed through the lens of relationality, where no element is given an a priori status above any other element, but where the meaning of each element emerges as part of a bigger whole.

The heterogeneity of entities is assumed in process thinking. Dewey (1934), for example, while emphasizing the precarious, transitory, and contingent nature of things, stated that things are never standalone entities, but are bound relationally to one another. And because they partake in the process over time, mutual value is attributed based on how the elements evolve—their processes of becoming. Thus the shaping of entities takes place over time through mutual experiencing. However, the ability to experience is not restricted to humans alone. According to Whitehead (1929/1978: 56–7), "all actual things are subjects, each prehending the universe from which it arises."

In mainstream organization studies, heterogeneity has referred principally to the diversity of social actors, whereas a process view of organization does not limit heterogeneity to social actors. Importantly, Chia and King (1998) referring to Bergson suggest that a process view invites heterogeneity that is infinitely varied and unique in each of its manifestations. Chia and King (1998) suggest, based on Bergson, that we should allow for heterogeneity in kind rather than in degree. From a perspective of becoming, heterogeneity in kind rather than degree would suggest that entities as different as people, artifacts, and concepts interact on an equal basis. Similarly Law (1994) works from the idea of organizing process, what he refers to as "modes of ordering" (1994: 110–11) involve different "materials," such as agents, devices, texts, social relations, and architectures. Organizing aims at coherence between different materials and is, in Law's view, an outcome of organizing processes in the sense of empirical appearance rather than a logical "fact." In a sense Law builds a bridge between a process view of organization as expressed by Chia and King, and ANT.

9.3.2 Heterogeneous relationality, ANT, and Callon's scallops

ANT is firmly founded in what may be called a relational sociology, not to be confused with the type of relational sociology that Emirbayer (1997) proposes. Whereas the relationality suggested by Emirbayer refers to social actors (humans, groups, organizations), ANT refers to heterogeneous sets of devices, humans, and concepts. ANT works from the assumption that the roles of connecting actors cannot be determined a priori. The extent to which actors come to play human or material roles is determined not by belonging to human or material categories, but by the ways in which they emerge from the associative work between them. A point, which was argued by Dewey (1934) and Whitehead (1929), and pursued by Latour and Callon, is that elements are given value neither by an omnipotent external observer, nor by any stable inherent qualities that they possess. Instead, value is given mutually by elements partaking in the process.

Callon offers a conceptual framework for explaining processes of becoming, which he applies to the process of domesticating scallops. The becoming of entities is relational, but takes place through a succession of processes. First, processes of *problematization*, during which actors define the overall project as well as criteria for becoming part of the network (Callon calls these "obligatory passage points," a term pursued by Latour and others). In Callon's account, problematization served to help researchers transpose the Japanese scallops project to France, while making themselves the indispensible architects of the process. Secondly, processes of *interessement* (a term also used by Akrich et al. (2002a) in the analysis of innovation and organization), during which actors seek to lock other actors into roles that can ensure the functioning of the network. In Callon's account, interessement took the form of using different devices. For example, the larvae and scallops were anchored to collectors, and the researchers' scientific colleagues were solicited during conferences and through publications. Thirdly, processes of *enrolment*, during which actors try to interrelate the roles of respective actors in the network. In Callon's account, enrolment took place through multilateral work of fitting actors' roles to one another, such as fitting anchorages and collectors to workable technologies for fishermen and researchers. Fourthly, processes of *mobilization* (a term also used by Akrich et al. (2002b) in the analysis of innovation and organization), during which "spokespersons" are selected and

171

activated so as to ensure the adhesion of the collectivities to the network. In Callon's account, mobilization takes place, for example, through working with representatives of the fishermen's association. Another process of mobilization takes place through the selection of scallops that can serve as reliable representatives for the population to be domesticated.

The four processes—problematization, interessement, enrolment, and mobilization—serve to distinguish activities by which the heterogeneous becoming (Chia and King, 1998) of entities is put into motion and upheld. Whereas heterogeneous becoming is an indispensible tenet of process-based organization studies, ANT, represented by Callon's study, provides an example of how it may be conceptualized and carried out in empirical analysis.

9.4 Contingency and time

9.4.1 Contingency and time, process thinking, and process-based organization studies

An important question confronting process thinking is "what keeps processes going?" Or "what causes continuity?" Events of processes are evanescent, making time irreversible. Thus the anti-essentialist position of process thinking is quickly confronted with the question of what forms a bridge from one event to the next. Lucretius, being concerned with explaining nature without the intervention of Man, explained the continuity of processes by the fact that atoms, through friction, get attached to one another, and that an emerging form, created by atoms, tended to attract more atoms, thus consolidating the form. Later process thinkers have turned to the associative powers of humans as the forces that keep processes going from one moment to the next.

Lucretius' atomic world was an open one, where the becoming of almost anything was possible. This left him with the problem of explaining how some things acquire consistent form, such as human beings, rain, and mountains. Consistent form was not possible in a world of disconnected flows of atoms. Thus Lucretius suggested the notion of *clinamen* (Lucretius, 2004: 41), which marks the moment at which atoms begin to swerve and things begin to take form. In chemistry, Prigogine (1996: 10) observed the deviation of processes without any observable reason for change, which he attributed to probability. Importantly, as things begin to take form, they attract flows that add to that form. Thus, form generates form, although the process is contingent, as new clinamen may occur.

The natural worlds of the early philosophers were not entangled with human action and understanding, hence processes were not seen to be influenced by human memory or intentions. More recent philosophers, such as Whitehead, Bergson, and Deleuze, while being influenced by Lucretius' writings, developed theories that took account of human meaning construction and the role of time. Importantly, continuity is achieved through the creation of abstractions, which endure from one moment to the next. Bergson (1988) argued that as humans we live in "pure durée," in which it is impossible to separate a seamless experience without the distinctions available to conscious reflection. From a seamless, moving world, human actors create abstractions and categories (such as markets, technologies, brands, institutions, organizations, etc.) which enable a sense of recognizability and regularity.

Still, clinamen is always possible, and processes may change, as "it belongs to the nature of a being that it holds a potential for every becoming" (Whitehead, 1929/1978). Thus, processes harbour contingencies, something which made it possible for Whitehead to speak of "creative advance," or the achievement of novelty (Hosinski, 1993). A key point is that although contingencies are constitutive of processes, they are not settled in advance. Rather they are latent and inherently uncertain. Although they may appear decisive to actors, their decisiveness cannot be assessed by actors at the time they make their selection, but can only be guessed at and brought into focus by actors. Choices are made as enacted working hypotheses, directed at how the world may possibly become. In Schutz's (1967: 59) words, "Every projection of action is rather a phantasying of action, that is, a phantasying of spontaneous activity, but not the activity itself. It is an intuitive advance picturing which may or may not include belief, and, if it does, can believe positively or negatively or with any degree of certainty."

In phenomenology, contingencies exist not as factors that influence the course of events, but rather as "horizons" (Heidegger, 1927) of possibilities from which actors draw in their phantasying (Schutz, 1967) of possible future actions. From horizons of lived experience, abstractions are made and converted into actual possibilities that are projected as possible futures, which become new horizons in turn with the passing of time. Projection onto a possible future is based on what is meaningful to actors from past experience. This is what confers the status of contingency upon these factors. Thus actors have some leeway in their choice of what to retain from the past, while at the same time being temporary products of that very past. However, human actors also have the competence to move on with a course of action while bracketing off other courses of action as future possibilities. Thus actors and things are products of their histories, but they are products that could have turned out differently. They could have turned out differently, not only because external conditions could have turned out differently, but also because they could have made different choices, producing different effects, which in turn would have made different horizons (Heidegger, 1927) of choice possible.

Whereas a traditional contingency theory of organizations (e.g. Pfeffer and Salancik, 1978) considers contingency as a spatial phenomenon, process-based organization studies considers contingency in time. In studies of organization and innovation, Van de Ven et al. (1999), for example, identified what they call cycles of convergent action and outcome events. Convergent behaviour, they argue, happens as choices are made to narrow development efforts towards a specific technical design or market niche for a given technology (1999: 204). Such decisions represent a transition from random to more linked events. In their papers on organizations and innovation, Akrich et al. (2002) observe that even insignificant decisions may turn out to be crucial for the shape that innovations take when they are launched on the market. A similar "clinamen logic" of contingency is also found in Lanzara and Morner (2005), who studied how the Open Source Software (OSS) development processes, towards which thousands of distributed users contribute, branch off as a result of the source code chosen. Source code contains basic programming rules that run the software and thus serve as temporary ordering around which development activities take place in OSS processes. Importantly, source codes may change as a result of software developments that were not anticipated at the time of the formulating of the source codes.

Although things like source code and other technologies, as well as rules (March, 1994) are binding on human actors to some extent, there is always an element of choice in the course of action to pursue. By the same token, a choice is also a non-choice in the sense that by choosing one course of action, a choice is made not to pursue another. The future is not known (Weick, 1995) because the possible effects of choosing another course of action cannot be evaluated (March, 1994). Therefore decisions in the present, while informed by the past, are oriented towards a *possible* future (Emirbayer and Mische, 1998), while other possible futures are considered. Even when managers are constrained by existing technologies they do not wish to change for economic reasons, they have virtual—but nonetheless real (Deleuze, 2004)—possibilities open to them. As time forces choices and non-choices upon them, actors create contingencies for future courses of action.

9.4.2 Contingency and time, ANT, and Callon's scallops

Contingency figures in ANT as the tentative yet consequential fixing of relationships between actors. Like Whitehead's process framework, major works in ANT are based on the assumption of a world where the identities of entities are not given at the outset, but become recognized as actors engage in interaction. Latour (2005) borrows explicitly from Whitehead (1929/ 1978) in using the term "propositions" to conceptualize how actors interact intentionally with other entities; an interaction from which actors and entities come to mutually define their roles ("enrolment") and qualities. His use of propositions is well articulated in his analysis of Pasteur's "discovery" of lactic yeast, describing how Pasteur interacted recursively with the substances involved in his experiments. Sometimes Pasteur would experiment based on hypotheses of what might happen. At other times the experiments would "speak back at him," forcing him to alter his course of experimentation. Sometimes he would be in charge, at other times the substances seemed to be in charge. Together they formed processes that separated, then blended, then emerged as something altogether different (Hernes, 2007).

The analytical assumptions of Callon's study correspond largely to those found in the kind of process thinking briefly described here. Similar to Lucretius's view, Callon assumes that there are flows, which while initially unconnected, may be made to converge given certain conditions. This convergence is mediated by attempts by human actors to impose order on the various flows, or bend the flows in their direction. The results of their efforts are sometimes unanticipated, and sometimes outside their control.

Callon's study illustrates a number of contingent factors, the most noticeable contingencies being found in what he calls "obligatory passage points" (Callon, 1986). Obligatory passage points serve to establish the identities of actors in relation to the network, and thus serve to assess their indispensability to the network. Unless actors pass the obligatory passage points, they are not enrolled into the network. If they do become enrolled, they modify the network by their presence and through the work of defining their identity and allocating their roles. An important obligatory passage point in Callon's account relates to the strength of the connection between larvae and their anchorage. Their ability to do so influences the technology used to ensure their cooperation in the project, and might also have a bearing on the roles of the fishermen and their project associations:

> Faced with these silent mutinies of scallops and fishermen, the strategy of the three researchers begins to wobble. Is anchorage an obligatory passage point? Even scientific colleagues become sceptical. The three researchers have now to deal with growing doubt on the part of their laboratory director and the organizations which had agreed to finance the experiment. Not only does the state of beliefs fluctuate with a controversy but the identity and characteristics of the implicated actors change as well. (Callon, 1986: 220)

The idea of obligatory passage points, used commonly in ANT studies, constitutes an empirical approach to contingency in processes. Obligatory passage points offer the possibility of drawing conclusions about why an actor has failed or not failed to be part of an actor-network. Compared to contingency as defined in phenomenology, where actors are seen to choose from horizons of possibilities, the notion of obligatory passage points, being tied to empirical actuality, seems somewhat limited. This reservation about ANT as a candidate for organization studies will be developed in the next section.

9.5 The making of meaning, process thinking, and ANT

In discussing the aspect of contingency and time above, the question is raised "What causes durability?" For example, Whitehead (1929/1978, 1933/1967), who conceptualized process as the becoming of events, located continuity in the immanence of events and the formation of abstractions. Works in phenomenology and pragmatism, both of which locate continuity in the meaning that actors attach to their actions, ascribe durability to the temporary stabilization of meaning structures. Meaning structures (Heidegger, 1927; Schutz, 1967) signify heterogeneous wholes that actors activate as a means to provide meaning to their actions. They may be compared with what Whitehead called enduring objects (Whitehead, 1929/1978: 211) which he defined as complexes of related material and non-material entities (Whitehead, 1920: 25). Whereas Whitehead conceived events as perpetually perishing, enduring objects are sufficiently stable to be identified as something that changes. Like actor-networks, meaning structures are heterogeneous configurations activated through articulation between their constituent parts. Actors operate within meaning structures and form part of them. Hence meaning structures are not to be seen as interpretative schemas through which human actors make sense of the world around them. Rather actors (human, material, and conceptual) form part of the meaning structures within which they operate.

Heidegger (1927), Foucault (1994), and Laclau and Mouffe (1985) extended thinking about meaning structures to include the idea of *articulation* between elements. Articulation takes place based on a sense of the unit *and* the whole, and is not exclusively a process of building the whole from its elements. In fact in Heidegger's thinking, while the unit takes part in building up the whole, it can only be perceived *through* the whole (Heidegger, 1927: 182). Although meaning structures cannot be seen in their totality, they can be sensed sufficiently in their totality. Heidegger (2000) uses the example of a school, which may be understood as a meaning structure. We can sense what the school "is," as a whole made up of many different parts. We may point at a school and say "There it is," and others will understand what we mean. We can see classrooms, children playing in the school yard, blackboards, teachers, books and pencils, etc. Still, the school as a whole cannot be seen, but can only be sensed in its fullness. Yet when we speak of a school we have a mutual understanding of what we mean, and the meaning of the school as a whole enables us to articulate elements within the school. Because we know that it is a school we can articulate, for example, the relationship between classrooms and pupils, and between blackboards and teachers.

Peirce (1878) described meaning structures from the perspective of time and situated actions by pointing to the act of playing a piece of music, in which each note represents an instant pertaining to that very note. A note may be present at an instant from which the past and future are both absent. It is different with the tune, Peirce insists. A tune occupies a certain time, during which only portions of it are played. To perceive the tune there must be some continuity of consciousness which makes the events of a lapse of time present to the listener. Thus, "Thought is a thread of tune running through the succession of our sensations" (Peirce, 1878: 290). The tune is the meaning that forms the context for the tone, and the tone forms part of the overall meaning. Thus there is an insoluble relationship between the tone and the tune, as between the part and the whole (Peirce, 1998).

Meaning structures enable meaning through the variety of possible articulations between elements. The fact that they exhibit more possibilities than what are actualized is what makes them meaningful to actors. Although meaning structures are made up of human as well as non-human actors, choice between different articulations based on assessment of the meaning associated with them is reserved to human actors. Human actors are able to play on a repertoire of articulations, and while engaging or focusing on some articulations they may keep other possible articulations open. In Weick's (2001) words, sense may be constructed from an indefinite number of plausible maps that can be constructed. The totality of articulations, some of which are actualized, others of which are left open as possibilities, provides a level of meaning that transcends local connections in a network.

The idea of meaning structures is analytically compatible with ANT, which is based on Greimas's semiotics, as mentioned above. Greimas's semiotic model addresses the relationship between the whole and its parts, in which parts may reveal themselves as persons, concepts, or material objects. ANT also works between the whole and the parts as actors connect into intelligible wholes (Latour, 2005). In ANT, however, meaning is located at the level of connections between actors, and relates to actors' interests in their respective connections. Hence the use of terms such as interessement, which aims to ensure that actors' interests are aligned in the network. When the actor's interest ceases to exist, the connection breaks down, because there is no meaning that transcends the local interest of the actor. This follows logically from the definition of actor-networks as made up of local orderings (Hoholm, 2009), illustrated in Latour's (1993) reading of organizations through the lens of local orderings:

> What, for example, is the size of IBM, or the Red Army, or the French Ministry of Education, or the world market? To be sure, these are all actors of great size, since they mobilize hundreds of thousands or even millions of agents. Their amplitude must therefore stem from causes that absolutely surpass the small collectives of the past. However, if we wander about inside IBM, if we follow the chains of command of the Red Army, if we inquire in the corridors of the Ministry of Education, if we study the process of selling and buying a bar of soap, we never leave the local level. We are always in interaction with four or five people; the building superintendent always has his territory well staked out; the directors' conversations sound just like those of the employees; as for the salespeople, they go on and on giving change and filling out their invoices. (Latour, 1993: 121)

Latour's observation suggests that once we begin to study the inside of organizations, we are not likely to see "the organizations," which remain constructs for facilitating analysis, if anything. What we do see are actions and people, interconnected largely through associations, in ways that make their connections more or less robust (Hernes, 2007).

In Callon's study, the opportunity to consider the broader meaning of the network is offered by the idea of problematization. The problematization of the network took the form of reports and analyses written by the researchers upon their return from Japan, in which they disclosed the impressions of their trip and the future projects they wished to launch. The central question they asked, according to Callon, was whether the experience in Japan was transposable to France, or more precisely, could larvae anchor themselves to collectors and grow undisturbed and sheltered from predators in St Brieuc Bay? The problematization that Callon focuses on is reduced to connections between, for example, the larvae and the collectors. The meaning of being part of the network is not elevated to a broader structure of meaning that would make sense in its wholeness *and* its parts.

The fact that ANT studies do not consider broader meaning structures explains why they sometimes conclude their analyses with network failure arising from the breakdown of individual connections. Consequently, when the larvae in Callon's paper, some years into the experiment, no longer adhere to the collectors, and fishermen break the rules by ceding to the temptation of a great Christmas Eve catch, Callon interprets it as "dissidence" and failure in the sense of broken network connections. The fishermen, for example, are seen as pursuing short-term economic goals rather than the long-term goal of a sustainable income. Hence Callon concludes that enrolment is rarely easy, as every process and every actor can break down or betray the enroller, as the ability to mobilize resources and forces is crucial (Hoholm, 2009).

ANT seems to rely on the idea that local disruption implies the overall collapse, downsizing, or reconfiguration of the network. The notion of meaning structures, on the other hand, implies that actors act out of a sense of wholeness as well as local articulation. This point becomes important if we accept Heidegger's (1927: 182) point that parts can only be seen through the whole. It opens the possibility that although actors may experience local disruption, they may remain connected to one another or to the whole because it makes sense from a perspective of wholeness. In cases where ANT might predict collapse of the network, actors may refer their work to a meaning structure that transcends the local level. In a sense, the idea of meaning structures offers a greater degree of plasticity to the network.

The insistence upon symmetry between material and human actors forces ANT to consider a flat ontology, illustrated by the title "How to keep the social flat" of one of the chapters in Latour's (2005) book *Re-assembling the Social*. The title is suggestive of "higher structural levels appearing merely as figments of actors' imaginations, as abstractions they make from their personal contexts, which in reality can be reduced to handfuls of mediators with whom they associate" (Elder-Vass, 2008: 465–6). Although ANT insists upon symmetrical treatment between human and non-human actors, however, it does not mean that asymmetry is excluded. It merely means that asymmetry is not to be taken as a starting point of analysis. As shown in ANT analyses, asymmetry may well emerge through the work of translation performed by actors. In other words, asymmetry shows itself through the work of mutual translation.

A key question is whether non-human actors can take part in the articulation of meaning structures in ways that transcend the level of connections between actors. That would imply that non-human actors convey meaning of articulations that represent virtual—but nonetheless real (Deleuze, 2004)—possibilities. It would imply that non-human actors, such as devices, convey a diversity of possible articulations in the meaning structure. Process-based views in organization studies (e.g. March, 1994) suggest that this is the case; that multiple sources of meaning patterns are open to actors. Translated back to ANT studies, this implies that the circulation of objects that provides for meaning conveys meaning of wholeness as well as of individual connections. With a focus on how wholeness is conveyed and experienced, a symmetrical view of actors may still be taken as a starting point, and one of the prime principles of ANT will not be violated.

9.6 Conclusion

ANT exhibits important traits of process thinking. More precisely, it emphasizes the ordering of heterogeneous wholes of entities in the making, making it a candidate for process-based organization studies. Its insistence on symmetry between human and non-human actors, and a corresponding tendency to seek to explain failure rather than continuity reflects a flat ontology, and would appear to reduce its usefulness as a theory of organization. To assume that a network breaks down because local connections break down does not hold for a process-based organization theory, because it ignores the possibility that meaning is also located beyond connections. Given that a guiding principle of ANT studies is to follow the work of actors assembling seemingly disparate and heterogeneous entities into *intelligible* assemblies (Latour, 2005), it should not compromise ANT principles to grant human actors the capacity for relating their work to wider meaning structures, and not limit it to the meaning of singular connections. Both material and human actors may well be seen as taking part in conveying wholeness in the work of connecting and reconnecting such intelligible assemblies. Conceptualizing wholeness would take ANT a step closer to becoming a most useful process-based theory of organization.

Note

I am grateful to several people, in particular Susse Georg, Kristian Kreiner, Kjell Tryggestad, Hari Tsoukas, and two anonymous reviewers, for their helpful comments.

References

Akrich, M., Callon, M., & Latour, B. (2002*a*). The key to success in innovation, part I: The art of interessement, *International Journal of Innovation Management*, 6(2), 187–206.

Akrich, M., Callon M., & Latour, B. (2002*b*). The key to success in innovation, part II: The art of choosing good spokespersons, *International Journal of Innovation Management*, 6(2), 207–225.

Bakken, T. & Hernes, T. (2006). Organizing is both a noun and a verb: Weick meets Whitehead, *Organization Studies*, 27(11), 1599–161.

Bergson, H. (1988). *Matter and Memory*, New York: Zone Books.

Bergson, H. (1998). The idea of duration, in D. Browning & W. T. Myers (eds) *Philosophers of Process*, Fordham University Press, 137–86.

Calas, M. B. & Smircich, L. (1999). Past postmodernism? Reflections and tentative directions, *Academy of Management Review*, 24(4), 649–71.

Callon, M. (1986). Some elements of a sociology of translation: Domestication of the scallops and the fishermen of St Brieuc Bay, in J. Law (ed.) *Power, Action and Belief. A New Sociology of Knowledge?* London: Routledge & Kegan Paul, 196–223.

Callon, M. (1991). Techno-economic networks and irreversibility, in J. Law (ed.) *A Sociology of Monsters: Essays on Power, Technology and Domination*, London: Routledge, 132–61.

Callon, M. (1992). The dynamics of techno-economic networks, in R. Coombs, P. Saviotti, & V. Walsh (eds) *Technological Change and Company Strategies: Economic and Sociological Perspectives*, San Diego: Harcourt Brace Jovanovich, Publishers, 72–102.

Callon, M. (1995). Technological conception and adoption network: Lessons for the CTA practitioner, in A. Rip, T. J. Misa, & J. Schot (eds) *Managing Technology in Society: The Approach of Constructive Technology Assessment*, London and New York: Pinter Publishers, 307–31.

Callon, M. (1998). An essay on framing and overflowing: Economic externalities revisited by sociology, in M. Callon (ed.) *The Laws of the Markets*, Blackwell Publishers/The Sociological Review, 244–69.

Callon, M. (1999). Actor-network theory: The market test, in J. Law and J. Hassard (eds) *Actor Network Theory and After*, Oxford: Blackwell, 181–92.

Callon, M. & Latour, B. (1981). Unscrewing the Big Leviathan: How actors macrostructure reality and how sociologists help them to do so, in K. Knorr Cetina & A. Cicourel (eds) *Advances in Social Theory and Methodology: Toward an Integration of Micro and Macro-Sociologies*, London, Routledge & Kegan Paul.

Carlsen, A. (2006). Organizational becoming as dialogic imagination of practice: The case of the indomitable Gauls, *Organization Science*, 17(1), 132–49.

Chia, R. (1999). A "Rhizomic" model of organizational change and transformation: Perspective from a metaphysics of change, *British Journal of Management*, 10, 209–27.

Chia, R. and King, I. W. (1998). The organizational structuring of novelty, *Organization*, 5(4), 461–78.

Chia, R. & Langley, A. (2005). Call for papers to the The First Organization Studies Summer Workshop on Theorizing Process in Organizational Research, 12–13 June 2005, Santorini, Greece.

Chia, R. & Holt, R. (2009). *Strategy without Design*, Cambridge: Cambridge University Press.

Clegg, S. R., Kornberger, M., & Rhodes, K. (2005). Learning/Becoming/Organizing, *Organization*, 12(2), 147–67.

Cooper, R. (2005). Relationality, *Organization Studies*, 26(11), 1689–710.

Cooper, R. & Law, J. (1995). Organization: Distal and proximal views, *Research in the Sociology of Organizations*, 13, 237–74.

Czarniawska, B. (1997). *Narrating the Organization: Dramas of Institutional Identity*. Chicago: University of Chicago Press.

Czarniawska, B. (2004). On time, space, and action nets, *Organization*, 11(6), 773–91.

Czarniawska, B. (2009). STS meets MOS, *Organization*, 16(1), 155–60.

Czarniawska, B. & Hernes, T. (eds) (2005). *Actor-Network Theory and Organizing*, Stockholm: Liber Ekonomi and CBS Press.

Czarniawska, B. & Sevón, G. (eds) (1996). *Translating Organizational Change*, Berlin: de Gruyter.

Czarniawska, B. & Sevón, G. (eds) (2005). *Global Ideas: How Ideas, Objects and Practices Travel in the Global Economy*, Stockholm: Liber.

Deleuze, G. (2004). *Difference and Repetition*, London and New York: Continuum Publishing Group.

Dewey, J. (1934). *Art as Experience*, New York: Minton.

Elder-Vass, D. (2008). Searching for realism, structure and agency in Actor Network Theory, *The British Journal of Sociology*, 59(3), 455–73.

Emirbayer, M. (1997). Manifesto for a Relational Sociology, *American Journal of Sociology*, 103(2), 281–317.

Emirbayer, M. & Mische, A. (1998). What is agency? *American Journal of Sociology*, 103, 1180–98.

Feldman, M. & B. T. Pentland (2003). Organizational routines as a source of flexibility and change, *Administrative Science Quarterly*, 48, 94–118.

Feldman, M. and Pentland, B. (2005). Organizational routines and the macro-actor, in B. Czarniawska & T. Hernes (eds) *Actor-Network Theory and Organizing*, Stockholm: Liber, 105–31.

Foucault, M. (1994). *The Order of Things: An Archeology of the Human Sciences*, New York: Vintage Books.

Gherardi, S. & Nicolini, D. (2002). Learning in a constellation of interconnected practices: Canon or dissonance? *Journal of Management Studies*, 39(4), 419–36.

Greimas, A. J. & Courtés, J. (1982). *Semiotics and Language: An Analytical Dictionary*, Bloomington, IN: Indiana University Press.

Hargadon, A. & Douglas, Y. (2001). When innovations meet institutions: Edison and the design of the electric light, *Administrative Science Quarterly*, 46, 476–501.

Hartshorne, C. (1965). Introduction, in D. Young (ed.) *Philosophers of Process*, New York: Random House.

Heidegger, M. (1927). *Being and Time*, Oxford: Blackwell.

Heidegger, M. (2000). *Introduction to Metaphysics*, New Haven: Yale University Press.

Hernes, T. (2007). *Understanding Organization as Process: Theory for a Tangled World*, London: Routledge.

Hoholm, T. (2009). The contrary forces of innovation: An ethnography of innovation processes in the food industry. Doctoral Dissertation, Norwegian School of Management, Oslo.

Hosinski, T. E. (1993). *Stubborn Fact and Creative Advance: An Introduction to the Metaphysics of Alfred North Whitehead*, Lanham, MD: Rowman & Littlefield.

James, W. (1890). *The Principles of Psychology*, New York: Dover.

James W. (1977). *A Pluralistic Universe*, Cambridge, MA: Harvard University Press.

Laclau, E. & Mouffe, C. (1985) *Hegemony and Socialist Strategy*, London: Verso.

Lanzara, G. & Morner, M. (2005). Artifacts' rule: How organizing happens in open source software projects, in B. Czarniawska and T. Hernes (eds) *Actor-Network Theory and Organizing*, Stockholm: Liber Ekonomi, 75–104.

Latour, B. (1987). *Science in Action*, Cambridge, MA: Harvard University Press.

Latour, B. (1993). *We Have Never Been Modern*, Cambridge, MA: Harvard University Press.

Latour, B. (1996). *Aramis, or the Love of Technology*, Harvard University Press.

Latour, B. (1999). *Pandora's Hope: Essays on the Reality of Science Studies*, Cambridge, MA: Harvard University Press.

Latour, B. (2005). *Reassembling the Social: An Introduction to Actor-Network Theory*, Oxford: Oxford University Press.

Latour, B. & Woolgar, S. (1979). *Laboratory Life: The Social Construction of Scientific Facts*, Los Angeles: Sage.

Law, J. (1994). *Organizing Modernity*, Oxford: Blackwell.

Law, J. (2004). *After Method: Mess in Social Science Research*, Oxon: Routledge.

Law, J. & Hassard, J. (eds) (1999). *Actor-Network Theory and After*, Oxford: Blackwells.

Lucretius, T. C. (2004). *On the Nature of Things*, New York: Dover.

Luhmann, N. (1995). *Social Systems*, Stanford: Stanford University Press.

March, J. G. (1994). *A Primer on Decision Making: How Decisions Happen*, New York: The Free Press.

Mead, G. H. (1934/1967). *Mind, Self, and Society*, Chicago: Chicago University Press.

Middleton, D. & Brown, S. (2005). Net-working on a neonatal intensive care unit: The baby as virtual object, in B. Czarniawska & T. Hernes (eds) *Actor-Network Theory and Organizing*, Stockholm: Liber, 376–402.

Peirce, C. S. (1878). How to make our ideas clear, *Popular Science Monthly*, 12, 286–302.

Peirce, C. S. (1998). *The Essential Writings*, New York: Prometheus Books.

Pfeffer, J. & Salancik, G. R. (1978). *The External Control of Organizations: A Resource Dependence Perspective*, New York: Harper and Row.

Prigogine, I. (1996). *The End of Certainty*, New York: Free Press.

Rescher, N. (1996). *Process Metaphysics: An Introduction to Process Philosophy*, New York: State University of New York Press.

Rogers, E. (1995). *Diffusion of Innovations*, 4th edn, New York: Free Press.

Rubino, C. A. (2001). The consolations of uncertainty: Time, change, and complexity, *Emergence*, 4(1/2), 200–6.

Russell, B. (1946). *History of Western Philosophy*, London: Routledge.

Schutz, A. (1967). *The Phenomenology of the Social World*, London: Heinemann Educational Books.

Schutz, A. (1982). *Life Forms and Meaning Structure*, London: Routledge and Kegan Paul.

Serres, M. (1980/1982). *The Parasite*, Baltimore, MR: Johns Hopkins University Press.

Sherburne, D. W. (1966). *A Key to Whitehead's Process and Reality*, New York: Macmillan.

Skærbæk, P. & Tryggestad, K. (2009). The role of accounting devices in performing corporate strategy, *Accounting, Organizations and Society*, 35, 108–24.

Styhre, A. (2004). Rethinking knowledge: A Bergsonian critique of the notion of tacit knowledge, *British Journal of Management*, 15, 177–88.

Tsoukas, H. & Chia, R. (2002). On organizational becoming: Rethinking organizational change, *Organization Science*, 13(5), 567–82.

Van de Ven, A. H., Polley, D., Garud, R., & Venkatamaran, S. (1999). *The Innovation Journey*, New York: Oxford University Press.

Weick, K. E. (1979). *The Social Psychology of Organizing*, 2nd edn, New York: Random House.

Weick, K. E. (1995). *Sensemaking in Organizations*, Thousand Oaks, CA: Sage.

Weick, K. E. (2001). *Making Sense of the Organization*, Oxford: Blackwell.

Weick, K. E., Sutcliffe, K. M., & Obstfeld, D. (2005). Organizing and the process of sensemaking, *Organization Science*, 16(4), 409–21.

Whitehead, A. N. (1920). *The Concept of Nature*, Cambridge: Cambridge University Press.

Whitehead, A. N. (1929/1978). *Process and Reality*, New York: The Free Press.

Whitehead, A. N. (1933/1967). *Adventures of Ideas*, New York: The Free Press.

10

Organizational Learning through Problem Absorption: A Processual View

Sergey E. Osadchiy, Irma Bogenrieder, and Pursey P. M. A. R. Heugens

Abstract: In organizations, existing codified rules are often used as the basis for solving new problems even when this means stretching those rules. Such "absorption" of new problems by rules reduces the need to explore and develop new solutions and to encode those solutions into new rules. In the present chapter we examine the phenomenon of "problem absorption" more closely from the process perspective and conceptualize it as a micro-level form of "semantic learning." Contrary to previous literature, we argue that problem absorption does not necessarily reinforce existing rules and prevent the search for alternatives. We thus contribute to the literature on organizational learning and rule dynamics by showing how under certain conditions the cumulative effects of semantic learning via repeated absorption of novel problems by formal rules can give rise to higher-level learning that has the potential to transform the organization's rule system.

Organizational learning is often conceptualized as a process by which organizations develop rules, procedures, and routines for solving recurring organizational problems (Cyert and March, 1992; Levitt and March, 1988; Nelson and Winter, 1982; Schulz, 1998; Weick, 1991). Over time, a repertory of "tried-and-tested" solutions is built up in organizational memory (Walsh and Ungson, 1991), and, insofar as these can be used to deal with or "absorb" new problems, the perceived need to search for alternative solutions is reduced (Levitt and March, 1988). In the literature on the dynamics of organizational rule systems in particular (March et al., 2000), this notion of "problem absorption" has been used to explain why the availability of codified and prescribed solutions to problems in the form of written rules tends to reduce the impetus for further learning and codification efforts (Schulz, 1998).

In the present chapter we examine the phenomenon of "problem absorption" more closely from the process perspective (e.g., Tsoukas and Chia, 2002), arguing that it need not always imply the absence of organizational learning. On the contrary, we suggest that insofar as it involves the ongoing construction and reconstruction of the very meaning of those rules in practice and calls for *reflexivity* on the part of the actors concerned (e.g., Antonacopoulou and Tsoukas, 2002; Archer, 2003), problem absorption may actually constitute a form of organizational learning in its own right. Furthermore, while the extant literature on problem absorption suggests that "[s]tretching old rules to deal with new problems reinforces the old rules" (Schulz, 1998: 853), we propose that such stretching can actually undermine those rules under certain conditions and thereby trigger higher-level organizational learning (Fiol and Lyles, 1985).

The intended contribution of this chapter is twofold. First, although the idea that rules absorb problems has already been introduced and briefly discussed in the literature on rules (Schulz, 1998; March et al., 2000), the concept of problem absorption remains underdeveloped. Our analysis helps to address this gap by reconceptualizing problem absorption as a reflexive process and integrating the concept more strongly with other literature that deals with related phenomena (Corley and Gioia, 2003; Tsoukas and Chia, 2002). Understanding problem absorption by rules is important for organization theory not only because such absorption constitutes a mechanism that limits bureaucratic growth (Schulz, 1998), but also because, as we argue in this chapter, problem absorption can be a source of both lower- and higher-level organizational learning. Thus, our second contribution is to challenge views that associate problem absorption with only lower-level learning (March et al., 2000) or codification traps (Schulz, 1998), by showing how the process of repeated and cumulative problem absorption can induce higher-level learning and thus release the organization from the codification trap. Our arguments suggest opportunities for advancing research on organizational learning through closer attention to learning in bureaucratic contexts.

Building on previous literature, we conceptualize problem absorption as involving reflexive extension of a rule's labeled categories to cases that are markedly different from the prototypical members of those categories (Tsoukas and Chia, 2002), which allows practitioners to maintain the pattern of practice and a sense of order in the face of ambiguity and situational variation. We further argue that problem absorption is a form of "semantic learning" or learning on the basis of meanings that emerges in a subtle and largely unintentional way from organizational members' practical coping (Corley and Gioia, 2003). When rules are extended to new cases repeatedly, semantic learning can become cumulative due to retention of precedents and new understandings in organizational memory (Walsh and Ungson, 1991). We suggest that it can have certain destabilizing effects on the relevant rule or rules and the broader understandings that underpin those rules and support their use in practice (Schatzki, 2006). Rule makers' recognition of these effects through reflection can lead to higher-level organizational learning, unlearning (Tsang and Zahra, 2008), and codification.

10.1 Theoretical background

10.1.1 Problem absorption and rule dynamics

The notion of problem absorption, as developed in the literature on rule dynamics (Schulz, 1998; March et al., 2000), has its roots in the "Carnegie School" research program, with its emphasis on the relationship between "human problem-solving processes" under bounded rationality and "the basic features of organization structure" (March and Simon, 1993: 190). According to this perspective, problem definitions, for example, do not constitute complete or fully accurate representations of all aspects of a problem, but rather simplified models that tend to be already constructed in light of potentially available solutions (March and Simon, 1993; Starbuck, 1983). Furthermore, many solutions, having once been developed through the process of search, become learned responses that can subsequently be routinely applied to similar situations, reducing the search process to the task of matching problems to solutions, and vice versa (Cohen et al., 1972; March and Simon, 1993; Levitt and March, 1988). Thus, an organization gradually accumulates a repertory of decision rules, procedures, and routines for dealing with recurring problems (Cyert and March, 1992; Nelson and Winter, 1982).

The rule dynamics research builds on these ideas, arguing that "[t]oday's rules are often the solution to yesterday's problems" (March et al., 2000: 48). The recognition or "social construction" of problems is sporadic and depends strongly on the allocation of organizational attention to different organizational task domains when performance in those domains falls below aspiration levels (March et al., 2000: 63; see also Cyert and March, 1992; Zhou, 1993). Once a solution to a problem situation has been encoded in a written rule, it is assumed that the rule can also help organizational members to deal with future problems "in a routine way," making such problems "less available for further rule production" (March et al., 2000: 65). This is what is meant by *problem absorption*.

Schulz (1998) identified two problem absorption mechanisms. The first of these, which he called *preemption*, has to do with the reluctance of rule makers to develop new rule-based solutions to a problem when a rule-based solution to the same problem already exists, because doing so could lead to inconsistencies between rules. The second mechanism involves a so-called *codification trap* stemming from the tendency of rule users to "stretch established rules to cope with new problems," which "reinforces the old rules and keeps experience with alternatives inadequate to make them rewarding to use" (Schulz, 1998: 853; see also Levitt and March, 1988). Schulz found indirect empirical support for problem absorption in the tendency for the rate of birth of new rules to decline as the total number of rules in a given domain grew larger. He also found that the rule birth rate increased when other rules were suspended, suggesting that such suspensions allowed problems that had previously been "absorbed" to be "released" and "recycled" into new rules (Schulz, 1998: 855).

In another study, Beck and Kieser (2003) attempted to extend the problem absorption argument to rule revisions, but could not find support for the hypothesis that rates of revision would decline with rule volume. March et al. (2000: 76) have suggested that rules are revised primarily in order to enhance their capacity to absorb new problems, describing this "refinement" process "as a case of learning by rules." Rule revision is also seen as a process through which experiences accumulated through rule use become formally incorporated into the rule (March et al., 2000: 76; see also Beck and Kieser, 2003; Schulz, 2003).

What are the main implications of these arguments and findings for the relationship between problem absorption by rules and organizational learning? Insofar as problem absorption involves *exploitation* of experiences already encoded in extant rules, it may prevent *exploration* of alternative solutions (March, 1991; Schulz, 1998). Note that such exploitation need not imply the absence of learning, since rule users can learn "how to operate within rules, extending the meaning of rules to new situations, molding them to encompass new problems" (March et al., 2000: 53). However, this kind of experiential learning *within* rules is seen as contributing to the stability of those rules (cf. Zhou, 1993), and thus to the codification trap mechanism mentioned above (Levitt and March, 1988; Schulz, 1998). Even when some of these learned experiences are formally incorporated into the rules via the revision process, such revisions may well only serve to further enhance the rule's stability through refinement (Beck and Kieser, 2003; March et al., 2000).

Despite considerable theoretical and empirical progress towards understanding both the problem absorption phenomenon itself, as well as its importance and consequences for organizations, we contend that important gaps in the theoretical treatment of the phenomenon still remain, and that filling those gaps from a process perspective will yield insights that may challenge some of the above conclusions regarding the relationship between problem absorption and organizational learning and change. In particular, extant treatments of problem absorption do not sufficiently address the micro-processes through which absorption occurs, the broader normative and cognitive foundations that underpin the organizational rule system, and the role played by reflexivity of organizational members. In the next section we further elaborate on these issues and explain how adopting a process perspective can both sensitize us to them, as well as provide a way to theorize about them.

10.1.2 A processual view of problem absorption

The meta-theoretical approach that we favor treats organizational rules as components of unfolding organizational practices (Schatzki, 2005, 2006). Moreover, it views the performative dimension (Feldman and Pentland, 2003) of such practices as inescapably open-ended and processual, and as having ontological primacy over the structure/organization/patterning of practice, which is a secondary accomplishment (Schatzki, 2005; Tsoukas and Chia, 2002). In line with this assumption, the meanings of artifacts like written rules are not "given" once and for all but are negotiated in and through practical activity, ever remaining open-ended and in a state of becoming (Tsoukas and Chia, 2002). As Tsoukas (1996) has forcefully argued, drawing on the work of Wittgenstein (1953) and other philosophers and social theorists, the knowledge that informs and directs the flow of practice can never be reduced to such rules, since "correct" use of any rule in a specific case always presupposes an unarticulated background of understandings, expectations, and embodied abilities.

How can this perspective contribute to our understanding of problem absorption? First, it provides a way of going beyond the truism that rules are extended or "stretched" to cope with new cases (Schulz, 1998) and of theorizing about this process. The very notion of "stretching" presupposes not only a view of rule use as involving attempts to subsume particular cases under general categories that correspond to the rule's domain (Schulz, 1998), but also a distinction between prototypical and non-prototypical cases, the former being more representative of a given category than the latter (Tsoukas and Chia, 2002). The "absorption" of a problem by a rule will thus often require "an imaginative projection of a category beyond prototypical cases to marginal ones," which in turn has "the potential of extending the radius of application of the concept, thus transforming it" (Tsoukas and Chia, 2002: 574). This conceptualization opens up new questions about problem absorption, such as the issue of the stability of prototypes, and the long-term effects of such conceptual micro-transformations.

Second, by emphasizing that rules are incomplete and so can never determine their own use (Reynaud, 2005; Tsoukas, 1996), the process perspective encourages us to look beyond the properties of the written rules themselves in analyzing problem absorption and its effects. For example, work on organizational routines and practices suggests that not only rules, but also general background assumptions and understandings about, for example, the nature of the task performed, the social roles of organizational members, organizational goals and priorities, and other relatively "enduring" aspects of organizational context, make an important contribution to the patterning of activities in organizations (e.g., Feldman and Rafaeli, 2002; Schatzki, 2006). This does not imply that all such understandings, if brought into focal awareness and reflected upon (Tsoukas, 1996), will be met with agreement by all participants in the routine or practice, but merely that there is sufficient implicit agreement to sustain mutual expectations and the patterning of activity.[1] Some of these understandings will also correspond to the cognitive and normative foundations underpinning certain sets of rules within the rule system; foundations that develop over time through theorizing and valorizing activities (Heugens and Osadchiy, 2007; Lawrence and Suddaby, 2006).

One of the reasons why these understandings cannot be neglected in the analysis of problem absorption is that they are likely to encompass lessons from past rule use experience, including stories about different prototypical and non-prototypical cases that have already been encountered and any precedents that may have been established (Levitt and March, 1988). As emphasized by Schatzki (2006), the concept of organizational memory[2] is necessary for explaining how general understandings about practice are preserved in organizations (Walsh and Ungson, 1991). While written rules may be regarded as the formal memory of the organization (Heugens and Osadchiy, 2007; Levitt and March, 1988: 327; Schatzki, 2006), it is also important to recognize that "organizations have memories in the form of precedents" (Cyert and March, 1992: 38). An analysis of problem absorption must take both these interdependent memory repositories into account.

Third, the analysis of problem absorption requires clarity in the assumptions regarding the scope for and role of human reflexivity in rule use (Tsoukas and Chia, 2002). While Schulz (1998: 853) suggests that problem absorption by bureaucrats might be "habitual" or the result of training (Merton, 1940), our view is that the constraints of bureaucracy can be mediated by reflexivity on the part of actors (Archer, 2003). Indeed, the view of rules as forming relatively enduring institutional structures with their own emergent causal powers, which constrain and enable the practice of agents (Archer, 1995), can be juxtaposed with the view of rules as "tools" that are "readily available" to practitioners who use them and that gradually come to be "internalized" or "dwelled-in" by those practitioners (Chia and Holt, 2006). While the language of "internalization" may appear to conflate people and rules (cf. Archer, 1995 on Giddens), this criticism need not apply. The analytic distinction between rules and rule users can still be maintained, since there is always a possibility of a "distancing of the individual from the phenomenon apprehended," a reflexive standing back, which characterizes the "occurrent" mode of engagement with the world (Chia and Holt, 2006: 641).

10.2 Problems, rules, reflexivity

The term "organizational problem" can have a variety of meanings, which poses a challenge for abstract theory. Typically, a problem is defined as "an undesirable gap between an expected and an observed state" (Tucker et al., 2002: 124; see also Cowan, 1990: 366). It is generally recognized that problems are social constructs that can be said to "exist" only insofar as they are "recognized as existing" (March et al., 2000: 63). Problem constructions are "imposed [on the ongoing flow of events], but not in total disregard of one's context and constraints" (Weick, 1995: 89). In light of the process perspective, where activity is seen as central to the phenomenon of organization (Schatzki, 2006; Tsoukas and Chia, 2002), it makes sense to conceptualize organizational problems as inextricably linked to activity. Indeed, as pointed out by William Starbuck (1983), organizational problems are often framed as "needs for action."

However, most of the activity that occurs continuously in organizations does not involve the imposition of problems or explicit search processes

(Starbuck, 1983). Rather, it takes place within what Chia and Holt (2006), following Heidegger, called the "dwelling" mode of engagement with the world, where circumstances and objects present themselves as "available" for activity. It is only when there is "a shift from the experience of immersion in projects to a sense that the flow of action has become unintelligible in some way" (Weick et al., 2005: 409) that "problematization" of activity is likely to take place (Emirbayer and Mische 1998: 998). Some elements within the unfolding situation are apprehended as unexpected, novel, or ambiguous, which prevents the continuation of activity in the "dwelling" mode. Instead, subsequent action with regards to the situation must take place within the "building" or "occurrent" mode of engagement, which allows for more disengaged reflexivity (Chia and Holt, 2006), at least until the momentarily disrupted sense of order is restored.

Given this understanding of organizational problems, we may say that a situation that has been problematized is "absorbed" when organizational members find a way of responding to that situation in a manner that both they and others within the organization might recognize as being in accordance with existing formal rules. Moreover, after the response, the situation is no longer regarded as problematic, and therefore does not become a pretext for proposals of new formal rules (Schulz, 1998). We believe that this interpretation of "problem absorption" is consistent with the arguments in the literature on rule dynamics (March et al., 2000; Schulz, 1998).[3]

A further and perhaps crucial point is that an attempt to respond to a situation in accordance with existing rules can generate problems of its own, which might be called *rule-related* problems. Specifically, the situation's novel or ambiguous features can make people wonder, *which* rule (if any) should be applied. Alternatively, or perhaps additionally, it may not be clear *how* a particular rule should be applied. As will hopefully become clear as we consider specific examples, these rule-related problems frequently have to do with categorization (Tsoukas and Chia, 2002). Indeed, difficulties of categorization are often the reason why situations are problematized in the first place (Emirbayer and Mische, 1998). How organizational members cope with such rule-related problems can make the difference between problem absorption and non-absorption. If no rule seems applicable or if some rules cannot be applied in the usual way, it becomes more likely that the response to the situation will be more "ad hoc" (Winter, 2003), improvisatory (Moorman and Miner, 1998) or "non-canonical" (Brown and Duguid, 1991). In some cases, this may entail an officially authorized exception to some rule or even an (unauthorized) rule violation (Lehman and Ramanujam, 2009). These non-absorption responses can alert organizational rule making agencies to the "problem" and motivate them to create new rules or adjust existing ones so as to enable the organization to handle similar problems in a more routine way in the future (Schulz, 1998).

10.2.1 Two examples of problem absorption

To clarify the types of situations that we have in mind, we shall make use of two examples of problem absorption. For the first example, we draw on the experiences of one of this chapter's co-authors in her role as a treasurer of a university department (see also Bogenrieder and Magala, 2007). The part of the treasurer's role relevant to our analysis consisted in evaluating and approving research-related expenditures that were to be financed from the department's budget. The applicant would fill out a form, providing details on the types of expenditure planned (e.g., conference visit, research collaboration, etc.) together with estimates of the expenses, which was then forwarded to the treasurer, who had to sign the application for approval. The treasurer was formally responsible for verifying that the expenditures were relevant to the department's research needs. In doing so, she naturally also had to take into account the department's financial situation. The treasurer's decisions were formally reviewed by the university's financial department, which made sure that these decisions were lawful and that the total expenditures remained within the budgetary limits.

The application form specified different categories of expenditure together with some rules and standards for ensuring that the expenditures remained relevant and the budget was not exceeded. In describing the case, we are specifically concerned with the category labeled "conference presentations." Recall that a case can be more or less prototypical relative to a category (Rosch and Lloyd, 1978, cited in Tsoukas and Chia, 2002). In this example, a prototypical application falling under the "conference presentations" category would involve a department member attending a conference with the aim of presenting a paper. The written rules stipulated that the category covered both conference fees and costs of travel and accommodation. However, as the treasurer was soon to discover, some conferences also required participants to be full members of the association linked to the conference, such as the AOM or EGOS. Attendance of such conferences thus entailed not only the usual conference registration fees, but also membership fees. This was the first problem or *non-prototypical* case faced by the treasurer, since the rules on the application form said nothing about membership fees.[4] Thus, the treasurer had to decide whether or not to extend the "conference presentations" category and interpret it as also covering membership fees. After careful reflection and consultation, the treasurer chose to extend the original category.

This example is a case of problem absorption, since the treasurer brought a non-prototypical request within the domain of existing rules (Schulz, 1998) and handled it by extending one of the categories. The problem was rule-related, since the request revealed (what the treasurer recognized as) a problematic ambiguity of the rules. The treasurer's decision resulted in a foregone opportunity for rule revision, such as the establishment of a separate category and procedure for membership fees (both related and unrelated to conferences). Later on in this chapter, we shall describe how this decision had the unintended consequence of attracting further non-prototypical cases for the treasurer cope with.

The second example is drawn from a historical study of the Rotterdam port (Van Driel and Bogenrieder, 2009). The focal rule is a by-law for regulating the use of berths in the Rotterdam port, adopted in 1883. The by-law stipulated that only "liner services" or "ships maintaining a scheduled service for many different customers" could be granted the right to a permanent berth (Van Driel and Bogenrieder, 2009: 654). The first truly problematic case in the history of the by-law involved the firm Wm. H. Müller & Co., which had filed a request for a permanent berth in 1891. While the municipal executive was in principle willing to grant the request, other important actors opposed such a decision on the grounds that Müller had initially failed to name specific ships that would use the berth, which was one of the official requirements. The case thus illustrates the role of disagreement between actors in the social construction of organizational problems. When Müller eventually did provide the details of the ships, further questions were raised about whether those ships were in fact true "liner services." In all likelihood, the actors viewed "the short sea traffic that dominated the Rotterdam liner shipping scene" as the prototype for the "liner service" category (Van Driel and Bogenrieder, 2009: 657). The prototypical "liners" were thus daily or weekly services, while the ships mentioned by Müller were primarily bi-weekly services (2009: 657). However, since the by-law did not explicitly specify the meaning of "liner service," it was also possible to interpret it in Müller's favor. In the end, the city council agreed to grant the request, thereby extending the radius of the category beyond the prototype (Tsoukas and Chia, 2002).

10.2.2 The role of reflexivity

As these examples illustrate, problem absorption is about "special cases that have to be fitted to a given repertoire of actions" (Levinthal and Rerup, 2006: 507). Actors recognize a case as ambiguous or non-prototypical when they are attentive to *both* the similarity *and* the difference (Weick and Sutcliffe, 2006: 516) between the prototypical cases that they have experienced in the past and the case they are faced with in the present. That is, the "systems of relevances" (Schutz, 1964, cited in Emirbayer and Mische, 1998: 979) acquired by actors through practical experience directs their attention to specific similarities and the differences that might be relevant in their work. For example, the similarity between membership fees and other conference-related expenses suggests to the treasurer the possibility of applying existing rules, while the fact that such fees have until now not been financed from the budget makes her hesitate. When a case is non-prototypical relative to a rule's domain, this can make actors uncertain as to *whether* the rule applies to the case. When a case is non-prototypical relative to a category that serves as a criterion for what should be done according to the rule, such as the "liner service" category in the port example, this can make actors uncertain as to *how* the rule applies to the case (i.e. which action would be consistent with the rule).

The fact that the non-prototypical case cannot be immediately subsumed leads actors to problematize the situation and to engage with the case more reflexively or mindfully (Levinthal and Rerup, 2006). An important component of this reflexive engagement will be what Emirbayer and Mische (1998: 971) called the "practical-evaluative element" of agency, which "entails the capacity of actors to make practical and normative judgments among alternative possible trajectories of action". Note that among these trajectories may be the action of *not* subsuming the case under any rule-related category. Thus, problem absorption is not inevitable and reflection can enable the exercise of agency with regard to whether and how the problem is absorbed.

Of course, in organizations with many rules, the frequency with which rules will be cited as legitimating reasons for action is likely to be quite high (Ocasio, 1999: 393). Rules will consequently tend to be seen as being "more or less exhaustive" and "gapless" (Weber, 1978: 958, 656, cited in Nass, 1986). Given these background understandings, actors may face strong normative pressure towards problem absorption that can constrain their agency. Empirical research can shed more light on the agentic choice between absorption and non-absorption, which is no doubt an important topic, but one that is beyond the scope of this chapter.

Even when the problem is absorbed, reflexive agency can still matter in the process. In reflecting on the possibility of subsuming the case under different rule-related categories, what is relevant is not only the similarities and differences between the case and the prototypical instances of the categories (Tsoukas and Chia, 2002), but also the overall variability of past instances still belonging to each of those categories (cf. Holland et al., 1986: 185–8). Both the sense of a category's overall variability and understandings about prototypical instances are developed through the use of the category in practice and can be brought to bear on the present situation through organizational remembering (Feldman and Feldman, 2006), in which actors' personal experiences, written organizational records (Walsh and Ungson, 1991), and storytelling (Boje, 1991) can all play a role. For example, there was ambiguity in the Müller case as to whether the ships in question could be categorized as "liners" or "irregular." In the debates that followed, actors considered the prototypical examples of liner ships and noted the variability within the category between daily and weekly services.

The last point we wish to highlight here is that reflection need not be completely retrospective, but will in most instances also cover the possible actions to be taken if a given rule is applied to the case and the anticipated consequences of these actions. This is the core of Emirbayer and Mische's (1998) practical-evaluative element. As Levinthal and Rerup (2006: 507) observed, "an important skill in the context of bureaucratic organizations is the art of manipulating the label or category with which a given request or initiative is encoded to elicit a desired outcome." Thus, reflexive evaluation of courses of action and anticipated outcomes in light of personal projects, understandings about organizational goals, and the teleological ordering of the relevant practice (Schatzki, 2006), clearly matters in problem absorption.

10.2.3 Stabilizing consequences

In the short run, problem absorption may be seen as contributing to the stability of both the individual rule and the rule system as a whole. First, extending the rule to new problems will tend to increase both its pragmatic and cognitive legitimacy (Suchman, 1995); it not only serves to reaffirm the rule's usefulness to the organization, but also contributes to its becoming increasingly taken for granted as part of organizational life, so that its abandonment seems almost unthinkable (Zucker, 1977). Second, problem absorption is an experiential learning process, whereby rule users become more skillful in interpreting and applying the rule, which in turn makes them less likely to challenge it (Zhou, 1993: 1138).

Third, problem absorption via rule extension to non-prototypical cases leaves far less scope for exploration of novel responses that could potentially be encoded into new rules (Schulz, 1998). Fourth, it is important to remember that the organizational rule system "is not some abstract chart but one of the crucial instruments by which groups perpetuate their power and control in organizations: groups struggle to constitute structures in order that they may become constituting" (Ranson et al. 1980: 8). Thus, as long as problems are absorbed and individual rules within the system remain unchallenged, the "rule regime" as a whole becomes more entrenched (March et al. 2000).

While acknowledging that problem absorption can have the stabilizing effects just described, what we would like to do in the remainder of this chapter is to focus on the more dynamic consequences of problem absorption. As we argue below, problem absorption can be seen as involving a special kind of organizational learning (March et al., 2000). Furthermore, repeated problem absorption by the same rule can lead to amplification of the small changes that problem absorption generates (Plowman et al., 2007), thereby giving rise to more radical forms of change.

10.3 Dynamic consequences and organizational learning

10.3.1 Semantic learning

Corley and Gioia (2003: 625) used the term "semantic learning" to refer to the "changes to the intersubjective meanings underlying the labels and actions constituting the core of a collective's understanding of themselves," and emphasized that such learning need not involve any changes to the actual labels. Although their discussion focused on the labels and meanings that form the basis for organizational identity, we suggest that an analogous learning process can take place at the micro-level when existing rules are extended to deal with non-prototypical cases, enabling the organization to maintain relative stability in its (rule-based) response in the face of variety in stimuli (Weick, 1991). While problem absorption does not generally lead to changes in the actual text of the written rule, including the labels used to specify its domain and the actions it prescribes, it can still modify the *categories* for those labels (Tsoukas and Chia, 2002). In the words of Corley and Gioia (2003: 622), "the meanings associated with these labels change to accommodate current needs." Because the intention of rule users in problem absorption is usually to deal with the new case, rather than to transform the rule's meaning, semantic learning is likely to be an unintended consequence of problem absorption. Thus we can also agree with Corley and Gioia's (2003: 625) assertion that semantic learning can take place "without explicit awareness of learning, without the recognition of learning, or even without the intention to learn by the members of the collective."[5]

One aspect of semantic learning that Corley and Gioia (2003) did not sufficiently emphasize is the cumulative nature of modifications of meaning. Similarly, discussions of problem absorption by rules do not address the implications of *repeated* absorption (March et al., 2000; Schulz, 1998). Only Tsoukas and Chia (2002: 576), while discussing empirical material from Feldman (2000), briefly mentioned that extensions of "current policies" to accommodate non-prototypical cases "provided opportunities for further changes." We believe that the temporal dimension of problem absorption and the tendency for later changes in the meaning/use of formal rules to build on earlier ones deserve greater attention. We also wish to highlight the role played by organizational remembering (Feldman and Feldman, 2006) in making it possible for semantic learning to become cumulative and have lasting effects.

As an illustration of our arguments, we return to our earlier example of the treasurer's work at a university department. Recall that the treasurer had found it necessary to interpret the "conference presentations" category as also covering conference-related membership fees, thus allowing such fees to be paid out of the department's budget under the existing rules. This decision set a precedent (Levitt and March, 1988) for subsequent uses of the application with regards to conferences requiring membership fees. Over time, visits to conferences requiring membership fees became more common, in effect making such cases part of the prototypical core of the category (Tsoukas and Chia, 2002). This in its turn paved the way for further category extensions.

The next non-prototypical request faced by the treasurer involved a membership fee that was not related to any conference, but had to be paid in order to enable the applicant to join a special association of researchers. In the absence of prior history of problem absorption, it would be very difficult to justify classifying such an expense under "conference presentations." However, given the fact that the category had already been extended to some membership fees, as well as the lack of any

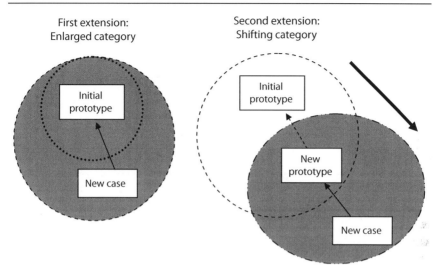

First extension: Enlarged category

Second extension: Shifting category

Fig. 10.1 Category enlargement and category shift

alternative category that could cover the case, the treasurer faced strong normative and political pressure from department members to extend the category once again, which she did. What happened was a category *shift*, where a case (or set of cases) that used to be treated as non-prototypical came to serve as the new prototype, to which future cases could be compared. Such a shift need not involve the complete unlearning (Tsang and Zahra, 2008) of the initial prototype, such that it no longer plays any role in the use of the rule in question, but it at least opens up the possibility of rule application to cases which would not have been included based purely on comparisons with the initial prototype.

We distinguish the phenomenon of category *shift* from (mere) category *enlargement*, as illustrated in Fig. 10.1. Category enlargement occurs when past category extensions modify organizational members' sense of the overall variability of the category, while category shift additionally involves an adjustment of the prototype, as in the above example. Pure category enlargement occurred when the treasurer was forced to also extend the category to conference visits that did not involve any paper presentations for the applicant. Essentially, the cases of membership fees enabled both the treasurer and the department members to see the category as encompassing more variability (and the category boundaries as being more broad and flexible) compared with the initial understanding of the category that was based solely on prototypical cases. Therefore, a seemingly unrelated extension to membership fees also paved the way for a further broadening of the category to cover conference visits for non-presenters.

As the example illustrates, problem absorption is a form of experiential learning insofar as it involves inquiry about how to respond to a mismatch between expected and observed situations or outcomes, as well as the retention of "learning agents' discoveries, inventions, and evaluations ... in organizational memory" (Argyris and Schön 1978: 19) in the form of new understandings and precedents for future rule applications. In the above example, the new understandings and precedents were relevant both for the treasurer (an actor formally charged with applying or enforcing the rule) and for the applicants (the actors directly affected by the rule). As participants in a common routine, both parties were able to learn about the others' "tasks and perceptions of the routine" (Feldman and Rafaeli, 2002: 314). The treasurer learned more about the kinds of expenses that applicants wanted reimbursed, while the applicants became more likely to submit further non-prototypical requests under an old category once they learned that the treasurer was sometimes willing to extend the category beyond the prototypical instances.

However, without broader reflection on the whole cumulative experience with the rule, semantic learning of the kind that we have described is likely to be limited in its impact on the organization and especially its more formal aspects, such as the rule itself. At best, it constitutes a form of practical drift (Snook, 2002) that leads to an increasing divergence between the abstract understandings about the rule-governed practice, which generally remains wedded to prototypical performances, and the actual pattern of practice itself, which has been transformed through problem absorption (Feldman and Pentland, 2003). In the next section we discuss how problem absorption can induce a higher-order learning process with more far-reaching effects for organizational rules.

10.3.2 Higher-level learning

Organizational learning theories often distinguish between different types or levels of learning. Fiol and Lyles (1985), building on Argyris and Schön's (1978) classification of single versus double-loop learning, postulate two levels of learning. Lower-level learning stems from repeated action within a given set of rules leading to new behavioral outcomes, while higher-level learning is a non-repetitive enquiry leading to the development of new rules and understandings (Fiol and Lyles, 1985). Nicolini and Meznar (1995) make a related distinction between learning as a continuous and often unconscious process of cognitive modification in the course of practice, which is especially close to the notion of semantic learning discussed above, and learning as a socially constructed product of organizational self-observation and abstraction. Finally, in developing their process perspective on organizational change, Tsoukas and Chia (2002: 579–80) appear to differentiate between "microscopic" change, which is pervasive and "ongoing" in organizations, and institutionalized change, which depends at least in part on the management's "declarative powers" to turn change into a potential institutional fact (Searle, 1995).

The relationship between the two levels of learning, however, is not entirely clear. Although it is recognized that lower-level learning "can provide the raw material" for higher-level learning (Lant and Mezias, 1992: 64; Nicolini and Meznar, 1995), the two processes have sometimes been presented as relatively independent (Fiol and Lyles, 1985), or even antagonistic (Levitt and March, 1988; March, 1991). Some have suggested that a transition from lower- to higher-level learning can be triggered when experience from lower-level learning is "equivocal" (Lant and Mezias, 1992: 64), when organizational performance falls below the aspiration level (Cyert and March, 1992; Lant and Mezias, 1992), or when the organization faces a crisis (Fiol and Lyles, 1985). In analyzing the consequences of problem absorption by rules we can better understand the process through which lower-level (semantic) learning can lead to higher-level organizational learning and change in written rules. The consequences we have in mind have to do with the emergence of new understandings and patterns of practice that can undermine the pragmatic, cognitive and normative bases of a rule's legitimacy (Suchman, 1995).

10.3.2.1 COGNITIVE BURDEN AND BREADTH

First, repeated problem absorption can impose a considerable cognitive burden on rule users and those whom they may consult and/or ask for authorization with regard to whether or not to extend the rule. This happens precisely because, as we argued above, problem absorption is often a reflexive (rather than mindless) process. Especially when people have to engage in such reflection frequently for the same rule (and thus encounter uncertainty in the expected results), the important purpose of the rule to provide a sense of order gradually becomes undermined by non-prototypical cases. The rule's use imposes a cognitive burden instead of reducing it (Simon, 1997), thereby undermining the rule's usefulness or pragmatic legitimacy in the eyes of rule users. In the example introduced above, the treasurer found after repeated extensions of the category that the rule was not helping her to reach a decision on a particular application, but rather that she had to consider each case in light of the whole history of past decisions.

Second, cumulative category enlargements and category shifts tend to make the rule quite broad or inclusive. Rule users may consequently find it increasingly difficult to draw the line and justify *not* extending the rule further given that it has already been extended so often in the past. Thus, the rule's usefulness in making distinctions can become undermined (Tsoukas and Vladimirou, 2001). Although each non-prototypical extension might be plausible in the concrete situation, nevertheless the sum of all extensions can generate problems for rule application, which in turn provide opportunities for learning and change. For example, after the rule has been extended to non-conference membership fees and to conference visits without paper presentations, the treasurer was asking herself: "Where does it stop?" She could no longer use the rule to justify turning down applications, even when their relevance to the department's research needs might be called into question. The reflexive attitude towards the rule induced by problem absorption makes it more likely that the rule's diminished usefulness (in making distinctions and reducing cognitive burden) will be recognized within the organization.

10.3.2.2 REFLECTION ON BROADER UNDERSTANDINGS

The same reflexive attitude can also contribute towards weakening the rule's cognitive legitimacy or taken-for-grantedness within the organization (Suchman, 1995). Because applications of a rule to non-prototypical cases are difficult to justify on the basis of the rule's text alone, other considerations, including especially the purpose or rationale behind the rule, are likely to be cited in accounting for such applications. Thus, problem absorption can bring the historical circumstances surrounding the rule's adoption into the focal awareness of organizational members (Tsoukas, 1996). More precisely, certain understandings about the rule's history and rationale will be re-constructed and elaborated through the process of organizational remembering (Feldman and Feldman, 2006). The very activity of reflecting on these matters can reduce the tendency to see the rule as a necessary or inevitable part of the organization (Suchman, 1995) or to value it for its own sake (Merton, 1940; Selznick, 1957). It can also make people more aware of potential alternatives to the rule.

Rationalized cultural understandings about formal organizational rules generally focus on the rules' relationship to organizational goals, technical expertise, or professional norms (Meyer and Rowan, 1977). However, organizational preferences and goals are frequently "ill-defined" and ambiguous (Cohen et al., 1972; Lindblom, 1959), while professional jurisdictions are often contested (Bechky, 2003; Reed, 1996). Thus, collective reflection on the rule's purpose can reopen old debates over what the relevant organizational goals and professional norms are, and how best to balance conflicting norms and goals. The normative underpinnings (Lawrence and Suddaby, 2006; Suchman, 1995) of the organizational rule (or even a whole set of organizational rules) may be called into question as a result. For example, the by-law regulating the use of permanent berths in the Port of Rotterdam was originally adopted in 1883 in order to prevent "independent middlemen [from] make[ing] money out of the right on permanent berths" (Van Driel and Bogenrieder, 2009: 654). However, by the end of the debates in the late 1890s, which were stimulated and informed by controversial extensions of the category "liner service" within the by-law, the relevant authorities came to the conclusion that the prosperity of the port was no longer "best served by an unmediated relation between the port and the end users of its berths," which in turn made it possible for a major revision of the by-law to be passed in 1900 (2009: 663).

10.3.2.3 TRANSITION TO HIGHER-LEVEL LEARNING

As this example shows, reflection on how the rule relates to broarder organizational goals can trigger higher-level learning and formal rule change when actors with formal authority over organizational rulemaking become involved in this reflection. This is consistent with the view that higher-level learning "occurs mostly in upper levels" of the organization (Fiol and Lyles, 1985: 810). If the organization has routines for monitoring and reviewing rule applications, then these can help to bring the non-prototypical rule applications to the attention of rule makers and thus ensure their involvement in the reflection induced by repeated problem absorption. Factors like organizational voice/silence (Milliken and Morrison, 2003) and the politics of issue selling (Dutton et al., 2001) can also affect whether reflection will become a collective process in which rule makers participate as well.

The transition to higher-level learning also implies the occurrence of a "cognitive breakdown" (Nicolini and Meznar, 1995: 739) or a "realization that certain experiences cannot be interpreted within the current belief system" (Lant and Mezias, 1992: 42; Argyris and Schön, 1978). In the context of problem absorption, this means that organizational members realize that the pattern of repeated category extensions cannot continue anymore. The sense of increased cognitive burden and of inability to make distinctions due to excessive broadening of the category can help to trigger such realization, as discussed above. The undermining of the rule's taken-for-grantedness and normative underpinnings can in turn make organizational members more willing to consider revising the rule or even suspending it altogether. Although the precise outcome of higher-level learning is difficult to predict ex ante, it is clear that the outcome will be affected by the organizational experience with category extensions. Given that higher-level learning is a response to a cognitive breakdown induced by this experience, it is likely to involve "the effort not to incur the same breakdown again" (Nicolini and Meznar, 1995: 739).

Indeed, one result of higher-level learning can be an attempt to reverse the process of category extensions that has taken place in the course of applying the rule. The rule might be revised so as to explicitly prohibit the kinds of extensions that have taken place by delineating more explicitly the boundaries of the relevant category.[6] Thus, if the setting of precedents through category extensions is a form of (semantic) organizational learning, as we maintain, then rule revisions that explicitly reject those precedents are a form of organizational unlearning (Tsang and Zahra, 2008). However, this is not what happened in the Rotterdam Port example. There, the rule makers actually embraced rather than rejected the results of semantic learning, since the revised by-law explicitly authorized the use of permanent berths by irregular ships, whereas prior to the revision such ships were only permitted to use permanent berths when the officials were willing to stretch their definition of liner service (Van Driel and Bogenrieder, 2009). Thus reflection on the process of semantic learning can reveal not only the inadequacy of the old rules in dealing with the problems that have been absorbed, but also the value of some lessons from the process of semantic learning for the organization.

The extent to which the consequences of semantic learning, such as the increased variety of users of permanent berths in the port example, are embraced or rejected in rule revisions is difficult to predict. Rejection may become less likely when broadening of rule categories over time generates organizational commitments that are difficult to reverse. Furthermore, as noted by March et al. (1991: 5), it can happen that the "preferences and values in terms of which organizations distinguish successes from failures are themselves transformed in the process of learning." Thus, the process of semantic learning can subtly modify the prevailing understandings of organizational goals and preferences, which can in turn pave the way for more radial forms of change, such as rule suspension (March et al., 2000).

10.4 Summary and discussion

The aim of this chapter was to further develop the concept of problem absorption and to explore the relationship between problem absorption and organizational learning. Building on the process view, we suggested that an important part of problem absorption is the extension of categories of existing rules to non-prototypical cases, which can transform the meaning of those categories in practice without changing the actual text of the rules (Tsoukas and Chia, 2002). Thus, our perspective on rules parallels Feldman and Pentland's (2003) argument that the performative aspect of a routine can vary even while its ostensive aspect (i.e. the abstract understanding of the routine) and the associated written rules, documents, and other artifacts, seem to remain relatively stable. In fact, variation at the performative level can actually contribute to stability at the ostensive and artifact levels (Essén, 2008), just as problem absorption in practice can sometimes contribute to the stability of a rule. Given that written rules are similar to technological artifacts (Adler and Borys, 1996), Orlikowski's (2000) arguments that technology's capacity to structure work is not inherent, but is *enacted* through "people's repeated and situated interaction with particular technologies," and that "technologies-in-practice" (2000: 407) can undergo subtle transformations that will not be apparent when technologies are examined apart from practice, also generalize to rules.

However, apart from Tsoukas and Chia's (2002) contribution, this literature fails to address the crucial role of categorization in the interaction between the performative and the ostensive or artifact levels. Category extensions are an important type of performative variation, which can to some extent modify people's shared understandings of the relevant categories (ostensive change), but without changing the associated labels and the normative link between categories of situations and categories of actions, as encoded in written rules (ostensive stability). We build on Tsoukas and Chia's (2002) arguments that extensions transform the *radius* of a category by affecting understandings about category variability, but further add that extensions can transform understandings about the *core* or prototype, leading to category shifts.

We also develop Tsoukas and Chia's (2002: 580) brief remark about the "agglomerative" nature of microscopic change and the possibility of such change being "amplified" (2002: 579; see also Plowman et al., 2007) by examining the effects of repeated extensions, each building on the previous one. We identified organizational remembering, and specifically reliance on precedents in rule use, as the crucial enabling condition for cumulative extensions. While our analysis echoes Feldman's (2000: 620) finding that continuous change in routines is possible when previous performances generate "outcomes [that] enable new opportunities," giving participants "the option of expanding" the routine, we specifically focus on category enlargements and shifts as the outcomes that provide opportunities for further change in the use of formal rules.

Finally, we explored the possibility of microscopic change (via problem absorption) leading to formal organizational change (in the form of rule revisions), which Tsoukas and Chia (2002: 580) mentioned as an "interesting topic...for further theoretical development". We framed the issue as one of a transition form lower- to higher-level learning (Fiol and Lyles, 1985). Like Feldman and Pentland (2003; see also Feldman, 2000), we argued that collective reflection on problem absorption and its outcomes (performative aspect) in relation to broader understandings that underpin the rule (ostensive aspect) matters in bringing about more fundamental changes. The crucial question that is not addressed in this literature, however, is why the performative variation cannot continue indefinitely without inducing any major changes to the ostensive aspect and the relevant artifacts. After all, research shows that flexible routines can persist in organizations (Howard-Grenville, 2005), and they may persist precisely because of (rather than in spite of) performative variation (Essén, 2008). What then might be the limits to the persistence of flexibly applied rules?

We argued that because rule application to non-prototypical cases requires reflection (Levinthal and Rerup, 2006; Tsoukas and Chia, 2002), it imposes cognitive burden on those who actually apply the rules or review rule applications. When rules have been extended repeatedly, the accumulated precedents add to the burden. This can make organizational members dissatisfied with the current version of the rule. Furthermore, repeated extensions can blur the boundaries between the categories and undermine the rule's role as a standard for drawing distinctions. Finally, reflection on the purpose of the rule can enable the organization to recognize that the purpose is no longer valid or that it would be best served by developing a different rule. It is these factors that, in our view, enable the transition to higher-level learning with regards to rules and can thus "release" the organization from the codification trap (Schulz, 1998).

An important issue for future research is how experience with problem absorption might affect the contents of the revised rules. While we agree with Feldman (2000: 624) that "rule changes may simply be the codification of changes that are already made," and specifically of the changes to rule-categories in problem absorption, we also suggest that the process of rule revision in response to problem absorption can entail more exploratory forms of learning (March, 1991), where the outcome cannot simply be inferred from prior organizational history or experience. Furthermore, the aim of codification might in some cases be to reverse some of the category extensions and to preclude their occurrence in the future.

10.5 Conclusion

The process perspective on organizations suggests that although change always has primacy, a sense of order can emerge temporarily when distinctions are made between different types of situations and systematically connected to distinctions between different types of actions (Tsoukas and Vladimirou, 2001). By serving as reminders of the imperative to continue making those distinctions and connections in practice, written rules contribute to the maintenance of the sense of order in organizations. In some situations, the distinctions and connections will be more difficult to make than in others. Such situations act as momentary disruptions of the sense of order and might be called "problems" by those who attend to them. Yet, organizational members can often find a way of acting in such situations that is consistent with the imperatives of the rules. Building on previous research, we called this phenomenon "problem absorption." Problem absorption subtly transforms the way in which distinctions are made within an organization, and thus constitutes a form of "semantic" organizational learning. Furthermore, when it occurs repeatedly, its cumulative consequences can lead to far greater disruptions to the sense of order and trigger a transition to higher-level organizational learning. We identified reflexivity as the crucial enabling condition in this process. We argued that through reflection on problem absorption both in situ, as well as retrospectively, organizations can develop new understandings about the relevant practice that can undermine existing rules and clear the way for the development of new distinctions and associations.

Notes

An earlier draft of this chapter was presented at the First International Symposium on Process Organization Studies (PROS) in Cyprus, June 2009. We thank two anonymous reviewers and volume editor Ann Langley for their helpful comments and suggestions. All errors remain our own.

1. A participant can feel a pressure to conform due to her *assumption* that such implicit agreement exists among others. However, this assumption may well overestimate the actual extent of the agreement.
2. The processual orientation sensitizes us to the danger of reifying organizational memory or conceptualizing it in substantialist terms. Perhaps "organizational remembering" would be a better term in this context (cf. Feldman and Feldman, 2006).
3. Still, perhaps this interpretation does not completely exhaust what these authors had in mind. One might argue that by enabling the enactment of a rationalized and patterned context of activity (Weick, 1995), and facilitating the emergence of organizational routines (Reynaud, 2005), formal rules make it less likely that situations will be problematized in the first place. While we acknowledge that it may well be worth exploring "problem absorption" in this second sense, we leave it as a task for future research.
4. At the time when these rules were adopted, EGOS (European Group for Organization Studies) did not require membership fees and visits to the AOM (Academy of Management) Conference by the department members were comparatively rare.
5. This, of course, does not mean that rule extension itself must be a completely tacit or unreflexive process. On the contrary, as should be clear from the previous sections, it rarely is in our view.
6. Of course, no amount of specification can eliminate the need for judgment in applying the rule to new cases, since the specifications themselves can only be made in abstract terms with the possibility of non-prototypical applications (Tsoukas, 1996; Wittgenstein, 1953). For example, changing the category "conference presentations" into "conference presentations excluding membership fees" will not help in cases where it is not clear whether the relevant expense is a membership fee or not.

References

Adler, P. S. & Borys, B. (1996). Two types of bureaucracy: Enabling and coercive, *Administrative Science Quarterly*, 41, 61–89.

Antonacopoulou, E. & Tsoukas, H. (2002). Time and reflexivity in organization studies: An introduction, *Organization Studies*, 23, 85–862.

Archer, M. S. (1995). *Realist Social Theory: The Morphogenetic Approach*, Cambridge: Cambridge University Press.

Archer, M. S. (2003). *Structure, Agency and the Internal Conversation*, Cambridge: Cambridge University Press.

Argyris, C. & Schön, D. A. (1978). *Organizational Learning: A Theory of Action Perspective*, Reading, MA: Addison-Wesley.

Bechky, B. A. (2003). Object lessons: Workplace artifacts as representations of occupational jurisdiction, *American Journal of Sociology*, 109, 720–52.

Beck, N. & Kieser, A. (2003). Complexity of rule systems, experience, and organizational learning, *Organization Studies*, 24, 793–814.

Bogenrieder, I. & Magala, S. (2007). Contested practices in routines, in *Proceedings of International Conference on Organizational Learning, Knowledge and Capabilities (OLKC 2007) —"Learning fusion"*.

Boje, D. M. (1991). The storytelling organization: A study of story performance in an office-supply firm, *Administrative Science Quarterly*, 36, 106–26.

Brown, J. S. & Duguid, P. (1991). Organizational learning and communities-of-practice: Toward a unified view of working, learning and innovation, *Organization Science*, 2, 40–57.

Chia, R. & Holt R. (2006). Strategy as practical coping: A Heideggerian perspective, *Organization Studies*, 27, 635–55.

Cohen, M. D., March, J. G., & Olsen, J. P. (1972). A garbage can model of organizational choice, *Administrative Science Quarterly*, 17, 1–25.

Corley, K. G. & Gioia, D. A. (2003). Semantic learning as change enabler: Relating organizational identity and organizational learning, in M. Easterby-Smith & M. A. Lyles (eds) *The Blackwell Handbook of Organizational Learning and Knowledge Management*, Oxford: Blackwell, 623–38.

Cowan, D. A. (1990). Developing a classification structure of organizational problems: An empirical investigation, *Academy of Management Journal*, 33, 366–90.

Cyert, R. M., & March, J. G. (1992). *A Behavioral Theory of the Firm*, 2nd edn, Cambridge, MA: Blackwell.

Dutton, J. E., Ashford, S. J., O'Neill, R. M., & Lawrence, K. A. (2001). Moves that matter: Issue selling and organizational change, *Academy of Management Review*, 44, 716–736.

Emirbayer, M. & Mische, A. (1998). What is agency?, *American Journal of Sociology*, 103, 962–1023.

Essén, A. (2008). Variability as a source of stability: Studying routines in the elderly home care setting, *Human Relations*, 61, 1617–44.

Feldman, M. S. (2000). Organizational routines as a source of continuous change, *Organization Science*, 6, 611–29.

Feldman, R. M. & Feldman, S. P. (2006). What links the chain: An essay on organizational remembering as practice, *Organization*, 13, 861–87.

Feldman, M. S. & Pentland, B.T. (2003). Reconceptualizing organizational routines as a source of flexibility and change, *Administrative Science Quarterly*, 48, 94–118.

Feldman, M. S. & Rafaeli, A. (2002). Organizational routines as sources of connections and understandings, *Journal of Management Studies*, 39, 309–31.

Fiol, C. M. & Lyles, M. A. (1985). Organizational learning, *Academy of Management Review*, 10, 803–13.

Giddens, A. (1984). *The Constitution of the Society: Outline of the Theory of Structuration*, Cambridge: Polity Press.

Heugens, P. P. M. A. R. & Osadchiy, S. E. (2007). Rule work: The mechanisms of organizational memorizing, paper presented at the 23rd EGOS Colloquium in Vienna, Austria, July.

Holland, J. H., Holyoak, K. J., Nisbett, R. E. & Thagard, P. R. (1986). *Induction: Processes of Inference, Learning, and Discovery*, Cambridge, MA: MIT Press.

Howard-Grenville, J. A. (2005). The persistence of flexible organizational routines: The role of agency and organizational context, *Organization Science*, 16, 618–36.

Huber, G. P. (1991). Organizational learning: The contributing processes and the literatures, *Organization Science*, 2, 88–115.

Lant, T. K. & Mezias, S. J. (1992). An organizational learning model of convergence and reorientation, *Organization Science*, 3, 47–71.

Lawrence, T. B. & Suddaby, R. (2006). Institutions and institutional work, in S. Clegg, C. Hardy, W. A. Nord, & T. B. Lawrence (eds) *The Sage Handbook of Organization Studies*, 2nd edn, Thousand Oaks: Sage, 215–55.

Lehman, D. W. & Ramanujam R. (2009). Selectivity in organizational rule violations, *Academy of Management Review*, 34, 643–57.

Levinthal, D. A. & Rerup, C. (2006). Crossing an apparent chasm: Bridging mindful and less-mindful perspectives on organizational learning, *Organization Science*, 17, 502–13.

Levitt, B. & March, J. G. (1988). Organizational learning, *Annual Review of Sociology*, 14, 319–40.

Lindblom, C. E. (1959). The science of "muddling through," *Public Administration Review*, 19, 79–88.

March, J. G. (1991). Exploration and exploitation in organizational learning, *Organization Science*, 2, 71–87.

March, J. G. & Simon, H. A. (1993). *Organizations*, 2nd edn, Cambridge, MA: Blackwell.

March, J. G., Schulz, M., & Zhou, X. (2000). *The Dynamics of Rules: Change in Written Organizational Codes*, Stanford: Stanford University Press.

March, J. G., Sproull, L. S., & Tamuz, M. (1991). Learning from samples of one or fewer, *Organization Science*, 2, 1–13.

Merton, R. K. (1940). Bureaucratic structure and personality, *Social Forces*, 18, 560–8.

Meyer, J. W. & Rowan, B. (1977). Institutionalized organizations: Formal structure as myth and ceremony, *American Journal of Sociology*, 83, 340–63.

Milliken, F. J. & Morrison, E. W. (2003). Speaking up, remaining silent: The dynamics of voice and silence in organizations, *Journal of Management Studies*, 40, 1353–8.

Moorman, C. & Miner, A. S. (1998). Organizational improvisation and organizational memory, *Academy of Management Review*, 23, 698–723.

Nass, C. (1986). Bureaucracy, technical expertise, and professionals: A Weberian approach, *Sociological Theory*, 4, 61–70.

Nelson, R. R. & Winter, S. G. (1982). *An Evolutionary Theory of Economic Change*, Cambridge, MA: Harvard University Press.

Nicolini, D. & Meznar, M. B. (1995). The social construction of organizational learning: Conceptual and practical issues in the field, *Human Relations*, 48, 727–46.

Ocasio, W. (1999). Institutionalized action and corporate governance: The reliance on rules of CEO succession, *Administrative Science Quarterly*, 44, 384–416.

Orlikowski, W. J. (2000). Using technology and constituting structures: A practice lens for studying technology in organizations, *Organization Science*, 11, 404–28.

Pentland, B. T. & Feldman, M. S. (2005). Organizational routines as a unit of analysis, *Industrial and Corporate Change*, 14, 793–815.

Plowman, D. A., Baker, L. T., Beck, T. E., Kulkarni, M., Solansky, S. T., & Travis, D. V. (2007). Radical change accidentally: The emergence and amplification of small change, *Academy of Management Journal*, 50, 515–43.

Ranson, S., Hinings, B., & Greenwood, R. (1980). The structuring of organizational structures, *Administrative Science Quarterly*, 25, 1–17.

Reed, M. I. (1996). Expert power and control in late modernity: An empirical review and theoretical synthesis, *Organization Studies*, 17, 573–97.

Reynaud, B. (2005). The void at the heart of rules: Routines in the context of rule-following. The case of the Paris Metro Workshop, *Industrial and Corporate Change*, 14, 847–71.

Rosch, E. and Lloyd, B. B. (1978). *Cognition and Categorization*, Hillsdale, NJ: Lawrence Erlabaum.

Schatzki, T. R. (2005). The sites of organizations, *Organization Studies*, 26, 465–84.

Schatzki, T. R. (2006). Organizations as they happen, *Organization Studies*, 27, 1863–73.

Schulz, M. (1998). Limits to bureaucratic growth: The density dependence of organizational rule births, *Administrative Science Quarterly*, 43, 845–76.

Schulz, M. (2003). Impermanent institutionalization: The duration dependence of organizational rule changes, *Industrial and Corporate Change*, 12, 1077–98.

Schutz, A. (1964). Tiresias, or our knowledge of future events, in Arvid Brodersen (ed.) *Collected Papers*, Vol. 2, *Studies in Social Theory*, The Hague: Martinus Nijhoff, 277–93.

Searle, J. R. (1995). *The Construction of Social Reality*, New York: The Free Press.

Selznick, P. (1957). *Leadership in Administration: A Sociological Interpretation*, New York: Harper & Row.

Simon, H. A. (1997). *Administrative Behavior: A Study of Decision-making Processes in Administrative Organizations*, 4th edn, New York: The Free Press.

Snook, S. A. (2002). *Friendly Fire: The Accidental Shootdown of U.S. Black Hawks over Northern Iraq*, Princeton, NJ: Princeton University Press.

Starbuck, W. H. (1983). Organizations as action generators, *American Sociological Review*, 48, 91–102.

Suchman, M. C. (1995). Managing legitimacy: Strategic and institutional approaches, *Academy of Management Review*, 20, 571–610.

Tsang, E. W. K. & Zahra, S. A. (2008). Organizational unlearning, *Human Relations*, 61, 1435–62.

Tsoukas, H. (1996). The firm as a distributed knowledge system: A constructionist approach, *Strategic Management Journal*, 17, 11–25.

Tsoukas, H. & Chia, R. (2002). On organizational becoming: Rethinking organizational change, *Organization Science*, 13, 567–82.

Tsoukas, H. & Vladimirou, E. (2001). What is organizational knowledge?, *Journal of Management Studies*, 38, 973–93.

Tucker, A. L., Edmondson, A, C., & Spear, S. (2002). When problem solving prevents organizational learning, *Journal of Organizational Change Management*, 15, 122–37.

Van Driel, H. & Bogenrieder, I. (2009). Memory and learning: Selecting users in the port of Rotterdam, 1883–1900, *Business History*, 51, 649–67.

Walsh, J. P. & Ungson, G. R. (1991). Organizational memory, *Academy of Management Review*, 16, 57–91.

Weber, M. (1978). *Economy and Society: An Outline of Interpretive Sociology*, Berkeley, CA: University of California Press.

Weick, K. E. (1991). The nontraditional quality of organizational learning, *Organization Science*, 2, 116–23.

Weick, K. E. (1995). *Sensemaking in Organizations*, Thousand Oaks, CA: Sage.

Weick, K. E. & Sutcliffe, K. M. (2006). Mindfulness and the quality of organizational attention, *Organization Science*, 17, 514–25.

Weick, K. E., Sutcliffe, K. M., & Obstfeld, D. (2005). Organizing and the process of sensemaking, *Organization Science*, 16, 409–21.

Winter, S. G. (2003). Understanding dynamic capabilities, *Strategic Management Journal*, 24, 991–5.

Wittgenstein, L. (1953). *Philosophical Investigations*, transl. G. E. M. Anscombe, Oxford: Basil Blackwell.

Zhou, X. (1993). The dynamics of organizational rules, *American Journal of Sociology*, 98, 1134–66.

Zucker, L. G. (1977). The role of institutionalization in cultural persistence, *American Sociological Review*, 42, 726–43.

11

Temporal Sensemaking: Managers' Use of Time to Frame Organizational Change

Elden Wiebe

Abstract: This chapter is a qualitative study exploring the relationship between time and organizational change, a recently emerging area of scholarly interest. Through the narrative analysis of managers' own stories of change, I discern five distinct "worlds" of organizational change within the "same" significant government mandated organizational change in the "same" organizational context. The analysis provides evidence that managers temporally make sense of their experiences of change, actively configuring the relationship between the past, present, and future in different ways. In doing so, managers construct the organizational change and their enacted reality of that organizational change in different ways. This research augments recent work linking time and agency, demonstrates a broader temporal basis than retrospection for sensemaking, and contributes to our knowledge of researching and implementing organizational change.

Burrell (1992) has lamented that time has been severely neglected in our handling of the management of change:

> Given that the whole notion of "change" relies heavily upon a conception of temporality, it is remarkable that the philosophy of time has been a neglected issue ... (Burrell, 1992: 165)

Indeed, the two major theories of organizational change within the domain of organizational studies, continuous and episodic (Weick and Quinn, 1999), belie a relationship to time in their very designations (Noss, 2002).

Yet, while greater attention has been paid recently to the relationship of time and organizational change (Purser et al., 2005; Tsoukas and Chia, 2002; Chia, 1999), this area remains under-studied and under-theorized (Pettigrew et al., 2001; George and Jones, 2000; Avital, 2000; Lee and Liebenau, 1999).

Hampering our efforts is the predominant notion of time in our Western culture, and especially that of business enterprises, namely, clock time, characterized as objective, linear, a-contextual, invariable, equally and infinitely divisible, measurable, and reversible (McGrath and Rotchford, 1983). As such we tend to think of time as absolute and external to ourselves, leading us to think we can "manage time, control it, spend it, save it, or waste it" (Hall, 1983: 36). Applying this conceptualization to organizational change, we find that change becomes a-temporal—time becomes nothing more than a tool of measurement and location of unchanging forms in static time–space (Adam, 1998: 40; Chia, 1999; Purser et al., 2005). Moreover, the clock disassociates time from human events (Mumford, quoted in Landes, 1983: 16), thereby imposing a "foreign" time on actions and processes, obscuring them and the presence of "other" times (Bluedorn, 2002), and heightening our alienation to time (Purser et al., 2005). As such, clock time actually keeps us from seeing the process of change (Tsoukas and Chia, 2002; Chia, 1999).

Yet the possibility exists to go beyond the limitations of clock time. Time is not singular, nor is it an invariant constant (Purser et al., 2005). Adam (1994: 509) observed that even within Western culture the dominance of clock time "does not obliterate the rich sources of local, idiosyncratic and context-dependent time-awareness that are rooted in the social and organic rhythms of everyday life." Likewise, Hall (1983: 13) observed that in "looking at what people actually do (in contrast to what they write and say when theorizing) one quickly discovers a wide discrepancy between time as it is lived and time as it is considered."

The purpose of this chapter is to explore the relationship between time as it is lived and organizational change. Understanding how organizational change is accomplished is not well served by variance theories; its dynamics require attention to time (Langley, 2007; Pettigrew et al., 1989). I do not privilege clock time, however, with its significant limitations for grasping the dynamics of organizational change (Tsoukas and Chia, 2002). Rather, I am seeking to privilege time that is context dependent, which better allows us to see the processes of organizational change. This is important not only because processes are largely missing or neglected in our research (Tsoukas and Chia, 2002; Avital, 2000; Langley, 2007), and thus represents a significant gap in our understanding, but also because it begins to make more visible how things come to be, thereby allowing for improvement of performance (Langley, 2007).

The remainder of the chapter is organized as follows. The next section situates the paper in two ways—first through a brief review of previous organizational studies using a time-lived approach, and second, through a brief reflection on various ways of conceptualizing the link between past, present, and future. I then describe the narrative method used, followed by the results of the analysis—an explication of the five "worlds" of organizational change within the "same" mandated change initiative. Next, I turn to a discussion of the temporal construction of organizational change. I conclude with some implications of the study, including the broader temporal basis for sensemaking, and future directions for research.

11.1 Time and organizational change

In the organizational change literature, time is often thought of as the context within which organizational change unfolds (Wiebe and Golden-Biddle, 2002; see also the comprehensive reviews of organizational change by Van de Ven and Poole, 1995; Weick and Quinn, 1999; and Armenakis and Bedeian, 1999). Increasingly, however, scholars have begun to examine time empirically in the events and processes of organizational change (i.e., time-lived). Organizational change has been linked to the rhythms of nature and culture rather than the artificial "foreign" time of the clock (Clark, 1985). It is also linked to establishing synchronized rhythms (entrainment) as well as being hindered once those rhythms are established and strengthened (Brown and Eisenhardt, 1997; Ancona and Chong, 1996). Altering periods of clock time (e.g., creating a quiet time) recontextualizes the a-contextual clock time metric, thereby changing people's work rhythms (Perlow, 1999; see also Mainemelis, 2001). Unexpected events change one's sense of time and thus create openness for change in organizations (Staudenmayer et al., 2002). Temporal dynamics are unconsciously at work and can cause radical changes in the behavior of groups and organizations (Gersick, 1988, 1994). The "right time" to introduce change into an organization is not necessarily determined by clock time coordination but by the confluence of circumstances recognized through knowledge of the social context (Dutton et al., 2001). Additional time-lived work has been done on other temporal features such as temporal horizons, time orientations, mono- and polychronicity, and temporal symmetry (Blue-dorn, 2002; Ancona et al., 2001; Barley, 1988).

Organization researchers have also approached lived-time from an interpretive stance (Chreim, 2007; O'Connor, 2000; Isabella, 1990). The present study is situated within this interpretive stream. Unlike Chreim (2007), this study does not compare entities at different points in time. Rather, it brings time into the foreground, seeking to understand how time is used by managers to frame the change they are experiencing. I refer to this as temporal sensemaking. By temporal sensemaking I mean the act of configuring (and reconfiguring) the relationship of past, present, and future.

This definition builds on Emirbayer and Mische's (1998) reconceptualization of human agency as

> a temporally embedded process of social engagement, informed by the past (in its habitual aspect), but also oriented toward the future (as a capacity to imagine alternative possibilities) and toward the present (as a capacity to contextualize past habits and future projects within the contingencies of the moment). (Emirbayer and Mische, 1998: 963)

Situating actors within the flow of time, Emirbayer and Mische (1998: 964) suggest that actors are able to exercise a particular orientation (past, present, or future) toward their particular contexts, and even to change those orientations (e.g., from past to future) thereby changing their relationship to their context. In addition to being in the flow of time, however, the notion of temporal sensemaking suggests that actors construct the flow of time in which they situate themselves and in which they subsequently orient to the past, present, or future. This fundamental difference is implied by philosophers of time who point out that we are not in time (like being in a box), but rather time is in us (Sherover, 2003: 107). If, as Sherover (2003: 96) argues, "temporality is radically pervasive," that "temporal activity would seem to be intrinsic to our experiences, to our capacity to engage in experiential activity, intrinsic to any particular experiences we might have" (2003: 97), then time is fundamental to our consciousness (George and Jones, 2000) and hence to our primary experiences of the continuously changing world and, importantly, our making sense of that world. We not only remember the past, imagine the future, and respond to present circumstances in any given situation; we also understand the present in a *certain way* as we are impacted by emergent events, shape the past to account for that present, and create trajectories for the future (Mead, 1932). In other words, we shape the very temporal framework of our particular contexts on the basis of our temporally infused primary perceptions, and in so doing create unique relationships to those contexts (Emirbayer and Mische, 1998).

11.1.1 A note on past, present, future

Sherover (2003) presents a succinct history of time in Western thought that highlights key ways in which we experience time. Natural processes that are cyclical suggest almost an "eternal present" (e.g., circadian rhythm, seasons). Other natural processes (e.g., aging) suggest a movement from past through present to the future. The time of human consciousness, however, seems to flow in the opposite direction—from the future, though the present and finally slipping into the past. Continental phenomenologists and American pragmatists brought these together in a "living present" (2003: 13) where determinism of the past and free will of an open future come together. Some, like Bergson, posited the concept of *dureé* (Purser et al., 2005; Tsoukas and Chia, 2002) which focuses on the internal experience of time as flow rather than as a discrete set of events. But while entering the flow is possible at times (e.g., Mainemelis, 2001), it does not appear to be the way we fully experience time. This chapter takes the position of Mead (1932) that our experience of time is social (Emirbayer and Mische, 1998). His focus is on the present where consciousness is impacted by emergence of the new. In this situation, a new present is formed from which we revise the past and newly project the future. This position seems to better allow for the confluence of human time and natural time.

11.2 Methods

This qualitative exploratory study utilizes narrative analysis to understand how managers, drawn from all levels of an organization, make sense of their experience of implementing significant organizational change from the perspective of time. In analyzing managers' narratives, I sought their individual experiences and constructions of meaning and whether these coalesced into discernable patterns. Accordingly, the unit of analysis is the individual manager's story of change. I approached the task from a constructivist rather than a realist perspective; I was not interested in the "real" story of organizational change, but rather the meanings ascribed by individual managers to the events within their experience of personal involvement in implementing change. The research questions for the study are (1) How do managers personally involved in implementing a significant organizational change narrate their experiences of that change?, and (2) How do managers involved in personally implementing a significant organizational change narrate their experiences of time in that change?

11.2.1 Research site

This study is part of a larger research program investigating organizational change in the health care system in "Province," Canada (note: personal names have been changed and place names genericized for anonymity). In 1994 the government of "Province" dissolved approximately 200 hospital and health boards, replacing them with 17 regional health authorities (RHAs). The administrative integration of all health care delivery within the respective regions provided a beginning point for service integration. This was especially pertinent for the delivery of long-term care. Facility-based long-term care was the norm, but with growing costs, an aging population, and the coming advent of the baby boomers reaching their retirement years, the government proposed a new approach. Long-term care was to become continuing care; that is, a "continuum of care" that seeks to integrate home care, local community supports, community health, supportive housing, and facility-based care. The nature of these changes provided an excellent context in which to observe managers' experience of significant organizational change. I use the word "significant" in order not to temporally determine the change taking place. The change is significant both in scope and in value-rationality (Dyck, 1997).

The specific site is a rural health region (ZRHA), which is a research partner within the larger research project. Access to managers at all levels was available through the partnership, established in 2000. At the time of this research in 2002, ZRHA served approximately 104,000 residents spread over an area of 38,000 km^2. Overall, ZRHA had a population over 65 years of age comprising 14.4 per cent of the total population, which was higher than the provincial average of about 9.8 per cent. Of those, 50 per cent were over 75 years of age. ZRHA identified these demographics as an important impetus for implementing the change in continuing care. Building on the recommendations in *Healthy Aging: New Directions for Care* ("Province" Health and Wellness, 1999), better known as the Grady Report, the government's mandated model of changing long-term care to continuing care,

ZRHA aggressively pursued this change. The Region's overall leadership and strength of commitment to implementing the Grady Report contributes to the value of ZRHA as the specific site for this research.

11.2.2 Data sources

This study utilizes 21 semi-structured interviews with managers directly involved in implementing the change in continuing care (henceforth "the change"). The importance of the managers' narratives for this study of time and organizational change is twofold. First, narratives capture organizational members' sensemaking, and they do so in members' own terms (Pentland, 1999). Through narratives we are able to access organizational members' cognitive processing (Tenkasi and Boland, 1993) of their first-hand, ongoing experience of organizational change. Second, narratives are replete with time, bringing together both objective and subjective time in the form of sequence (chronology) (Pentland, 1999) and identification of, and ascription of meaning to, consequential events (kairology) (Riessman, 1993). In narratives of organizational change obtained in the course of actively implementing that change, we have access to organizational members' use of time in making sense of organizational change.

All managers interviewed work within ZRHA. Seventeen managers are directly employed by ZRHA. The other four managers represent three types of partner organizations providing delivery of continuing care in the region: a not-for-profit voluntary organization (two managers), a non-profit foundation (one manager), and a for-profit private organization (one manager). Together, the twenty-one managers represent all three streams of care that constitute continuing care; that is, home-living, supportive living, and facility-based. The home living and supportive living streams collectively fall within the community care stream, in which eighteen managers are involved; the facility-based stream involves nine managers (some managers are involved in more than one care stream). The interviews were conducted from August 8 to September 6, 2002 in each person's place of work during their normal working hours. The interviews were triangulated with several other data sources, including observational data, archival documents, and additional interviews from the larger research project.

11.2.3 Data analysis

11.2.3.1 GATHERING THE PRIMARY INTERVIEW DATA

Given that different settings, different people, and different developments of the relationship between researcher and respondent all contribute to producing differing narrative accounts, I made the following decisions to elicit stories of change from managers. I met with each respondent individually in the context of their own workplace. Underscoring confidentiality and the voluntary nature of the interview assisted respondents in freely discussing the change however they wished. I also encouraged them to tell me *their* story of the implementation of change in continuing care and to frame their story in whatever way seemed appropriate to them, rather than attempting to conform to some conception of the "official" story of change. Finally, I also sought to convey a sense of valuing who they were and the story they had to tell, which I hoped would help them to share their stories freely. I felt a sense of guarded conversation on only one occasion. The questions were open ended. I sought as much as possible to "get out of the way" of the person telling the story so that the resulting story would reflect more of their own construction of the narrative rather than be a response to my continual shaping.

I tape recorded each interview when given permission; otherwise I manually recorded the interview, taking detailed notes which were typed as soon as possible in order to capture as much of the interview as possible from notes and memory. Taped interviews were transcribed verbatim with a high level of detail. Wanting to have a full sense of respondents' "telling," including emotions, I included pauses, additional emphasis on words, unfinished sentences, verbal fillers, nonverbal emotions expressed (e.g., laughter, sighing), repetitions of words, and interruptions. These features of speech can carry additional meaning that would otherwise be lost. While this made transcripts more difficult to read, it better reflected the interaction creating the interview data and better captured the verbal, on the spot constructed character of the narratives. The transcribed interviews yielded approximately 300 single-spaced pages of text.

11.2.3.2 ANALYZING AND INTERPRETING THE NARRATIVE INTERVIEWS

Approaching the narrative data, I practiced "analytic induction" (Riessman, 1993). This requires, first, considerable time scrutinizing the rough data across a number of interviews to allow a focus for analysis to emerge. I began with the narrative's structure. This helps the researcher to "start from the inside," which attends to the meanings "encoded in the form of talk"

(Riessman, 1993: 61). The intent is to privilege the speaker's voice and attend to their construction of the story. To do so, I drew on the work of Gee (1999), who takes an oral approach to the analysis of interview data, to undertake an in-depth structural analysis of two interviews that represented extreme cases from the perspective of demographics. I then returned to the content to better understand what was being said in light of the way it was being said. Again I turned to Gee, who suggests that in telling stories the teller engages in building their "reality" (1999: 12, 86); that is, through his/her speech, the teller delineates their social world, making certain aspects relevant while making others irrelevant. What we see, then, in the interviews is not their world "as it is" but the world of the teller as it has meaning for the teller at the time of the interview.

Having honed my attention through the lengthy and detailed analysis of the two interviews, I then proceeded to analyze the remainder much more quickly. As I examined and re-examined the stories, I developed five "worlds of organizational change." Within this framework, I again compared the central issues and themes from within each world and across worlds to validate the distinctiveness of the worlds. Being satisfied that the five worlds were indeed distinct, I created composite portraits of each world from its members, thereby identifying the general story of change for each world and the temporal construction of that change.

11.3 Temporal construction of managers' worlds of organizational change

The five "worlds of organizational change" emerging from the analysis are the following: "Now = Then", with little hope for meaningful change (World 1); "We'll See": Practical assessment at the local level (World 2); "Hitting a Wall" (World 3); "A Rocky Road" (World 4); and "It Never Stops": Massive and unrelenting change (World 5). The titles of the worlds come from managers' own words as they described their experiences of organizational change.

I begin with some demographic observations as they relate to the five worlds. Then, for each world, I provide the general characterization of each world's story of change followed by identifying the world's temporal construction of the change (see Table 11.1).

The five stories of change are interesting demographically since they do not fall along functional, role, or other demographic lines. For example, senior managers (those of ZRHA and partner organizations) are found in

Table 11.1 Central characteristics of managers' worlds of organizational change

World	Central story	Central issue	Key elements in story of change	Construction of time	Managers' responses/actions
Now = Then	No change	What is real change	Real change: • Relevance to manager • Fundamental difference in underlying philosophies • Known through comparison of states: Hindrances to real change: • Instability leading to reversals – fluctuating provincial budget, – political aspirations of politicians – turnover of top management • Shutting out front line staff – Ignoring – Actively excluding	• Identity of present and future with past ("sameness" across time) • Continuous temporality • Past is dominant	Raw emotions: • Cynicism • Anger • Despair Managers feel shut down and shut out
We'll See	This might be a change eventually	What is real change	Real change: • Different goals than those already being pursued • Fundamental difference from the past • Takes considerable time to accomplish • Planning must meet practice	• Deliberately slow pace • Evolutionary, incremental progress • Continuous temporality • Engagement in the present; present is dominant	Making it possible to involve front line staff • Provide time (deliberately slow down the change initiative) • Share ideas • Provide training and education • Listen to their ideas and feedback
Hitting a Wall	Have made real change but now hit a wall	Helplessness in the face of an insurmountable barrier	• Grady Report defined a new (good) world which was fully supported by ZRHA • Real accomplishments already achieved	• Demarcation of new era • Discontinuous temporality	With framing of new world: • Positive emotions, energy, and accomplishments, even if stressful at times

Theme	Sub-narrative	Storyline	Temporality	Actions / Emotions
A Rocky Road — We are progressing, though it is very difficult at times		• Now facing insurmountable barriers (institutional players) that threaten all that has been accomplished – Fiscal constraint and instability – Lack of supportive legislation	• Past is dominant within a future perfect tense • However, the past of the old era may yet dominate	In the face of barriers: • Negative emotions: cynicism, fear, frustration • Loss of motivation: tinkering around the edges or inaction • Searching for alternatives
	Making it work	• Pragmatic approach to implementing change ("doing what makes sense here") • Engaging the context day-to-day while keeping eye on future goal • Metaphors of contextually engaging change • Sense of continuous change in the world around them	• Engagement in the present with future goal in mind • Continuous temporality • Present is dominant • Sense of continuous change	Numerous actions conveyed: • Taking control of the change • Creativity in the face of barriers • Translation of change initiative to "front line" • Feedback to higher levels • Real achievements • Lots of emotion, positive and negative; at times intense
It Never Stops — Massive and unrelenting change	**Seeking stability**	• Downloading from "Province" Health and Wellness • Early discharges to home care which greatly expanded the program • Fiscal restraints placed on managers that minimized provision of service	• Cutting ties to the past and instilling new behavior • Insufficient time (Clock Time construction) • Massive turbulence in the present • Discontinuous temporality • Future dominant	• Downloading onto staff • Insufficient time for training, and learning new ways of doing things • Burnout pending for both manager and staff; growing inability to handle more changes

Worlds 1, 3, and 4. Facility managers are found in Worlds 1, 2, 3, and 4. The top management team of ZRHA is found in both Worlds 3 and 4. Home care managers are found in Worlds 1, 3, 4, and 5. Managers with many years of experience are in all five worlds; managers with relatively less experience (i.e., ⟨ 5 years) are in Worlds 3 and 4. Even managers reporting to the same superior (e.g., facility managers and home care managers) did not experience or construct the change in the same way, and hence did not enact the change in the same way. With this in mind, we now turn to the worlds themselves.

11.3.1 World 1: Now = Then, with little hope for meaningful change

World 1 is a story of non-change in the midst of all the talk and activity of implementing the Grady Report in ZRHA. Even more, it is a story of little to no hope for real change in the future, based on the experience of the government's present activities and the history of change in the organization and delivery of health care. Three managers share this world's characteristics.

> We've been talking about change probably for the last eight or nine years, and it's been going on and on and on, and I haven't seen a lot of change, quite honestly. . . . In the services to the clients, I haven't seen a lot of change. And I guess that's—you know, we were providing basic services then. We're still providing basic services now. (Debbie)
>
> I don't know if it's going to mean anything at the end of the day about change. I just don't—it's not clear to me yet the significance of calling things different. I don't want to be facetious here. We are heavily involved in activities and discussions and in fact implementation around what people think might be a change. It's just not clear whether it really is a change yet. (Susan)

The central issue in this world's story is, "what constitutes real change?" Much activity, new structures, and new terminology in and of themselves do not constitute real change for managers telling this story of change. Real change, in this world, is a matter of two issues: relevance to the manager and fundamental difference in underlying philosophies, which becomes visible through comparison of states in different time periods. States of affairs can be compared either with a future time (a pending comparison) or a past time (near or distant past), or even fine-grained day to day comparisons. Hindering real change in this world stems from a perceived lack of stability and reversals in the direction of change over time, and managers' exclusion from involvement in shaping the change.

11.3.1.1 CONSTRUCTION OF TIME: CONTINUITY—THE PRESENT (AND FUTURE) IS THE PAST

World 1 exemplifies the temporal construction of continuity where the present and future are substantially the same as the past. When managers equate "now" with "then" and "this" with "that," they create continuity between time and between events such that those times and events become equivalent, and the present substantially becomes the past (Zerubavel, 2003). The future may also come to be represented as "sameness" with the past/present when eventually compared with an earlier point in time. The likelihood of parallels being drawn between the future and the past/present is enhanced by managers framing the future in the context of a trajectory of identity and continuity between these temporalities. The past, then, is actively constructed as dominating the present and, in expectation, the future.

11.3.2 World 2: We'll see: Practical assessment at the local level

> Well, the expectation certainly is that we make long-term care facilities a more home-like atmosphere where we provide a higher level of, certainly, choice, resident involvement, family involvement in the care of those people. In some ways, I don't see it as a huge change because that's always been the goal, but certainly provincially, we seem to think it's a huge change, so (trailing off) . . .

This excerpt is the beginning of the story of change for the one manager, Mark, in World 2. While sharing the same central issue and some features with World 1, what distinguishes this world is the sense that real change may yet come, though it will take substantial time to accomplish. Mark advocates working slowly toward change. Central to taking time is the involvement of front line staff and managers, who bring an understanding to the change implementation from their day-to-day experience which is missing from the planning at higher levels.

> Generally speaking, the people who do the work are best able to help change it, or I find anyway. They truly understand what they've been seeing and what people who they care for have been telling them or what would be better for them, and if we make it possible for them to do that, we will see choice and change and the Eden Alternative and all of those things. But we have to make it possible . . .

This is not to say that planning at the higher levels is not needed. But change in this world occurs when planning is complemented by the full involvement of those at the front line.

11.3.2.1 CONSTRUCTION OF TIME: CONTINUITY—THE FUTURE MAY EVENTUALLY BE DIFFERENT FROM THE PRESENT

World 2 exemplifies an evolutionary change whose pacing is imposed by the manager. While not always able to control the pace ("telling people how we're going to change—that may happen when I'm on the unit but that's not where we wish to be. . . ."), Mark strives to attain the insights of the front line, and to fully involve them in the process. Like the managers of Now = Then (World 1), Mark constructs continuity between the past, present, and future. However, unlike the managers of World 1, Mark does not equate the present or the future with the past; he acknowledges the present as different from the past as well as the possibility of real change in the future. The present has grown out of the past and the future will grow out of the present as ideas are thought through, tested, and implemented at the interface of practice. By locating real change at the practice interface and controlling the pacing of the change to include those at the front line, Mark assures, as much as possible, the evolutionary nature of change.

11.3.3 World 3: Hitting a wall

> I guess for me, to sum up my experience with the change in continuing care and the transition, there's been some real highs—it's been really, really exciting, challenging. It's probably the best work I've done in my career in terms of being able to see some positive outcomes and to be able to have a really, really strong vision. But there've also been some real lows because there is so much we could do if we could just get all the ducks in a row. If we could get the—if the politicians could agree, if the departments could work together, if we could get the legislative changes, if we could get some agreement among the regions that they will all buy into the same system so that we have a system that's across the Province—not, you get something different if you're in "Major City 1" and "Major City 2" than you do if you're in ZRHA. And if some of those things came together, I think we're positioned really well to make some big changes . . .

Catherine's summary depicts the central characteristics of implementing change in continuing care as construed in this world, shared by six managers. Given the Grady Report, which brought "a whole new vision" and energized people working in continuing care, Catherine's work has been a time of real highs. The positive side is characterized by accomplishment. But it has also been a time of real lows: there is so much more that they could do. The negative side is characterized by a significant blockage in progress caused by inconsonance among external actors in the change initiative, a situation that appears to be remedied only by the fulfilment of a series of difficult conditions ("if … if … if … if … if … ") that lie outside the realm of one's influence. Answers to key questions are not forthcoming, initiatives are put on hold, resources shift to other projects, and clarity and energy are lost:

> So we had this great momentum for eight to ten months and then we kind of hit a wall and we can't go over—can't address any more ideas because there's a bunch of unknowns, so … the momentum was there, there was a lot of momentum. We had a lot of buy-in and we dissipated because we haven't got any more answers to the questions that we're waiting on still. (Jesse; community level)

11.3.3.1 CONSTRUCTION OF TIME: DISCONTINUITY—THE DEMARCATION OF NEW WORLDS

World 3 is characterized by discontinuity over time. The creation of discontinuity is the act of punctuating the continuousness of on-going experience into distinct periods. Typically, demarcation of specific periods is accomplished through retrospective identification of a "watershed" event that marks the end of one period and the beginning of another (Zerubavel, 2003). In this world, the watershed event used to denote discontinuity is the Grady Report. It gathered up the wide and loosely connected discussions in continuing care, providing coherence and energy as it raised its profile. Managers in this world, however, may be facing yet another new "era" with the potential watershed event of government inaction. While still uncertain, signs are appearing: managers have become fearful and are no longer energized in the face of seemingly insurmountable roadblocks.

It is important to note that along with bifurcating time, managers in this world are working toward a future goal that is understood to be the future consummation of an already existing "reality." In other words, managers are working in the "future perfect" tense (Gioia et al., 2002). It is a new world—a future envisioned as already having happened. This justifies and energizes the present actions taken to achieve what is considered a "reality" but at the moment is manifested only as a new orientation.

11.3.4 World 4: A rocky road

> The change, in itself, has been a rocky road—a rocky road.

Fay begins her story by describing it as a rocky road, which is representative of how the ten managers in this world tell their stories of change. The work has been difficult; there have been ups and downs. But they continue to make progress. In this world managers use a very pragmatic approach to change, paying careful attention to the context within which change must take place. This orientation is well represented by the following short quotes, oft repeated in this world: "Well, we will do what makes sense here," "and that really works well in here." Rather than waiting on others to act to create the best framework for the change, these managers become proactive. They will go ahead with changes, finding solutions to problems faced now, in the moment.

Within this world, more so than other worlds, managers use a variety of metaphors, such as "the dance," "walking through mud," and "paddling upstream" to communicate their pragmatic, daily experience of implementing change. In so doing they are struggling to express their experience with the vagaries of the flux and flow of a world in continuous change while attempting to continuously move forward toward the final goal outlined in the Grady Report. The "dance" in particular captures the sense well, directing attention to the day-to-day exigencies and contingencies of carrying out one's normal work responsibilities while also anticipating changes that may come and shaping those that do. It is a metaphor that elegantly captures the responsiveness to the myriad contextual issues involved in implementing change while keeping an eye on the future.

> ... doing that dance between ... the principles that we're operating under now and the anticipated ones is kind of grey sometimes, and so that becomes a dance to stay clear about what we're trying to do in the moment and still think about how it may be and how we can position ourselves to be ready to move, 'cause I think that's one of the things that we've tried to do in this office is be in a position where we're ready to move—structure ourselves and structure our processes so that they aren't so cumbersome, that we can move when we have to. And that's the dance. (Grace)

In World 4, managers work within their contexts and within continuous change to pragmatically carry out the implementation of change.

11.3.4.1 CONSTRUCTION OF TIME: CONTINUITY—ENGAGING CONTINUOUS CHANGE IN THE PRESENT

World 4 exemplifies an evolutionary change, but one that is much more convoluted than World 2. Overall there is a sense of progression toward a future goal; yet the progress is not smooth, nor is it evenly paced. The convoluted nature of the progress in this world seems to be the result of consciously engaging the past and the future in the midst of attempting planned implementation in the present. Managers characterize their world as a place of continuous change in which they must operate. To depict this sense, managers both directly claim that their world is continuously changing, as well as use numerous metaphors to attempt to convey their experience of engaging continuous change while implementing planned change.

Continuity in this world, then, is constituted differently than in the other worlds. Here it seems to be based especially on engaging all three temporal dimensions—the past and the future in an ever-changing present. More so than other worlds of organizational change, this world seems to embrace an undergirding reality of continuous change, as opposed to stability. The world is in constant flux, and in the midst of that constant flux planned change is implemented in all of its convolutions. To do so successfully requires day-by-day engagement of continuous change while at the same time holding out a future goal and dealing with a persistent past. In this way, the past and the future are engaged within a continuously changing present.

11.3.5 World 5: It never stops: Massive and unrelenting change

> And it just never seems to stop. We think, well, once we've got the writ implemented, and once we've got the home-bound status implemented, and once we're on track with doing case reviews, and once we've got all the new assessment forms for palliative care down pat and everybody's doing it, then we should be okay. But it never stops. And I understand that change is a good thing and that we need to keep upgrading ourselves, but it's just been massive in the last couple of years probably.

Change in this world is experienced as massive and unrelenting. Within this short excerpt, Ray, the one manager in this world, mentions four changes that he has had to implement with his staff. Implementing these changes should lead to a level of stability ("then we should be okay"). But bracketing the entire sentence is the poignant recurring phrase capturing his present reality: "it just never seems to stop.... But it never stops." What hope of stability might have come with fully implementing the four changes is non-existent. More of the same is coming in the form of the Grady Report, which will mean continual change as that fully rolls out. There is no end in sight, and the result is significant stress for Ray and his staff.

11.3.5.1 CONSTRUCTION OF TIME: DISCONTINUITY—CUTTING THE TIES TO THE PAST

Ray's narrative utilizes the before and after bifurcation characteristic of discontinuity. Ray easily speaks of the time previous to the present situation where there was a greater sense of stability, more leeway in meeting budgets and where there was ample money for meeting people's needs in home care. That has fundamentally changed. Now, for Ray, instability is the unhappy norm because of continual changes in policy that must be implemented. Unlike the energizing future perfect goal of World 3, the prevalent future orientation of World 5 is a new world of instability where ties to the past are cut. Ray describes his task as a manager in exactly this way. He is there to make sure that staff understand the changes they need to implement, and then to reinforce those changes in their work and behavior. Helping staff move into this new world demands deliberate reinforcement of new policy and procedure which carries the strong implication of severing and discarding links to old behavior (Zerubavel, 2003; Biggart, 1977).

11.3.6 How worlds shape managers' actions

The practical importance of the different temporally constructed worlds of organizational change is evident in their differing enactments (Weick, 1995; Pentland, 1999; Emirbayer and Mische, 1998). Given space considerations, I will simply point the reader to Table 11.1. It is worth noting that among the worlds there are some similarities, but also important differences in the actions taken by managers. Most important of these perhaps is the greater sense of control in the actions of those who predominantly engage the present (Worlds 2 and 4).

11.4 Discussion

Managers' stories of the "same" government mandated change within the "same" organizational framework reveal very different constructions of the organizational change they are experiencing. Some managers equate the present with the past resulting in a story of no change. Some tell a long, slow, evolutionary tale of change, while others see periods of time framed by events defined as turning points, periods during which change was first enabled and then hindered. Still other managers see an ongoing convoluted day-to-day effort resulting in an overall progression that combines elements of both ongoing change and planned change. Finally, others view the change as dramatic and unrelenting in its pace.

I suggest that managers' temporal sensemaking can account for this surprising display of difference. Recall that by temporal sensemaking I

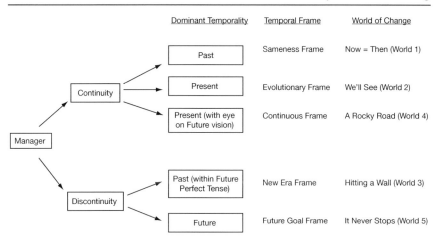

Dominant Temporality	Temporal Frame	World of Change

Fig. 11.1 Temporal framing of the five worlds of organizational change

mean the act of (re)configuring the relationship of past, present, and future. In temporal sensemaking, managers seem to draw first on continuity/discontinuity, the two basic modes of understanding the progression of time (Zerubavel, 2003), and then, second, predominantly on one of the three central dimensions of time—past, present, or future—thereby creating the distinct worlds of change (see Fig. 11.1). The results both confirm—in the predominant use of different dimensions of time—and extend—in the formation of continuity or discontinuity and thus a different past–present–future linkage—Emirbayer and Mische's (1998) theoretical linkage of agency and time.

For managers in Worlds 1, 2, and 4 what is happening now is constituted as continuity. Those in Worlds 3 and 5, however, determine that what is being experienced is different enough from the past to warrant a bifurcation in time. Both continuity and discontinuity are contrived (Zerubavel, 2003), and this done from the perspective of the knower (Adam, 2004: 66; Mead, 1932). In both cases, continuity/discontinuity appears to be created through attention to both the past and the future in the present. Theoretically, as people make sense of emergent phenomena in the present, they appear to draw on memory to determine whether what is now perceptual to the senses is in continuity with what *was* perceptual to the senses but is now in the past (Sherover, 2003). However the future is also involved:

> Human cognitive activity is founded on the capacity to anticipate futurity and bring that anticipation into the constitution of the present activity. (Sherover, 2003: 99)

The change implementation for each of the managers in this study is a planned, mandated change whose broad aspects are embodied in the Grady Report. With the anticipation and active involvement of its implementation, managers assess the emerging present against that expectation as well as the past. Continuity/discontinuity, then, appears to be determined by drawing on the future and the past in making sense of perceptual elements in the present. What is sensed in the present is assessed by our anticipation of the future; and elements of the past (in our memory), as they pertain to the anticipated future, are utilized to determine the meaning of what is emerging in the present.

Managers also seem to link what is happening in the present to a particular dimension of temporality. The managers in World 1 focus predominantly on the past where the emphasis is on the iteration of past actions and thought (Emirbayer and Mische, 1998: 971). Interestingly, they are not the ones seeking iteration. In their world, higher levels in the organization and those outside the organization (i.e., government) are responsible for what amounts to iteration (sometimes because of reversals of direction), and these managers are unhappily negated in their attempts to implement the change.

Managers in Worlds 2 and 4 predominantly focus on the present where the emphasis is on the practical-evaluative element, described as

> ... the capacity of actors to make practical and normative judgments among alternative possible trajectories of action, in response to emerging demands, dilemmas, and ambiguities of presently evolving situations. (Emirbayer and Mische, 1998: 971)

The manager in World 2 constantly evaluates the mandated changes in light of what is already happening, and tests ideas with front line staff to see what they might really mean in the nexus of practice. The managers in World 4 are highly pragmatic and creative, seeking to keep moving forward in spite of difficulties encountered. Here higher levels within and outside the organization are part of the evolving situation rather than dictating the situation. There is also an obvious sense of control over the change implementation, more so than in the other three worlds.

The manager in World 5 predominantly focuses on the future where the emphasis is on "projectivity" (Emirbayer and Mische, 1998: 971). In World 5, the manager's imagined, hoped-for future is stability in the organization (longing for iteration). However, this trajectory is being overridden by a feared and undesired trajectory—that of constant change implementation imposed from higher levels in the organization. The strength of this sense is reinforced with the bifurcation of time—it is presently a new time that does not resemble the more stable old time. Indeed, the old is being destroyed; instability is the new reality.

A special situation exists in World 3. Here the predominant temporal dimension is the past, but it is a past of a future not yet manifest (Purser et al., 2005; Schutz, 1967; Gioia et al., 2002). The managers in this world are seeking to establish the iterations that will make that future a stable reality. They are assisted in this project by bifurcating time. They are working in a new era in which the old iterative elements no longer apply and can be modified, ignored, dismantled, or destroyed. The projective element in this world is grounded in a new era that is already here, so all that needs to be done is to "make it so" by establishing new routines. The threat and fear in this narrative is that the "new era" will not materialize, and the iterations of the past era will predominate. If this latter situation materializes, it seems likely that the dominant temporal dimension for these managers will shift from the future-perfect past to the future because of real gains already made. The worst case scenario, however, is that the past era will predominate, destroying even existing hard-won gains. This world could become World 1.

11.4.1 Implications and Future Directions

An important theoretical implication of this research is that cognition is fundamentally temporal. Tenkasi and Boland (1993) recognized that narrativizing is the central cognitive activity in making sense of our lived experiences (Polkinghorne, 1988). This research extends that insight by highlighting and affirming the inherent and holistic (time-lived) temporality of narrative. Thinking narratively means thinking temporally. This observation is supported by similar evidence elsewhere. Organizational behavior researchers have noted that time is "an intrinsic property of consciousness" (George and Jones, 2000: 659). Philosophers are even more poignant—"every facet of our lives is soaked in time" (Unger, 2009: 78; Sherover, 2003). Anthropologists ground these assertions in observations of lived time in our own and other cultures (e.g., Hall, 1983; Smith, 1982).

Widespread observations of "time-soaked" cognition suggest that sensemaking is also thoroughly temporal, not just retrospective (Weick, 1995). If thinking and narrativizing is pervasively temporal, then our experiences and our sensemaking of those experiences suggests more than retrospection. Appealing to Schutz, Weick locates the action of sensemaking in the backward glance, noting that we can only pay attention to that which has already happened, even if a fraction of a second in the past. Yet this ignores the real present—that dimension of time in which events take place (Mead, 1932). The present is not an abstraction—some thin line between the infinitely extended future rushing to meet us and the infinitely extended past into which all things immediately pass. Rather, as Mead (1932: 32) asserts, the present is the "seat of reality" in which the past and future have their existence. Weick (1995) comes close to this position when he encourages us to:

> think of the act of reflection as a cone of light that spreads backward *from a particular present*. This cone of light will give definition to portions of lived experiences. Because the cone starts in the present, *projects and feelings that are under way* will affect the backward glance and what is seen. ... *Whatever is now, at the present moment, under way will determine the meaning of whatever has just occurred.* (Weick, 1995: 26–7, my emphasis)

I suggest there is no need then to narrow sensemaking down to retrospection. It is in the present that we encounter the "flowing soup" and become cognizant of new events, and from this experience, we readjust the "what it is" we are experiencing as well as the past and future as it relates to it. Is this continuous with the past (World 2)? Is this something entirely new—a new world discontinuous from the past (World 3)? Is it yet another event convoluting the road on the way to our future goal (World 4)? Is there really no change taking place in spite of all the activity and change talk (World 1)? Encountering new events in the present, managers draw on all three dimensions of temporality in making sense of those events.

Methodologically, this study suggests that clock time is limited in its usefulness for understanding and characterizing organizational change as it is understood and enacted by the organization's members. From the perspective of clock time, change researchers have pointed out that we see different things using different periodicities (Ranson et al., 1980; Pettigrew, 1985; Zaheer et al., 1999). In this study, however, "getting up close" to the action through narratives has given us polar opposites of "no change" and "massive and unrelenting change" as well as three other stories in between. We also see both continuity and discontinuity across time. This research suggests that the relative position of the *research observer* is not as important as the temporal construction and enactment by organizational members themselves. Different stories of change contain different elements, common elements (e.g., the Grady Report) related to in different ways, and different managerial actions and emotions. Pettigrew et al., (1989), commenting on strategic change, made this pertinent observation of the importance of temporality for understanding organizational change and its outcomes:

> the management of strategic change must pay attention to the wealth of temporal features involved ... The way time is socially constructed by people and the way such active perceptions of time may transform the detailed course of projects and their processes is a vital concern ... it may be in this process where the competitive performances of companies are either made or broken. (Pettigrew et al., 1989: 129)

In this study we have seen how the "same" organizational change is temporally constructed in different ways. These observations would be invisible to clock time. Examining organizational change from the perspective of time lived will enhance our understanding of how organizational change is experienced and accomplished.

Finally, given different temporal constructions of change, how might we better manage organizational change? One practical implication is that we cannot assume all managers at the same level or function in the organization will temporally make sense of the change in the same way, even if a particular sense has been given by upper management (Gioia and Chittipeddi, 1991; Chreim, 2005) and even by government, as was the case in this research.

It may be important, then, for a change agent to identify those with a similar (positive) temporal construction to champion the change. As observed, the temporal construction of the change varied drastically across any single function and level (e.g., facility managers). That similar constructions existed at various levels and functions presents an opportunity to tap into similarly held frames throughout the organization. In particular, managers who temporally construct their world as continuity with a focus on the present (Worlds 2 and 4) appear to be more in control of implementing change, even if they face setbacks, delays, disappointments, and surprises. These managers will continue to creatively seek ways forward in spite of difficulties. They will also better manage the inevitable emotion that arises in significant organizational change (Huy, 2002).

Less effective is to attempt sense-giving through verbal temporal reframing. In this research, reframing seemed to come with changed budgets, new policies, and action/inaction, and not with verbal sense-giving. Moreover, when reframing did happen (e.g., insurmountable blocks in World 3), it occurred through assessment from experience. Since temporal sensemaking stems from the consciousness of the knower, their experiences will shape the temporal sense of the change initiative more than verbal directives or promises from superiors (Labianca et al., 2000).

Another practical implication is that in the midst of implementing organizational change, we are able to see resistance to change in relation to different temporal constructions of the change. For example, resistance may be an erroneous attribution of slowing down the pace of change to fully include those at the front lines (World 2). Such managers actually strengthen the implementation over the long term by creating continuity and shielding their staff and daily routine from perturbations (Huy, 2002). Resistance may also be an erroneous attribution of cynicism, fear, and tentativeness resulting from a loss of sense of direction (Worlds 1 and 3) engendered through the actions of upper management and/or government. Managers in these worlds actually wanted change and had worked hard at implementation. Reaffirming the "new reality" (e.g., Grady Report in World 3) or the original direction (World 1) for employees, especially through enacting supporting frameworks (e.g., necessary legislation, appropriate budgets), imparts the confidence that actions taken are not in vain and renews energy for the change initiative. Finally, resistance may be the result of a manager's construction of change as an unrelenting onslaught of the "brave new world" (World 5). These managers, who seek stability and thrive on iteration, may more readily embrace rather than resist change if the change is experientially reframed as evolutionary—for example, making connections to the past routines, slowing the pace of change, and actively seeking feedback.

This leads to a third practical implication. In this research I observed a high degree of emotion in each world (with the stark exception of World 2). While emotion is inevitable, it appears some temporal constructions are more susceptible to becoming negatively charged. In particular, those managers who constructed their stories with an external referent (e.g., the government, upper management) experienced a great deal more negative emotion (Worlds 1, 3, 5). In contrast, those who constructed their stories with reference to themselves tended to experience no emotion or more positive than negative emotion. These were the managers who also temporally constructed their worlds as continuity with a focus on the present. To diffuse negative emotion and to increase efficacy in implementing change, it seems important to fully include managers and employees in determining the change in which they are involved. In doing so, managers and employees will not feel shut down and shut out (World 1), and their suggestions will add necessary practical nuance and feedback to the change implementation (e.g., "choice" in the context of dementia patients; World 2). Granting greater involvement may create an experience shift for managers that could lead to a change of managers' temporal constructions; it may also alleviate some of the negative emotion often associated with significant change.

Future directions for research are suggested by limitations of this study. First, I have approached this research thoroughly immersed in Western temporal thinking, making it difficult to see time from another vantage point. Anthropologists have shown us that Western time is not universal (Smith, 1982; Hall, 1983). Thus future studies examining "time-lived" should include researchers from other ethnic/national temporal contexts. In the same vein, other philosophical approaches could be utilized. Our Western view of time is arbitrary (McGrath and Rotchford, 1983). Thus, while Westerners think of time as flowing incessantly from the future and that time is a pre-requisite of change, we might seek insight from Mead's (1932) conception that change is a pre-requisite of time and so perhaps time does not come at us as we suppose. What might we see with different philosophical orientations that would help us better understand organizational change (Tsoukas and Chia, 2002; Purser and Petranker, 2005; Wiebe and Golden-Biddle, 2002)? Another temporal orientation stems from this study being located in health care. There may be a different sense of time in this context shaped by a mandate for care rather than pure production. Future research should include other sectors (e.g. Staudenmayer et al., 2002).

Second, this study is essentially cross-sectional. Further research should incorporate a longitudinal design to see if and how temporal constructions change (Isabella, 1990; Chreim, 2007). Third, this research focused on the individual manager's sensemaking. Future research should examine the interaction of "worlds of organizational change" and the accomplishment (or not) of a collective interpretation. An obvious site for the conflict or collision of "presents" is meetings. Supporting data from the larger research project suggests that managers bring their temporal construction of the change initiative to bear on subjects discussed in meetings. The investigation of the interaction of temporal perspectives would illuminate how individual temporal constructions may become reconstituted, and how "objects" within the change initiative may be used in that work of reconstitution. It may also provide insight into the temporal basis for conflicted groups (e.g. Barley, 1988).

Note

I gratefully acknowledge the research funding provided by the Canadian Health Services Research Foundation and the "Province" Heritage Foundation for Medical

Research through the Health Organization Studies research team at the University of "Province" School of Business. I aslo gratefully acknowledge the guidance provided by Karen Golden-Biddle on an earlier version of this chapter. Finally, I also gratefully acknowledge the editorial guidance of Tor Hernes and two anonymous reviewers whose suggestions greatly strengthened the paper.

References

Adam, B. (1994). Perceptions of time, in T. Ingold (ed.) *Companion Encyclopedia of Anthropology: Humanity, Culture and Social Life*, London: Routledge, 503–26.

Adam, B. (1998). *Timescapes of Modernity: The Environment and Invisible Hazards*, London: Routledge.

Adam, B. (2004). *Time*, Cambridge, UK: Polity Press.

Ancona, D. & Chong, C.-L. (1996). Entrainment: Pace, cycle and rhythm in organizational behaviour, in B. M. Staw & L. L. Cummings (eds) *Research in Organizational Behavior*, Greenwich, CT: JAI Press, 18, 251–84.

Ancona, D., Okhuysen, G., & Perlow, L. (2001). Taking time to integrate temporal research, *Academy of Management Review*, 26 (4), 512–29.

Armenakis, A. A. & Bedeian, A. G. (1999). Organizational change: A review of theory and research in the 1990s, *Journal of Management*, 25 (3), 293–315.

Avital, M. (2000). Dealing with time in social inquiry: A tension between method and lived experience, *Organization Science*, 11 (6), 665–73.

Barley, S. R. (1988). On technology, time, and social order: Technically induced change in the temporal organization of radiological work, in F. A. Dubinskas (ed.) *Making time: Ethnographies of High-technology Organizations*, Philadelphia: Temple University Press, 123–69.

Biggart, N. W. (1977). The creative–destructive process of organizational change: The case of the post office, *Administrative Science Quarterly*, 22, 410–26.

Bluedorn, A. C. (2002). *The Human Organization of Time: Temporal Realities and Experience*, Stanford, CA: Stanford University Press.

Brown, S. L. & Eisenhardt, K. M. (1997). The art of continuous change: Linking complexity theory and time-paced evolution in relentlessly shifting organizations, *Administrative Science Quarterly*, 42, 1–34.

Burrell, G. (1992). Back to the future: Time and organization, in M. Reed & M. Hughs (eds) *Rethinking Organizations*, London: Sage, 165–83.

Chia, R. (1999). A "rhizomic" model of organizational change and transformation: Perspectives from a metaphysics of change, *British Journal of Management*, 10, 209 27.

Chreim, S. (2005). The continuity–change duality in narrative texts of organizational identity, *Journal of Management Studies*, 42 (3), 567–93.

Chreim, S. (2007). Social and temporal influences on interpretations of organizational identity and acquisition integration: A narrative study, *Journal of Applied Behavioral Science*, 43 (4), 449–80.

Clark, P. A. (1985). A review of the theories of time and structure for organizational sociology, in S. B. Bacharach & S. M. Mitchell (eds) *Research in the Sociology of Organizations*, Greenwich, Conn.: JAI Press, 4, 35–79.

Dutton, J. E., Ashford, S. J., O'Neill, R. M., & Lawrence, K. A. (2001). Moves that matter: Issue selling and organizational change, *Academy of Management Journal*, 44 (4), 716–36.

Dyck, B. (1997). Understanding configuration and transformation through a multiple rationalities approach, *Journal of Management Studies*, 34 (5), 793–823.

Emirbayer, M. & Mische, A. (1998). What is agency? *American Journal of Sociology*, 103 (4), 962–1023.

Gee, J. P. (1999). *An Introduction to Discourse Analysis: Theory and Method*, New York: Routledge.

George, J. M. & Jones, G. R. (2000). The role of time in theory and theory building, *Journal of Management*, 26, 657–84.

Gersick, C. J. G. (1988). Time and transition in work teams: Toward a new model of group development, *Academy of Management Journal*, 31, 9–41.

Gersick, C. J. G. (1994). Pacing strategic change: The case of a new venture, *Academy of Management Journal*, 37 (1), 9–45.

Gioia, D. A. & Chittipeddi, K. (1991). Sensemaking and sensegiving in strategic change initiation, *Strategic Management Journal*, 12, 433–48.

Gioia, D. A., Corley, K. G., & Fabbri, T. (2002). Revising the past (while thinking in the future perfect tense), *Journal of Organizational Change Management*, 15 (6), 622–34.

Hall, E. T. (1983). *The Dance of Life: The Other Dimension of Time*, New York: Anchor Books/Doubleday.

Huy, Q. (2002). Emotional balancing of organizational continuity and radical change: The contribution of middle managers, *Administrative Science Quarterly*, 47, 31–69.

Isabella, L. A. (1990). Evolving interpretations as a change unfolds: How managers construe key organizational events, *Academy of Management Journal*, 33 (1), 7–41.

Labianca, G., Gray, B., & Brass, D. J. (2000). A grounded model of organizational schema change during empowerment, *Organization Science*, 11 (2), 235–57.

Landes, D. S. (1983). *Revolution in Time: Clocks and the Making of the Modern World*. Cambridge, MA: Harvard University Press.

Langley, A. (2007). Process thinking in strategic organization, *Strategic Organization*, 5 (3), 271–82.

Lee, H. & Liebenau, J. (1999). Time in organizational studies: Towards a new research direction, *Organization Studies*, 20 (6), 1035–58.

McGrath, J. E. & Rotchford, N. L. (1983). Time and behavior in organizations, *Research in Organizational Behavior*, 5, 57–101.

Mainemelis, C. (2001). When the muse takes it all: A model for the experience of timelessness in organizations, *Academy of Management Review*, 26 (4), 548–65.

Mead, G. H. (1932). *The Philosophy of the Present*, Chicago: Open Court Publishing Co.

Noss, C. (2002). Taking time seriously: Organizational change, flexibility, and the present time in a new perspective, in R. Whipp, B. Adam, & I. Sabelis (eds) *Making Time: Time and Management in Modern Organizations*, Oxford: Oxford University Press.

O'Connor, E. S. (2000). Plotting the organization: The embedded narrative as a construct for studying change, *The Journal of Applied Behavioral Science*, 36, 174–92.

Pentland, B. T. (1999). Building process theory with narrative: From description to explanation, *Academy of Management Review*, 24 (4), 711–24.

Perlow, L. (1999). The time famine: Toward a sociology of work time, *Administrative Science Quarterly*, 44 (1), 57–82.

Pettigrew, A. M. (1985). Contextualist research: A natural way to link theory and practice, in E. E. Lawler, A. G. Mohrman Jr., S. A. Mohrman, G. E. Ledford Jr., & T. G. Cummings (eds) *Doing Research that is Useful for Theory and Practice*, San Francisco: Jossey-Bass, 222–74.

Pettigrew, A. M., Whipp, R., & Rosenfeld, R. (1989). Competitiveness and the management of strategic change processes, in A. Francis & P. K. M. Tharakan (eds) *The Competitiveness of European Industry*, London: Routledge, 110–36.

Pettigrew, A. M., Woodman, R. W., & Cameron, K. S. (2001). Studying organizational change and development: Challenges for future research, *Academy of Management Journal*, 44 (4), 697–713.

Polkinghorne, D. E. (1988). *Narrative Knowing and the Human Sciences*, Albany: State University of New York Press.

"Province" Health and Wellness (1999). *Healthy Aging: New Directions for Care*, "City": Communications Branch, "Province" Health and Wellness, November.

Purser, R. E. & Petranker, J. (2005). Unfreezing the future: Exploring the dynamic of time in organizational change, *Journal of Applied Behavioral Science*, 41 (2), 182–203.

Purser, R. E., Bluedorn, A. C., & Petranker, J. (2005). The times of cause and flow in organizational change, *Research in Organizational Change and Development*, 15, 1–29.

Ranson, S., Hinings, C. R., & Greenwood, R. (1980). The structuring of organizational structures, *Administrative Science Quarterly*, 25, 1–17.

Riessman, C. K. (1993). *Narrative Analysis*, Newbury Park, CA: Sage.

Schutz, A. (1967). *The Phenomenology of the Social World*, trans. G. Walsh & F. Lehnert, Toronto: Northwestern University Press.

Sherover, C. M. (2003). *Are We in Time? And Other Essays on Time and Temporality*, Evanston, IL: Northwestern University Press.

Smith, M. F. (1982). Bloody time and bloody scarcity: Capitalism, authority, and the transformation of temporal experience in a Papua New Guinea village, *American Ethnologist*, 9 (3), 503–18.

Staudenmayer, N., Tyre, M., & Perlow, L. (2002). Time to change: Temporal shifts as enablers of organizational change, *Organization Science*, 13 (5), 583–97.

Tenkasi, R. V. & Boland, R. J., Jr. (1993). Locating meaning making in organizational learning: The narrative basis of cognition, *Research in Organizational Change and Development*, 7, 77–103.

Tsoukas, H. & Chia, R. (2002). On organizational becoming: Rethinking organizational change, *Organization Science*, 13 (5), 567–82.

Unger, R. M. (2009). *The Self Awakened: Pragmatism Unbound*. Cambridge, MA: Harvard University Press.

Van de Ven, A. H. & Poole, M. S. (1995). Explaining development and change in organizations, *Academy of Management Review*, 20 (3), 510–40.

Weick, K. E. (1995). *Sensemaking in Organizations*, Thousand Oaks: Sage.

Weick, K. E. & Quinn, R. E. (1999). Organizational change and development, *Annual Review of Psychology*, 50, 361–86.

Wiebe, E. & Golden-Biddle, K. (2002). *Change in Time and Time in Change: Addressing Temporal Dualism in the Study of Organizational Change*, Presented at the Dynamic Time and Creative Inquiry in Organizational Change Conference, Boston, June.

Zaheer, S., Albert, S., & Zaheer, A. (1999). Time scales and organizational theory, *Academy of Management Review*, 24 (4), 725–41.

Zerubavel, E. (2003). *Time Maps: Collective Memory and the Social Shape of the Past*, Chicago: University of Chicago Press.

12

Studying *Metaphors-in-Use* in their Social and Institutional Context: Sensemaking and Discourse Theory

Silvia Jordan and Hermann Mitterhofer

Abstract: This chapter seeks to relate sensemaking and sensegiving processes to their social and institutional context by describing and explaining the effects of diverse metaphors of change used by organizational members during the implementation of lean production and TQM in an internationally operating manufacturing company. We explore how organizational members made sense of these strategic changes in terms of their understanding of the process as an incremental or rather a radical organizational change. We analyze what kind of "conceptual metaphors" are associated with these divergent understandings and explain the relative power of certain conceptual metaphors of change as compared to others by analyzing the social and institutional context of these metaphors-in-use. Adopting a "contextualized metaphor" analytical approach which expands Lakoff and Johnson's conceptual metaphor theory with the discourse analysis of linguist Jürgen Link, we analyze the link of dominant metaphors-in-use to institutionalized meanings as represented in "collective symbols" apparent in "interdiscursive" charts. Conceptual metaphors were particularly powerful when they referred to institutions that enable identification by virtue of taken-for-granted favorable connotations and by means of interpretive flexibility.

12.1 Introduction

Several authors have recently pointed out that cultural-cognitive institutions are an implicit but under-theorized component of current theories of sensemaking (Sutcliffe et al., 2006; Weber & Glynn, 2006; Weick et al., 2005). In this paper, we relate sensemaking and sensegiving processes to their social and institutional context by describing and explaining the effects of diverse metaphors of change used by organizational members during a strategic change initiative in a manufacturing company. We explore the relative power of these metaphors-in-use by analyzing their connection to institutionalized meanings, adopting a "contextualized metaphor analysis" informed by Jürgen Link's (1982, 1996) discourse analysis.

Sensemaking studies focusing on the use of metaphors in organizations have described *how* and *by whom* certain metaphors were used to give and make sense of events and *what effects* this use of metaphors had on individual and collective actions (Gioia et al., 1994; Gioia & Thomas, 1996; Greenberg, 1995; Watson, 2003). However, they did not relate these usages and effects to social and institutional contexts in order to explain *why* certain metaphors are more powerful than others. This chapter seeks to address this gap in that it investigates the use of socially and institutionally situated metaphors in sensemaking and sensegiving in the course of an organizational change initiative. The implementation of lean and total quality management (TQM) in the production company studied was prompted by the newly appointed Chief Operating Officer (COO) and entailed diverse change initiatives, comprising among other things changes in plant layout, production processes, supplier relations, and the product portfolio. Organizational members theorized about this organizational change differently, viewing it either as an extensive change initiative or as a minor initiative reinforcing the company's existing strategies and shared ways of thinking and acting. We explore what kind of metaphors of change were drawn upon in organizational members' talk and writing about the change process, and analyze the relation of dominant metaphors to institutionalized meanings in order to explain their relative power.

The chapter is organized as follows. In the next section, we review extant research on metaphors in organization studies and outline current gaps in this literature with regard to the study of cultural-cognitive institutions. In the following section, we introduce Jürgen Link's discourse analysis and develop a "contextualized metaphor analysis" as a framework for studying metaphors-in-use. We then describe the research context of our case study of metaphors of change and stability in a manufacturing company, and we present the methods of data collection and analysis. Thereafter, we identify relevant metaphors-in-use and analyze their institutionally situated use based on our analytical framework. In the concluding section, we discuss how the study informs our understanding of the impact of the institutional context on metaphors, and our understanding of sensemaking in organizations more generally.

12.2 Metaphor analysis in organization studies

By emphasizing the interactive talk and the resources of language in organizing processes, Karl Weick's concept of sensemaking (Weick, 1979, 1988, 1993, 1995; Weick et al., 2005) forms part of the "linguistic turn" in organization studies (Alvesson and Kärreman, 2000; Bakken and Hernes, 2006; Czarniawska, 2006; Weick et al., 2005). This approach is prominently expressed by the saying *how can I know what I think until I see what I say?* (Weick, 1995) and in the notion that "situations, organizations, and environments are *talked into existence*" (Weick et al., 2005: 409, emphasis added). Metaphors have, among other things, been pointed out as relevant linguistic devices applied in order to make sense of events, be it in everyday or in academic theory construction (Cornelissen, 2006; Czarniawska, 2004). Rather than being mere linguistic forms, metaphors are characterized as expressions of certain shared "world views," that is, as cognitive schemes that form part of the social construction of reality (Cornelissen et al., 2008; Heracleous and Jacobs, 2008; Lakoff and Johnson, 1980).

Within organization studies, metaphors have been used on the one hand for theory building, as authors have *projected* metaphors as "second-order" constructs onto empirical settings in order to describe and explain the "first-order" lived experience of people within organizations (Cornelissen, 2006; Hatch and Yanow, 2008; Morgan, 1986; Putnam et al., 1997; Tsoukas, 1991; Weick, 1989). On the other hand, organization scholars have also more inductively analyzed how metaphors are used by organizational actors themselves. In these studies, processes of meaning-making around metaphors are elicited at the level of people's language use: "The objective is to identify the symbolic and interpretive uses of metaphors in people's sensemaking and communication with one another" (Cornelissen et al., 2008: 10). Most of these studies contextualize metaphors-in-use in emphasizing locally-specific uses and meanings of metaphors and highlighting their potential social impact in terms of impression management, normative judgments, and legitimacy. Such research often looks at how metaphors are involved in processes of promoting and adopting new perspectives, or maintaining established ways of thinking and acting during organizational change. Gioia and his colleagues, for instance, examine the use of an "excellence" metaphor by the incoming president of a university in order to promote a strategic change initiative (Gioia, 1986; Gioia and Chittipeddi, 1991; Gioia et al., 1994; Gioia and Thomas, 1996). Watson (2003) studies the use of symbols by managers in order to legitimate and defend organizational change that entails downsizing measures, and Greenberg (1995) investigates how symbolic processes associated with the separation of "blue" and "grey" employees constrained sensemaking during a departmental restructuring.

While such research has revealed important micro-dynamics of language use in specific settings, studies of sensemaking and sensegiving by means of metaphors have not systematically taken into account the wider social and institutional context so far. According to Weick et al. (2005), sensemaking studies tend to ignore the role of institutionalization. They assert that extant research neglects processes of socialization to "accepted" sensemaking activities as well as cognitive, normative, and regulatory forces that shape firm behavior and are enforced by actors such as mass media, governmental agencies, professions, and interest groups. Weber and Glynn (2006) similarly stress that sensemaking studies tend to exaggerate agency and ignore the effects of institutionalization.

Institutionalized language and discourse are essential elements of cultural-cognitive institutions, since language mediates certain taken-for-granted meanings and connotations. Studying socially and institutionally situated metaphors-in-use thus responds to recent calls for studies of organizational sensemaking that acknowledge the role of institutions.

The most prominent metaphor theory that has been drawn upon in organization studies so far is Lakoff and Johnson's conceptual metaphor theory (Lakoff, 1987, 1993; Lakoff and Johnson, 1980). In contrast to other linguistic metaphor theories such as comparison, substitution, and interaction theories (cf. Black, 1979), Lakoff and Johnson are not primarily interested in "living metaphors": noticeable, unusual linguistic forms, as they appear for instance in poems, such as calling old age *the evening of life* or *life's setting sun* (Aristotle, 1996). Rather, conceptual metaphor theory is concerned with *systems* of "dead metaphors," taken-for-granted metaphors that are used in everyday speech which are organized along conceptual domains, such as expressions that form part of the conceptual metaphor "argument is war" or "time is money." Such "conceptual metaphors" express certain shared mental maps or cognitive schemes which frame people's understanding of the world and consequently influence the way people act. Conceptual metaphors are thus regarded as systems of statements that express shared ways of thinking and acting, as opposed to single metaphorical expressions. They refer to the understanding of one idea, or conceptual domain (target domain) in terms of another (source domain).

By highlighting dominant as well as potential alternative conceptual metaphors, conceptual metaphor analysis reveals currently shared as well as alternative ways of thinking and associated behavioral patterns. As such, conceptual metaphor analysis reveals interesting *potential* impacts of conceptual metaphors, but does not study metaphors as they are used in a specific local context such as an organization. Empirical organization studies on metaphors used in a specific context therefore do not adopt conceptual metaphor *analysis*, but refer to conceptual metaphor theory in that they rest on Lakoff and Johnson's premise that metaphors function as organizing principles of thought, rather than being simply regarded as figures of speech or as linguistic ornaments (e.g. Heracleous and Jacobs, 2008). Furthermore, Lakoff and Johnson's metaphor theory also disregards the role of social interaction and the power of institutionalized meanings. As some linguists (e.g. Leezenberg, 2001; Niedermayr, 2001) have pointed out, conceptual metaphors do not precede linguistic expression, but require an intermediate level of socially organized and therefore linguistically communicated experience. To conceptualize "argument" in terms of "war," for instance, does not necessarily require the actual physical experience of war, but rather diverse narrations of war, making up a discursive entity about "war." In this regard, conceptual metaphor theory conflicts with process organization studies which adopt a sensemaking perspective and it lacks a critical, historical discussion, as metaphors are analyzed abstracted from their social and institutional contexts.

When studying the use of socially and institutionally situated metaphors in sensemaking and sensegiving, conceptual metaphor theory is therefore only helpful to a limited extent. It draws attention to everyday metaphors-in-use, but it does not take into account broader institutionalized discourses that affect the power of certain conceptual metaphors used in a specific context. We therefore extend the perspective of conceptual metaphor theory in this paper with the discourse theoretical approach of German linguist Jürgen Link (1982, 1986a, 1986b, 1996, 2007). As we will explain in the next section, Link's discourse analysis is specifically concerned with the institutionalized discursive context of *symbols* and therefore is better suited to analyze institutionally situated metaphors than related approaches, such as other critical discourse theories (Foucault, 1981, 1995, 2008; Fairclough, 1995, 2005, 2007; Fairclough and Wodak 1997) or more conversation analytical approaches (e.g., Boje, 2001; Iedema and Wodak, 1999; Phillips and Hardy, 2002; for an overview see Heracleous, 2004, 2006).

12.3 Studying *metaphors-in-use* in their social and institutional context: Metaphor theory and Jürgen Link's discourse theory

Building upon Foucault's (1981, 2008) and Pecheux' (1982) work, Link's (1982, 1996) discourse analysis particularly focuses on unconsciously perceived and processed verbal images. Such images are called "collective symbols" ("Kollektivsymbole") and are conceived as shared figurative elements of talk that play a part in constructing identity. They affect sensemaking of current and past events and processes by acting as institutionalized, that is, historically developed and collectively taken-for-granted, interpretive frames.

Link defines discourse as an institutionalized, ordered mode of speaking and writing (a practice) that is bound to actions and is capable of exerting power (Link, 1982: 71). He differentiates between "specialized discourses" and "interdiscourse." Specialized discourses, similar to Foucault's discursive formations, consist of statements that relate to each other in specific, rule-based ways. The concept of interdiscourse, on the other hand, is based on Foucault's (2002, 2008) notion of "interdiscursive configuration" which denotes regularities that are common across diverse discourses. In contrast to Foucault, Link conceives interdiscourse not only as common regularities between different specialized discourses, but conceptualizes it on a discrete discursive level which is related to institutionalized cultural everyday knowledge or "senso commune" (Gramsci, 2000). Interdiscourse is thus located between specialized discourses, comprising selective cultural everyday knowledge: elements, relations, and procedures which characterize several "Spezialdiskurse" simultaneously.

The most significant elements of interdiscourses are called collective symbols. Collective symbols are conceived as a cultural "topos" which is collectively passed on and used (Drews et al., 1985: 265). Topos, deriving from Greek (and meaning location or place) and specifically from Aristotle's (2007) "Topics," denotes in literature studies a stable motif, an image, or a pattern of thought and expression. Link regards collective symbols as figurative elements of talk, as an umbrella term for the so-called *Bildhaftigkeit* (pictoriality) of a culture: the universe of its most widely shared allegories, emblems, exemplars, illustrative models, comparisons, and analogies (Link, 1996: 25). Also, symbolic numbers can form part of collective symbols, for instance on a continuum, such as "a thousand dead soldiers" and "IQ beneath 100." Collective symbols contain in a condensed and simplified form historically developed images of our society. They are most prominently represented in caricatures, graphs, and pseudo-scientific charts—but also in texts. They are often combined in such interdiscursive configurations with other collective symbols and other interdiscursive elements such as metaphorical expressions.

A newspaper caricature might for instance depict a well-known company which suffers from the financial crisis as a "ship which got into distress" with a sub-text such as "will [the company] succeed in steering the course despite the stormy ups and downs?" Here, meaning is transferred in that a company is discursively related to a vehicle: the ship as a collective symbol represents a completely different entity, an organization or the processes conducted by organizational agents. This is similar to a metaphorical transfer. However, collective symbols are more comprehensive. They are (i) complex verbal imageries which consist of several elements: figurative, graphical elements, called "Pictura" (e.g., the pictured boat in the example above) and verbal signs in a more specific sense, comparable to a legend, called "Subscriptio" (e.g., the accompanying text in the caricature). Both image and text contain numerous further elements and details, such as the type of ship and emblems on the ship, each endowed with meaning. Metaphorical expressions can be combined with these complex symbols. Furthermore (ii), collective symbols are characterized by connotations that derive from their socio-historical context. The type of ship represented, for instance, plays a relevant role. A pleasure boat evokes very different connotations compared to a heavily armed warship. Related to their connotative character, (iii) collective symbols can in principle be visualized and (iv) they allow for analogies, that is, the ship could be replaced by other collective symbols such as a burning house or a patient.

Collective symbols allow for such analogies because their use in interdiscursive configurations expresses a catachresis ("Bildbruch"), a disturbance or disruption in the visual logic of a symbol that juxtaposes different levels of content. A ship in stormy waters, a sick patient, or a burning house are not logically related to the financial crisis. Yet, these representations make sense to the recipient, since they evoke related connotations. According to Link, catachresis is therefore an aspect of symbols which enables and furthers sensemaking as it allows the linking of seemingly contradictory elements to a meaningful whole. Thus, similar to metaphors, collective symbols are characterized by a transfer of meaning, such as the transfer of meaning from the culturally anchored symbol "ship" to "processes." In addition, collective symbols always refer to a certain *collective*, in our example this can be the broader public, citizens of a state in which the organization is based, or more specifically members of the organization itself. The connotative symbol of a sinking ship or a burning house enables both potential groups to identify with the symbol. Such connotations are however not naturally inherent in the symbol, but are embedded in a socio-historical context.

One important element of Link's discourse analysis is therefore investigating the historical meaning of symbols and the respective development of meaning over time. This *semantic analysis* builds the basis for a *pragmatic analysis* of potential performative effects of symbols. By means of their value-laden connotations, collective symbols affect processes of identification, constructing or threatening certain identities. An "ill-equipped, sinking boat in stormy waters" for instance has unfavorable connotations, whereas a boat which resists the storm has more favorable connotations. In this way, elements of interdiscourse serve as "Applikationsvorlage," as interpretive frames for the identification processes of individuals. By means of identification with certain systems of collective symbols, individuals adopt them as interpretive frames, make sense of events and processes that they encounter, and perform actions against this background.

This leads us to propose an extension of sensemaking studies on metaphors-in-use in local contexts in terms of a "contextualized metaphor analysis" informed by Link's discourse analysis. We suggest studying conceptual metaphors-in-use in their social and institutional context on three levels of analysis: local-interactive, semantic, and pragmatic.

1. On a local, interactive level, the analysis focuses on the concrete use of conceptual metaphors in a specific setting, for example, in an organization, with regard to power effects, legitimation, and strategies of sensegiving. This focus on micro-practices has been characteristic of research on sensemaking and can be seen as a valuable extension of discourse analysis.
2. On a semantic level, discourse theory broadens the analysis of conceptual metaphors in that their links to institutionalized collective symbols and interdiscursive configurations at large are explored and the historical meaning and the development of meaning over time of these interdiscursive elements are taken into account.
3. On a pragmatic level, these links are further explored by analyzing the potential performative effects of identified relevant institutions in terms of value-laden processes of identification. Semantic and pragmatic

analyses taken together can shed light on the power of certain conceptual metaphors as compared to others in a specific local setting. A contextualized metaphor analysis therefore looks at local strategies involved in using metaphors, but in addition takes a socio-historical perspective and identifies links between local metaphors-in-use and institutionalized collective symbols.

12.4 Research focus

This chapter seeks to relate sensemaking and sensegiving processes to their social and institutional context by describing and explaining the effects of diverse metaphors of change used by organizational members during the implementation of lean production and TQM in an internationally operating manufacturing company. More specifically, we explore how organizational members made sense of these strategic changes in terms of their understanding of the process as a minor or rather a major organizational change. We analyze what kind of conceptual metaphors are associated with these divergent understandings, and we explore their relative power, that is, which metaphors dominated others. Our main analysis seeks to *explain* the relative power of certain conceptual metaphors of change as compared to others by analyzing the social and institutional context of these metaphors-in-use. Adopting a contextualized metaphor analytical approach, as outlined above, we explore the link of dominant metaphors-in-use to institutionalized meanings, as represented in collective symbols that were drawn upon in interdiscursive charts when the new COO and his supporting consultants presented the new initiative.

12.5 Research context

The case organization, hereafter called MetalsOrg, is one division of a globally operating manufacturing company in the metal and plastics processing industry that maintains production sites and sales organizations all over the world and employs more than 7,000 people. The corporate headquarters are located in a German-speaking country where the company was founded as a family firm in the 1950s. Meanwhile, the company has grown considerably and is organized in three main divisions that manufacture products within six major brands. The company offers both mass-market products and project-specific realizations. It markets its products as high-quality, innovative products and has established a top market position, being ranked among the top three companies in this industry in terms of market share worldwide. The divisional headquarters are also located in the German-speaking country where MetalsOrg was founded, together with one of its production plants. In addition, there are five further production plants, all located in Europe.

Our field work started in May 2008, shortly after the company's management had appointed a new Chief Operating Officer for MetalsOrg in the January. One of the first decisions of this new COO, who was experienced with lean manufacturing and TQM, was to launch a lean production agenda, termed "lean six sigma." He presented the "lean six sigma" strategy as being in line with the principles of the Toyota Production System (TPS), as pioneered by the Japanese car manufacturer in the 1970s. Generally speaking, the TPS is characterized by just-in-time production in terms of a "one-piece-flow," market pull instead of push, zero defects, continuous improvement, employee empowerment, multifunctional teams, and customer orientation (Ohno, 1988). Lean six sigma as a label for the strategic change introduced by the new COO combines Lean Management (Åhlström and Karlsson, 1996; Krafcik, 1988) and Six Sigma Quality Management.[1] Although the new COO and his consultants stressed that they did not intend to implement TPS to the letter, but only apply some of its principles and tailor them to the specific context of MetalsOrg, they distributed books and flyers on TPS within MetalsOrg (notably Womack and Jones (2003): *Lean Thinking: Banish Waste and Create Wealth in Your Corporation*, Liker (2003): *The Toyota Way*, and Goldratt and Cox (1986): *The Goal: A Process of Ongoing Improvement*.

In order to implement lean six sigma, four key performance indicators—on-time-delivery, cycle efficiency, six sigma quality, and productivity—were introduced and targets for these indicators were set. The implementation was delegated to project groups in each production site which were responsible for taking initiatives that would improve the performance of the plant in terms of one of the four relevant indicators. These groups consisted mainly of middle managers and engineers. The team leaders were often "black belts," that is, qualified experts in six sigma methodology (see Taylor, 2008). Also involved in this process were a small number of external consultants, specialized in lean management and total quality management. We followed the implementation process from May 2008 onwards at the main production site (which is also where division and company headquarters are located).

The more general objectives of the study comprised exploring how strategic changes are introduced, how they evolve, and how they are received and co-constructed by the employees. In this respect, one focus has been on the enactment of performance indicators (Jordan and Messner, 2009). One thing that struck us during interviews and observations was the rather divergent views that organizational members expressed concerning the perceived extent and significance of the strategic change towards lean six sigma. That is, we encountered diverse sensemaking and sensegiving mechanisms concerning this strategic initiative (conceived as incremental or rather radical change). As outlined above, our focus in this paper is on these different patterns of theorizing upon the strategic changes by analyzing various metaphors of change and their relative power.

12.6 Research design

As we are interested in the organizational members' viewpoints in terms of their perceptions of strategic changes as enacted in processes of sensegiving and sensemaking, we adopted a qualitative methodology. Qualitative research typically examines the emic view (Pike, 1967) of the participants, focusing on individuals' interpretations of events and processes and their enacted consequences (Denzin and Lincoln, 2005; Isabella, 1990; Maitlis, 2005).

Data were collected by reviewing company-internal documents, including presentation slides, newsletters, and management books on lean production that were distributed within the organization, by attending project team meetings and by conducting semi-structured interviews with project team members and other employees over a period of 16 months. Table 12.1 gives an overview of the collected data.

Data were analyzed by first selecting all data in which the lean six sigma initiative was addressed and organizing the statements into expressions of radical change, incremental change and statements which are ambiguous or inarticulate with regard to the *extent* of change. Such data comprised interviewees' statements and observation protocols about the strategic change as well as the senior management's presentations of lean six sigma in the company newspaper and presentation slides. The second analytical step consisted of categorizing these statements along conceptual metaphors of change. Most statements regarding the strategic change towards lean six sigma could be categorized as expressing one of four conceptual metaphors. We then analyzed which conceptual metaphors were expressed by whom

Table 12.1 Summary of data sources

Data source	Quantity
Interviews (conducted from May 2008 to August 2009)	
Members of senior management (including human resources manager, chief management accountant, supply chain manager)	8
Project managers (team leaders of the four lean six sigma implementation teams)	10
Other project team members	9
Organizational members who were not directly involved in the project teams (production line manager, management accountant, foreman at the production site)	4
Lean six sigma specialists (internal and external consultants)	2
Total	33
Meetings observed	
Project team meetings (from June 2008 to February 2009)	7
Production layout and production review meetings (July 2009)	2
Total	9
Documents	
Internal company newsletters (issued during the study period)	7
Sets of presentation slides (used by the COO when presenting "lean six sigma")	3
Other documents (such as presentation slides and handouts used during team meetings, public company reports, internal memos, corporate code of conduct, and company values)	25
Total	35

and when and which concepts were prevalent and shared to a higher extent than others (analysis on the local-interactive level). In order to explain the pervasiveness of certain metaphors, we analyzed in a fourth step the dominating metaphors in more detail by exploring their link to institutionalized meanings, as manifested among others in collective symbols used as a means of sensegiving by the senior management. We analyze the historical development and associated taken-for-granted beliefs and connotations of these collective symbols beyond the boundaries of the studied organization. That is, we finally relate the local interactive level of analysis to semantic and pragmatic levels of discourse analysis. Table 12.2 displays the stages of our data analysis.

12.7 Theorizing upon organizational change and stability

Views on the extent to which the introduction of lean six sigma presented a radical or only an incremental change differed widely among organizational members during the first sixteen months of its implementation. While the COO's strategic direction was sometimes framed as radically different from the previously followed strategy, it was at the same time framed as an incremental change being conceived as reinforcing previous aspirations

Table 12.2 Stages of data analysis

Stages of data analysis	Output
1. Selecting all statements which frame the lean six sigma initiative in terms of change (or stability) and organizing them into expressions of radical change, incremental change, and statements which are ambiguous or inarticulate with regard to the extent of change	Selected statements organized into "views of radical change," "views of incremental change/stability," and "statements of change which are unclear about the extent of change," indicating the source and the date of each statement
2. Categorizing the statements with regard to different conceptual metaphors of change	Statements grouped according to four conceptual metaphors of change
3. Contextualized metaphor analysis (local-interactive level): Analyzing patterns of metaphor use (which conceptual metaphor(s) dominated over others, to what extent did the use of conceptual metaphors differ over time, settings and types of stakeholders)	Patterns in the way conceptual metaphors are used; identified dominating conceptual metaphors
4. Contextualized metaphor analysis (semantic and pragmatic levels): Analyzing the dominating conceptual metaphors with regard to their institutional embeddedness	Link of dominant conceptual metaphors to related institutionalized "collected symbols" (historical development of these symbols, connotations and potential impacts on people's sensemaking and actions due to these connotations)

and business principles. The following two quotations are indicative of such contradictory views, with the first one expressing the perception of incremental change and the second one indicating a more radical understanding of the ongoing changes:

> The company veered towards this direction (lean six sigma) already before the arrival of the new COO. It has gained in importance since his arrival. (project manager of the Cycle Efficiency Team, July 23, 2008)

> The current management setting does not correspond to lean six sigma...It necessitates a team approach, continuous improvement, excellent quality, absolute customer orientation, the customer is close to the process, not only the person who buys the product. These are all things that have to be implemented. Currently, the classic hierarchical relationship prevails: top-down. And with lean six sigma it's exactly inverted...the shopfloor has to be empowered, they have to contribute, and executives have to let that happen, they have to take a completely different role, being the ones that ask questions rather than giving answers. (human resources manager, July 24, 2008)

Throughout the collected data, these distinct rationalities are rather evenly distributed. About a third of the statements on the lean six sigma initiative express an understanding of an incremental change, while one-third frame it as a radical change, with another third being ambiguous with regard to the extent of change perceived. From an organization research perspective, how can we make sense of this divergence in organizational members' sensemaking? One could assume that these divergent framings express diverse interests: for example, those being supportive of the COO frame the change as minor change, while those being skeptical frame it as a major change and thus express resistance towards change, or even the other way around, in the sense that skepticism is expressed by framing it as "only" a minor change. However, the data do not support any of these hypotheses. The following quotations exemplify that "incremental change" was connoted in both ways, favorably as well as unfavorably:

> I don't believe that anybody regards this initiative as problematic … because these are *topics* that *are known and that have been worked on already*, just not within this framework (project team structure). (team member, Cycle Efficiency Team, November 14, 2008)

> It would be fatal if we employ large teams and finally come up with *only minor changes*. That would be fatal. (Service and coordination manager with regard to a sub-project on product complexity, Cycle Efficiency Meeting, December 4, 2009)

In general, a very favorable attitude towards lean six sigma prevailed, especially among middle managers and overall in administrative areas, largely independent of whether they conceived of the new strategy as radical or incremental change. At the shopfloor level, some employees expressed a more negative attitude towards the new strategic focus, however, less in terms of resistance to lean six sigma, but rather in vague terms such as "It's once again some kind of reorganization" or "who knows when the next COO will arrive, presumably coming up with a new strategy again." A few middle managers also expressed certain concerns. They worried for instance whether the new strategy ignored relevant areas such as innovation. However, in general, the attitude towards lean six sigma was rather friendly and supportive and many organizational members were actively involved in its implementation. Surprisingly, this was also the case for activities that could be easily resented as they were concerned with productivity and as such with efficiency gains resulting in lower staff requirements (based on lean factory layouts).

Secondly, we could not discern any pattern of development in the course of the implementation period. That is, distinctive perceptions about the extent of the strategic change persisted in the beginning of the implementation period as well as throughout the following months. Thus, divergent sensemaking was not due to a collectively changed perspective caused by certain events during implementation. In some instances, divergent views were actually expressed by the same person during one and the same interview or meeting. Such apparent inconsistency was, however, never explicitly discussed by the respective individuals or their colleagues. So, at first sight it remains unclear how these divergent views can be explained. A content analysis of interview material and other linguistic data drawn from observations does not advance the analysis in this respect, since the divergence of perspectives was not consciously reflected upon by the actors in place.

In the following, we will therefore turn from a content analysis towards a metaphor analysis, aimed at shedding light on the empirical phenomena presented above by investigating what kind of conceptual metaphors-in-use are associated with divergent understandings of change.

12.8 Metaphors of change

In order to analyze diverse theorizing on the COO's strategic initiatives, we searched for the occurrence of conceptual metaphors in the organizational members' talk (and writing) about the new strategic thrust since its announcement in March 2008. We found four different conceptual metaphors associated with this change process: (i) change as putting things under one common roof, (ii) change as speeding up and improving what has been done before, (iii) change as moving up a constitutional staircase, and (iv) change as a horizontal and vertical turn.

The metaphor of "change as putting things under one roof" framed change as a process of enhancing existing initiatives by giving them a common name in terms of a "roof." As such, it constitutes the least radical understanding of the change process, as indicated for instance in a statement by a project team member as follows:

> We do still follow the same goals. We have to deal with the same topics ... I just see it (lean six sigma) as a guidance system (Leitsystem). You can find all existing activities *underneath* it ... I see the four topics of lean six sigma as *columns* and you find all that we had before *underneath these columns* ... no real difference, a clearer focus only. (team member Cycle Efficiency, July 2, 2008)

Similar to the first metaphor, "change as speeding up and improving what has been done before" frames the lean six sigma initiative as described here as a process that does not fundamentally change what has been done before. Lean six sigma is seen predominantly as an incremental change that seeks to make *existing* processes a bit faster and generally "better," as exemplified in the following statements:

> One intention of lean six sigma is certainly to make the business *faster* in order to be able to react more timely to market needs . . . the basic goal is to *improve*, simply *continuous improvement*. (On-Time-Delivery manager, July 23, 2008)

> Six Sigma is based on the concern to *improve existing products and processes*. There is no more to it than that: analyzing what is already there . . . nothing fundamentally new. (team member of the quality team, November 25, 2008)

More ambiguous in terms of the extent of change perceived is the third metaphor which conceives of change as moving up on a constitutional staircase. Similar to the metaphor of change as speeding up, lean six sigma is represented here as a long-term, rather steady, and continuous process "in the same direction as before," however, it is likewise associated with a more or less significant "step" to be taken.

> In principle, it is not fundamentally new to us . . . it is only a bit more comprehensive. For instance, with regard to productivity, we are now also taking into account administrative jobs. And yes, these modifications will bother us in the next years. These are rather challenging tasks . . . to *step* from a rather high level *further upwards* will be difficult. (production line manager, April 27, 2009)

> Well, he (the new COO) has truly struck *a new path* which was unknown to MetalsOrg so far. . . . I fully support this strategy. Otherwise we would not sustainably *step forward* in this type of project-based business. But it will take some time, because it requires a different mindset. (supply chain manager, August 18, 2009)

Finally, some statements characterized the change process as a complete change in direction, adopting the metaphor of "change as a vertical or horizontal turn" which stands somewhat in opposition to the conceptual metaphors described above.

> Currently, the classic hierarchical relationship prevails: top-down. And with this approach (lean six sigma) it's *exactly inverted*. (human resources manager, July 24, 2008)

We intend to turn the factory *upside-down* … quite mundanely you have to put it that way. It will entail extreme changes, for instance in terms of the production philosophy. (chief management accountant, November 26, 2008)

12.9 Patterns in metaphor usage

In order to identify the dominant conceptual metaphors of change, we now turn to the local-interactive level of metaphor analysis focusing on how the conceptual metaphors of change presented above have been used during the implementation process in MetalsOrg.

Out of the four conceptual metaphors of change presented above, the "roof" metaphor was the least prevalent in our data. Only two project managers and one project team member drew upon this concept of change, expressing explicitly perceived stability rather than change. Likewise, a very clear conception of change was conveyed by the "turn" metaphor, here however with reference to a radical change. Interestingly, this metaphor was used mainly by senior managers, project managers, and lean consultants, and was expressed exclusively in interviews, appearing in neither project team meetings nor internal documents such as company newsletters. Furthermore, this rather radical concept of change is mostly expressed by those organizational members that identify themselves as "change agents" rather than as being subject to changes introduced by others. This is visible in the phrasing of statements such as "*we* intend to turn the factory upside-down."

The two most prevalent metaphors of change, however, are those which are not unambiguously related to rationalities of incremental or radical change. This applies to the metaphor of "change as speeding up and improving what has been done before," and most notably to the metaphor of "change as moving up on a constitutional staircase." While "change as speeding up" is mostly, but not exclusively, related to incremental change, "change as a moving up on a staircase" is primarily related to statements which are ambiguous with regard to the extent of change perceived. In contrast to the other metaphors, these two metaphors appear not only in interviews, but are mobilized as well during presentations in meetings and in newsletters that report the new strategic orientation. In quantitative terms, both were used to a similar extent. However, the "staircase" metaphor was most widely shared, as it was used by such different groups as production foremen, middle managers, senior managers, and lean consultants, while the "speeding up" metaphor was mostly used by middle managers and appeared within some internal documents, but was not used by the group of consultants at all. In the following, we take a closer look at how the two most prevalent metaphors materialized in documents which were used as sensegiving devices by senior management during presentations or in company newsletters.

As is shown in Fig. 12.1, the new strategic focus was presented by the COO as a combination of Lean Management and Six Sigma, where Lean is linked to the notion of "speed," while Six Sigma is referred to as ensuring high quality via continuous improvement. The combination of both elements was presented as ensuring "breakthrough profit performance." "Lean Six Sigma" was first announced by the new COO in March 2008, two months after his appointment. The implementation process was organized along four performance indicators, expressing six sigma by means of "six sigma quality" and "on-time delivery," and lean by means of "cycle efficiency" and "productivity."

Later on, in July 2008, an additional label for the strategic change emerged: "Excellerate," combining "accelerate" (speed up) and "excellence." The label "Excellerate" actually already existed before the introduction of Lean Six Sigma. It had been used as a reassuring label in communication to the company's shareholders, expressing the company's commitment to increase shareholder value (in publicly available reports

Combine
Lean Speed
and
Six Sigma

and
Creating Breakthrough
Profit Performance

Fig. 12.1 Opening slide of the presentation of the new strategic focus
Source: Internal company document, March 2008

and letters to shareholders). The originally promoted initiative "excelle-rate" could be easily linked to "lean six sigma" as it stresses speed (lean) as well as quality. However, it originally incorporated more elements, for instance innovation which does not appear within the four lean six sigma performance indicators.

Thus both labels, "lean six sigma" and "excellerate," express the new strategic initiative in terms of speeding up and improving *what has been done before*. Even though the labels represent a new initiative, at the same time they entail strong linkages to existing ways of thinking and acting, as existing processes "just" have to be accelerated and improved. Such signifi-cation was enhanced by the use of symbols: "excellerate" was written on slides as "exce>>erate," stressing the notion of improvement in terms of "speeding up" (expressed in a slide shown in a meeting in July 2008 as a response to fierce competition and dynamic technological environments as "Speed is a major success factor—Speed up!"). In addition, the sign ">>" was also used as a stand-alone symbol as represented in Fig. 12.2, indicating a movement from bottom left to top right, created by a hand without a body.

Communication from top management to employees in terms of month-ly company newsletters also incorporated these notions. The following excerpt from an article which appeared in a newsletter in November 2008 is indicative of the reference to the COO's strategic initiative in terms of speeding up and improving what has been done before:

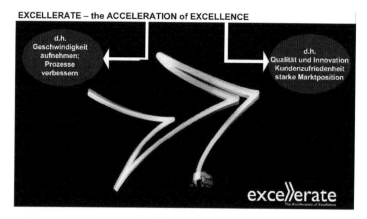

Fig. 12.2 Slide on the initiative "excellerate"

The left-hand bubble says: "acceleration means to speed up and improve process"; the right-hand bubble says: "excellence means quality and innovation, customer satisfaction and a strong market position".

Source: Internal company document, July 2008

12.9.1 Interview with the group CEO, Mr Maier:[2] "Improvement at Every Workplace"

*Recently, an organizational value initiative has been started, and now again the "**Excellerate**" initiative, in order to become conjointly better and faster. Doesn't that result in less time to sustainably implement such initiatives?*

That would be a wrong conclusion. Our everyday actions are based on our values. Excellerate *builds on our values so that we can jointly become faster and better.* The essential part of our new initiative is to emphasize and focus on our main goals and those goals—such as *"becoming more efficient"*—are translated into clear action initiatives.

We will then forcefully implement these initiatives.

Why do we need a new label, then?

We can discuss a lot about labels and terminology. However, it is important that we all comprehend that we are facing major challenges and "more of the same" ["weiter so"] will not be sufficient any more. We have to *improve many practices* thoroughly, to *purge* and *accelerate* our processes and daily *live* customer orientation—not just write it down in brochures.

To become faster and better, motivation and enthusiasm are necessary. How are you going about these issues?

I believe success is the best motivation. Every single one contributes to our joint success. This applies for instance to the lean six sigma workshops that are currently running in all production sites. Every employee can bring in his knowledge concerning opportunities for *improvement*, and can then experience how *processes become better and faster.* This applies to our production sites as well as to distribution and administration. If everybody contributes enthusiastically to workplace improvements, we will be successful with *Excellerate.* (Company newspaper article, November 2008, emphasis added)

Becoming faster and better by means of Excellerate is framed here in an attempt at *sensegiving* (Gioia and Chittipeddi, 1991), as change and stability at the same time, as it is said to "build on current values and main goals," which is still clearly distinguished from "keep doing the same" (see excerpt above).

Similar to the metaphor of change as speeding up, lean six sigma/excellerate was represented as a step that forms part of a long-term, rather steady and continuous process. Fig. 12.3 represents the promoted strategic initiative as a consistent and necessary step on a "staircase." In order to advance on this staircase (again from bottom left to top right), the next "step" in terms of Excellerate has to be taken.

Strategic Position

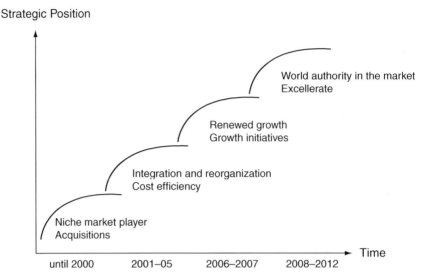

Fig. 12.3 Graph presented in a meeting to promote the new strategic focus, with the headline: "Our common challenge: We have to take action now and we have to consistently take the next step!"

The idea of advancement on a staircase can be linked to other statements in sensegiving devices that characterize lean six sigma initiatives as heading *in the same direction* as initiatives before, and as *progression*. A company newspaper article features this metaphor and is like the staircase image in the way that it is indicative of the ambivalence of stability and change ("The goals are not new. What has changed?"):

12.9.2 Our four fingerposts in the business year 2008/2009

Plant manager (main production site), Mr. Müller [picture]: *"It is important that all employees know the goals so that we can pull together."*

Mr. Müller, what goals do our plants pursue?

Our main directions of impact are clearly four factors: Six Sigma quality, nearly zero defects, 100% On Time Delivery (OTD), reduction of cycle times and increase of productivity. We have explained these goals to all our employees in workshops and face-to-face conversations.

How shall these goals be attained?

We continuously develop initiatives that will further strengthen our customers' trust. First positive results could be attained for OTD and quality.

In addition, we need some initiatives that lead to long-term improvement. Our project teams are about to implement them. Six Sigma tools assist them in their task. What is important is to note: We integrated employees from product lifecycle management and distribution. They represent the "voice of the customer".

The goals are not new. What has changed?

Certainly we have *always headed in this direction*. However, focusing on these four key topics enables us to concentrate all [our] energy on these projects. I am confident that we will *progress quickly* in such a way.

Source: Company newspaper article, June 2008, emphasis added.

It is remarkable that sensegiving strategies drew upon such ambiguous conceptions of change rather than taking a clear standpoint as to what extent the new initiative would involve minor or major changes. Neither radical "turns" nor a clear conveyance of incremental change as "focusing existing initiatives under a common roof" appear in public communication with organizational members. The extent of change resulting from the new initiative is in these sensegiving statements thus very much open to the recipients' interpretation. Apparently, the "staircase" and the "speeding up" metaphors were particularly powerful, as many interview statements reproduced these views. The "staircase" metaphor was furthermore shared among different groups of organizational actors, as explained above and in some statements, the difference between the staircase metaphor and the "speeding up" metaphor is blurred, as the former is somewhat inclusive of the latter. The staircase incorporates for instance the movement from bottom left to top right as represented in the ">>" image (Fig. 12.2).

In this way, the new COO's initiative was framed as a *new* initiative that, however, builds heavily on what had been done before, and was welcomed as a favorable initiative, even though the planned changes were most likely to have rather significant effects on plant layout, hierarchical structures, and productivity, decreasing among other things the need for a direct and indirect workforce. In order to explain the power of the two dominating conceptual metaphors, we expand the analysis on the local-interactive level to semantic and pragmatic levels of analysis, investigating the dominating metaphors with regard to their link to institutionalized meanings as represented in collective symbols.

12.10 The impact of institutionalized meanings

According to Link (1982, 1996), institutionalized meanings, shared and taken-for-granted beliefs as materialized in collective symbols and interdiscursive configurations at large, influence people's sensemaking of concrete events by acting as interpretive frames. We discuss in this section to what extent the dominating metaphors of change in MetalsOrg were related to institutions, analyzing on a semantic level their meaning and historical development and on a pragmatic level, their potential performative effects in terms of value-laden processes of identification.

The two dominating metaphors of change, "change as speeding up and improving" and "change as moving up on a staircase" feature several links to institutionalized meanings. In particular, we identified concepts of progression and mathematical-statistical symbols, as well as combinations of such concepts and symbols within interdiscursive charts. Two performative effects account for the power of the associated conceptual metaphors. First, references to institutionalized concepts potentially decrease the need to justify strategic changes. Such decreased efforts of justification are visible in sensegiving as well as sensemaking statements in MetalsOrg in that they lack references to concrete events or specified competitors that would call for that specific change. Identification with the change initiative is achieved by virtue of institutionalized favorable connotations which make detailed justifications obsolete. Furthermore, identification is further enhanced by institutions that convey interpretive flexibility and are thus able to reconcile different interests of diverse local agents.

Both dominating metaphors represented the change process by means of symbols of progression: the sign ">>" indicating a movement from bottom left to top right as well as acceleration (Fig. 12.2) and the growth curve which is at the same time a staircase (Fig. 12.3). Progression or "evolution" to higher "levels" is particularly alluded to in the staircase metaphor as represented in the growth curve. Growth curves originated in specialized mathematical and statistical discourses and when they have been combined with images, these combined graphs rapidly permeated all kinds of social discourse. In 1786, William Playfair was the first to "translate" tables that had been used since the Middle Ages into growth curves (Link, 1996). Thereby, one of the most important representational devices of modernity had been created. In no time, all areas of society had been pervaded by growth curves, be it curves on remuneration, profit, deficit, or forecast. Approximately one trillion statistical graphs were printed in the year 1980 alone (Tufte, 2006; qtd. by Link, 1996: 198). The use of growth curves went along with new terminology that is full of metaphors and other collective symbols: curves are "steep," "flat," there are "turning points," "areas of excess/surplus and deficit," and there is always the danger of "limits to growth" (scarce resources). Early on, "symbolic curves" including "symbolic numbers" emerged that worked even without exact mathematical calculation, since the "graphical" statement was most important (Link, 1996: 198). For instance, Otto Neurath, a representative of the neo-positivistic Vienna Circle, claimed with an emancipatory and pedagogical intention that "pure" curves should be substituted by "animated groups"—they should be combined with images. The resulting ISOTYPE diagrams (see Fig. 12.4 for an example) are precursors of information graphs such as the one used by MetalsOrg (Fig. 12.3).

From a discourse analytical perspective, data that stem from the specialized discourse on statistics and mathematics are related to pictographic, interdiscursive elements. This relation can be linked to processes of identification of individuals with these graphs: according to Neurath, the aim of such graphs is to activate the observer's feeling of "that's me" (Neurath, 1991; qtd. by Schulte-Holtey, 2001: 106).

The growth curve used by the COO to promote the change process in MetalsOrg can be likewise regarded as an interdiscursive document: on the one hand it shows a tool of a specialized discourse, the Cartesian coordinate system with an x-coordinate (abscissa) and a y-coordinate (ordinate). On the other hand, however, there is a third axis, a z-coordinate (applicate). On

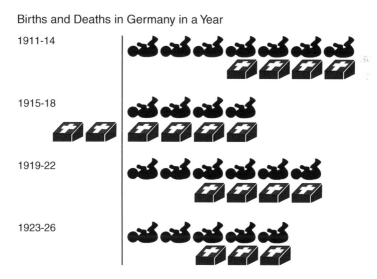

Births and Deaths in Germany in a Year

1911-14

1915-18

1919-22

1923-26

1 child for 250,000 births a year
1 coffin for 250,000 deaths a year

Fig. 12.4 Example of an "ISOTYPE-Mengenbild" (ISOTYPE diagram)
Source: Neurath (1936: 87)

this axis, statistics are combined with a metaphor to a collective symbol which generates a narration:

1. First, there is the catachresis typical for the use of collective symbols: "non-sense" that nevertheless makes sense to the recipient. The rudimentary, symbolic "curves" do not correspond with the intervals on the x-coordinate, creating the *impression of a steady* growth, with the connotation of "every other year the next step has to be taken."
2. The actual "curve" appears rather as a "staircase" or "ladder," without explicitly calling it that.
3. The graph thus represents analogies by means of the figurative metaphors mentioned above.
4. Of major significance is the connotation: as a collective symbol, the graph creates a scenario with a clear orientation, a goal termed "Excellerate." This metaphoric linear growth curve tells an evolutionary story, a story of "growing (up)" from a niche market player to a world-authority in the market. Like any kind of story, it evolves in stages—visualized in the graph—or "milestones" that are marked by changes. This is supported by the uneven presentation of years and time intervals that would not make sense outside that context.
5. These taken-for-granted connotations potentially affect organizational members' sensemaking in that they can be expected to interpret the left–right growth curve as something "favorable" (it goes up), thus easily identifying themselves with this process and the highest strategic "step," Excellerate, presented at the top-right of the curve. Growth curves can be assumed to exert power by means of normalization: the curve suggests a development that represents a certain normality (this is a "natural development"), and at the same time normativity ("we *have to* take the next step").
6. Furthermore, by placing the staircase in a Cartesian coordinate system, despite not resulting from a calculation, the curve alludes to mathematical-statistical institutions. Thus, the discourse of natural science is mobilized which conveys authority and reliability by means of "objective" and neutral measurement. Organizational members can be expected to be familiar with this type of representation and to interpret it as something "proven" (because it has been objectively calculated).

Thus, dominating conceptual metaphors of change were related to symbols which conveyed taken-for-granted favorable connotations of progression and objective calculation which potentially enable favorable identification with this change process. Illustrations of the new strategic program as an outcome of the change (the Toyota Production System) in books that were distributed within the company allude to the same type of institutions as the representations of the change process as such. Multiple references to favorable "progress" are made by means of catch phrases such as "continuous improvement," "being ahead of the competitors" and "breakthrough performance" (Goldratt and Cox, 1986; Liker, 2003; Womack and Jones, 2003). Likewise, reference to statistical-mathematical discourses is made by presenting the TPS as resting upon tools of statistical process analysis such as SixSigma (σ, standard deviation, indicating a "normal," allowable distribution of defects). Critical literature on Lean and TQM have repeatedly pointed out that these concepts have become widely accepted and considered as benign and universally beneficial despite some inherent contradictions such as employee empowerment versus top-down management control (De Cock and Hipkin, 1997; Kerfoot and Knights, 1995, McArdle et al., 1995).

Against this background, the local sensegiving strategies can be better understood. The new COO and his consultants did remarkably little to justify the need for change, other than referring to anonymous "increased competition" and some "obvious" benefits of the TPS, such as increased customer orientation. Furthermore, the COO referred during presentations to his experience and competence in lean six sigma and to its "successful" implementation in the company where he had been employed before, without showing in concrete detail what exactly had been done in that company and in what sense it had been successful. This is consequential within the logic of the growth curve: it is a *natural* step to be taken which does not require a specific justification. This view was widely reproduced within the organization. Most interviewees were puzzled by our questions regarding justifications for the change initiative and replied that there had been none given by the COO, and furthermore, that they didn't require one as the proposed change appeared to be the right and logical thing to do.

The first set of effects by institutionalized meanings on organizational members' sensemaking can be subsumed as positive identification with the promoted change due to favorable taken-for-granted connotations, with an associated minor need for justification of change. Besides favorable connotations, catachresis as a characteristic of collective symbols entails a second type of performative effect on identification. Catachresis can render collective symbols ambiguous so that they exhibit interpretive flexibility. Such symbols are thus able to reconcile the different interests of diverse local agents. The "staircase graph" is indicative of this ambiguity: it depicts change as a necessary step to be taken upwards on a constitutional staircase. In this sense, it builds upon what has been done before (it belongs to a broader "big plan" in the same direction), but it still constitutes a change (a loop upwards, a step).

The change-as-a-step-on-a-staircase metaphor as represented in this graph thus features ambiguity in terms of interpretive flexibility. Consequently, organizational actors can easily identify with the depicted process, as the metaphor reconciles different perspectives, such as those of senior managers conceiving themselves as change agents who bring about major change, but build on existing values, of consultants who have to initiate major change in order to justify their presence and fees, and those of middle managers who are keen to stress the incremental nature of change in order not to scare employees and in order not to blame themselves for having done something fundamentally wrong in the past.

The specific history of COO changes in this company further explains why it was "useful" for the new COO, even if not necessarily explicitly intended, to frame his strategic initiatives in two seemingly contradictory ways simultaneously, both as change and stability. On the one hand, it was relevant for the new COO to differentiate his strategy from the former COO's strategy, since the previous COO was strongly resented due to some rather unpopular plans of re-locating production to low-wage countries. The new COO stopped these initiatives and was thus welcomed in this respect. On the other hand, however, recent history featured a high turnover of COOs (four different COOs in the last eight years). Some employees asserted that due to these frequent COO changes they were tired of committing again to another COO with another strategic orientation. In this regard, the rhetoric of stability had a reassuring effect.

We conclude from this analysis more generally that such metaphors that relate to favorably connoted and ambiguous institutions are particularly powerful as sensemaking as well as sensegiving devices. In our specific case, they can be seen as at least one explanatory factor for only minor resistance towards change in a setting that presumably could feature more doubts and scepticism.

12.11 Conclusion

We sought to relate sensemaking and sensegiving processes to their social and institutional context by describing and explaining the effects of diverse metaphors of change used within a production company during the implementation of lean production and TQM. The framework of a "contextualized metaphor analysis" informed by Link's (1982, 1986a, 1986b, 1996) critical discourse analysis allowed us to analyze the relative power of different conceptual metaphors-in-use. This was motivated by recent calls to contextualize sensemaking studies in order to move beyond an exclusive focus on micro-practices and to study metaphors-in-use in their social and institutional context (Sutcliffe et al., 2006; Weber and Glynn, 2006; Weick et al., 2005). We have shown that powerful metaphors-in-use are related to institutionalized collective symbols that have favorable connotations and that feature interpretive flexibility.

By integrating "lean six sigma/Excellerate" in a staircase of continuous growth, the strategic initiative appeared as a natural "step" to be taken and as a part of a broader movement upwards, heading in the same direction as before in accordance with the second dominating metaphor as represented by the sign ">>". At the same time, the most widely shared staircase metaphor allowed the recipient to interpret the strategic initative as a change, for example, as a milestone or a step. The mobilized institution in this metaphor thus features "interpretive flexibility"—the progression on a staircase which is at the same time referred to as a natural evolution cannot be unambiguously interpreted in terms of change or stability. Consequently, organizational actors can easily identify with that process. As connotations (left–right movement upwards, objectivity due to statistical/numerical "proof") can be assumed to be mostly favorable, this identification is also likely to be a favorable one. We argued that communicating conceptual metaphors that draw upon such institutions are powerful sensegiving (Gioia and Chittipeddi, 1991) strategies. In our specific case, they can be seen as an explanatory factor for only minor resistance towards change in a setting that presumably could feature more doubts and scepticism.

Institutions effect organizational sensemaking in terms of which interpretive schemes are pervasive and regarded as legitimate within organizations. We conceived of institutions as collective taken-for-granted beliefs within and across organizations, such as the connotations of statistical-mathematical tools as conveying neutrality and objectivity. To be sure, acting as interpretive frames, institutions do not *determine* a specific kind of sensemaking and specific actions, since they do not exist in isolation and individuals draw upon a diversity of interpretation and action repertoires. Furthermore, institutions are constituted and changed by means of sensemaking themselves (e.g. Munir and Phillips, 2005; Weber and Glynn, 2006). Still, at one point in time (or one period of time) they can be analytically distinguished from local sensemaking processes that are shaped, but not determined, by their institutional context.

Collective symbols can be seen as interpretive frames that affect identification processes, in our example in terms of a favorable or unfavorable identification with organizational change processes. An individual confronted with the growth curve discussed above can identify him/herself with the narration represented in the graph—he/she can feel part of the story or be unaffected by the story. Whether the individual identifies with the narration will, at least to a certain degree, depend on the more or less shared *connotations* of this collective symbol. From a discourse-theoretical point of view, connotations are not "inherent" in symbols as such, but are socially constructed during their historical development and use.

We focused our analysis in this paper on institutionalized collective symbols, their connotations and the resulting effects on identification processes. This is a fruitful, but by no means an exhaustive analysis of the institutional impact on sensemaking. This line of research could be further developed by extending the analysis to taken-for-granted power relations as conveyed by *broader* discourses such as prevalent managerial discourses (see for example Edelman et al., 2001 on the discourse of "diversity" and Miller and O'Leary, 1993 on the discourse of "economic citizenship"), as well as the interrelation of different collective symbols within such broader discourses.

Notes

We want to thank Martin Messner, Iain Munro, Richard Weiskopf, participants of the first International Symposium on Process Organization Studies in Pissouri, Cyprus, Sally Maitlis, and two anonymous reviewers for their helpful suggestions and comments on drafts of this paper.
1. Similar to TQM, six sigma, as a business strategy originally developed by Motorola, seeks to identify and remove the causes of defects and errors in manufacturing and business processes. Statistics and project management tools as well as formal training sessions with the objective of setting up an infrastructure of experts in using these tools ("green belts" and "black belts") form part of this business strategy (Lee-Mortimer, 2006; Taylor, 2008).
2. All names have been changed.

References

Åhlström, P. & Karlsson, K. (1996). Change processes towards lean production: The role of the management accounting system, *International Journal of Operations and Production Management*, 16(11), 42–56.

Alvesson, M. & Kärreman, D. (2000). Taking the linguistic turn in organizational research: Challenges, responses, consequences, *Journal of Applied Behavioral Science*, 36(2), 136–58.

Aristotle (1996). *Poetics*, London: Penguin Books.

Aristotle (2007). *Topics*, Translated by W. A. Pickard-Cambridge. eBooks@Adelaide. The University of Adelaide Library. http://ebooks.adelaide.edu.au/a/aristotle/a8t/ (accessed October 20, 2009).

Bakken, T. & Hernes, T. (2006). Organizing is both a verb and a noun: Weick meets Whitehead, *Organization Studies*, 27(11), 1599–616.

Black, M. (1979). More about metaphor, in A. Ortony (ed.) *Metaphor and Thought*, Cambridge: Cambridge University Press, 19–43.

Boje, D. (2001). *Narrative Methods for Organizational and Communications Research*, London: Sage.

Cornelissen, J. P. (2006). Making sense of theory construction: Metaphor and disciplined imagination, *Organization Studies*, 27(11), 1579–97.

Cornelissen, J. P., Oswick, C., Christensen, L. T., & Phillips, N. (2008). Metaphor in organizational research: Context, modalities and implications for research, *Organization Studies*, 29(1), 7–22.

Czarniawska, B. (2004). Metaphors as enemies of organizing, or the advantages of a flat discourse, *International Journal of the Sociology of Language*, 166, 45–65.

Czarniawska, B. (2006). A golden braid: Allport, Goffman, Weick, *Organization Studies*, 27(11), 1661–74.

De Cock, C. & Hipkin, I. (1997). TQM and BPR: Beyond the Beyond Myth, *Journal of Management Studies*, 34(5), 660–75.

Denzin, N. K. & Lincoln, Y. S. (2005). Introduction: The discipline and practice of qualitative research, in N. K. Denzin & Y. S. Lincoln (eds) *The Sage Handbook of Qualitative Research*, London, Sage, 1–32.

Drews, A., Gerhard, U., & Link, J. (1985). Moderne Kollektivsymbolik. Eine diskurstheoretisch orientierte Einführung mit Auswahlbibliographie, *Internationales Archiv für Sozialgeschichte der deutschen Literatur (IASL), 1. Sonderheft*, Forschungsreferate, Tübingen, 256–375.

Edelman, L. B., Fuller, S. R., & Mara-Drita, I. (2001). Diversity, rhetoric and the managerialization of law, *American Journal of Sociology*, 106(6), 1589-1641.

Fairclough, N. (1995). *Critical Discourse Analysis*, London: Longman.

Fairclough, N. (2005). Discourse analysis in organization studies: The case for critical realism, *Organization Studies*, 26(6), 925–39.

Fairclough, N. (2007). *Critical Discourse Analysis*, Harolow: Longman.

Fairclough, N. & Wodak, R. (1997). Critical discourse analysis, in T. Van Dijk (ed.) *Discourse as Social Interaction*, London: Sage, 258–84.

Foucault, M. (1981). The order of discourse, trans. I. McLeod, in R. Young (ed.) *Untying the Text: A Post-Structuralist Reader*, London and New York: Routledge & Kegan Paul, 48–78.

Foucault, M. (1995). *Discipline and Punish: The Birth of the Prison*, trans. A. Sheridan, New York: Vintage Books.

Foucault, M. (2002). *The Order of Things: An Archaeology of the Human Sciences*, London and New York: Routledge.

Foucault, M. (2008). *The Archaeology of Knowledge*, 7th edn, London: Routledge.

Gioia, D. A. (1986). Symbols, scripts, and sensemaking: Creating meaning in the organizational experience, in H. P. Sims, Jr. & D. A. Gioia (eds) *The Thinking Organization*, San Francisco: Jossey-Bass, 49–74.

Gioia, D. A., & Chittipeddi, K. (1991). Sensemaking and sensegiving in strategic change initiation, *Strategic Management Journal*, 12, 433–48.

Gioia, D. A., & Thomas, J. B. (1996). Identity, image, and issue interpretation: Sensemaking during strategic change in academia, *Administrative Science Quarterly*, 41, 370–403.

Gioia, D. A., Thomas, J. B., Clark, S. M., & Chittipeddi, K. (1994). Symbolism and strategic change in academia: The dynamics of sensemaking and influence, *Organization Science*, 5, 363–83.

Goldratt, E.M., & Cox, J. (1986). *The Goal: A Process of Ongoing Improvement*, Great Barrington, MA: North River Press.

Gramsci, A. (2000). *The Antonio Gramsci Reader: Selected Writings 1916–1935*, New York: University Press.

Greenberg, D. N. (1995). Blue versus gray: A metaphor constraining sensemaking around a restructuring, *Group and Organization Management*, 20, 183–209.

Hardy, C. (2004). Scaling up and bearing down in discourse analysis: Questions regarding textual agencies and their context, *Organization*, 11(3), 415–25.

Hatch, M. J. & Yanow, D. (2008). Methodology by metaphor: Ways of seeing in painting and research, *Organization Studies*, 29(1), 23–44.

Heracleous, L. (2004). Interpretivist approaches to organizational discourse, in D. Grant, N. Phillips, C. Hardy, L. Putnam, & C. Oswick (eds) *Handbook of Organizational Discourse*, Beverly Hills: Sage, 175–92.

Heracleous, L. (2006). *Discourse, Interpretation, Organization*, Cambridge: Cambridge University Press.

Heracleous, L. & Jacobs, C. (2008). Understanding organizations through embodied metaphors, *Organization Studies*, 29(1), 45–78.

Iedema, R. A. & Wodak, R. (1999). Introduction: Organizational discourses and practices, *Discourse & Society*, 10(1), 5–20.

Isabella, L. A. (1990). Evolving interpretations as a change unfolds: How managers construe key organizational events, *Academy of Management Journal*, 33(1), 7–41.

Johnson, M. (1987). *The Body in the Mind: The Bodily Basis of Meaning, Imagination, and Reason*, Chicago/London: The University of Chicago Press.

Jordan, S. & Messner, M. (2009). The problematisation of performance indicators. Paper presented at the 5th conference on performance measurement and management control, Nice, France.

Kerfoot, D. & Knights, D. (1995). Empowering the "quality worker"? The seduction and contradiction of the total quality phenomenon, in A. Wilkinson & H. Willmott (eds) *Making Quality Critical*, London: Routledge, 219–38.

Krafcik, J. F. (1988). Triumph of the lean production system, *Sloan Management Review*, 30(1), 41–52.

Kristeva, J. (1980). *Desire in Language: A Semiotic Approach to Literature and Art*, New York: Columbia University Press.

Lakoff, G. (1987). *Women, Fire, and Dangerous Things*, Chicago: University of Chicago Press.

Lakoff, G. (1993). The contemporary theory of metaphor, in A. Ortony (ed.) *Metaphor and Thought*, Cambridge: Cambridge University Press, 202–51.

Lakoff, G. & Johnson, M. (1980). *Metaphors We Live By*, Chicago: University of Chicago Press.

Lee-Mortimer, A. (2006). Six Sigma: Effective handling of deep rooted quality problems, *Assembly Automation*, 26(3), 200–4.

Leezenberg, M. (2001). *Contexts of Metaphor. Current Research in the Semantics/Pragmatics. Interface* Vol 7, Amsterdam: Elsevier.

Liker, J. (2003). *The Toyota Way: 14 Management Principles from the World's Greatest Manufacturer*, New York: McGraw-Hill.

Link, J. (1982). Kollektivsymbolik und Mediendiskurs. Zur aktuellen Frage, wie subjektive Aufrüstung funktioniert, *kultuRRevolution*, 1.

Link, J. (1986*a*). Kleines Begriffslexikon, *kultuRRevolution*, 11, 71.

Link, J (1986*b*). Noch einmal: Diskurs, Interdiskurs, Macht, *kultuRRevolution*, 11, 4–7.

Link, J. (1996). *Versuch über den Normalismus. Wie Normalität produziert wird*, Göttingen: Vandenhoeck & Ruprecht.

Link, J. (2007). Dispositiv und Interdiskurs. Mit Überlegungen zum "Dreieck" Foucault–Bourdieu–Luhmann, in C. Kammler & R. Parr (eds) *Foucault in den Kulturwissenschaften. Eine Bestandsaufnahme*, Heidelberg: Synchron, 219–38.

Link, J. & Link-Heer, U. (1990). Diskurs/Interdiskurs und Literaturanalyse, *Zeitschrift für Literaturwissenschaft und Linguistik, LiLi* 77, 88–99.

McArdle, L., Rowlinson, M., Procter, S., Hassard, J., & Forrester, P. (1995). Total quality management and participation: Employee empowerment or the enhancement of exploitation?, in A. Wilkinson & H. Willmott (eds) *Making Quality Critical*, London: Routledge, 156–72.

Maitlis, S. (2005). The social process of organizational sensemaking, *Academy of Management Journal*, 48(1), 21–49.

Miller, P. & O'Leary, T. (1993). Accounting expertise and the politics of the product: Economic citizenship and modes of corporate governance, *Accounting, Organizations & Society*, 18(2/3), 187–206.

Morgan, G. (1986). *Images of Organization*, Newbury Park: Sage.

Munir, K. A. & Phillips, N. (2005). The birth of the "Kodak Moment": Institutional entrepreneurship and the adoption of new technologies, *Organization Studies*, 26 (11), 1665–87.

Neurath, O. (1936). *International Picture Language—The First Rules of Isotype*, London: Kegan Paul (Facsimile reprint: Department of Typography & Graphic Communication, University of Reading, 1980).

Neurath, O. (1991). Bildliche Darstellung gesellschaftlicher Tatbestände, in R. Haller & R. Kinross (eds) *Gesammelte bildpädagogische Schriften*, Wien: Hölder-Pichler-Tempsky, 118–25.

273

Niedermayr, K. (2001). Metaphernanalyse, in T. Hug (ed.) *Wie kommt Wissenschaft zu Wissen? Band 2: Einfuehrung in die Forschungsmethodik und Forschungspraxis*, Baltmannsweiler: Schneider Verlag Hohengehren.

Ohno, T. (1988). *The Toyota Production System: Beyond Large-Scale Production*, Portland, OR: Productivity Press.

Pecheux, M. (1982). *Language, Semantics, and Ideology*, New York: St. Martin's Press.

Phillips, N. & Hardy, C. (2002). *Discourse Analysis: Investigating Processes of Social Construction*, London: Sage.

Pike, K. L. (1967). *Language in Relation to a Unified Theory of Structure of Human Behavior*, The Hague: Mouton.

Putnam, L. L., Phillips, N., & Chapman, P. (1997). Metaphors of communication and organization, in S. Clegg, C. Hardy, & W. R. Nord (eds) *Handbook of Organization Studies*, London: Sage Publications, 375–408.

Schulte-Holtey, E. (2001). Über Kurvenlandschaften in Printmedien, in U. Gerhard, J. Link, & E. Schulte-Holtey (eds) *Infographiken, Medien, Normalisierung. Zur Kartographie politisch-sozialer Landschaften*, Heidelberg: Synchron, 93–114.

Sutcliffe, K., Brown, A. D., & Putnam, L. L. (2006). Introduction to the Special Issue "Making Sense of Organizing: in Honor of Karl Weick", *Organization Studies*, 27 (11), 1573–8.

Taylor, G. (2008). *Lean Six Sigma Service Excellence: A Guide to Green Belt Certification and Bottom Line Improvement*, New York, NY: J. Ross Publishing.

Tsoukas, H. (1991). The missing link: A transformational view of metaphors in organizational science, *Academy of Management Review*, 16, 566–85.

Tufte, E. R. (2006). *The Visual Display of Quantitative Information*, 2nd edn, Cheshire: Graphics Press.

Watson, G. W. (2003). Ideology and the symbolic construction of fairness in organizational change, *Journal of Organizational Change Management*, 16(2), 154–68.

Weber, K., & Glynn, M. A. (2006). Making sense with institutions: Context, thought and action in Karl Weick's theory, *Organization Studies*, 27(11), 1639–60.

Weick, K. E. (1979). *The Social Psychology of Organizing*, 2nd edn, Reading, MA: Addison-Wesley.

Weick, K. E. (1988). Enacted sensemaking in crisis situations, *Journal of Management Studies*, 25(4), 305–17.

Weick, K. E. (1989). Theory construction as disciplined imagination, *Academy of Management Review*, 14, 516–31.

Weick, K. E. (1993). The collapse of sensemaking in organizations: The Mann Gulch Disaster, *Administrative Science Quarterly*, 38, 628–52.

Weick, K. E. (1995). *Sensemaking in Organizations*, Thousand Oaks: Sage.

Weick, K. E., Sutcliffe, K., & Obstfeld, D. (2005). Organizing and the process of sensemaking, *Organization Science*, 16(4), 409–21.

Womack, J. P. & Jones, D. T. (2003). *Lean Thinking: Banish Waste and Create Wealth in Your Corporation*, New York: Simon & Schuster.

13

Future-oriented Sensemaking: Temporalities and Institutional Legitimation

Robert P. Gephart, Cagri Topal, and Zhen Zhang

Abstract: Sensemaking is the process by which people construct, interpret, and recognize meaningful features of the world. Although retrospective sensemaking is a key property of the Weickian approach, sensemaking can also orient to the future. This chapter explores the social processes and practices of future-oriented sensemaking to understand how it is accomplished, how it relates to other temporal dimensions, and how it legitimates institutions. To do so, we discuss five sensemaking perspectives relevant to temporality: Weickian sensemaking, post-Weickian sensemaking, institutional rhetoric, agentivity, and ethnomethodology. We use the ideas in these perspectives as a means to conceptualize future-oriented sensemaking and to understand the potential influence that temporal modalities of sensemaking hold for legitimation. Next, we conduct an ethnomethodological investigation of future-oriented sensemaking in a public hearing where future-oriented sensemaking was a primary focus. Our investigation of inquiry discourse finds that the construction of plans, expertise, hypothetical entities, institutionalized sequences, and conventional histories are important practices in future-oriented sensemaking that produce and sustain institutional legitimation.

Sensemaking refers to "comprehending, understanding, explaining, attributing, extrapolating and predicting" (Starbuck and Milliken, 1988: 10). It is a means "intentional agents faced with equivocality" use to structure the unknown (Brown and Jones, 2000: 662). The retrospective nature of sensemaking is a distinguishing feature of Weick's influential model of sensemaking (Weick, 1995; Weick et al., 2005): "sensemaking involves the ongoing retrospective development of plausible images that rationalize what people are doing" (Weick et al., 2005: 409). Sensemaking is retrospective since the attention necessary for sensemaking requires experience to pass before attention can occur (Weick, 1995: 24).

Weick's approach to sensemaking has provided organization studies with important insights into the retrospective dimension or aspects of sensemaking. Only a few previous studies recognize the importance of future-oriented sensemaking. For example, Gioia et al. (1994) explore sensemaking that has a "future-oriented focus" involving "the conscious and intentional consideration of the probable future impact of certain actions...on the meaning construction processes" of social actors (Gioia et al., 1994: 378). Clarke (1999: 40) shows how organizations use rhetoric to create legitimate images of the future world, using planning and expertise to describe, substantiate, and produce these future worlds. Emirbayer and Mische (1998: 1963) theorize how actors engaged in agentic, interpretive processes are "oriented to the past, future and present at any given moment." And ethnomethodology (Gephart, 1978) has shown how "the organization" is constructed as an open-ended scheme of interpretation using a combination of retrospective, situated or present and prospective sensemaking.

Our chapter explores the social processes and practices that constitute future-oriented sensemaking. Further, future-oriented aspects of sensemaking have been shown to be relevant to organizational and institutional legitimacy in public hearings conducted by social institutions to assess plans for large-scale energy projects (Kemp et al., 1984; Kemp, 1985) since the public acceptability of these plans influences institutional legitimacy (Clarke, 1999). We thus undertake an empirical study of sensemaking during a government-organized public hearing to assess plans for energy projects since this is an appropriate site to study future-oriented aspects of sensemaking and to relate temporal orientations in sensemaking to institutionally produced processes of meaning creation and legitimation. This chapter therefore addresses three issues: (i) how prospective or future-oriented sensemaking is accomplished; (ii) how future-oriented sensemaking relates to other temporal orientations used in sensemaking; and (iii) how prospective sensemaking legitimates institutions.

13.1 Literature review

Our literature review addresses five perspectives on sensemaking developed in the organizational and social science literature that provide insights into temporal aspects of sensemaking. We first review two cognitive-psychological perspectives used extensively in organizational research—Weickian and post-Weickian sensemaking—to provide background information on the dominant models used in the field. Next we address three sociological perspectives that are complementary in nature. These perspectives address social aspects of sensemaking and provide elements of the analytical framework used to explore temporal orientations in this chapter. The perspectives are institutional rhetoric, agentivity, and ethnomethodology. We then compare the different perspectives, and offer a more fully developed conceptualization of future-oriented sensemaking to guide our research. Finally, we discuss how future-oriented sensemaking relates to institutional legitimation which is an important topic addressed in past sensemaking research and an important issue in the sensemaking examined in the current study.

13.1.1 The Weickian perspective on sensemaking

The Weickian perspective conceives sensemaking as a retrospective, cognitive process bound to the present where attention and meaning creation are "directed backward from a specific point in time" (Weick, 1995: 26). Events that occur during retrospective sensemaking influence "what is discovered when people glance backwards" (Weick, 1995: 26). Sensemaking is occasional: it "starts with chaos" (Weick et al., 2005: 411) or disruptions, occurs "when the world is perceived to be different from the expected state of the world" (Weick et al., 2005: 409) and stops once feelings of order, clarity, and rationality emerge (Weick, 1995: 25). Weick's retrospective emphasis may explain "why students of sensemaking find forecasting, contingency planning, strategic planning and other magical probes into the future wasteful and misleading if they are decoupled from reflective action and history" (Weick, 1995: 30).

Nonetheless, Weick has noted that prospective (1969: 196) and future perfect thinking "can make speculation more manageable" (1969: 199). Sensemaking can extend "beyond the present" (Weick, 1995: 29) as a "mixture of retrospect and prospect" (Weick et al., 2005: 413) used to answer practical questions such as "now what?" that address the future (Weick et al., 2005).

13.1.2 Post-Weickian sensemaking

A large body of research has extended Weick's sensemaking perspective to new concepts, dimensions, and domains. However, only a few studies have explored future-oriented aspects of sensemaking. Key studies were done by Gioia and associates who developed the concept of prospective sensemaking to address anticipatory sensemaking uncovered in a study of university strategic change. Prospective sensemaking considers "the probable future impact of certain actions and especially nonactions, on the meaning construction processes" of people (Gioia et al., 1994: 378). Two major dimensions emerged—sensemaking and sensegiving. Sensemaking was the prospective "meaning construction and reconstruction by the involved parties as they attempted to develop a meaningful framework for understanding the nature of the intended strategic change" (Gioia and Chittipeddi, 1991: 442). Sensegiving sought to influence "the sensemaking and meaning construction of others toward a preferred redefinition of organizational reality" (Gioia and Chittipeddi, 1991: 442) and involved an intentional process of influence using "staged actions" to "provide a viable interpretation of a new reality," to influence others to adopt it and thus it involved "making sense to others" (Gioia and Chittipeddi, 1991: 443).

More recently, sensegiving (Pratt, 2000; Maitlis, 2005; Maitlis and Lawrence, 2007) has been described as "an interpretive process in which actors influence each other through persuasive and evocative language" (Maitlis and Lawrence, 2007: 57). Maitlis's (2005) research provides strong evidence of temporal dimensions in sensegiving. Her research found evidence of retrospectively oriented sensegiving behaviors (justifying a view, gossiping) and prospective sensegiving actions (promoting a position). However, her work is not primarily oriented to understanding temporal dimensions of sensegiving and thus does not explore these dimensions in detail. This research does however clarify three properties of sensemaking that will be explored in detail later in the paper. First, sensegiving emerges from and is a form of sensemaking. Thus in the present chapter, our focus is on sensemaking as a general concept. Second, because sensegiving refers to and includes both prospective and retrospective behaviors and interpretations, the present chapter seeks to identify and distinguish or separate these temporal orientations in sensemaking. Third, sensegiving highlights rhetorical or persuasive aspects, uses, or forms of sensemaking. Hence in this chapter, we are concerned to address the rhetorical aspects and implications of sensemaking. We turn now to social perspectives on sensemaking used to pursue these topics.

13.1.3 Sociological perspectives on sensemaking

The next three perspectives take a sociological approach and focus on sensemaking as a social process. The first is the agentivity perspective of Emirbayer and Mische (1998) that offers an integrative model to analytically differentiate temporal orientations. The model explicitly incorporates sensemaking practices from ethnomethodology and facilitates exploration of all orientations simultaneously in a given study. The second perspective of ethnomethodology offers a model of sensemaking practices that can be used to explore how temporal dimensions are created and used in discourse. Finally, the institutional rhetoric perspective focuses on plans and expertise as important resources for constructing future dimensions of sensemaking. We then provide a model that integrates key elements of the views into a single framework.

13.1.3.1 AGENCY AND TEMPORALITY

A key paper that conceptualizes temporal dimensions of sensemaking is provided by Emirbayer and Mische (1998) who initiate a re-conceptualization of agency as "the temporally constructed engagement by actors of different structural environments—temporal-relational contexts of action" that use "habit, imagination and judgement" to transform structures in response to problems (1998: 970). Agency "is always a dialogical process" by which actors "engage with others" (Emirbayer and Mische, 1998: 973). Emirbayer and Mische (1998) identify three temporal dimensions of agency: future, past, and present. These are addressed respectively by the projective element, the iterational element and the practical evaluation element.

The central focus of the agentivity perspective is projectivity, that is, the future-oriented dimension of sensemaking. Projectivity is the imaginative generation by actors of possible future trajectories of action where received structures are reconfigured in relation to the future (Emirbayer and Mische, 1999). It includes the ways people imagine, negotiate, talk, and make commitments that invent the future. Emirbayer and Mische (1998: 988) offer a concrete account of how projectivity, the future orientation of agency, works in social processes. They also seek to rescue projectivity "from the subjectivist ghetto" (Emirbayer and Mische, 1998: 991) by demonstrating how it is an intersubjective phenomenon undertaken in social interaction and communication. Further, they note how projectivity relates to the past and present since actors are oriented to past, present, and future at any given moment and all orientations are found in any given situation. And projectivity is influenced by social conflict.

Key words that describe the projective ability are (organizational) goals, plans, and objectives (Emirbayer and Mische, 1998: 987). "Projects" are projective action expected to be completed in the future. A key feature of projectivity examined here is anticipatory identification that draws on past experiences to identify appropriate actions (Emirbayer and Mische, 1998: 989) and identify patterns or trajectories of possible developments. The projective dimension has been given limited consideration in organizational research including Weickian sensemaking. And institutional theory eclipses projectivity by arguing "institutional processes are embedded in routines that come to light only in post-hoc accounting practices" (Emirbayer and Mische, 1998: 993).

The iterational element is the past orientation of social action (Emirbayer and Mische, 1998: 971). This involves selective reactivation of past routines and habits to provide stability and order in social life. The iterative dimension uses recall, selection, and taken-for-granted schemes of past action to ground other dimensions of agency. Key elements of the iterational moment are selective attention and recognition of types or typifications where actors identify typical patterns of experience and predict their recurrence in the future (Emirbayer and Mische, 1998: 979); categorical location (Emirbayer and Mische, 1998: 980) where actors try to correctly locate where experiences fit; and the future expectation that past patterns will repeat themselves and be sustained over time.

The present-oriented or practical evaluation dimension refers to practical judgments made to select trajectories of action and respond to emerging demands in the present (Emirbayer and Mische, 1998). This domain of practical decision making in face to face, everyday life contexts is the focus of ethnomethodology, described below. That is, the present or practical evaluation dimension of agentivity is the site where iterations of past experience are created and where projections of the future are accomplished. Thus practical evaluation in present settings is done using ethnomethodological sensemaking practices discussed below and these sensemaking practices give meaning to present settings as they construct and (re)create the past and the future. We now address ethnomethodology in more detail.

13.1.3.2 ETHNOMETHODOLOGY

Ethnomethodology is "a descriptive science of sensemaking and practical reasoning" (Heap, 1976: 107) that studies the interpretive methods that members of society use to construct social reality (Garfinkel, 1967) and to create and sustain the factual "sense" or character of the social world (Leiter, 1980: 14). "Sense" refers to the idea that the social world is a product of how people look and talk about the world (Leiter, 1980: 69) and the assumption or sense that we are being understood in conversation even if we lack substantive agreement with others. Ethnomethodology thus conceives sensemaking as an intersubjective process accomplished through conversation and social interaction. The intersubjective world is the world "known and held in common by some collectivity of persons" (Schegloff, 1992: 1296).

The sensemaking practices and the production of social reality are ongoing and "must be continually enacted . . . geared and re-geared to the unfolding events of the everyday world" (Leiter, 1980: 173): there is no time out from sensemaking. "When the practices . . . are used undisturbed, the facticity of the social world is taken for granted. When the practices are interrupted, that facticity can no longer be assumed, and the subject actively seeks to restore it" using sensemaking practices (Leiter, 1980: 171). The interpretive process is central to the constitution of social interaction and is not merely an intervening variable (Leiter, 1980: 231). The only place to find sensemaking methods is in people's talk and behavior (Leiter, 1980: 240). Thus ethnomethodology focuses on settings where social reality is carried out to observe how talk constructs a sense of shared social reality.

Leiter (1980) describes four sensemaking practices. The first sensemaking practice is the *reciprocity of perspectives* where members assume that if they were to change places with one another during communication each would see what the other sees or at least that specific differences can be treated as idiosyncratic "until further notice" (Leiter, 1980: 174). This present-oriented practice helps actors respond to demands and contingencies of the present interaction and make practical judgments that consider the other party or parties to conversation.

The practice of *normal forms* directs each person in a conversation to expect others to emit recognizable, intelligible utterances that are part of common knowledge and to attempt to understand what is being said. The production of normal forms invokes the past by requesting schematization and typification of social experience (Emirbayer and Mische, 1998: 975). The practice of normal forms uses the iterational dimension to invoke tacit knowledge that directs speakers to extend past typfications and interpretive schemas to interpret present action. The practice requests actors to use attention selectively and employ past typfications or schemas to maintain past expectations.

The *etcetera principle* sustains the normal form appearance of talk even when it is vague by using two sub-practices. The *etcetera assumption* presumes the speaker can fill in un-stated meanings or background knowledge intended by the other by using simplifying idealizations where past meanings are recognized and assimilated into present interaction and the continuity of past and present is produced. The *retrospective-prospective sense of occurrence* practice invites the hearer to assume the speaker will say things later in the conversation to clarify ambiguous statements. This practice addresses how the present will be informed by future talk and how the past is the source of typifications to map future trajectories of action (Emirbayer and Mische, 1998: 989).

Finally, the practice of *descriptive vocabularies as indexical expressions* assumes the specific sense or meaning of conversational expressions requires linking kernel meanings of expressions to particular contexts including who is the speaker, the setting where talk is occurring, and the relationship the speaker has with the hearer. This practice emphasizes the construction of meanings for expressions and is a present- or future-oriented task. The present is constructed by using this practice to describe the speaker, the setting, and the current relationships among parties to the present interaction. But past typifications are used to construct the speakers' biographies and to fill in vague descriptive statements.

There is debate concerning whether sensemaking practices are situationally specific (Heap, 1976) or situationally invariant (Zimmerman and Pollner, 1970: 95; Leiter, 1980). We view Leiter's sensemaking practices as an abstract summary of core ethnomethodological tools used to understand intersubjective communication. Use of these practices to explore discourse uncovers local sensemaking practices that operate in specific contexts. The goal is to describe how members' sensemaking practices are used to construct an intersubjective world.

Ethnomethodology's concern with the future orientation of sensemaking is evidenced by research on how institutional schemes are used to interpret future events. For example, Gephart (1978) and Bittner (1965) have demonstrated how members use the concept or schema of organization to make acts meaningful during interaction. The organization as an interpretive scheme is reconstructed and continuously negotiated in real scenes of action to fit problems at hand (Gephart, 1978: 558). The organization is thus a prospective, open-ended sensemaking resource used in talk to explain behaviors, prescribe and justify sanctions, and give organizationally relevant meanings to phenomena. Sensemaking is prospective and seeks to create reality.

13.1.3.3 INSTITUTIONAL RHETORIC

The third sociological perspective, institutional rhetoric, has been concerned with the role of plans and planning in future-oriented sensemaking. Rhetoric, a basic feature of all communication, is the act of speaking and the study of how people persuade others to accept particular interpretations of the world (McCloskey, 1985). Rhetoric is an important feature of organizational documents (Brown, 2000; Gephart, 2007*a*, 2007*b*) and is particularly important in organizational plans and planning that have future orientations (Clarke, 1999). "Plans are the means by which organizations know what the future will entail" (Clarke, 1999: 40). Two general types of planning are functional planning and symbolic planning. Functional planning (Clarke, 1999) requires a meaningful history to estimate probabilities of events. If decision makers cannot assign definite probabilities to events, planning becomes symbolic and "fantasy documents" are often created since events are uncertain. Fantasy documents are imaginative fictions about what people hope will happen. One cannot know if the promises made by the documents can be fulfilled until a crisis emerges and plans are implemented. Thus fantasy documents are "a form of rhetoric, tools designed to convince audiences they ought to believe what an organization says" (Clarke, 1999: 2). Plans are task oriented, they project resources into the future, they claim to incorporate expertise, they promise organizations can reduce uncertainty and control things. Plans thus do things for managers and organizations including legitimating organizational action and managerial control of the future (Clarke, 1999: 152).

Fantasy documents are compelling because they are developed by "experts" who "predict" (Clarke, 1999: 158) and this expertise is manufactured by esoteric knowledge and muting competing voices (Clarke, 1999: 129) in contexts where contested interests emerge (Clarke, 1999: 103). Plans fashion political rhetoric in the guise of technical language to persuade others of particular views (Clarke, 1999: 102). Experts thereby define acceptable plans and risks for others. Experts and the fantasy documents they create shield elites and organizations from responsibility (Clarke, 1999: 167), create the impression that problems have been covered, stifle objections, and shape contexts so critics are viewed as extremists. Planning can thus be more "symbolic" than real and can use fantasy documents to produce symbolic control (Clarke, 1999).

Plans are thus future-oriented sensemaking devices constructed through the rhetoric of technical competence. They use significant political interests including national interests to persuade audiences of their legitimacy

(Clarke, 1999: 16). If things go wrong stakeholders may lose trust in institutions and institutional legitimacy can be threatened (Clarke, 1999: 170). Plans, experts, and expertise are thus important, future-oriented resources for legitimating the ability of organizations to control the future (Clarke, 1999: 152).

13.1.4 Comparing perspectives

The literature review shows that different sensemaking perspectives conceptualize temporal dimensions of sensemaking, the locus of sensemaking, and the concept of sensemaking itself in different ways. The Weickian and post-Weickian perspectives emphasize retrospection and locate sensemaking in cognitive psychological processes and subjective states. In contrast, sociological perspectives orient to future- and present-oriented sensemaking, they are directly addressed to social aspects of intersubjective sensemaking, and thus find sensemaking in documents, social interaction, and conversations.

The meaning of sensemaking for Weickians and ethnomethodologists also differs substantially. In Weickian views sensemaking occurs only after it is triggered by the breakdown, collapse, or disruption of meanings due to unusual environmental events or to sensebreaking. Sensemaking is then done to restore meaning and ends when meaning is restored. Weickian conceptions of sensemaking limit sensemaking to situations where meaningful interaction has collapsed. In contrast, ethnomethodology and agentivity view sensemaking as an ongoing process of producing and sustaining a sense of shared meaning. Reality disjunctures or breaches that disrupt sensemaking lead to the use of repair practices to restore a sense of shared meaning. Ethnomethodology thus views sensemaking as a foundational process of human action that is describable, ongoing, and compels attempts at restoration if it is disrupted.

13.1.5 Conceptualizing future-oriented sensemaking

We can now define and explain future-oriented sensemaking more fully. In this chapter, we use the three sociological perspectives to address future-oriented sensemaking. We conceptualize sensemaking in a manner consistent with ethnomethodology. Sensemaking is an ongoing process that creates an intersubjective sense of shared meaning through conversation and non-verbal behavior in face to face settings where people seek to produce, negotiate, and sustain a shared sense of meaning. Future-oriented sensemaking is thus sensemaking that seeks to construct intersubjective meanings, images, and schemes in conversation where these meanings and interpretations create or project images of future objects and phenomena. These meanings are also used to understand the implications of the projected entities. Following agentivity, we assume that future-oriented sensemaking uses past and present temporal orientations to provide contexts and histories for proposed entities. Future-oriented sensemaking can be undertaken in settings where the future is a prominent concern and in settings where the future is less prominent. Future-oriented sensemaking is always embedded in or related to past and present temporal states and is undertaken using present-oriented sensemaking practices identified in part by ethnomethodology. Finally, following institutional rhetoric perspectives, we address planning, expertise, and fantasy documents as resources used in future-oriented sensemaking. Table 13.1 summarizes the elements of the conceptual framework used to explore future-oriented sensemaking in this chapter.

13.1.6 Sensemaking and institutional legitimation

The focus of this chapter is future-oriented sensemaking. However, sensemaking and legitimation are often inter-related in institutional settings and sensemaking research has addressed organizational legitimation (Gioia et al., 1994; Gephart, 1992). Thus in the chapter we also seek to explore

Table 13.1 Analytical framework for exploring temporal orientations in sensemaking

Orientation	Past	Present	Future
Dimension	Iteration	Practical evaluation	Projection
Sensemaking practices		Reciprocity of perspectives Normal forms Etcetera assumption Descriptive vocabularies as indexical expressions Retrospective–prospective sense of occurrences Institutionalized schemes as interpretive devices	
Sensemaking tools or resources	Typifications and schematization including structures Habits, routines, documents	Contexts, practical decision making	Plans, projects, experts and expertise, fantasy documents

how temporal dimensions of sensemaking are relevant to institutional legitimation.

Legitimacy is a concept that addresses how organizations and institutions justify their right to exist (Suchman, 1995: 573). It is: "the generalized perception or assumption that the actions of an entity are desirable, proper or appropriate within some socially constructed system of norms, beliefs and definitions" (Suchman, 1995: 574). Legitimacy is a generalized concept or attribution reflecting observers' perceptions or assumptions about an organization or institution (Suchman, 1995). The socially constructed nature of legitimacy is emphasized: it is intersubjectively transmitted through communication and discourse (Suchman, 1995).

Legitimation involves providing accounts that support the state or key institutions, buttress important social norms, and keep people from testing and examining the claims made by the state and key institutions in discourse. Thus organizational legitimacy is based in and related to broad, societal level events and issues (Habermas, 1973, 1979; Offe, 1984, 1985) because serious legitimation crises can emerge from these events and threaten social institutions with disintegration and even violence. This large scale de-legitimation may be rare. But de-legitimation remains a critical threat to institutions and so is managed continuously, in part by management of impressions (Elsbach and Sutton, 1992). Hence institutional actors develop sensemaking frameworks to respond to past and present legitimacy threats and anticipate future threats. For example, Brown (2003) noted that the Piper Alpha offshore oil platform disaster produced public anxiety by challenging cherished assumptions that corporations and regulatory agencies could control organizational operations and prevent disasters. In the Piper Alpha case, the government report repaired the legitimacy of the state and the regulatory institutions through sensemaking that made the events appear to be comprehensible and controllable (Brown, 2003: 108). Thus institutions are sensitive to legitimation threats and need to manage legitimacy on a continuous basis.

13.1.7 Research questions

Our literature review leads to the following questions that guide the present study. First, how is future-oriented sensemaking produced in conversational interaction in institutional settings? That is, how are key words, vocabularies, organizational documents, and sensemaking practices used to create meaningful images of the future? Second, how are past and present sensemaking orientations used to project the future and to manage implications of future images? Third, how does future-oriented sensemaking legitimate institutions?

13.2 Methodology

13.2.1 Setting

This chapter examines an Alberta Energy & Utilities Board (AEUB) public hearing into applications by Elk Point Resources Limited to drill and operate two sour gas wells and associated facilities on the Skocdopole farm in Alberta, Canada (AEUB, 2002: 4). The Skocdopole family had contested the applications. The first phase of the hearing was held November 26, 2002 in the Royal Canadian Legion Hall in Evansburg, Alberta. The hearing reopened on May 1, 2003 to transfer Elk Point's license to a different company. The government's final report was issued on June 24, 2003.

Skocdopole Farms is a third generation, family owned and operated business (AEUB, 2002: 216) that moved its operations to the current property three years prior to the hearing. The property was "a pristine, unique piece of land, which is rare, hard to find nowadays. Another thing that attracted us ... was there was not a lot of petroleum development on it" (AEUB, 2002: 217).

The AEUB conducted the hearing. It regulates oil and gas development in Alberta to "ensure that the discovery, development and delivery of Alberta's energy resources take place in a manner that is fair, responsible, and in the public interest" (AEUB, 2009). This means "giving people who may be directly and adversely affected by proposed developments ... an opportunity to be heard." (AEUB, 2000: 26). AEUB hearings are quasi-judicial events conducted in a formal legal manner and result in an official AEUB report. The official proceedings reproduce all testimony at the hearing as recorded by Court Reporters. In the current hearing, official participants were introduced at the outset by the Board. Elk Point provided an overview of their applications then its panel of five expert witnesses was examined by company counsel and cross-examined by counsel for landowners and the Board. A second panel of five Skocdopole family members was then sworn, examined, and cross-examined.

Public hearings orient to interpretation and sensemaking (Brown and Jones, 2000; Lynch and Bogen, 1996; Gephart, 1993), use sensemaking to legitimate social institutions (Brown, 2000, 2003; Brown and Jones, 2000; Kemp, 1985; Kemp et al., 1984; Gephart, 1992, 1993; Bogen and Lynch, 1989), and hearings can be conducted to assess plans for energy projects

(Kemp, 1985; Kemp et al., 1984). Public hearings (Kemp, 1985; Brown and Jones, 2000; Gephart, 2007a, 2007b) are a useful site for research on future-oriented sensemaking and institutional legitimation (Brown, 2000, 2003).

13.2.2 Data, sampling, and methods of analysis

The first author attended the hearing. Electronic copies of the official proceedings (518 pages) and the final report (23 pages) were obtained and compiled into a textual data base using T.A.C.T. software (Lancashire, 1996). The software was used to search documents and display key segments of data and associated contextual information.

Two data displays (sub-samples of data) were created for detailed, fine-grained analysis. The first display sample was a narrative overview of the project constructed with key document passages and organized by themes to show the views of each party at the hearing (see Appendix 1). An expansion analysis (below) was done for this table to understand the projective dimension of sensemaking, to identify other temporal orientations, and to interpret how temporal orientations were presented and discussed in hearing talk and documents. Second, we used a key segment of hearing testimony to explore the use of sensemaking practices in the unfolding interaction and to better understand discourse about planning (see Appendix 2).

We used expansion analysis (Cicourel, 1980) to write interpretations of the data displays. The analysis describes how particular sensemaking practices operate in the text, how participants use background knowledge to interpret the discourse and how concepts and processes of interest to the researcher operated in the data segments (Gephart, 1993: 1485). It is important to show readers the bases for analysis and the contextual particulars used to produce it (Leiter, 1980: 210). The expansion analysis provides explicit links between the actual hearing discourse and concepts drawn from the literature, in particular sensemaking practices, temporal orientations, and expert planning.

13.3 Analysis

13.3.1 Contextual Themes

13.3.1.1 THE COMPANY'S VIEWS

Segment 1 (Appendix 1) presents testimony by Mr Wade, operations manager for Elk Point. The statements construct the present ("this proceeding") and "our company" as open-ended interpretive schemes linking the company's existence and hearing participation to a substantial past documented in an Annual Report. The statement that this is Elk Point's "first hearing" before the AEUB invites the reader to use background knowledge to understand Elk Point is unusual. Most companies with a lengthy history of operations have been involved in hearings.

Segment 2, from the direct testimony of Elk Point's expert witness panel, illustrates how panellists described their qualifications, experience, and current work assignments. Mr Wade invokes several schematized entities—graduate, University of Regina, the Association of Professional Engineers Geologists and Geophysicists of Alberta, and the designation of professional engineer. The biographies display how their institutionally certified expertise in oil and gas production is appropriate to the current application. They extend the expertise from past operations to the present and future.

Segment 3 constructs "two new wells" as schematized entities. These "new wells" are hypothetical entities that project the known schemes of "wells" drilled in the past into "proposed" or future wells. Locating the targets in the Notikewin and Nordegg subsurface formations connects geological formations to hypothetical actions that target the formations. The two hypothetical wells are objectified with specific locations, and verbally constructed as separate entities through future perfect or prospective-retrospective discourse—"In the event that the wells will ultimately prove successful." The commercial potential of the wells is uncertain but it is extended from past practices and successes into the possible future. The hypothetical objects are stabilized and reified by practices that label the wells and connect the prospective entities to standard objects and operating practices from the past and present: an "existing" gas battery and an existing pipeline. These statements construct future-oriented entities with a history that includes past and present operations and facilities as well as expectations that the wells may prove successful. If so, secondary hypothetical facilities to operate the well would be needed and thus applications for these entities are warranted.

Segment 4 constructs Elk Point's submission as the source of future, hypothetical wells that "will produce sweet gas." This future projection is based on past experience documented in the submission. The statements construct a sense of certainty about the wells and are based in expectations from the past extended forward to hypothetical entities. This certainty is tempered by "the prospect of sour gas...clearly recognized at this time." Given the risks of sour gas, "prudence"—a cautious approach to the future—is invoked to prospectively warrant official construction of an alternative image of enhanced risk due to the potential for "sour gas." This prospect is "considered remote at this time and does not correspond" with Elk Point's "current drilling plans."

Segment 5 constructs the interpretive schema of "wells targeting sweet gas." Targeting sweet gas but "encountering sour gas" is common in the industry and "must be considered" given past knowledge and expertise. Expertise is documented by constructing two distinct hypothetical wells then differentiating them in terms of technical knowledge including past geological knowledge and projected estimates of H_2S content. The first hypothetical well is the "16 of 23" well (the designation refers to land co-ordinates) constructed as a sweet gas well with potentially 0.29 per cent H_2S. The projected features of the well are grounds for secondary projections including a small emergency planning zone (EPZ) during drilling and "no EPZ (for) operations." The projected, hypothetical entity creates the expectation of little risk and leads to facilities for low risk operations.

The "10 of 25" well is a hypothetical projection with "slightly sour gas, less then 0.8 per cent H_2S" with a worst case of 1.46 per cent H_2S. The projected sour content range becomes grounds for further secondary projections since "depending on completion results" the company may determine a small EPZ is appropriate. Normal form technical schemes—well designations, subsurface formations, H_2S concentrations, and emergency planning zones—create future projections by embedding them in technical background knowledge of oil and gas professionals including engineers. The technical terms are expected to be comprehensible to oil and gas personnel but less so to local residents.

Segment 6 addresses an uncertain contingency that emerges from typification of the well as sour. The uncertainty is created by using "if" and "only potentially the case" to describe the possibility of "slightly sour gas." By typifying one well as "potentially" sour, normal form facilities for sour wells (e.g. "flare stack") are identified as future solutions to sour gas issues. Elk Point thereby constructs an image of itself as a responsible and well prepared firm.

Segment 7 addresses previous consultations with the landowners and other agencies. Elk Point has worked with stakeholders to create a shared agreement, it met the expectations of the Board, and it made amendments to the applications, thus Elk Point is responsive to stakeholder concerns. The passage also constructs an orderly, linear sequence of events and a conventional historical account where past consultations led to pre-filing of amendments to applications. The past, present, and future are discussed in talk and actors do work to create a conventional linear history of consultations.

Segment 8 is oriented to the present. Landowners' concerns are only one of many factors to address. These factors are constructed as technical entities or schemata that exhibit the convergence of three temporal orientations on the topic of concerns. Past structures, typifications, and practices include landowner concerns, regulations that require compliance, good engineering practices, and compatability with other systems. Present issues include available data. Future-oriented concerns include landowners' preferences, drilling and production information, and potential impacts on other stakeholders. Several other factors are temporally vague. Elk Point's testimony refers to one past and one present concern of the Skocdopoles in contrast to numerous technical factors Elk Point faces that are not Skocdopole concerns. Elk Point thus displays that it would be unreasonable to ignore other factors or to privilege Skocdopole family concerns.

Segment 9 translates Skocdopole family concerns into future-oriented institutional categories used by the Board. The concerns are issues from the past that were already addressed. Segment 10 thus constructs limits to Skocdopole family actions. Elk Point followed an appropriate sequence, for example by using alternative dispute resolution before filing an application and applying for licenses in a proper manner. Elk Point is thus acting appropriately to meet the regulatory demands of the AEUB. Nonetheless, the landowner refuses to support the license applications.

13.3.1.2 LANDOWNERS' VIEWS

Segment 1 shows Hugh Skocdopole's background. The farm is constructed as a "family-owned and operated business," grounded in two past generations, with a continuous history of farming and a new farm that has operated for four years. In contrast to Mr Wade's autobiographical account, the family account is brief, constructs the family farm as the only institutional scheme mentioned, notes its existence over generations and does not discuss credentials or special expertise. The family has extended its farming business from the past into the present but the farm is not highly institutionalized.

Segment 2 addresses the hypothetical wells. Mr Carter highlights the ambiguous nature of the wells: "it may be sweet and it may not be sour." He directs Mr Skocdopole's focus to the understanding of the wells "in this hearing." Mr Skocdopole invokes documented, retrospective actions: "the applications have been made for sour facilities." This statement extends past interpretations into a projected future—"there is going to be some sour content." This projection is simple and offers few documentary details in contrast to Elk Point's account employing technical language to invoke numerous documents, past practices, and future expectations to interpret the wells as mainly sweet gas (Segment 4, above).

Segment 3 constructs the family's plans. The family is now ready to "start developing" longer range plans and has goals from the past. "The land" is an interpretive scheme to contextualize future goals that include: leave the land healthier for future generations, produce healthy products, and have a healthy life and business. Jonas Skocdopole describes a plan for film production, his past training in film, current work on a film script to be made on "our land," and a future cost advantage from filming to show "we are in, midway through the process." Jonas constructs schedules and steps to establish the movie is not "speculative."

Segment 4 explores the past consultation process. Jonas Skocdopole constructs two interpretive schemes, the "extensive consultation process" and "sour" gas. In the past, sour content "was not divulged" by the company as easily as in the present hearing. A correct typification of the well as "sour" ("call a spade a spade") would lead to future, secondary projections to manage sour development. Mr Skocdopole criticizes the vague language that extends past expectations into future potentialities: it lacks foresight. "Our operation" is thus likely to experience future, "severe" impacts from the wells.

13.3.1.3 THE ALBERTA ENERGY AND UTILITIES BOARD'S VIEWS

Segment 1 addresses the Skocdopole concern with reclamation of land. Past rules and requirements will be extended into the future "when the sites were ready to be reclaimed." It constructs Elk Point as a company that has agreed to undertake institutionally legitimate reclamation using the expertise of "an accredited soil inspector" and will provide a report to assist "future reclamation." Past structures created by the Board and another agency will be extended into the future to steer Elk Point's actions.

Segment 2 addresses consultation about reclamation. Elk Point is constructed as having "failed" to provide information or address concerns and thereby failed to build effective community relations. Elk Point does not renew its own legitimacy or that of the Board. The Board faults the Skocdopoles by typifying them as Albertans who own the resources but fail to perform the duty to allow energy developments.

Segment 3 projects past evidence into the future to demonstrate the need for the hypothetical wells, to show they can be safely constructed and operated, and to show future impacts can be mitigated. The applications are approved and the "public interest" is served.

13.3.2 Sensemaking and the reclamation plan

Appendix 2 provides cross-examination of Mr Wade, an Elk Point expert witness, concerning a reclamation plan for a proposed pipeline on Skocdopole property. Mr Clarke, counsel for the Skocdopoles, begins cross-examination (1) by locating the speech acts in the present: "I want to ask you at this point" to provide details. He asks Mr Wade to fill in the essentially vague details of the hypothetical, institutional scheme of a "reclamation plan": "if you had done one." This statement creates the expectation that a reclamation plan is appropriate but absent. It invites a reciprocity of perspectives ("if you can point this out to me") to request Mr Wade use the etcetera assumption and elaborate the meaning of Elk Point's plan. The statement also invites use of the indexicality of descriptive vocabularies to go beyond kernel meanings.

Mr Wade (2.) references the opening statement to re-construct the plan "not produced for this well" since unspecified "Alberta guidelines" do not necessitate a reclamation plan. The plan and Alberta guidelines are produced as normal form entities that Mr Wade uses to provide a truncated iteration of meaning—no plan was created. He describes construction "details" (2.1) in the present ("are") and notes future contingencies ("if") to which a plan would orient. He describes how the prospect of unsuccessful wells and past sensemaking form a rationale for the lack of a plan—pipelines are only needed if the wells "were" successful hence the plan lacks "that level of detail." The projected future could lead to drilling success (a contingency) that "would" require assessment of local conditions (a contingency) before a plan could be done.

Mr Carter (3) affirms the reciprocity of perspectives ("okay"). He constructs "the landowner" with a point of view, invokes the reclamation plan as a sensemaking resource, and asks again for details. He relates details to fairness, a key issue in formal proceedings. Mr Wade agrees that sharing details is "not unreasonable" (4). Mr Carter (5) acknowledges this sense of shared meaning. He then addresses the present to state that the details are not available. Since these typifications from the past that do not exist are necessary for practical decision making, he provisionally reconstructs the "pipeline proposal" as a proposal "on hold" that would meet a prior legal expectations of fairness. He asks for a reciprocity of perspectives to confirm this.

Mr Wade (6) rejects the reciprocity of perspectives and its link to institutional expectations. Mr Carter (7) hears the statement ("okay") and Mr Wade elaborates by providing a normal form temporal sequence (8): look at conditions, develop plans, share them. The sequence requires unspecified prospective events and the passage of time to occur before "conditions" are known.

Mr Carter (11) expresses partial reciprocity: "I appreciate that … but you don't go the next step." He projects a sequence of planning as an institutionally formed interpretive scheme and suggests the company has conceived the temporal order of events incorrectly. Approval comes after, not prior to, constructing plans. Mr Wade (12) shows he has heard Mr Carter but he rejects the proposed action and counters by extending government guidelines and codes of practice from the past to the present project, refers to them as normal form "premises" and extends this institutional scheme to the future.

Mr Carter (13) tries a second time to produce explicit, shared agreement about the assumption the reclamation will be successful and notes that landowners need to accept the assumption with limited evidence.

Mr Carter (15) offers a present-oriented statement that implies details are absent thus "you don't know what you are going to do." He constructs "trust" as an interpretive scheme. Mr Wade (16) rejects the suggestion Elk Point lacks a plan: "It is not to say that we don't know what we are going to do." He specifies the contingency that makes the plan vague: conditions are not known. Past "reasonable practices" and regulations are projected into the future as interpretive schemes to be used to "construct" the future. He continues (18) by rejecting the "trust" of the family as an interpretive scheme then projects expectations, trust in institutions, and guidelines as alternative interpretive schemes for the future.

Mr Carter (19) seeks to elaborate the scheme of industry regulation to address conditions that require a reclamation plan and invites a reciprocity of perspectives that Mr Wade accepts (20). Mr Carter then states "there is nothing preventing you from preparing such a plan even in a pipeline such as this" (21). The statement elaborates the pipeline as an interpretive scheme that makes a reclamation plan reasonable but optional. This view is accepted (22).

Mr Carter requests another reciprocity of perspectives with explicit agreement on shared meaning (23) "would you agree with me?" He constructs the landowner as a scheme of interpretation and invites the company expert witness to develop a hypothetical reciprocity of perspectives with the landowner: "as far as the landowner is concerned." This includes the assumption that any pipeline will have unacceptable impacts no matter the length.

Mr Olthafer, counsel for Elk Point, argues that the request for a reciprocity of perspectives between Mr Wade and the landowner is "impossible"

(24) due to challenges of creating intersubjectivity ("read the landowner's mind"). At this point, Mr Carter produces a reciprocity of perspectives (26) to recognize the question is objectionable, that is it lacks normal and appropriate form, a claim that is accepted (27). The inability to overcome different views leads Mr Carter to abandon this line of questioning.

13.4 Discussion

The first research question asked how future-oriented sensemaking is produced in conversational interaction in institutional settings. The "hearing" into energy project applications is constructed as an institutionalized interpretive scheme in conversation. Actors thus actively construct the setting as a hearing and also use the hearing to interpret the setting. This is done by constructing normal form projective devices including plans and experts as expected features of discourse in this setting. Sensemaking practices maintain the setting as "a hearing" by insuring that normal legal and industry schemes of interpretation and key terms are expected, comprehended, and used in the setting and that interaction unfolds in ways that are comprehensible to participants. Vocabularies and key words are thus critical to constructing the setting as a hearing with a specific character and are employed through the use of the descriptive vocabularies practice to produce the meaning of the setting as a hearing where future issues are addressed.

Second, actors construct hypothetical entities, objectify them with labels, construct them as discrete entities, project their existence in the future, and construct a history for the hypothetical entities based in an unfolding trajectory that appears compelled to continue into the future. Once primary hypothetical entities are constructed they acquire a sense of incipient reality based on their embeddedness in the past and present and secondary hypothetical entities can then be constructed to elaborate the primary entities and concretize the expectation that projected entities will become real.

Third, hearing participants construct linear, conventional history of the entities including applications and wells (Lynch and Bogen, 1996). These conventional histories use two types of sequencing. First, temporal events described in accounts are assembled into an orderly sequence of events moving from past to present to future hence the linear sequence then seems to extend itself into the future. The second sequencing process uses standardized institutional step-sequences from past organizational practices and structures to fashion future, next steps that are expected to occur. For example, Elk Point constructed a step-sequence as a rationale for the lack of a plan—the first step of determining local conditions had not been completed and the plan was a second step that could not yet be taken.

Finally, individuals' biographies, technical qualifications, credentials, and work experience are assembled into interpretive schemas that establish particular individuals as professionals and experts. Experts are depicted and understood as appropriate "types" of people to make future projections about the current project.

The second question was how are past and present sensemaking orientations used with future-oriented sensemaking to project or substantiate images of the future? Actors construct schemes for action developed in the past, employ these in the present, and shape these into future projections. These schemes create hypothetical entities. Future-oriented projections are thus shaped through selective reconstruction and creative elaboration of prior entities or through the invention of new ones. Because past meanings are indexical and the future is untestable in the present, there is a great latitude for innovative construction and projection from past entities. The indexicality of past meanings makes future projections more open to innovation.

In addition, experts link past- and present-oriented sensemaking to future orientations and are constructed in terms of temporalities. For example, experts are constructed through statements about past degrees and qualifications, by their role as experts in hearing settings and by their authoritative, future projections. Experts also construct expertise by using past–present–future assemblages to describe established practices, produce expert testimony on current concerns, and suggest how to plan and manage future projects. Experts and expertise—as well as plans, organizations, and institutions—are situated accomplishments created by using past and present sensemaking resources to project sensible images of the future. Extensive and significant links to past and present appear to make future projections more certain and sensible than projections without such links.

The third question is how does future-oriented sensemaking legitimate institutions? Our data show future-oriented sensemaking is grounded in extensions and inventions of past typifications, routines, expectations, and structures in present settings. Resources from the past are used to produce plans and images of the future in discourse. Experts are authorities who are institutionally sanctioned to engage in future-oriented sensemaking including planning for organizations. They can project hypothetical future entities that are technical in nature and credible due to links to past sensemaking. But these future projections can be vague and difficult for non-experts to challenge. Other experts share similar background knowledge and are unlikely to mount such challenges. Thus future-oriented sensemaking is sensible to experts and industry professionals and this institutionally buttressed comprehensibility makes the future-oriented projections legitimate (Suchman, 1995). Experts manage legitimation threats by extending institutional recipes into the future and warranting new recipes based on past ones. The future projections legitimate institutions and organizations by showing how organizations will extend past expertise to reduce uncertainty and thus manage or control the future.

13.5 Conclusions

Future-oriented sensemaking is common in organizational and institutional life. It has distinct aspects: plans, experts and expertise, hypothetical entities, projectivity, sequencing, and constructing conventional histories. Future-oriented sensemaking is part of an unfolding sensemaking process that incorporates past and present orientations. Future-oriented sensemaking can be understood metaphorically as a dimension of a "chordal triad" (Emirbayer and Mische, 1998: 972) where three temporal dimensions "resonate as separate but not always harmonious tones . . . in any given case, one or another of these three aspects might well predominate."

Our primary goal was to explore the future dimension of sensemaking and to show it has a significant role in sensemaking research. Understanding this role requires studying sensemaking as a social process (Maitlis, 2005) to address how future-oriented sensemaking is intersubjectively produced and sustained. We thus contribute to sensemaking research by showing that future-oriented sensemaking is an important, describable and analysable feature of sensemaking. We also contribute insights into how to study future-oriented sensemaking as it unfolds in actual conversational interaction.

This chapter offers several specific contributions to research on sensemaking, institutions, and legitimacy. First, we show sensemaking is a visible feature of communication in institutional settings that can be analyzed with sensemaking practices and methods of qualitative research. This social view differs from the Weickian view of sensemaking as a psychological or cognitive process operating at an individual level that is difficult to observe. Therefore, we conceptualize sensemaking in a manner that invites systematic, comprehensive, and exhaustive analyses of conversation, conducted at a fine-grained level that appear difficult to undertake using Weickian approaches.

Second, we contribute insights into sensemaking as rhetoric. We show how sensemaking practices create interpretive schemes and produce one rather than another scheme as dominant in a given setting. An integration or juxtaposition of rhetorical analysis with ethnomethodological sensemaking practices therefore seems possible and important (see Gephart, 2007*b*). Our chapter also shows how hypothetical entities are produced and substantiated in institutional contexts, thus providing an understanding of how fictions are produced that later become embedded in "fantasy documents" (Clarke, 1999).

Third, we contribute to research on sensegiving (Maitlis and Lawrence, 2007), sensebreaking (Pratt, 2000) and related domains of framing (Fiss and Hirsch, 2005) and impression management (Elsbach and Sutton, 1992). We propose that key concepts in these domains can be understood by uncovering the situated practices of sensemaking that produce them. For example, framing (Fiss and Hirsch, 2005) examines how different meanings compete for support and how a dominant framework is constructed and used. Ethnomethodological sensemaking practices have explored this domain (see e.g. Gephart, 1978) and demonstrate that framing uses a process composed in part of constructing and using descriptive vocabularies to compose interpretive schema. Fiss and Hirsch (2005) assert framing and sensemaking "combine to create the meaning of events" whereas we view sensemaking as a basic process that produces framing and frames. Research on sensegiving, sensebreaking, framing, and impression management also needs to distinguish the different temporal orientations of the concepts.

Fourth, we contribute to the integration of institutional views and sensemaking. The integration of institutional theory and Weickian sensemaking (Weber and Glynn, 2006) explores how priming, editing, and triggering bring institutional context into sensemaking. In contrast, our chapter explores how sensemaking practices assemble institutions as interpretive schemes to produce and sustain a sense of shared meaning during interaction in specific contexts. Ethnomethodology is an institutional perspective on sensemaking (Scott, 1992: 108–9). Our recommendation is that organizational scholars should broaden their views of institutional perspectives and sensemaking and explore how sensemaking practices produce and sustain institutions. This will provide another and perhaps more direct path to the integration of sensemaking and institutional perspectives sought by Weber and Glynn (2006).

Fifth, we contribute insights into the role temporal orientations in micro-level sensemaking play in the legitimation of institutions. We describe how micro-level sensemaking practices use temporal orientations to construct experts, expertise, and plans that actors employ to show organizations can manage the future. These future-oriented actions create the sense that the organizations involved in a hearing are legitimate. But legitimacy is not enduring and must be produced and reproduced by organizations in actual settings on an ongoing basis. We therefore conceive legitimacy as a snap-shot of the ongoing process of legitimation (Habermas, 1973). This distinction is apparent in the hearing given that the company and the Board had legitimacy at both the start and end of the hearing. The implicit goal of the hearing was to enact or reproduce institutional legitimacy through a pro-cess of legitimation in which competing accounts and views were presented and countered. The legitimation of the projects was needed because of actual and potential challenges to the legitimacy of the company and the Board that resulted from "concerns" of the landowners. By conducting a hearing which legitimated current plans and projects, the Board extended the legitimacy of the company operations into future projects and pre-empted challenges to the legitimacy of the Board itself.

Finally, the chapter contributes to process theories of organization (Langley, 1999) that explore how things evolve over time. Process data are difficult to collect and analyse since they focus on events, involve multiple levels of analysis simultaneously, are embedded in broader aspects of orga-nizations and organizing, and are eclectic in nature. Past process organiza-tional research has explored "forms" of sensemaking including meanings and stories. Our paper contributes by providing a means to collect and analyze process data and to address multiple levels of analysis. We show how process data are temporally embedded and we offer a framework for understanding sensemaking using temporal modalities. Ethnomethodolo-gy also provides an additional strategy for making sense of process data to complement the seven forms of process-oriented sensemaking Langley (1999) articulates. Our approach moves an understanding of processes to a deep level of analysis—to sensemaking practices that are foundational to the construction of meaning—a goal that is consistent with process organi-zation studies. Thus process organization studies can be advanced by de-veloping insights into organizational processes using ethnomethodological sensemaking practices.

Boundary conditions for ethnomethodological sensemaking in different temporal modalities can be specified. Sensemaking practices are disrupted by systematically creating environments where the practices cannot be produced or sustained as demonstrated in Garfinkel's (1967) famous study of medical school applicants. Beck and Beck-Gernsheim (2002) suggest individualization, de-routinization, and sub-politics in contemporary society have led to the "disappearance of any sense of mutual obligation" (Beck and Beck-Gernsheim, 2002: xi) and conditions for producing intersubjective meanings in society are disintegrating. Society could thus implode through actors' inability to produce a sense of shared meaning. The limits to sensemaking and its temporal orientations are also therefore the boundary conditions for producing a sense of shared social reality.

To conclude, the chapter has shown how organizations and institutions create plans for the future that are vague and hence difficult to challenge. Public hearings provide institutionally sanctioned settings in which to use sensemaking practices to create projections of the future. A close examination of these institutional sensemaking processes reveals they are less fully developed than members of the public expect or desire. However, these institutionalized, future-oriented sensemaking practices are the only means available to create future worlds and develop means to make them safe. As such, future-oriented sensemaking in critical institutional settings warrants much future exploration.

Note

Funding support from the Social Sciences and Humanities Research Council of Canada and the University of Alberta Roger S. Smith Research Fellowship are gratefully acknowledged. Thanks to Manley Sharifian, Mia Yan, and Keith Zubot-Gephart for research assistance. Special thanks to Sally Maitlis and to two anonymous reviewers for insightful and helpful comments.

References

Alberta Energy and Utilities Board (2000). *Alberta Energy and Utilities Board, 1999–2000 Annual Report*, Edmonton: Government of Alberta.

——(2002). *Proceedings of Notice of Hearing Application Nos. 1253701, 1253703 and 1261233 Elk Point Resources Inc., Wildwood Field*, Evansburg, Alberta, November 26, 2002 and Stony Plain, Alberta, May 1, 2003.

——(2003). *Decision 2003-050 Applications No. 1253701, 1253703 and 1261233*. Calgary, Alberta, June 23, 2003.

——(2009). *About the ERCB*. Downloaded from http://www.ercb.ca/portal/server.pt?open=512&objID=260&PageID=0&cached=true&mode=2, accessed June 4, 2009.

Beck, U. & Beck-Gernsheim, E. (2002). *Individualization*, Thousand Oaks, CA.: Sage.

Bittner, E. (1965). The concept of organization, *Social Research*, 32, 239–55.

Bogen, D. & Lynch, M. (1989). Taking account of the hostile native: plausible deniability and the production of conventional history, *Social Problems*, 36, 197–224.

Brown, A. D. (2000). Making sense of inquiry sensemaking, *Journal of Management Studies*, 37, 45–76.

Brown, A. D. (2003). Authoritative sensemaking in a public inquiry report, *Organization Studies*, 25 (1), 95–112.

——& Jones, M. (2000). Honorable members and dishonorable deeds: Sensemaking, impression management and legitimation in the "Arms to Iraq Affair", *Human Relations*, 55 (5), 655–89.

Cicourel, A. V. (1980). Three models of discourse analysis: The role of social structure, *Discourse Processes*, 3, 101–32.

Clarke, L. (1999). *Mission Probable: Using Fantasy Documents to Tame Disaster*, Chicago: University of Chicago Press.

Elsbach, K. D. & Sutton, R. I. (1992). Acquiring organizational legitimacy through illegitimate actions: A marriage of institutional and impression management theories, *Academy of Management Journal*, 35, 699–738.

Emirbayer, M. & Mische, A. (1998). What is agency? *American Journal of Sociology*, 104 (4), 962–1023.

Fiss, P. C. & Hirsch, P. M. (2005). The discourse of globalization: Framing and sensemaking of an emerging concept, *American Sociological Review*, 70 (1), 29–52.

Garfinkel, H. (1967). *Studies in Ethnomethodology*, Englewood Cliffs, NJ: Prentice-Hall.

Gephart, R. P. (1978). Status degradation and organizational succession: An ethnomethodological approach, *Administrative Science Quarterly*, 23, 553–8.

——(1992). Sensemaking, communicative distortion and the logic of public inquiry legitimation, *Industrial and Environmental Crisis Quarterly*, 6, 115–35.

——(1993). The textual approach: Risk and blame in disaster sensemaking, *Academy of Management Journal*, 38 (6), 1465–514.

——(2007a). Hearing discourse, in M. Zachry & C. Thralls (eds) *The Cultural Turn: Perspectives on Communication Practices in Workplaces and the Professions*, Baywood Press, 239–60.

——(2007b). Crisis sensemaking and public inquiry, in C. Pearson, C. Roux-Dufort, & Judith Clair (eds) *International Handbook of Organizational Crisis Management*, Sage Publications, 123–60.

Gioia, D. & Chittepeddi, K. (1991). Sensemaking and sensegiving in strategic change implementation, *Strategic Management Journal*, 12, 443–8.

Gioia, D. A., Thomas, J. B., Clark, S. M., & Chittipeddi, K. (1994). Symbolism and strategic change in academia: The dynamics of sensemaking and influence, *Organization Science*, 5 (3), 363–83.

Habermas, J. (1973). *Legitimation Crisis*, Beacon Press, Boston, MA.

Habermas, J. (1979). *Communication and the Evolution of Society*, Heinemann, London.

Heap, J. (1976). What are sense making practices? *Sociological Inquiry*, 46, 107–15.

Kemp, R. (1985). Planning, public hearings, and the politics of discourse, in J. Forester (ed.) *Critical Theory and Public Life*, MIT Press: Cambridge, MA, 177–201.

Kemp, R., O'Riordan, T., & Purdue, M. (1984). Investigation as legitimacy: The maturing of the big public inquiry, *Geoforum*, 15, 477–88.

Lancashire, I. (1996). *Using TACT with Electronic Texts*, New York: Modern Language Association.

Langley, A. (1999). Strategies for theorizing from process data, *Academy of Management Review*, 24 (4), 691–710.

Leiter, K. (1980). *A Primer on Ethnomethodology*, Oxford University Press, New York.

Lynch, M. & Bogen, D. (1996). *The Spectacle of History: Speech, Text, and Memory at the Iran-Contra Hearings*, Durham, NC: Duke University Press.

Maitlis, S. (2005). The social processes of organizational sensemaking, *Academy of Management Journal*, 48 (1), 21–49.

Maitlis, S. & Lawrence, T. B. (2007). Triggers and enablers of sensegiving in organizations, *Academy of Management Review*, 50 (1), 57–84.

McCloskey, D. N. (1985). *The Rhetoric of Economics*, Madison, WI: University of Wisconsin Press.

Offe, C. (1984). *Contradictions of the Welfare State*, Cambridge, MA: MIT Press.

Offe, C. (1985). *Disorganized Capitalism: Contemporary Transformations of Work and Politics*, Cambridge: Polity Press.

Pratt, M. (2000). The good, the bad, and the ambivalent: Managing identification among Amway distributors, *Administrative Science Quarterly*, 45 (3), 456–93.

Scott, W. R. (1992). *Organizational Sociology*, Aldershot: Dartmouth Publishing.

Schegloff, E. (1992). Repair after next turn: The last structurally provided defense of intersubjectivity in conversation, *American Journal of Sociology*, 97, 1295–345.

Starbuck, W. H. & Milliken, F. J. (1988). Challenger: Fine-tuning the odds until something breaks, *Journal of Management Studies*, 25 (4), 319–40.

Suchman, M. C. (1995). Managing legitimacy: Strategic and institutional approaches, *Academy of Management Review*, 20 (3), 571–610.

Weber, K. & Glynn, M. A. (2006). Making sense with institutions: Context, thought and action in Karl Weick's theory, *Organization Studies*, 27 (11), 1639–60.

Weick, K. (1969). *The Social Psychology of Organizing*, Reading, MA: Addison-Wesley.

——(1995). *Sensemaking in Organizations*, Thousand Oaks, CA: Sage.

——Sutcliffe, K. M., & Obstfeld, D. (2005). Organizing and the process of sensemaking, *Organization Science*, 16 (4), 409–21.

Zimmerman, D. H. & Pollner, M. (1970). The everyday world as a phenomenon, in J. D. Douglas (ed.) *Understanding Everyday Life: Toward the Reconstruction of Sociological Knowledge*, London: Aldine Publishing, 80–104.

KEY TRANSCRIPT SEGMENTS

I. COMPANY VIEWS: ELK POINT RESOURCES

Mr Richard Wade, Operations Manager, Elk Point Resource Inc.

1. Elk Point's first hearing

"Mr Chairman, members of the board, this proceeding constitutes Elk Point Resource Inc.'s first hearing in front of the Alberta Energy and Utilities Board. On the assumption that not everyone is familiar with our company, I thought I should begin by providing a brief overview of who we are and what it is we do. To that end, I don't think I can do much better than to quote from the Elk Point Resource Inc.'s 2001 annual report." (p. 25).

2. Biography: expertise

"I'm a graduate with distinction from the University of Regina, majoring in industrial systems engineering. I'm a member of the Association of Professional Engineers, Geologists, and Geophysicists of Alberta, and I'm entitled to practice professional engineering within the Province of Alberta and to take and use the title of professional engineer. My previous work experience has included . . ." (p. 20).

3. Two wells

"Elk Point has proposed to drill two new wells, the first at 10 of 25-54-9-West of the 5th Meridian and targeting both Notikewin and the deeper Nordegg formations. The second at 16 of 23-54-9-West of the 5th Meridian, targeting the Notikewin only. Neither location is contingent on the success of the other. In the event that the wells will ultimately prove commercially productive, and at the suggestion of the board, Elk Point has also applied for wellsite facilities and pipelines to connect the proposed wells to the existing 14 of 26-54-9-West of the 5th Meridian gas battery." (pp. 27–8).

4. Sweet gas is expected

"As indicated in Elk Point's submission, it is expected that the new wells that are proposed will produce sweet gas from the Notikewin formation; however, the prospect of sour gas produced from the 10 of 25 well, which also targets the slightly sour Nordegg formation, is clearly recognized at this time. As well, prudence dictates that Elk Point consider the future possibility in the context of the 16 of 23 well, though it is considered remote at this time and does not correspond with its current drilling plans at that location." (pp. 28–9).

5. Estimated hydrogen sulfide concentrations

"Of course, even for wells targeting sweet gas production, the possibility of encountering sour gas during drilling operations must be considered. While the proposed 16 of 23 well consists of a vertical well targeting sweet gas production from the Notikewin, the application takes into account the maximum H_2S content from any zone expected to be encountered during the course of the drilling is 0.29 per cent from the Lower Manville formation. A cumulative drilling H_2S rate of 0.0014 cubic meters per second was determined for the 16 of 23 well, which corresponds to a drilling and completion emergency planning zone, or EPZ, of 44 meters. Given the sweet target of the well, there would be no EPZ associated with expected production operations." (p. 30). "The 10 of 25, like the 16 of 23, is a proposed vertical well targeting sweet gas production from the Notikewin, but it also targets slightly sour gas, less than 0.8 per cent H_2S, producing from the deeper Nordegg formation. The maximum H_2S content of 1.46 per cent that may be encountered during the course of the drilling of 10 of 25 is not associated with the Nordegg target, but with the Pekisko formation. The cumulative drilling H_2S release rate of 0.0341 cubic meters per second was determined for the 10 of 25 well, which corresponds to a drilling and completion EPZ radius of 282 meters. Depending on completion results, an EPZ associated with production operations at the 10 of 25 well would typically be smaller, if there is one at all." (p. 31).

6. Potential facilities if there is sour gas

"If there is a need for the proposed wellsite facilities to handle slightly sour gas and associated water from the Nordegg formation, as is only potentially the case for 10 of 25, then a flare knock-out drum and flare stack would also be stalled for emergency and maintenance depressurization events. Provision would also be made for a remote terminal unit with remote and local shutdown capability, H_2S detection, and a small storage tank for the continuous injection of corrosion inhibitor in the sour gas production." (p.31).

7. Consultations with stakeholders

"Elk Point's applications were the subject of extensive consultations with, and input from, various stakeholders including area landowners, residents, and Alberta Environment. This input resulted in several amendments to Elk Point's proposals before the applications were initially filed." (p. 33).

8. Competing factors

"Elk Point must concern itself not only with particular landowners' concerns and preferences, but many other factors. Some of these factors include regulatory compliance, public and environmental safety, available geological data, drilling and production information, good engineering practices, technological limitations, construction and operability difficulties, potential impacts on other stakeholders, compatibility with downstream third party systems, costs, and perhaps less tangible assessment of business and geological risk." (pp. 33–4).

9. Addressing stakeholder concerns

"In Elk Point's submission, the concerns articulated by Skocdopole Farms can be distilled into the following categories: Protection of water resources, health impacts to people and animals from fugitive and flaring emissions, interference with farming operations and impacts on land value and future development plans." (pp. 36–7). "Elk Point addressed each of those identified concerns in its submission." (p. 37).

10. A reluctant landowner

"Notwithstanding these efforts in advance of filing the applications and a subsequent attempt at mediated alternative dispute resolution, Skocdopole Farms maintains objection to the applications and has not been prepared to grant the necessary land rights for the proposed wells, wellsite facilities and pipelines to Elk Point." (p. 36).

II. STAKEHOLDER VIEWS: THE SKOCDOPOLE FAMILY

1. Biography: expertise

Hugh Skocdopole: Skocdopole Farms is a family-owned and operated business. Jonas, Bruce and myself are the third generation in the family to be in the agricultural business. We recently moved the family business to a property, to the property of Wildwood from Olds, Alberta. We are in our fourth year at the Wildwood property. (p. 216)

2. Two wells: sour gas expected

Mr Carter, counsel for the Skocdopole family, asks Jonas Skocdopole: "could you comment on the discussions that we heard earlier about, well, it may be sweet and it may not be sour, and just what you believe that we are dealing with or what you feel you are dealing with in this hearing?"

Jonas Skocdopole: I guess our opinion on the matter is that, on the simplest level, the applications have been made for sour facilities and pipelines that can accommodate for that. And from our perspective, that seems to be, that we are working under the assumption that there is going to be some sour content involved in the development of these facilities. (p. 222).

3. Plans

Hugh Skocdopole: We are just now settling in enough that we can start developing some more specific longer-term plans and goals. Some of the general goals that we currently have and have had for some time are to leave the land in a healthier state for the next generation than we found it. This would mean improving the soil nutrients and water and water cycles, et cetera, as well as sustaining air quality in the area. We also want to produce products from the land that are healthy and natural. And in the end, all we want to make a healthy life for ourselves in the area, and this is going to depend on the health of our business. (pp. 217–18).

Mr Olthafer, counsel for Elk Point: Okay. I just wanted to review with you some of the various uses of the lands that you were postulating. Would you characterize them generally though at this time as speculative uses?

Hugh Skocdopole: Could you give us specifics?

Jonas Skocdopole: Well, I—one of the ones we listed was film, used for film production. And I—just to qualify that a little bit, I have trained in the film and television industry. There is currently a script that I have been working on with another fellow that was in the works prior to any of this other stuff; and had a verbal, I guess, agreement with the family that I would have access to the use of our land for that purpose. And location cost is a fairly significant advantage to me to save by being able to do that…and so I wouldn't say it is speculative. That's one example.

Mr Olthafer: Just exploring that a little bit. So it is a certainty? You have—your movie is going ahead? There is a schedule or—

Jonas Skocdopole: Yes, there is a—we are in, midway through the process. The script is very close to being first draft being finished. After that is completed we'll move on to the next step. I am working under the assumption that we will be able to film it next summer. (pp. 271–2)

4. Consultation

Jonas Skocdopole: And in the extensive consultation process that we have been exposed to, I would suggest that the sour aspect of the conversation was not divulged as easily as it perhaps was indicated. And I guess our feeling is, let's call a spade a spade and address the fact that we are talking potentially about sour development here and what the ramifications of that are if that does arise.

I mean, there is a lot of this language of expected and its potential. It is a vague, vague language, I guess, and in a lot of cases it lacks what we see as foresight. And some of the implications of these things are fairly severe to our operation, I guess— (pp. 222–3).

III. THE VIEWS OF THE ALBERTA ENERGY AND UTILITIES BOARD HEARING PANEL

1. Reclamation

"Elk Point said that it would comply with the relevant notification, guidelines, and code of practice requirements when the sites were ready to be reclaimed. In addition, Elk Point stated that it would have an experienced construction inspector on the project and would commit to having an accredited soil inspector of its choosing on site during construction, topsoil salvaging operations, and cleanup. Further, AENV Conservation and Reclamation Information Letter 00-08, Pre-construction Assessment Report for Wellsites (November 2000) calls for the preparation of a report to serve as a record for future reclamation of a well site. While not a regulatory requirement, Elk Point said that it was prepared to commit to have such reports prepared with respect to the 16–23 and 10–25 well sites and to share them with the Skocdopoles." (AEUB, 2003, p. 10)

2. Consultation

"The Board was concerned to hear that transferring the pipeline to another area operator led to problems with reclamation. In the Board's view, Elk Point failed to recognize that a key element to building and sustaining constructive community and stakeholder relations is providing information, listening to concerns, and then trying to resolve those concerns in a meaningful manner. In addition, as resource owners, Albertans need to be aware of the importance of energy resources to Alberta's economy and society." (AEUB, 2003, p. 20)

3. Decision

"Having carefully considered all the evidence, the Board finds that Elk Point and Burmis have demonstrated the need for the proposed wells, facilities, and pipelines and that those can be drilled, constructed, and operated in a safe and environmentally acceptable manner. The Board finds that the associated impacts can be properly addressed and mitigated. As a result, the Board is of the view that the subject applications are in the public interest and, therefore, approves the applications subject to Burmis meeting the conditions set out in the appendix." (AEUB, June 24, 2003, p. 21)

CROSS EXAMINATION OF ELK POINT BY SKOCDOPOLE COUNSEL CONCERNING THE LAND RECLAMATION PLAN

1. *Mr Carter*: And I want to ask you at this point about the pipeline proposal, and I am wondering if you can point this out to me, and it would be the details regarding construction practices for the pipeline, how the right of way would be stripped, what would happen if you encountered wet conditions, what the plans are for reclamation with respect to the right of way. Really, the kind of detail that one would find in a conservation and reclamation plan if you had done one.

2. *Mr Wade*: As noted in the opening statements, the conservation and reclamation plan was not produced for this well as it doesn't fall under Alberta guidelines for such a plan being necessary.

2.1 Construction details are very season, time and weather dependent, depending on the conditions. If the proposed pipeline is conducted in the winter time or the spring or the summer, you would utilize very different construction methods. Given that the pipelines are only necessary in the event that the proposed wells were successful, that level of detail has not been undertaken at this time.

2.2 If it were deemed necessary that the pipelines would be put into place, we would do an assessment, a prior assessment of the conditions to determine the actual conditions and develop our plan.

3. Okay. Now, would you agree with me, and you may want to defer to Mr Hurst, that from the landowner's point of view, it would only be fair for them to know what these details are?

4. I think sharing of those details prior to construction is not unreasonable.

5. Okay. And since they are not available, would you agree with me that, at least from the landowner's point of view, it would make sense and, again, be fair and reasonable to say, well, let's just put this pipeline proposal on hold until the well is drilled and we know whether it is successful and then we know what we are facing? That would be fair, wouldn't it?

6. No, I don't think that would be fair.

7. Okay.

8. I think it would be fair to take a look at the conditions that we are proposing the pipelines in, develop the plans and then share them with the Skocdopoles; but those cannot be developed until we know what conditions we are facing.

9. No, and I appreciate—

10. So I don't—sorry.

11. I appreciate that you have acknowledged that. But you don't go the next step and say that, in view of that, we shouldn't expect the go-ahead from any board until we have got those plans and they have been presented to the landowners. You wouldn't agree with that?

12. I would not agree with that. As stated in our opening statement, we comply with all Alberta Environmental protection guidelines and code of practice. This project is not an exception to that. We conducted our operations previously on these lands under those premises; and we will conduct our operations, if permitted, under those premises again.

13. But you agree with me that that requires that the landowners and the board, I guess, accept that whatever these plans might be, are going to be totally successful and you are going to carry out your job in the best way possible? They would have to be taking your word for it. Right?

14. Sorry. Can you restate the question?

15. Well, if you don't have the details to look at, don't know what you are going to do, you are really saying, trust us. Just give us the go-ahead and trust us.

16. It is not to say that we don't know what we are going to do. We don't know the conditions we are going to encounter and, therefore, we will have to construct according to reasonable practices for the conditions we face. And we will comply with all the regulations set forth by the government agencies. So—

17. Well, what—

18. —it is not a matter of trust. We expect and trust that the agencies had developed codes and practices and guidelines to undertake those circumstances, so we followed the guidelines.

19. Okay. Now, in certain cases, depending upon the length of the pipeline, you would have to have a conservation reclamation plan. Right?

20. If the pipeline is of sufficient diameter and sufficient length, then a reclamation plan to be filed is necessary, that is correct.

21. Okay. There is nothing preventing you from preparing such a plan even in a pipeline such as this, is there?

22. There's nothing preventing us from doing that plan, no.

23. And would you agree with me that, as far as the landowner is concerned and the impact on the landowner, it doesn't matter how long the pipeline might be?

24. *Mr Olthafer*: Mr Chairman, with all due respect, my friend is asking Elk Point to put themselves in the position of the landowner; and the landowner's perspective will, I'm sure, be offered later on; but for Mr Wade to read the landowner's mind as to what perspective they have in that context, I think it is pretty impossible for him to answer. As well, the answer has already been given that what the guidelines are, and that Elk Point is following those procedures.

25. * QUESTION OBJECTED TO *

26. *Mr Carter*: So you are objecting to the question?

27. *Mr Olthafer*: Yes, I am, to the extent that it is asking Mr Wade to postulate what the landowner might think.

28. *Mr Carter*: Okay. I will leave it at that.

Source: Alberta Energy and Utilities Board, 2002: 74–9.

Index

Appendices, figures and tables are indexed in bold.

Index

Index

Pfeffer, J. 174
phenomena/ology 15, 33, 34, 44, 131, 162,
    166, 176
  and atoms 28–9
  contingency 173, 175
  future 35
  oblique approach 128, 130
  ontology 45
  social 116
Phillips, J. R. 85, 86, 90
Phillips, N. 244, 247, 269
philosophy 38, 39, 43, 46–7, 48–9, 50–1,
    73, 141
  early 173
  to non-philosophy 39, 48
  of the future 32, 40
  thinking 46, 52
  of time 32, 40–41, 44
Pike, K. L. 252
Pipan, T. 149
planes (*"durée"*) of time 43
plans/planning 283–4, 285, 287–8, 296–7
Plato 46, 128
  Ideals 119
  realm 120
  thought 73
Playfair, William 264
Plowman, D. A. 12, 197, 206
pluralism 45, 49, 50
poetry 93, 110, 120, 121
  China 124
poetics of process 102
Polkinghorne, D. E. 7, 8, 233
Polley, D. 174
Pollner, M. 282
polysemic words 64
Poole, M. S. 8, 15, 16, 215
Porsander, L. 149
Porter, M. E. 19
potentiality-actuality 29
pragmatism/ists 27, 30, 34, 162, 176
Pratt, M. G. 14, 16, 17, 278, 298
predictions 65, 67, 68, 73
prehensive unities 5, 77, 82, 83, 84, 85
  determinate meanings 92–3
*Presence: Exploring Profound Change in People,
    Organizations and Society* (Senge et al) 88
Prigogine, I. 5, 20, 119, 172
printing press 134
problem absorption 34, 185, 187, 188,
    189–91, 193–4, 195, 205, 206, 207
  learning:
    experiential 197, 200;
    higher-level 200–1

microscopic change 201, 206
  and non-absorption 192, 195–6
    repeated 198, 201
  by rules 198, 201
    codification 188;
    dynamics 187;
    repeated 198
  semantic learning 186–7
  stability 196–7
problem solving 72, 74, 80–1, 84, 90, 185,
    187, 189
problemization 171, 172, 179, 192
process/es 16, 52, 55, 57, 64, 68, 75, 89, 112,
    114, 118, 120, 140, 150, 155
  and *immanent movement* 40
  knowledge 10, 14
  metaphysics 2, 3, 7, 8, 13, 29, 162
  ontology 8, 14, 32
  poetics 102
  pure 59, 69, 106
  and radical impermanence 119
  world 74–5
process organization 8–11, 20, 48–9
  retrospective studies 11–12, 13, 14
  studies 2, 39, 299
process orientation 5, 8, 19, 32, 33, 56, 57,
    58, 64, 67, 68–9, 72, 76–7, 80
  in practice 70, 71, 73, 74–5, 76, 88, 92,
    95–6
process perspective 109, 189, 190, 191,
    201, 207
process philosophy 40, 43, 47, 48, 162
process practitioners 103, 109
process reducibility thesis 117
process research 17, 18, 19
process theories/theorists 6, 8, 9–10, 13, 16,
    17, 20, 29, 31, 32, 34, 58, 102, 103–4,
    105, 106, 107, 109, 110, 112, 167
  Enron 18
process thinking 5, 27, 30, 32, 33, 34, 35, 36,
    48, 102, 103, 107, 109, 161, 162, 165,
    166, 172, 176–80
  Aristotle on 28
  Callon on 168
  heterogeneity of entities 170
  Whitehead on 166
process view 163, 170, 205
process vs. substance metaphysics 2
process vs.variance theorizing 2, 6
Procter, S. 267
projectivity 279, 280, 297
public hearings 287, 295, 299, 300
punctuated equilibrium model/theory
    15, 16

Index

9035779R00198

Printed in Germany
by Amazon Distribution
GmbH, Leipzig